T0227553

Evaluating Information Systems

Evaluating Information Systems

Public and Private Sector

Edited by
Zahir Irani and Peter Love

Routledge
Taylor & Francis Group

LONDON AND NEW YORK

First published 2008 by Butterworth-Heinemann

2 Park Square, Milton Park, Abingdon, Oxon OX14 4RN
711 Third Avenue, New York, NY 10017, USA

Routledge is an imprint of the Taylor & Francis Group, an informa business

First issued in hardback 2016

British Library Cataloguing in Publication Data
A catalogue record for this book is available from the British Library

Library of Congress Cataloging-in-Publication Data
A catalog record for this book is available from the Library of Congress

ISBN: 978-0-7506-8587-0 (pbk)
ISBN: 978-1-138-15264-9 (hbk)

Contents

■ Preface

The discipline of Information Systems (IS) began to emerge in the late 1950s and early 1960s. It was driven by the increasing use of digital computers in business – the first business applications were rolled out in 1953 (Hally, 2005). Specialist consultants like Isaac Auerbach (Auerbach Associates were founded in 1957) had began to formalise what practitioners had been doing under the heading of Electronic Data Processing (EDP) and Automatic Data Processing (ADP). The earliest textbooks on 'how to do it' were being published (Gregory and Van Horn, 1965). By the mid-1960s, universities began to establish courses, and research and develop a theoretical base for scholars and for practitioners (Langefors, 1966).

From the earliest days the problem of justifying and auditing investments in developing and operating these EDP systems was recognised and addressed by the burgeoning IS community. Textbooks for practitioners were published as early as 1961 (Frielink, 1961) covering the auditing of systems, and symposia and conferences on the economics of EDP held, sponsored, for example, by the International Federation for Information Processing (IFIP) (Frielink, 1965; Frielink, 1974). In the UK, the National Computing Council set up a working party comprising practitioners from commerce and administration, consultants and academics to report on the state of practice in the UK regarding both justification of investment and the measurement of the outturn from the implementation of IS systems. Their study (Morris et al., 1971) reported on the lack of systematic practice and, in particular, on the failure to measure the value of the outturn compared to expectation. It noted that the business community was expressing concern about the problem of evaluating the worth of its innovative IS.

In the decades that followed surveys of computer managers, conducted by academics and consultants, listed evaluation as one of the top issues of concern (Brancheau and Wetherby, 1987; Grindley, 1991). The academic community, hardware and software vendors, and consultants responded by publishing prescriptions on how to solve the problem (Emery, 1973; King and Schrems, 1978; Lincoln, 1986; Parker and Benson, 1987; Kaplan and Norton, 1992 and many others). The UK civil service, for example, developed a standard project management framework, PRINCE2 (Office of Government Commerce, 2005), incorporating a methodology for assessing the 'business case' for use by government departments proposing new investments in computer-based systems. At the same time a profusion of literature grew up including reviews of the methods formulated, reviews of practice, theoretical and pragmatic insights into the problems, and case studies for students and practitioners.

By the 1980s, it was becoming apparent that the growing investment in Information Technology (IT) systems was not having the sought after and expected benefit either at the level of the economy or the level of the enterprise. Whereas previous economic trans-formations involving the application of capital, such as the agrarian and industrial revo-lutions had yielded notable increases in productivity, macro-economic studies suggested that white-collar productivity, rather than rising from the impact of investment in com-puter technology, was over the decades 1950–1980 actually declining (Strassmann, 1985; Brynjolfsson, 1993; Landauer, 1995; Land 1996). The paradox to be explained was to rec-oncile the continuous year-on-year rise in investment in IT with the inability of individual companies to demonstrate a positive return on their investment in terms of profit, and the stubborn failure of significant improvements in productivity at the national level. But the paradox defied rational explanation. Why would the business community and government administrations continue to increase the proportion of resources devoted to information and communication technology (ICT), if adequate returns could not be demonstrated?

Further research may have resolved the paradox (Brynjolfsson and Hitt, 1996; Brynjolfsson and Hitt, 2000). Problems with econometric measurement techniques plus observed lags in the yield from ICT provide an explanation for the paradox and suggest that the current yield from these investments is actually earning a return in excess of those from other busi-ness investments. If these measurements can be fully validated, far from over-investing in ICT, the business community should probably be increasing its investments.

Given the rich literature on evaluation, which is constantly being added to, the wide choice of evaluation methods available and the apparent resolution of the productivity paradox, why is there a need for yet another book?

Perhaps, the most compelling reason is that the world of ICT is rapidly changing. Much of the extant literature refers to an age when evaluation was relevant only to the organisa-tion implementing new ICT systems. Today systems span organisational boundaries, add-ing a new dimension to the way costs and benefits are distributed. By and large systems were confined within an organisation and developed inside that organisation. Today the dominance of Internet and Web-based systems brings vastly more stakeholders into the value equations. Development and operations are globally outsourced increasing the com-plexity of evaluation. At the same time more applications depend on infrastructures which themselves are major systems such as Enterprise Resource Planning (ERP) systems, adding another layer of uncertainty and complexity.

Together with developments in technology the range of applications is widening. Today's technology is ubiquitous and serves a variety of new purposes. Radio frequency identifica-tion technology (RFID) provides a good example of such possibilities. Each new innovation in technology and its field of application poses new challenges in terms of measurement of outcomes and evaluation, both at the justification – *ex ante* stage, and at the outturn – *ex post* stage.

The second reason is the continuing concern expressed by executives from private enter-prise and the public sector about the problems they face in setting a value on ICT. Management invests in new systems to stay competitive by improving services to custom-ers and reducing costs. However, they often find demonstrable evidence of value added elusive and, further, find it difficult to compare the return from investments in ICT with other investments. ICT executives express concern about the low esteem they enjoy in their organisations coupled with the problems they face in convincing their management peers about the value of the services and systems they provide.

These concerns are a reflection of the gap between what happens in practice and the normative solutions provided by academia. Too often systems' justification is seen and treated as a ritual which has to be complied with but which is manipulated to achieve intended outcomes. And rigorous post-implementation reviews are far too often neglected (Kumar, 1990), partly because they are regarded as burdensome while adding little value, partly for instrumental reasons. Anecdotal evidence suggests that there is little correspondence between predicted outcomes and actual achievements, throwing doubt on the value of attempts at justification.

There is a clear need for closer collaboration between academia and practitioners, and it is hoped that a book such as this one can help to close the gap.

Yet another reason for bringing out another book on evaluation is the lack of balance in the literature. Much of the literature, particularly that from the USA, focuses on the private sector. Indeed, in an interesting essay entitled *Business Value of IT: An Essay on Expanding Research Directions to Keep Up with the Times* (Kohli and Grover, 2008), the authors define the topic as one exclusively concerned with the private sector. They place the public sector and evaluation of the private sector as being different and therefore in a different realm. Public sector systems serving government administration and the citizen, absorb huge resources and systems such as the UK National Programme for Information Technology designed to serve the National Health Service are larger in scale than any other civilian system worldwide (Wikipedia). In addition, public sector systems also represent some of the most innovative users of the Internet. It is clear that in terms of evaluation the public and private sectors have much to learn from each other.

This book brings some new insights relevant to practitioners and students to the problem of evaluation.

■ References

Brancheau, J. and Wetherby, J. C. (1987), *Key Issues in Information Systems Management: A Delphi Study of IS Executives and Corporate General Managers*, University of Minnesota, Carlson School, MIS Research Center, Working Paper 87–09.

Brynjolfsson, E. (1993). 'The productivity paradox of information technology'. *Communications of the ACM*, 36(12), 66–77.

Brynjolfsson, E. and Hitt, L. M. (1996). 'Paradox lost? Firm-level evidence on the returns to information systems spending'. *Management Science*, 42(4), 541–558.

Brynjolfsson, E. and Hitt, L. M. (2000). 'Beyond computation: Information technology, organizational transformation and business performance'. *Journal of Economic Perspectives*, 14(4), 23–48.

Emery, J. (1973). *Cost Benefit Analysis of Information* Systems, SMIS Workshop, No. 1.

Frielink, A. B. (1961). *Auditing Automatic Data Processing*. Elsevier, Amsterdam.

Frielink, A. B. (1965). Economics of Automatic Data Processing, Amsterdam, North Holland.

Frielink, A. B. (1974). *Economics of Informatics: Symposium Proceedings*. Mainz, Amsterdam, North Holland.

Gregory, R. H. and Van Horn, R. L. (1965). *Automatic Data Processing Systems: Principles and Procedures*. Wadsworth, Belmont.

Grindley, K. (1991). *Managing IT at Board Level: The Hidden Agenda Exposed*. Pitman, London.

Hally, M. (2005). *Electronic Brains: Stories from the Dawn of the Computer Age*. Granta Books, London.

Kaplan, R. and Norton, D. (1992). 'The balanced scorecard'. *Harvard Business Review*, January–February, 71–79.

King, J. L. and Schrems, E. L. (1978). 'Cost–benefit analysis in information systems development and operation'. *ACM Computing Surveys*, 10(1), 19–34.

Kohli, R. and Grover, V. (Forthcoming). "Business value of IT: An essay on expanding research directions to keep up with the times". *Journal of the Association of Information Technology*.

Kumar, K. (1990). 'Post implementation evaluation of computer-based information systems: Current practices'. *Communications of the ACM*, 33(2), 203–212.

Land, F. F. (1996). 'Information revolution'. In Warner, M. (ed.) *International Encyclopaedia of Business and Management*. Thomson Business Press, London Volume III, pp. 2093–2102.

Landauer, T. K. (1995). *The Trouble with Computers: Usefulness, Usability and Productivity*. MIT Press, USA

Langefors, B. (1966). *Theoretical Analysis of Information Systems*. Studentlitteratur, Lund.

Lincoln, T. (1986). 'Do computer systems really pay off?'. *Information and Management*, 11(1), 25–34.

Morris, W., Hawgood, J., Land, F. F., Mumford, E. and Reddington, C. M. (1971). *Economic Evaluation of Computer-Based Systems, Working Party Report*, Vol. 1, NCC, April.

Office of Government Commerce (2005). Managing Successful Projects with PRINCE2.

Parker, M. M. and Benson, R. J. (1987). *Information Economics*. Prentice Hall, Englewood Cliffs, NJ.

Strassmann, P. A. (1985). *Information Payoff: Transformation of Work in the Electronic Age*. The Free Press, New York.

Wikipedia, *National Programme for Information Technology*, http://en.wikipedia.org/wiki/National_Programme_for_IT (Downloaded 11/12/2007).

List of contributors

F. Bannister, Trinity College, Ireland
W. L. Currie, Warwick University, UK
A. Esfahanipour, McMaster University, Canada
I. Entwistle, University of Salford, UK
Z. Irani, Brunel University, UK
S. Jones, Conway County Borough Council, UK
R. Heeks, University of Manchester, UK
B. Light, University of Salford, UK
M. M. Kamal, Brunel University, UK
V. Mantzana, Brunel University, UK
V. Morabito, Bocconi University, Itlay
A. R. Montazemi, McMaster University, Canada
P. Kawalek, University of Manchester, UK
P. E. D. Love, Curtin University of Technology, Australia
M. Nijland, London School of Economics, UK
J. J. Siam, McMaster University, Canada
C. Standing, Edith Cowan University, Australia
R. Stockdale, Massey University, New Zealand
M. Themistocleous, Brunel University, UK
D. Wastell, Nottingham University Business School
L. P. Willcocks, London School of Economics, UK
A. Ghoneim, Brunel University, UK
S. Sahraoui, American University of Sharjah, UAE
A. Gunasekaran, University of Massachusetts, USA
E. W. T. Ngai, The Hong Kong Polytechnic University, China
R. E. McGaughey, The University of Central Arkansas, USA
S. Ozkan, Brunel University, UK
R. J. Paul, Brunel University, UK
T. Eldabi, Brunel University, UK
R. El-Haddadeh, Brunel University, UK
H. Al-Yaseen, Al-Ahlliyya Amman University, Jordan
G. Thomas, The Australian National University, Australia
P. B. Seddon, The University of Melbourne, Australia
W. Fernandez, The Australian National University, Australia
K. Soulioutis, University of Peloponnesus, Greece

Information systems evaluation: A crisis of understanding

Zahir Irani and Peter E. D. Love

Introduction

Information Systems (IS) are a primary enabler to initiate business change within and between organisations and are considered pivotal to the efficient and effective running of a modern business. Indeed, the argument once posed to justify such investment '…to sustain a competitive advantage in today's global marketplace' has now been surpassed, as such systems are needed often just to stay in business. Yet despite the ever increasing investment in IS infrastructures, particularly enterprise-wide applications such *Extended-Enterprise Resource Planning* and *Customer Relationship Management* (CRM), organisations have not been able to gain immediate commensurate financial returns – other than being able to simply trade, on par, with their competitors. This seems paradoxical considering the plethora of reported research in the literature that has propagated investment justification and benefits management models and frameworks.

The importance of investing in new IS architecture and infrastructures has become a topical issue within organisations. Largely motivated by the need to deliver better value products and service through robust and responsive supply chains. With this in mind, business managers are seeking to use *appropriate* methods and techniques to appraise and justify the financial contribution of IS at strategic, operational and tactical levels. Yet, managers often express concern regarding their ability to appraise IS investments prior to committing financial and emotional resources (Raymond et al., 1995; Irani et al., 1997).

Many of the problems identified by Farbey et al. (1993) are still prevalent today, exacerbated yet further because of the complexity associated with linking intra- and interorganisational IS. Notably, the proliferation of IS has often coincided with lower macroeconomic figures of productivity and profitability in sectors such as agriculture, construction, manufacturing and service delivery (Baily and Chakrabarti 1988; Roach 1991). The term *productivity paradox* has thus been used to describe the alleged inability of IS to deliver in *practice* the benefits they promise in *theory* (Brynjolfsson, 1993). Indeed, according to Stratopoulos and Dehning (2000), it is more important *how* organisations manage and utilise their IS assets than *how* much they invest in technology. This is now considered fundamental, with Irani and Love (2001) demonstrating through their research that it is often the soft, human and organisational factors associated with the adoption and implementation process, which lead to organisational learning and improved readiness which, in turn, support the efficient and effective utilisation of the IS resource.

However, the experiences of businesses reported in the normative literature should provide the foundations for learning and improvement and thereby assist with the evaluation process, but unfortunately this has not occurred. Indeed, organisational learning is rarely seen as a 'spin-off' benefit from a robust evaluation process.

As a consequence of the inherent problems consistently identified with IS evaluation, it would appear that there is a 'crisis of understanding' confronting the private and public sectors regarding its' *importance, role* and *relevance* throughout a project's life cycle. A lack of understanding as to *why, how,* and *when* to evaluate IS appears to be the central issue facing managers with little consensus among the academic community, as represented by Irani and Love (2002) in their presentation of taxonomies of IS evaluation approaches. Fundamentally, it appears that managers need to have a better understanding about the impact of IS on organisational performance and a better understanding of the benefits, costs and risks associated with financial and social capital investments in developing such infrastructures. Such understanding can help an organisation better utilise resources and improve its position *vis-à-vis* its competitors. Failure of such understanding can have disastrous consequences such as inappropriate resource allocation and competitive disadvantage (Farbey et al., 1993). With this in mind, the chapters presented hereafter seek to provide readers with an ameliorated understanding of the importance, role and relevance of IS evaluation in today's challenging and complex business environment.

■ Defining IS and then, evaluation

The literature is awash with definitions and scope of what constitutes an IS. In reviewing such definitions, one needs only to pick up an undergraduate text to get a feel for the difference between Information Technology (IT) and its often confused but close relative, [the] IS. One such definition from a leading IS Journal stood out quite profoundly, as it resonated with the authors' own personal views of what constitutes an IS. Paul (2007; 194) explains that:

> '[An] information system is what emerges from the usage that is made of the IT delivery system by the users (whose strengths are that they are human beings not machines)'.

The article by Paul (2007) then goes on to explain that this notion of an IS is made up of two parts:

'1 First the formal processes, which are assumed to be pre-determinable with respect to the decisions about what IT to use. However, these processes will then need to change quite quickly in two ways: first whenever the system is found not to work as anticipated and second so that the IS can appropriately be adapted to the changing world around it, in particular its host organisation.
2 Second the informal processes, which are what the human beings who use the IT and the formal processes create or invent in order to ensure that useful work is done'.

What is important when extrapolating from this view of what constitutes an IS is that there is a significant 'human' dimension that underpins [its] appropriate and successful use thus, resulting benefits, costs and risk. It is these three dimensions that need to form the cornerstones of an evaluation process.

Things are not much different when it comes to defining what constitutes a definition of IS evaluation, with Ramage (1997) explaining that such definitions abound in the literature. For example, Remenyi et al. (1997) focus on the determination of worth and value of something judged according to appropriate criteria and offer the following definition:

> 'a series of activities incorporating understanding, measurement and assessment. It is either a conscious or tacit process which aims to establish the value of or the contribution made by a particular situation. It can also relate to the determination of the worth of an object' (p. 46).

Farbey et al. (1999: 205), however, explain that IS evaluation needs to be seen as

> 'a process that takes place at different points in time or continuously, for searching for and making explicit, quantitatively or qualitatively, all impacts of an IS project'.

Other definitions of evaluation take a narrower perspective and emphasis is placed upon improved learning and understanding as a desired goal for an evaluation activity, and addressing organisational learning. However, this dimension needs to be seen as a significant benefit resulting from an IS evaluation process, especially during post-implementation evaluation (PIE).

Forss et al. (1994) and Serafeimidis and Psoinos (1995) suggest that evaluation is, by definition, synonymous with feedback and that feedback is the link between performance and knowledge structures. Serafeimidis and Psoinos (1995), Farbey et al. (1999) and Irani and Love (2002) do not consider the process of IS evaluation to be solely rational, but interwoven with an array of social activity that is influenced by the human bias of behaviour. Indeed, demonstrating its link back to the earlier definition [of an information system] preferred by Paul (2007).

Prior to commencing any IS evaluation exercise, there must be well-defined goals (Brown and Wallnau, 1996), which should be aligned with the organisation's business strategy (Willcocks and Graeser, 2001). In particular, businesses should articulate their strategic, tactical and operational expectations of the technology to their immediate stakeholders and supply chain partners. Symons and Walsham (1988) consider evaluation as a process to be *understood* and argue that such an understanding should include an awareness of why it is undertaken, the nature of the process which is undertaken and also its inherent complexity (i.e. limitations and problems). Viewed from a systems perspective, evaluation provides the basic feedback function to managers as well as forming a fundamental component of the organisational learning process (Smithson and Hirschheim 1998).

IS investment

IS investments differ in nature from other capital investments as there is a substantial human and organisational interface (Irani et al., 2001). In addition, they are characterised by high risk, erratic timing of cash flows, several portfolio benefits, and significant intangible costs (Milis and Mercken, 2004). Regardless of these challenges that place IS investments in a space that is quite different to other capital investments, for example, in plant and equipment, IS projects are often evaluated using the same traditional appraisal techniques. And here lies much of the dilemma facing IS evaluation. Appraisal techniques that form part of a broader capital budgeting process are typically used by decision-makers to support their evaluation of an investment case. The reasons why organisations appraise their IS investments are explained by Irani and Love (2002) as being:

■ comparison between different projects;
■ rank projects in terms of organisational priorities;
■ justify investment requests by management;
■ control expenditure, benefits, risk, development and implementation of projects;
■ provide a framework that facilitates organisational learning; and
■ mechanism to decide whether to fund, postpone or reject investment requests.

Although these reasons demonstrate the importance of an investment appraisal process and add weight to the use of such techniques, Primrose (1991) noted that many managers view project appraisal as a financial hurdle that has to be overcome and not as a technique for evaluating a project's worth.

IS projects are increasingly a multi-stakeholder investment that has an impact not only on the organisation but, increasingly, its supply chain. The reason is that the decision to adopt a particular technology is often cascaded down throughout the supply chain thus ensuring issues of interoperability. According to Milis and Mercken (2004), there are a number of stakeholders involved with the IS investment process; each having their own set of objectives and expectations. If the evaluation of IS investments is only financially based, and centres on the use of traditional appraisal techniques then the process only serves the objective of management; often limited solely to financial management. This means neglecting all other parties' objectives and, accordingly, failing to incorporate critical factors that might affect the willingness of these parties to cooperate in realising the objectives of the investment for the greater good of the business and thus, possibly impacting on its sustainability.

Choosing an evaluation approach that seeks to go beyond the traditional boundaries of financial evaluation is increasingly important, and many factors associated with developing a robust IS requires a business, user and technology context. Therefore, providing decision-makers with direct cost analysis, cash flow projections, financial figures etc, will not be enough, as there are other strategic (grounded in long-term objectives), softer, political and social factors that need to be considered during the evaluation process. Notwithstanding, it remains important to ensure that financial transparency exists, as organisations cannot afford to fund investments that provide little or no financial return and clearly need to stay in business (financially liquid) until the medium and longer-term benefits can be realised.

A further perspective is a move away from *generic* appraisal techniques to *sympathetic* techniques where IS projects are based on their characteristics. For example, Hochstrasser (1990) classified IS and IT projects based on their objectives:

■ *Infrastructure*: Hardware or software systems installed to enable the subsequent development of front-end systems.
■ *Cost replacement*: IT systems introduced to automate manual activities.
■ *Economy of scale*: Systems introduced to allow a company to handle an increased volume of data.

- *Economy of scope*: IT systems introduced to allow a company to perform an extended range of tasks.
- *Customer support*: IT systems introduced to offer better services to customers.
- *Quality support*: IT introduced to increase the quality of the finished product.
- *Information sharing and manipulation*: IT systems introduced to offer better information sharing and information manipulation.
- *New technology*: IT systems introduced to exploit strategically the business potential of the new technology, to do things that were not possible before.

The view here could be to match a particular appraisal technique to one of the above project characteristics. For example, if the project was a *cost replacement project*, where the costs are direct in nature, and benefits largely efficiency gains, then such an investment can be evaluated using traditional economic appraisal approaches such as ratio based or discounted approaches. However, if the investment is a *new technology project* with a substantial strategic dimension which would translate into intangible benefits and indirect costs, then approaches like the balanced scorecard might well be more appropriate. Selecting the most suitable approach to use remains a challenging task for managers but it is imperative that stakeholders' views are taken into account and decisions are not made purely from a traditional cost accounting perspective.

IS have always taken too long to develop, cost too much to implement and maintain, and are frequently not perceived to be delivering the business benefits that were initially intended (Mahmood 1993; Byrd and Marshall 1997; Irani and Love, 2001; Irani et al., 2001). In recent years the changing role of IS in organisations has given new impetus to the problem of its evaluation. The high expenditure on IS, growing usage that penetrates to the core of organisational functioning, together with unrealistic expectations about its impact, have all served to raise the profile of *how* IS investments should be evaluated and, the benefits that should be expected.

The role and scope of technology investment decision-making is complicated and ever changing. The reason for this is that there has been a continuous expansion of the boundaries surrounding the evaluation domain often grounded in the changing impact that IT offers through its advancement. The change in such boundaries is in part attributable to new technology (increased, scope, functionality and flexibility) and its impact (in human and organisational terms) on developing a new organisational IS infrastructure, juxtaposed with the many interacting socio-technical dimensions that support an organisation. Hence, investment decision-makers not only need to have the skill to evaluate the *nuts and bolts* of the technology sought but also need the foresight to assess its impact on the future of the organisation, and the people that rely on and use the system. Such impact may lie, in terms of the integration links, with existing and future systems, benefit realisation, stakeholder exploitation, cost (direct and indirect) management and risk minimisation.

Benefits, costs and risks of IS

Benefits associated with investing in IS _____

Benefits management comprises a range of management activities designed to ensure that an organisation realises the benefits it plans to achieve from an IS investment. Managers can use an array of appraisal techniques to quantify the amount and timing of cost–benefits associated with implementing IS. This enables decision-makers to decide between competing investments. Some of the most common techniques used for evaluation by business managers have been identified as return on investment, internal rate of return and net present value methods. Such methods, however, are built on the underlying rationale that the costs of an investment need to be related to the benefits that the investment seeks to realise. One of the problems with this *balancing act* is that the costs tend to be incurred immediately, whereas benefits arise in the future. The longer the delay in receiving the desired financial benefits, the greater the risk and this also needs to be factored into the justification of IS investments. Unfortunately, actual realisation of benefits will be modified by future prevailing conditions, and countless other factors that are beyond the control of decision-makers. Indeed, often those that take such investment decisions are not around to see the benefits of the long-term decisions they took years earlier. Additionally, those involved with the IS justification process will invariably make subjective judgements, based on their different interpretations of future costs, quantification of tangible and intangible benefits and their perspective as to how the technology will affect the work activities of all the stakeholders.

Assessing the effective delivery of useful benefits from these services to the business is a complex task and has proven to be very difficult to implement. To assist managers and decision-makers with the IS benefits management process a number of frameworks have been developed. For example, IS benefits have been classified as strategic, tactical and pecuniary (Demmel and Askin, 1992; Demmel and Askin, 1996). Similarly, Peters (1994) argued that the benefits of IS typically fall into three categories: enhanced productivity, business expansion and risk minimisation. Farbey et al. (1995) and Irani and Love (2000) categorised IS benefits as strategic, tactical and operational but acknowledged that benefits at the strategic level are arduous to quantify in as much as they are 'soft' and uncertain and therefore confidence in attributing a financial figure to such benefits is low. Indeed, it has been suggested that traditional investment appraisal techniques are no more accurate than a manager's intuition when it comes to measuring strategic benefits. Tactical and operational benefits focus on efficiency gains within specific processes, functions or departments and so are able to be identified and quantified much more readily.

The evaluation process has become even more complex with the emergence of sophisticated interorganisational systems. Previously, benefits relating to efficiency could be measured with a transparent financial business case made for the investment of IS. As noted above, with the emergence of e-business and IT applications focusing on CRM, and Enterprise Resource Planning (ERP), the identification and quantification of benefits have become an even more complex and challenging issue for managers. The payoffs from implementing such technologies are not controllable and invariably depend upon other business functions within the organisation. Similarly, Changchit et al. (1998) suggest that the 'dynamic nature of IS, the variety of technical options readily available, the uncertainties of projected payoffs, the potential presence of intangible benefits and stakeholders contribute to the problem of benefit identification' (p. 145). While the process of benefits identification can itself contribute to the success of an IS implementation, organisations find the evaluation process difficult and, as a result, tend to use notional arbitrary values for assessing benefits. In large organisations, for example, Lin and Pervan (2003) found that 45% of organisations did not prepare a benefits delivery plan. Furthermore, more than half of the organisations could not determine whether expected benefits were being achieved. Inadequate and inappropriate appraisals/evaluation processes have been found to be the most important inhibitors to effective IS evaluation (Levy et al. 2002).

Costs associated with investing in IS

Difficulties in measuring costs lead to uncertainty about the expected benefits of IT investment and hence are a major constraint on IT investments. Although these costs often go beyond the initial user specification of the system, it is the focus adopted by management on these aspects that often dictates the project's budget and ultimate justification (Renkema and Berghout, 1997).

Direct IT costs are those that can be attributed to the implementation and operation of new technology. Interestingly, Ballantine et al. (1998) suggest that straightforward payback investment evaluation techniques are particularly appropriate for small-to-medium sized enterprises since the majority of them use IT for automation purposes and thus the benefits are short term and often financially quantifiable. Even so, direct IT costs are often underestimated and go beyond the obvious hardware, software and installation costs. Initial cost estimates that contribute towards determining the level of IT investment required are often governed by the performance characteristics that are established by an organisation's IT manager during the system requirements planning stage. These can easily increase during the testing and implementation stages. They may include unexpected additional hardware accessories, increases in processing power, memory and storage devices. Installation and configuration costs are also classified as direct costs, and typically include consultancy support, installation and maintenance engineers and networking hardware/software support.

The indirect costs associated with the adoption of IT are more significant than the direct costs. However, it is the elusive nature of these costs that make their identification and control difficult to determine. Indirect costs are not simply restricted to human factors, but encompass organisational issues as well. Organisational costs relate to the transformation from old to new work practices and the influence of the new system on work activities (Hochstrasser, and Griffths, 1991; Irani and Love, 2001). At first, a temporary loss in productivity may be experienced, as all employees go through a learning curve while adapting to new systems, procedures and guidelines. This involves employees being trained and training others to use and exploit the system. Additional organisational costs may also be experienced once the basic functions of the system are in place. These costs are associated with management's attempts to capitalise on the wider potential of the system at the business and project level. Further costs may include management's attempt to integrate information flows and increase its availability. Companies with extensive IS infrastructures in place tend to change their corporate shape by reducing their number of management levels which may bring benefits such as improved communication, although there are short-term costs associated with restructuring. This is often achieved by redefining the role of many management functions, through increasing their flexibility and overall contribution to the organisation. The costs of organisational restructuring are considered expensive, particularly if isolated groups within the company resist change, and are unwilling to make the transition to the new structure.

Management time has been found to be the most significant indirect cost experienced by many organisations (Irani and Love, 2000). Invariably, management time is spent leading, planning and organising the integration of new systems into current work practices or where relevant, new work practices. The result of implementing newly adopted technologies may also force management to spend additional time revising, approving and subsequently amending their IS-related strategies and deployment plans. A significant amount of resource may also be used to investigate the potential of the IS and in experimenting with new information flows and modified reporting structures, especially workflow; often being built up from data and information flow. Unfortunately, the majority of organisations cannot afford the time or resources to perform systematic evaluation of benefits and likely impacts of IS on organisational processes often because by the time it comes to evaluating the investment decision, there is significant momentum to support the investment decision. Another indirect cost may result from employees developing new skills, thus increasing their flexibility/overall contribution towards the organisation. Once employees have developed new skills they may request revised pay scales or retention allowances or leave to join competitors – here there is a clear cost and risk cross-over. Clearly, such indirect costs associated with employee pay and rewards, together with the cost implications of increases in staff turnover need capturing, and bringing into the IT decision-making arena because they are directly attributable to the investment.

Risk associated with investing in IS

IS projects are renowned for their high *failure* rate although the authors are mindful that defining success and failure is nebulous. Given this, it is prudent for organisations to improve their ability to manage their IS risks so that projects can be delivered against the objectives with which they were justified. According to Willcocks and Margetts (1994), risk refers to exposure to the possibility of failure to obtain some, or all, of the anticipated benefits due to:

■ implementation costs being higher than expected;
■ technical systems performance significantly below the estimate; and
■ incompatibility of the system with selected hardware and software.

Risk management is hence an essential process for the successful delivery of IT projects, yet evidence indicates that the lack of risk identification and management during a project's life cycle is a major contributing factor to the project failure or inability to realise all its objectives. Risks are typically associated with the feasibility of an IT project and the consequent payoffs (i.e. the likelihood of not finishing on time or to budget). However, this is often a myopic view. The assessment of risk during the justification process can enable managers to identify those outcomes that may adversely influence behavioural, structural and strategic aspects within the organisation before they materialise. In addition, it is important to take into account the risk of computer systems security breach and the costs of computer systems breakdown for the organisation. In doing so, managers can put in place mechanisms to manage and mitigate their risks while also acknowledging the costs of not doing so.

In seeking to explore this challenging area of research, the editors of this book approached leading international scholars in this field to offer their own perspectives and insights through their research. The result is this edited book that seeks to act as the focus of knowledge in the area of IS evaluation and thus a reference for those wishing to seek a deeper insight. The book has been carefully sectioned with the following abstracts acting as useful pointers to help navigate through the book.

Chapter 1: *Information technology and systems justification*
A. Gunasekaran, E.W.T. Ngai and R.E. McGaughey

Abstract

Information Technology (IT) such as Electronic Data Interchange (EDI), Radio Frequency Identification Technology (RFID), wireless, the Internet and World Wide Web (WWW), and Information Systems (IS) such as Electronic Commerce (e-commerce) systems and ERP systems have had a tremendous impact in education, healthcare, manufacturing, transportation, retailing, pure services and even war. Many organisations turned to IT/IS to help them achieve their goals; however, many failed to achieve the full potential of IT/IS. These failures can be attributed, at least in part, to a weak link in the planning process. That weak link is the IT/IS justification process. The decision-making process has grown more difficult in recent years with the increased complexity of business brought about by the rapid growth of supply chain management, the virtual enterprise and e-business. These are but three of the many changes in the business environment over the past 10 to 12 years. The complexities of this dynamic new business environment should be taken into account in IT/IS justification. A. Gunasekaran, E.W.T. Ngai and R.E. McGaughey conducted a review of the current literature on IT/IS justification. The purpose of the literature review was to assemble meaningful information for the development of a framework for IT/IS evaluation that better reflects the new business environment. A suitable classification scheme has been proposed for organising the literature reviewed and directions for future research are indicated.

Chapter 2: *Revisiting the content, context and process of IS evaluation*
R. Stockdale, C. Standing, Peter E.D. Love and Z. Irani

Abstract

Irani (2002) argued that generic Information Systems (IS) evaluation is not an effective process and that there is a need for specific models. Thence, in this chapter Rosemary Stockdale, Craig Standing, Peter E.D. Love and Zahir Irani build on the context, content and process (CCP) to develop a parsimonious framework for building individual IS evaluation models. Realising that one of the major challenges for IS evaluation is to develop frameworks that are sufficiently generic to be applicable to a wide range of circumstances, but also sufficiently detailed to provide effective guidance, they favour the use of CCP as an overarching approach to evaluation. This allows for questions of what is being measured, by whom and for what purpose, to be asked. Furthermore, the interaction and linking between *context*, *content* and *process* allow for the complicated procedure of evaluation to be explored in multiple dimensions. The chapter presents a framework for examining the key issues of IS evaluation. The concepts of content, context and process are divided into elements of *what, why, who, how* and *when* to enable the influences within an interpretive evaluation approach to be reflected upon. Stockdale, Standing, Love and Irani emphasise the fact that the use of the proposed framework requires an approach that supports understanding of the nuances, influences and perceptions of those involved in the evaluation, and the way they are, in turn, influenced by the context of the organisation. A review of the CCP framework's strengths and limitations is also presented.

Chapter 3: How IT evaluation methods are used: Examining case research from an ANT perspective
M. Nijland and L.P. Willcocks

Abstract

In this chapter, Menno Nijland and Leslie P. Willcocks explore the apparent paradox of Information Technology (IT) evaluation methods not being broadly employed despite their potential to assist organisations in improving the management of IT costs and benefits. This is paradoxical since organisations look for improvement in that area; a multitude of evaluation methods exists and both academic and professional literature suggests their use will lead to beneficial effects. Nijland and Willcocks argue that such methods do not manifest their expected employment due to limited understanding of evaluation methods and unrealistic assumptions about evaluation employment. The study builds on actor-network theory (ANT) to explore an in-depth case study of the use of an IT evaluation method at a major European insurance company. Far from an evaluation method being neutral, with innate qualities, with use progressing as planned, the study demonstrates that during a process of mutual translation both the evaluation method and its surrounding actors enter into a dynamic negotiation mutually translating each other. The resulting process of use has emergent properties and is characterised by improvisation rather than blueprint planning. The chapter also assesses the value ANT brings to such an analysis.

Chapter 4: IT project evaluation: Why more formal evaluation is not necessarily better
G. Thomas, P.B. Seddon and W. Fernandez

Abstract

Motivated by the high failure rates that IT projects continue to experience, Graeme Thomas, Peter B. Seddon and Walter Fernandez strive to gain a better understanding of which Information Technology (IT) evaluation methodologies and practices are being used today. In this chapter, they explore effective IT project evaluation practices in Australia among 36 companies operating in three industry sectors: finance and insurance; mining; and electricity, gas and water supply. Qualitative analysis of in-depth interviews with 72 senior managers was used to determine the characteristics of effective evaluation practices. Graeme Thomas, Peter B. Seddon and Walter Fernandez found that effective IT project evaluation outcomes are more closely related to governance structures and leadership behaviours than formal processes or methods. While some level of formality helped improve evaluation, processes that were too formal resulted in dysfunctional behaviours. It was only when simple and flexible evaluation processes were combined with six key organisational drivers that positive behaviours were reinforced, actions were aligned, and evaluation processes were used effectively. The conclusions offered in this chapter provide both theoretical and practical insights into the evaluation of IT projects in complex environments.

Chapter 5: Don't mention the war: Managing disbenefits
F. Bannister

Abstract

There is a large literature, including several weighty books, on benefits realisation and benefits management. In contrast, the concept of disbenefits management is something of an orphan in IS value research and the IS value literature. Disbenefits, like hidden costs, is an under-researched and poorly understood topic. In this chapter, Frank Banister explores the concept of disbenefits. According to Bannister, the problem with disbenefits management is that many disbenefits are hidden. They are often harder to find than benefits and the link between their elimination and better organisational performance is not always immediately obvious or simple to trace. Furthermore, it is argued that the disbenefits of (Information Communication Technologies) ICT are significantly greater than is generally realised, particularly if increased business risk is taken into account. Bannister argues that like benefits, disbenefits need to be managed and the difference is that, in the case of disbenefits, the objective is minimisation. The chapter presents and discusses several illustrative examples of common disbenefits and an outlines a six-stage methodology for disbenefits management which is pre-emptive as well as competitive. If properly applied, this methodology will result in material productivity improvements and cost savings.

Chapter 6: Spot the difference: Evaluation of custom and package applications
I. Entwistle and B. Light

Abstract

With the motivation of spurring the location of package software studies more squarely within the field of Information Systems (IS), Ian Entwistle and Ben Light aim at illustrating the similarities between the package software evaluation process and the more traditional custom-developed approaches. Packaged software is now a common approach for IS provision in work organisations. A key aspect of the selection of packages is the process of evaluation. However, much of the literature on the selection of packages does not relate to the broader base of work on evaluation within the field of IS. Through a case study investigation, Entwistle and Light attempt to bridge the gap between packaged software studies and other IS studies that incorporate an element of evaluation. The main point of the chapter is that although there are differences, packaged software evaluation also shares many similarities with traditional custom-oriented practices (and vice versa). In this case at least, custom and package applications were evaluated in tandem. Entwistle and Light call for the opening up of discussions in this area and further research which emphasises the theoretical and practical similarities and differences between these two forms of software.

Chapter 7: Post-implementation evaluation of IT Systems: A close review of practice
H. Al-Yaseen, T. Eldabi, R.J. Paul and R. El-Haddadeh

Abstract

In this chapter, Hussein Al-Yaseen, Tillal Eldabi, Ray J. Paul and Ramzi El-Haddadeh attempt to obtain insights into post-implementation evaluation (PIE) in order to identify the real extent to which PIE is practised and what lessons can be learned to improve knowledge about it. In doing so, they add to the knowledge base by reviewing the current state of practice of the IT evaluation process and its types (prior-implementation and PIE) in business organisations. Secondly, understanding this complex phenomena: to explain and understand the findings of this research to gain a comprehensive picture of IT evaluation. In the chapter they identify several factors that affect the evaluation process, such as: timing of evaluation types; stakeholders and their role in the evaluation process; evaluation criteria; and the gap between Prior Operational Use evaluation (POU) and PIE outcomes.

Furthermore, propelled to research practitioners' perceptions of the evaluation process and the practices associated with the evaluation adopted within large organisations, they present the findings of a survey conducted on the FTSE 500 companies. The survey shows that around two-thirds of the 123 respondent organisations gave less importance to the PIE than POU evaluation. Of those organisations who did use PIE, some thought of it as a mechanistic process for signing off the project. The chapter demonstrates that practitioners do not appreciate the full benefits of PIE and need to be aware of such benefits. Such lack of appreciation is evidently behind the apparent scarcity of implementations of PIE, which negatively feeds back into perceptions and so forth.

Chapter 8: Evaluation of information service providers in support of the fixed-income market
A.R. Montazemi, A. Esfahanipour and J.J. Siam

Abstract

The objective of this chapter is to evaluate three different information systems (IS). These IS, considered global information service providers to (Fixed Income) FI-Market actors, are: Bloomberg, Reuters, and Action Economics. The question raised in this chapter is: How valuable are these three systems to FI-Market actors? Montazemi, Esfahanipour and Siam compare and contrast the functionality of each system to highlight their advantages/disadvantages towards usage. While both private and public information are critical to profitable trade in FI markets, the question arises as to the significance of different information sources in support of different stages of FI actors' decision-making processes (i.e. information categories). The aim is to investigate the value of information sources to actors in the FI market for pre-trade that may lead to an execution of trade and post-trade to assess the quality of their previous transactions. Montazemi, Esfahanipour and Siam examine the FI information providers based on a human computer interaction (HCI) framework to understand the way people interact with computers in terms of the processes they engage in, resources they use, and tasks they intend to accomplish. The framework identifies four levels of interaction within the context of FI information providers namely; tasks level, semantic level, syntax level and lexical level. The findings show that the platform that seemed to serve on FI trader best was Bloomberg followed by Reuters and then Action Economics. Reuters and Bloomberg provide the essential information that FI traders require for their daily involvement in the markets. The chapter provides a detailed analysis of the three platforms in support of the above assessment.

Chapter 9: Evaluating actors and factors associated with healthcare information systems
V. Mantzana, M. Themistocleous, V. Morabito and K. Soulioutis

Abstract

Enterprise Application Integration (EAI) has emerged to support organisations overcoming their integration problems and it has been adopted by many organisations in various sectors. Despite its importance, the healthcare domain develops EAI solutions at a slower pace compared to other sectors. The small number of EAI applications in healthcare has resulted in limited research in this area with many issues requiring further investigation. The normative literature analyzes the factors that influence EAI adoption in healthcare (MAESTRO model) but it has not yet explored the role of actors during the adoption process. In this chapter, Vasiliki Mantzana, Marinos Themistocleous and Vincenzo Morabito take a step forward and contribute to the body of knowledge as they: (a) highlight the role of healthcare actors and attitudes towards EAI adoption, (b) identify the actors involved in this process, by using the proposed IGOHcaps method and (c) combine the actor-oriented approach with the factors influencing EAI adoption. They believe that such an approach is significant and novel as it: (a) enhances existing EAI adoption models (MAESTRO) by incorporating an actor-oriented analysis and (b) facilitates healthcare organisations in making robust decisions for EAI adoption. Mantzana, Themistocleous, and Morabito aim to contribute in this area by presenting and validating a model that incorporates human actors (IGOHcaps method) (Mantzana et al., 2007) into an existing model on EAI adoption (MAESTRO) (Khoumbati et al., 2006). Sections 1 and 2 describes accordingly, Healthcare Information Systems (HIS), their potential and challenges. In Section 3, the need for HIS integration is presented. In the sections that follow, the adoption of EAI is analyzed and the authors derive and propose a conceptual model that incorporates human, organisational and technical factors. Thereafter, the research methodology and the case study used to evaluate the conceptual model are described. The findings and their analysis are presented and explained before conclusions are drawn in Section 7.

Chapter 10: Evaluating the governance structure for public sector IT: The UK National Programme in the Health Service
W.L. Currie

Abstract

The National Programme for Information Technology (IT) is the largest civil IT programme worldwide at an initial estimated cost of £6.2 billion over a 10-year period. Launched in 2002, it provides standardised IT solutions across the National Health Service (NHS). Traditionally, the NHS has witnessed under investment in IT with a proliferation of disparate IT systems implemented at the local level. But while the National Programme aims to change this, the top-down, government-led approach is coming under increasing media interest as all planned IT systems implementations are running late. Nearly 5 years on – and under pressure from government and senior hospital managers to deliver working systems – the relationship between public sector organisations and private sector firms is once again under increasing scrutiny. Wendy L. Currie presents the findings from a longitudinal study on the National Programme covering the period between 2001–2006. With the aim of examining the relationship between the various stakeholders involved in developing and implementing the National Programme, Currie has evaluated the formal governance structure that comprises the development of an agency charged with running the National Programme – Connecting for Health. The empirical findings suggest that Connecting for Health has focused almost entirely on developing a rigid governance structure where IT vendors enter into tight procurement contracts to the detriment of the softer, change management issues including relationship building and user engagement. The chapter begins with an overview of the governance structure in UK healthcare and the identification of five key stakeholders, each of whom plays an important role in the fulfilment of the National Programme. Next, a brief overview of the research methods, data collection and analysis is presented. The findings from the case study on the National Programme are presented. The chapter concludes by highlighting a number of critical pressure points that are seriously damaging the progress of the National Programme and offer some insights for theory and practice.

Chapter 11: Strategic alignment and a culture innovation: Using the SPRINT methodology to meet two challenges of information age government
P. Kawalek and D. Wastell

Abstract

The task of encouraging innovation while ensuring the alignment of information systems (IS) and organisational goals is central to all organisations in this ongoing 'information age'. In this chapter, Peter Kawalek and David Wastell place this problem in the context of organisational change through Business Process Reengineering (BPR). The domain is government. They describe a BPR methodology which attempts to address the key issues of alignment and innovation. The methodology is known as SPRINT (Salford Process Reengineering method Involving New Technology) and was developed collaboratively with the IT department of a local public administration, the City of Salford (a novel feature in itself, which was seen as key to its adoption in practice). This work recognises the contested, problematic nature of the term 'BPR'. It has also been influenced by recent thinking in the area of change management and strategic alignment, principally the need to adopt a participative, improvisational approach to change, a bottom-up 'design approach' to strategic alignment, and the need to embed a culture of innovation across organisational layers. The findings presented in the chapter illustrate just how difficult it is to meet the challenge of remaking so-called information age government, which will be made up of a huge number of projects as people try to apply new technologies and ideas to their organisations.

Chapter 12: Social dimension of IT/IS evaluation: Views from the public sector
S. Jones

Abstract

This chapter was motivated by a concern for the use of IS evaluation methods in the public sector. Stephen Jones contends that there are a significant number of methods and techniques available to enable both public and private sector organisations to undertake IS evaluation. However, it is mechanistic IS evaluation methods based upon economic factors that dominate. This is particularly an issue in the public sector, because economic factors are mainly irrelevant and inappropriate in this domain. Furthermore, these methods are often misused, underused or not used in practice due to their complexity. Mechanistic IS evaluation approaches contain little or no social and organisational dimensions with regard to the usefulness and impact of the IS. This is a major omission because user perspectives on IS evaluation are useful to public sector bodies. This aspect is becoming critically important due to central government modernisation and improvement initiatives, which require increasing public sector IS investment and assessment, together with increasing citizen use of e-Government systems to interact and transact with public sector organisations. The primary objective of the chapter is to discuss the UK central government improvement agenda, IS deployment and evaluation in public sector organisations, IS evaluation methods, and to argue for more widespread development and use of interpretive IS evaluation approaches that contain social and organisational perspectives. The chapter also presents tentative guidelines for interpretive IS evaluation that have been elicited from the discussion.

Chapter 13: Benchmarking e-Government: Improving the national and international measurement, evaluation and comparison of e-Government
R. Heeks

Abstract

There is little explicit evidence about the demand for benchmarking studies, though in some cases they arise out of e-Government practitioner forums or are conducted by e-Government agencies. One can make an assumption in such cases that benchmarking has been demand-driven. However, in general, there is a knowledge gap around the demand for benchmarking data. In this chapter, Richard Heeks targets those involved – in planning, in undertaking, in using or in evaluating – the benchmarking or measurement of e-Government. Heeks draws on models of e-Government and current practice of benchmarking e-Government to answer four questions namely: Why benchmark e-Government? What to benchmark? How to benchmark? and How to report? The chapter provides an extended series of recommendations based on good practice or innovative practice, backed up by a set of conceptual frameworks and statistical findings. Furthermore, checklists are provided for those planning and for those evaluating e-Government benchmarking studies.

Chapter 14: Evaluating e-Government infrastructure through enterprise application integration (EAI)
M.M. Kamal, M. Themistocleous and V. Morabito

Abstract

During the past few years public organisations have adopted CRM applications to improve both their services and relationships with their citizens. The application of CRM is beneficial for local government authorities (LGAs) as it results in improvements in information sharing and cost reduction. Recently, many LGAs have attempted to link together their e-Gov and CRM applications to deliver better services. Nonetheless, public organisations have realised that they can gain significant advantages when they integrate their CRM and e-Gov IS with their disparate back-office solutions. Thus, they are seeking ways to integrate their applications and IT infrastructures. Kamal, Themistocleous and Morabito suggest that public organisations can focus on integration technologies like Enterprise Application Integration (EAI) to incorporate their systems and processes, and thus, achieve their goals. In this chapter, they present and analyze one case study that focuses on the development of integrated e-Gov and IT infrastructures in an LGA. The case organisation has initially incorporated its e-Gov-IS with CRM to improve its services. Such interconnectivity has resulted in a partial integration solution, as there was no linkage between the front- (CRM, e-Gov) and back-office systems. Thus, the organisation collaborated with its software supplier to apply an EAI solution and piece together its IS. The extracted results may seem less as they are based on one pilot case study. In addition, all factors reported by Kamal and Themistocleous were not analyzed in this one case study. However, it is considered a starting point in comparing and analyzing EAI adoption factors when analyzing further case studies within LGAs.

Chapter 15: t-Government for benefit realisation: A research agenda
S. Sahraoui, A. Ghoneim, Z. Irani and S. Ozkan

Abstract

This chapter proposes a model for t-Government and highlights the research agenda needed to increase understanding of transformational government and the processes involved in furthering the agenda of t-Government. In particular, both an operational and a conceptual model for effective involvement of citizens and businesses in government functioning have been proposed. This will help to define an agenda for t-Government research that emerges from national UK strategy and policy for e-Government. The main threads of t-Government encompass: (1) A citizen-centric delivery of public services or e-inclusion, (2) A shared services culture to maximise value added to clients (3) The effective delivery and management of resources and skills within government or professionalism. All three threads should be addressed principally from the perspectives of delivery, evaluation and participation in view of benefits realisation as envisioned by government strategic planning and policy directives (Cabinet Office, 2005). The management of change dimension of these phenomena have been included in the research agenda. In particular, research is needed to reshape the discourse towards emphasising a citizen-centric approach that defines, develops, and benefits from public service. Decision-makers in government will need models of governance that fulfil transformational objectives. They will also need models of benefits realisation within a strategic governance framework. It has been argued that t-Government research should be addressing these relative voids.

References

Baily, M. N. and Chakrabarti, A. (1988). *Innovation and the Productivity Crisis*. Brookings Institution, Washington, DC.

Brown, A. W. and Wallnau, K. C. (1996). 'Framework for evaluating software technology'. *IEEE Software*, 13(5), 39–49.

Brynjolfsson, E. (1993). 'The productivity paradox of information technology'. *Communications of the ACM*, 36(12), 67–77.

Byrd, T. A. and Marshall, T. E. (1997). 'Relating information technology investment to organisational performance: A causal model analysis'. *Omega*, 25(1), 43–56.

Cabinet Office (2005). Transformational Government-Enabled by Technology Strategy Document.

Changchit, C., Kshiti, J. D. and Lederer, A. L. (1998). 'Process and reality in information systems benefit analysis'. *Information Systems Journal*, 8, 145–162.

Demmel, J. G. and Askin, R. G. (1992). 'A multiple-objective decision model for the evaluation of advanced manufacturing technologies'. *Journal of Manufacturing Systems*, 11(3), 79–194.

Demmel, J. G. and Askin, R. G. (1996). 'Multiple-objective evaluation of advanced manufacturing system technology with risk'. *IIE Transactions*, 28(3), 225–249.

Farbey, B., Land, F. and Targett, D. (1993). *How to Assess your IT Investment: A Study of Methods and Practice*. Butterworth-Heinmann, Oxford.

Farbey, B., Targett, D. and Land, F. (1995). 'Evaluating business information systems: reflections on an empirical study'. *Information Systems Journal*, 5, 235–252.

Farbey, B., Land, F. and Targett, D. (1999). 'IS evaluation: a process of bringing together benefits, costs and risks'. In Currie, W. and Gallier, R. (Eds.), *Rethinking Management Information Systems*. Oxford University Press, New York, pp. 204–228.

Forss, K., Cracknell, B. and Samset, K. (1994). 'Can evaluation help an organization learn?'. *Evaluation Practice*, 18(3), 253–266.

Hochstrasser, B. (1990). 'Evaluating IT investments – matching techniques to projects'. *Journal of Intelligent Systems*, 5, 215–221.

Hochstrasser, B. and Griffths, C. (1991). *Controlling IT Investment: Strategy and Management*. Chapman and Hall, London.

Irani, Z. (2002). 'Information systems evaluation: Navigating through the problem domain'. *Information and Management*, 40(1), 11–24.

Irani, Z. and Love, P. E. D. (2000). 'The propagation of technology management taxonomies for evaluating information systems'. *Journal of Management Information Systems*, 17(3), 161–177.

Irani, Z. and Love, P. E. D. (2001). 'The propagation of technology management taxonomies for evaluating investments in information systems'. *Journal of Management Information System*, 17(3), 161–177.

Irani, Z. and Love, P. E. D. (2002). 'Developing a frame of reference for *ex-ante* IT/IS investment evaluation'. *European Journal of Information Systems*, 11(1), 74–82.

Irani, Z., Ezingeard, J.-N. and Grieve, R. J. (1997). 'Integrating the costs of an IT/IS infrastructure into the investment decision making process'. *The International Journal of Technological Innovation, Entrepreneurship and Technology Management (Technovation)*, 17(11–12), 695–706.

Irani, Z., Sharif, A. M. and Love, P. E. D. (2001). 'Transforming failure into success through organisational learning: An analysis of a manufacturing information system'. *European Journal of Information Systems*, 10(1), 55–66.

Khoumbati, K., Themistocleous, M. and Irani, Z. (2006). 'Evaluating the Adoption of Enterprise Application Integration in Healthcare Organisations'. *Journal of Management Information Systems*, 22(4), 69–108.

Levy, M., Powell, P. and Yetton, P. (2002). 'The Dynamics of SME information stations'. *Small Business Economics*, 19(4), 341–354.

Mahmood, M. A. (1993). 'Associating organisational strategic performance with information technology investment: An exploratory research'. *European Journal of Information Systems*, 2(3), 185–200.

Mantzana, V., Themistocleous, M., Irani, Z. and Morabito, V. (2007). 'Identifying Healthcare Actors involved in the Adoption of Information Systems'. *European Journal of Information Systems*, 16(1), 91–102.

Milis, K. and Mercken, R. (2004). 'The use of the balanced scorecard for the evaluation of information and communication technology projects'. *International Journal of Project Management*, 22, 87–97.

Paul, R. J. (2007). 'EDITORIAL: Challenges to information systems: time to change'. *European Journal of Information Systems*, 16(3), 193–195.

Peters, G. (1994). 'Evaluating your computer investment strategy'. In Willcocks, L. (Ed.), *Information Management: The Evaluation of Information Systems Investments*. Chapman and Hall, London, pp. 99–111.

Primrose, P. L. (1991). *Investment in Manufacturing Technology*. Chapman and Hall, UK.

Ramage, M. (1997). Developing a methodology for the evaluation of cooperative systems. Proceedings of the 20th Information Systems Research Conference in Scandinavia, Department of Informatics, University of Oslo, Norway, pp. 769–789.

Raymond, L., Pare, G. and Bergeron, F. (1995). 'Matching information technology and organisational structure: An empirical study with implications for performance'. *European Journal of Information Systems*, 4, 3–16.

Remenyi, D., Sherwood-Smith, A. M. and White, T. (1997). *Achieving Maximum Value From Information Systems*. John Wiley and Sons.

Renkema, J. W. and Berghout, E. W. (1997). 'Methodologies for information systems investment evaluation at the proposal stage: a comparative review'. *Information and Software Technology*, 39, 1–13.

Roach, S. S. (1991). 'Services under siege: The restructuring imperative'. *Harvard Business Review, September/October*, , 83–91.

Serafeimidis, V. and Psoinos, A. (1995). Emerging issues and a holistic approach for information technology investments evaluation into the 1990s. Proceedings of the 5th Hellenic Conference Symons, V.J., and Walsham, G. (1988). The evaluation of information systems: A critique. Journal of Applied Systems Analysis, 15, pp. 119–132 on Informatics, 7th–9th December, Athens, Greece.

Smithson, S. and Hirschheim, R. (1998). 'Analysing information systems evaluation: Another look at an old problem'. *European Journal of Information Systems*, 7(3), 158–174.

Stratopoulos, T. and Dehning, B. (2000). 'Does successful investment in information technology solve the productivty paradox'. *Information and Management*, 38(2), 103–117.

Willcocks, L. P. and Margetts, H. (1994). 'Risk assessment and information systems'. *European Journal of Information Systems*, 5(2), 127–138.

Willcocks, L. P. and Graeser, V. (2001). *Delivering IT and e-Business Value*. Butterworth, Oxford, UK.

Chapter 1 ■■■

Information technology and systems justification

A. Gunasekaran, E. W. T. Ngai and R. E. McGaughey

■ Introduction

Globalisation, together with the development of information technology/information systems (IT/IS), have had a tremendous impact on the way organisations function. These developments influence the strategies, tactics and operational decisions of organisations. The application of marketing principles to the transfer and commercialisation of technology is a vital policy issue in the highly competitive global marketplace (Drury and Farhoomand, 1999). IT has spread to the extent that it is hard to envision any organisation in an industrialised nation, and even in a developing nation, not using some form of IT/IS. The rapid growth of IT investments has put pressure on management to take into account investment risks and payoffs in decision-making (Kim and Sanders, 2002). Comprehensive but understandable methodologies are needed to solve the complicated project justification problems arising from the complexity of new technologies.

Selecting and effectively pursuing the right IT/IS investments can be a key factor in sustaining corporate viability and prosperity (Bacon, 1992). Managers have employed various methods for evaluating the cost and benefits of IT/IS investment, ranging from simple computational formula to very complex techniques that blend quantitative and qualitative analysis into one. Quantitative techniques have been used mainly for capital investment decisions, but they do not necessarily capture the entire impact of new technology adoption (Shank and Govindarajan, 1992). Justification difficulties are linked to the intangible nature of the benefits promised by IT, such as improved communication and control, enhanced capabilities, and competitive advantage (Senn, 1989), and likewise to costs that are difficult to quantify.

The original version of this chapter has been published in *European Journal of Operational Research*, Volume 173, No. 3 (2006), 957–983.

Existing models for IS project selection typically do not reflect interdependencies among criteria and candidate projects. Careful and deliberate consideration of these interdependencies among criteria captures valuable cost savings and benefits that accrue to organisations from the use of IT/IS. Lee and Kim (2000) argue that IS project selection problems are multi-criteria, decision-making (MCDM) problems. They suggest that it is very important to incorporate multiple opinions in order to understand the interdependence among criteria and candidate projects. They further suggest an improved IS project selection methodology, which reflects interdependencies among evaluation criteria and candidate projects, using an analytic network process (ANP) within a zero-one goal programming (ZOGP) model. Their rather complex approach highlights the importance of considering the implications of IT/IS from multidimensional perspectives and the combined impact of IT/IS in all areas.

The level of investment and the associated risks involved in planning and implementing IT/IS, coupled with less than stellar results reported by many companies, highlight the need for improved understanding of the IT/IS justification process. A company's success, or lack thereof, in this important area can have a significant impact on its competitiveness. In the literature, there is a considerable volume of research reported on IT/IS evaluation, but a balanced and practical framework has yet to be established. What is proposed here is a simple, balanced, and more complete framework for IT/IS evaluation.

The chapter is organised as follows: First, IT/IS evaluation and justification is discussed. Second, the details of the research methodology are presented. Third, the classification scheme used for reviewing the selected literature available on IT/IS evaluation and justification is discussed. Fourth, a brief review of the literature on IT/IS evaluation and justification is presented. Fifth, a framework has been developed for the design and implementation of IT/IS justification. Finally, it concludes.

■ IT/IS evaluation and justification

IT investment studies are important, especially in the current business environment, because of the large sums of money spent on IT/IS projects as well as the risks. The benefits are expected to be of strategic value. In the published literature there is little consensus about why some IT projects succeed and others fail. A common criticism is that companies do not give due consideration to intangibles which produce long-term strategic and operational benefits (Anandarajan and Wen, 1999). Anandarajan and Wen (1999) concluded that IT investment evaluation is very complex, and because IT becomes more sophisticated over time, we may never have a complete understanding of the full range of costs and benefits associated with it. This suggests that there is a need to develop a balanced approach to evaluating investment in IT/IS projects. For example, if the evaluation relates to IT/IS in services, one might need to assign more weight to intangibles, and if it is in manufacturing, one might need to assign higher weight to tangibles. With services or manufacturing, different situations will require different weights be assigned to financial, non-financial, tangible and intangible criteria. For example, when evaluating IT/IS projects in marketing, more weight might be given to financial performance and intangibles like customer satisfaction, but an IT/IS project in manufacturing might necessitate more weight be assigned to non-financial performance measures like capacity utilisation, and intangibles like flexibility.

The use of traditional appraisal techniques to justify investments in IT and IS has received a lot of attention in recent years. This is due to the increased worldwide investment in IT/IS. Companies need to justify the investment in IT/IS taking into account costs and benefits, both short-term and long-term. Small and Chen (1995) and Alshawi et al. (2003) argue that a lack of management guidelines for use in investment decisions could encourage decision-makers to:

- refuse to implement an IT infrastructure that could be beneficial to the long-term competitiveness of the organisation;
- invest in IT as an 'act of faith'; or
- use creative accounting (assigning arbitrary values to benefits and costs) as a means of passing the budgetary process.

The justification process is a major concern for those organisations considering the development of an IT/IS infrastructure. Weak justification may be putting the competitive advantage of many companies at risk. The reason is management's inability to evaluate the holistic implications of adopting new technology, both in terms of the benefits and costs. The adoption of new technology, especially IT/IS, can clearly be one of the most lengthy, expensive and complex tasks that a firm can undertake. The level of investment and high degree of uncertainty associated with the adoption of this technology implies that issues involving project justification should assume great importance (Irani et al., 2002).

Although there is a considerable body of literature on IT/IS evaluation, gaps still exist regarding the application of the research findings. The following are some of the deficiencies discovered in the existing literature:

- No precise definition of various performance measures and metrics based on the organisational characteristics.
- No clear distinction among strategic, tactical and operational performance measures and metrics.
- Identification and measurement of intangibles and other non-financial performance measures relevant in IT/IS justification is problematic and often neglected.
- No good framework for assessing the implications of IT/IS on organisational performance measures during the implementation of IT/IS.
- Absence of risk measurement and management models for IT/IS implementation.
- No proven optimisation models for IT/IS evaluation.
- No good framework for selection of suitable tools or techniques for IT/IS investment evaluation.

The current literature is reviewed in an effort to develop a contemporary framework that sheds more light on these deficiencies and moves us in the direction of bridging these gaps.

Research methodology

A literature review was the research methodology employed for developing the proposed framework for IT/IS evaluation. The literature review focused on articles in scholarly journals published over the last 14 years. In addition to classifying the literature on IT/IS evaluation, techniques and tools used to model and analyze IT/IS projects environments were identified. The following were the major objectives of this study:

- Highlight the significance of IT/IS justification and its implications for organisational performance.
- Identify the major performance criteria that should be considered in evaluating and justifying IT/IS.
- Identify the techniques and tools used for evaluating and justifying IT/IS projects.
- Focus attention on evaluating the implementation stage of IT/IS projects.

The literature review was undertaken to identify articles and provide information that should be helpful to researchers and practitioners studying, or involved in, IT/IS evaluation. The literature on IT/IS evaluation and closely associated topics was reviewed and classified in the following sections.

Classification of the literature on IT/IS evaluation

There are several survey-type articles on the evaluation of IT/IS investment. Included among them are the works of Ezingeard et al. (1999), Irani (2002) and Irani and Love (2001). Most articles focus on different types of performance measures such as strategic, tactical and operational, tangibles, intangibles, financial and non-financial. Some articles focus on the techniques and tools used in evaluating IT/IS projects and investments; however, there are few that provide a comprehensive review of articles ranging from the conceptual, to IT/IS investment evaluation, to evaluating the implementation of IT/IS projects. From this review of literature on IT/IS evaluation, a generic framework is proposed which could assist researchers and practitioners in studying or evaluating the costs and benefits of IT/IS.

IS can improve organisational efficiency and effectiveness, thereby providing competitive advantage. Irani (2002) argues that, although many of the savings resulting from IS are considered suitable for inclusion within the traditional accountancy framework, it is the intangibles and non-financial benefits, together with indirect project costs, that complicate the justification process. Irani (2002) reviewed the normative literature in the area of IS justification, and then proposed a set of conjectures. Many managers now appreciate the wider strategic implications of developing a robust and responsive IT infrastructure, yet businesses still wrestle with the dilemma of how to assess, quantify and accommodate the implications of infrastructural investments within traditional methods of appraisal. Managers still struggle with identifying and measuring the strategic implications of IT/IS. There is no suitable framework to guide them.

The literature on IT/IS justification has been divided into four major areas (gleaned from the literature review) that are considered essential for developing and managing IT/IS justification (see Table 1.1). The four major areas include: (i) general IT/IS evaluation and justification concepts, (ii) evaluation criteria for justifying IT/IS projects, (iii) techniques and tools used for evaluating and justifying IT/IS projects and (iv) evaluation of the implementation of IT/IS projects. The proposed framework for IT/IS justification addresses these four areas. The major classifications and articles that come under each are presented in Table 1.1. The details of the four areas of interest are discussed in the next section.

Table 1.1 Classification of the literature available on IT/IS justification

Classification criteria	References
General IT/IS evaluation and justification concepts	Clemons (1991); Willcocks (1992a, b); Sethi et al. (1993); Hitt and Brynjolfsson (1996); Grover et al. (1998); Ballantine and Stray (1999); Lubbe and Remenyi (1999); Bharadwaj (2000); Chircu and Kauffman (2000); Devaraj and Kohli (2000); Larsen and Bloniarz (2000); Sircar et al. (2000); Massey et al. (2001); Alshawi et al. (2003); Khoumbati et al. (2006); Connell and Young (2007)
Evaluation criteria emphasised for justifying IT/IS projects	Chokhani (1992); Davis et al. (1992); Banker et al. (1993); Belcher and Watson (1993); Powell (1993); Ballantine and Stray (1999); Drury and Farhoomand (1999); Ryan and Harrison (2000); Sarkis and Sundarraj (2000); Tallon et al. (2000); Croteau and Bergeron (2001); Gunasekaran et al. (2001); Kushniruk et al. (2001); Love and Irani (2001); Benaroch (2002); Chatterjee et al. (2002); Hitt et al. (2002); Irani et al. (2002); Kazanjian and Green (2002); Ryan et al. (2002); Ammenwerth et al. (2003); Cavusoglu et al. (2004); Milis and Mercken (2004); Wagner (2004), Lu and Yang (2007)
Techniques and tools used for evaluating and justifying IT/IS projects	Kassicieh et al. (1993); Powell (1993); Kauffman and Wang (1994); Willcocks (1995); Lichtenstein (1996); Irani et al. (1997); Lefley and Sarkis (1997); Small and Chen (1995); Sarkis and Sundarraj (2000); Thatcher and Oliver (2001); Irani and Lovo (2002); Irani et al. (2002); Suwardy et al. (2003); Love et al. (2004); Phillips-Wren et al. (2004); Hamill et al. (2005)
Evaluation of the implementation of IT/IS projects	Rackoff et al. (1985); Kumar (1990); Belcher and Watson (1993); Powell (1993); Farbey et al. (1994); Davis and Venkatesh (1996); Apostolopoulos and Pramataris (1997); Hitt and Brynjolfsson (1997); Anandarajan and Wen (1999); Ballantine and Stray (1999); Dixon (1999); Gottschalk (1999); Huerta and Sanchez (1999); Sarkis and Sundarraj (2000); Croteau and Bergeron (2001); Gunasekaran et al. (2001); Love and Irani (2001); Hitt et al. (2002); Irani (2002); Irani et al. (2002); Fink and Shoeib (2003); Love and Irani (2004); Milis and Mercken (2004); Wagner (2004); Love et al. (2005)

In order to be more precise in identifying the detailed areas/criteria for IT/IS justification, the literature in the four major areas of interest was further classified into detailed decision-making areas (see Table 1.2). The first area, general IT/IS evaluation and justification concepts, includes justification of investment in IT/IS projects, costs and benefits of IT/IS implementation, and implications of IT/IS evaluation. The second area, evaluation criteria emphasised for justifying IT/IS projects, includes performance measures and metrics under strategic impact, tactical considerations, operational performance, financial measures, non-financial indicators, tangibles and intangibles. The third area, techniques and tools used for evaluating and justifying IT/IS projects, includes tools and techniques under economic approaches, strategic approaches and analytic approaches. The fourth area, evaluation of the implementation of IT/IS projects, includes performance measures that are financial, non-financial, tangible and intangible.

Table 1.2 Summary of references under detailed classification scheme for the literature on IT/IS justification

Major classification	Sub-classification	References
General IT/IS evaluation and justification concepts	Justification of investment in IT/IS projects	Willcocks (1992b); Hitt and Brynjolfsson (1996); Lubbe and Remenyi (1999); Massey et al. (2001)
	Costs and benefits of IT/IS investments	Devaraj and Kohli (2000); Larsen and Bloniarz (2000); Sircar et al. (2000); Massey et al. (2001); Alshawi et al. (2003)
	Implications of IT/IS evaluation	Sethi et al. (1993); Ballantine and Stray (1999); Bharadwaj (2000); Chircu and Kauffman (2000)
Evaluation criteria emphasised for justifying IT/IS projects	Strategic impact	Powell (1993); Sarkis and Sundarraj (2000); Croteau and Bergeron (2001); Benaroch (2002); Wagner (2004)
	Tactical considerations	Belcher and Watson (1993); Kassicieh et al. (1993); Apostolopoulos and Pramataris (1997); Cronk and Fitzgerald (1999); Drury and Farhoomand (1999); Ezingeard et al. (1999); Lubbe and Remenyi (1999); Bharadwaj (2000); Larsen and Bloniarz (2000); Gunasekaran et al. (2001); Irani and Love (2001); Hitt et al. (2002); Alshawi et al. (2003)
	Operational performance	Clemons (1991); Willcocks (1992b); Sethi et al. (1993); Farbey et al. (1994); Small and Chen (1995); Grover et al. (1998); Anandarajan and Wen (1999); Ezingeard et al. (1999); Tallon et al. (2000); Gunasekaran et al. (2001); Irani and Love (2001); Love and Irani (2001); Thatcher and Oliver (2001); Hitt et al. (2002); Irani et al. (2002); Khoumbati et al. (2006)
	Financial measures	Ballantine and Stray (1999); Love and Irani (2001); Hitt et al. (2002); Cavusoglu et al. (2004); Milis and Mercken (2004)
	Non-financial indicators	Chokhani (1992); Davis et al. (1992); Belcher and Watson (1993); Ballantine and Stray (1999); Ryan and Harrison (2000); Ryan et al. (2002)
	Tangibles	Clemons (1991); Willcocks (1992b); Sethi et al. (1993); Farbey et al. (1994); Small and Chen (1995); Grover et al. (1998); Anandarajan and Wen (1999);

(*Continued*)

Table 1.2 (Continued)

Major classification	Sub-classification	References
		Ezingeard et al. (1999); Irani and Love (2001); Love and Irani (2001); Thatcher and Oliver (2001); Chatterjee et al. (2002); Hitt et al. (2002)
	Intangibles	Clemons (1991); Willcocks (1992b); Sethi et al. (1993; Farbey et al. (1994); Small and Chen (1995); Grover et al. (1998); Anandarajan and Wen (1999); Ezingeard et al. (1999); Irani and Love (2001); Kushniruk et al. (2001); Love and Irani (2001); Thatcher and Oliver (2001); Hitt et al. (2002); Ammenwerth et al. (2003)
Techniques and tools used for evaluating and justifying IT/IS projects	Economic approaches	Kauffman and Wang (1994); Willcocks (1995); Irani et al. (1997); Small and Chen (1997); Irani et al. (2002); Love et al. (2004); Hamill et al. (2005)
	Strategic approaches	Powell (1993); Lefley and Sarkis (1997); Sarkis and Sundarraj (2000); Irani et al. (2002); Fink and Shoeib (2003); Suwardy et al. (2003)
	Analytic approaches	Kassicieh et al. (1993); Lichtenstein (1996); Thatcher and Oliver (2001); Phillips-Wren et al. (2004)
Evaluation of the implementation of IT/IS projects	Financial	Apostolopoulos and Pramataris (1997); Ballantine and Stray (1999); Gottschalk (1999); Love and Irani (2001); Thatcher and Oliver (2001); Hitt et al. (2002); Milis and Mercken (2004); Phillips-Wren et al. (2004); Wagner (2004)
	Non-financial	Watson et al. (1991); Belcher and Watson (1993); Powell (1993); Apostolopoulos and Pramataris (1997); Hitt and Brynjolfsson (1997); Huerta and Sanchez (1999); Gunasekaran et al. (2001); Irani et al. (2002)
	Tangibles	Powell (1993); Sethi et al. (1993); Farbey et al. (1994); Apostolopoulos and Pramataris (1997); Huerta and Sanchez (1999); Sarkis and Sundarraj (2000)
	Intangibles	Davis and Venkatesh (1996); Anandarajan and Wen (1999); Dixon (1999); Croteau and Bergeron (2001); Gunasekaran et al. (2001); Irani (2002); Ryan et al. (2002)

In the following section, the selected literature on IT/IS evaluation and some very closely related literature are reviewed briefly to:

- Identify the contribution and relevance of each article to IT/IS justification.
- Group the papers under each major and sub-classification based on their contribution and relevance.
- Extract from the articles a list of the tools for and approaches to IT/IS justification.

In the paragraphs that follow, an explanation is given of the criteria used for reviewing the literature on the evaluation of IT/IS.

General IT/IS evaluation and justification concepts

This classification criterion deals with the importance of investment justification in IT/IS projects and the implications for organisational performance. The evaluation process itself should not become too complicated. If it does, it will be counter-productive; therefore, it is necessary to employ an approach that will produce sufficient benefits that warrant the time and effort devoted to making the decision. A lack of understanding of the process and range of choices in method and criteria can cause managers to waste time and energy on an approach that yields no better results than simple 'rules of thumb'. The situation must be adequately understood if sound, timely, efficient and effective investment decisions are to be made. General IT/IS evaluation and justification concepts include: (i) justification of investment in IT/IS projects, (ii) costs and benefits of IT/IS investment and (iii) implications of IT/IS evaluation.

Evaluation criteria emphasised for IT/IS project justification

Evaluation criteria should be based on the organisational strategies, goals and objectives. Traditional criteria that do not 'fit' the situation should not be used, and non-traditional criteria that are relevant should not be left out. A sound approach to investing in IT/IS should foster knowledge development and encourage high-quality decisions that improve organisational performance. Commonly employed criteria for IT/IS investment justification can be grouped as follows: (i) strategic impact, (ii) tactical considerations, (iii) operational performance, (iv) financial measures, (v) non-financial indicators, (vi) tangibles and (vii) intangibles.

Techniques and tools used for evaluating and justifying IT/IS projects

Different techniques and tools have been used for evaluating IT/IS projects and the performance resulting therefrom. Economic, strategic and operational approaches are popular, but analytic approaches and the associated tools and techniques are most popular for IT/IS project justification. The following classification scheme, derived from the literature review, was used for classifying the techniques and tools used to evaluate IT/IS investments: (i) economic approaches, (ii) strategic approaches and (iii) analytic approaches.

Evaluation of the implementation of IT/IS projects _____

Many companies experience difficulty in IT/IS implementation due to their lack of experience in evaluating implementation performance. Evaluation of the implementation of IT/IS projects has been not given due consideration as managers often fail to recognise the implications of evaluation and justification during the implementation of IT/IS projects. The life cycle of the project should be considered. Criteria used in evaluating the implementation of IT/IS projects can be categorised as follows: (i) financial, (ii) non-financial, (iii) tangibles and (iv) intangibles.

In the following section, the literature available on IT/IS evaluation has been reviewed to: understand the importance, context and current state of IT/IS justification; identify, examine and organise the performance measures and metrics for IT/IS evaluation and justification; identify, examine and organise suitable tools and techniques for evaluating and justifying IT/IS investments; and explore if and how the implementation of IT/IS is evaluated.

Review of previous research on IT/IS justification

In this section the results of this review of the journal literature on IT/IS justification are summarised. Although this review is not exhaustive, it does provide reasonable insight into the state of IT/IS justification.

General IT/IS evaluation and justification concepts _____

The evaluation of IT/IS investments should be based on purpose, relevance and contribution. The need to manage a rapidly changing resource such as IT requires effective management of change. It is not enough to cost justify each element of a myriad of technologies separately. In the face of dynamic technological change, IT/IS investments have to be prioritised and evaluated from a holistic organisational perspective (Grover et al., 1998). A fundamental starting point is examination of the following: alignment with business/organisational needs, what is done with IT, plans for human resources, organisational structure and processes (Willcocks, 1992a). Khoumbati et al. (2006) discuss the evaluation and adoption of Enterprise Application Integration (EAI) systems in healthcare organisations, highlighting methods for evaluating the integration level, quality of services and integration costs.

Justification of investment in IT/IS projects

The business value of IT has been discussed at length in the literature. In particular, IT's contribution to productivity, business profitability and consumer surplus have been examined. Willcocks (1992b) defines systems evaluation as the 'process of establishing by quantitative and/or qualitative techniques the worth of IT/IS projects to the organisation'. IT/IS evaluation assesses the contribution of an IT/IS investment. Hitt and Brynjolfsson (1996) focused on the fact that while productivity, consumer value and business profitability are related, they are ultimately separate areas of concern. Their empirical findings indicate that

IT has increased productivity and provided substantial value for consumers. However, they did not find any evidence that these benefits have resulted in supernormal business profitability. Furthermore, there is no inherent contradiction between increased productivity, increased consumer value and unchanged business profitability. There are two potential insights one could derive from the work of Hitt and Brynjolfsson (1996): (i) when cost is the central strategic issue in an industry, productivity gains from IT may make IT investment desirable as a means of pursuing a cost leadership strategy, provided that the cost reductions cannot be emulated by other firms; and (ii) the managers of companies should look beyond productivity to focus on how IT can address other strategic levers such as product position, quality or customer service. Their results suggest that on average, IT spending alone does not determine success – whether or not the IT has facilitated an opportunity for business process reengineering (BPR), improved teamwork and innovation in product design, etc. seems important. This research highlights the importance of a MCDM approach for IT/IS evaluation, employing a variety of performance measures and metrics (financial, tangible, intangibles and non-financial performance measures).

Lubbe and Remenyi (1999) addressed approaches to IT/IS evaluation and assessment of the effectiveness of IT investment in organisations, to develop a thesis of good practice in this area. They tested their thesis with a focus group comprised of practitioners and found that successful realisation IT outcomes (benefits) hinges on careful planning and review. They concluded that organisations should spend more time and money on planning for the realisation of IT outcomes (benefits). IT investment and the realisation of expected outcomes require appropriate staffing (the right people involved at the right time in the right thing) and this requires a lot of detailed planning and precise execution.

Massey et al. (2001) examined how different stakeholder perspectives on innovative IT influence the implementation process, attitudes towards usage and perceived benefits in mandatory use situations. Employing a case study, they found that innovative IT applications involve change that is inherently a long-term endeavour, requiring transformation of individual skills, and organisational processes and practices. The following are the lessons learned from their study:

- The reasons for IT innovation must be uniformly communicated to all relevant stakeholders.
- There must be opportunities for stakeholders to share their understandings of the nature and magnitude of the change associated with the innovative IT.
- The change process must be matched to the nature and magnitude of the innovation.
- IT innovation must be treated as an ongoing process that continues after technical installation.

Costs and benefits of IT/IS investment

Most companies fail to consider the total costs in IT/IS. They tend to focus more on the benefits, and those are often viewed from a much too narrow perspective. This is not to argue that firms must consider all minor costs and benefits, along with major costs and benefits, in order to have an effective IT/IS performance evaluation system, but rather that relevant costs and benefits be considered. Larsen and Bloniarz (2000) described a set of support tools to help assess important factors in Web services and discussed their experience using them in a number of public sector organisations. They considered various criteria including: (i) organisational readiness, (ii) access for employees and other users, (iii) end-user support,

(iv) content development and maintenance, and (v) hosting site infrastructure. Each criterion was considered, along with start-up costs and annual maintenance costs. The categories not only included the cost of technical design and system development, but also decisions about which users of a system to target and what service to provide. The technical details and required user skills should be aligned, so that employee use of the system produces valuable information for making better decisions that contribute to improved organisational competitiveness.

Developing a strategic application with the aim of making a company more agile in a competitive environment is different from automating the back office to reduce costs or increase capacity. Clemons (1991) offered the following suggestions for evaluating proposed alternatives in this context: (a) rank alternatives, (b) work with the numbers, (c) balance the many forms of risk, (d) actively manage the risks, (e) examine the role of critical resources, (f) promote sustainable competitive advantage and (g) do not forget the down-side. Strategic systems can have enormous impact on a firm and its entire industry, but with potential gain goes commensurate risk. The following questions should be asked:

- What are benefits, both tangible and intangible of the proposed strategic programme?
- What are the costs of undertaking the programme?
- What are the risks of moving forward with the programme?
- What is the competitive impact?
- What is the possibility of duplication?

Devaraj and Kohli (2000) examined monthly data collected from eight hospitals over a three-year period. They set forth propositions that relate investments in IT to performance such as productivity, quality and customer satisfaction, and the combined effect of technology and BPR on performance. They argued that without sufficient control variables, annual aggregation of data may fail to account for other influences or factors that can affect the firm. Furthermore, they made an important point that three to five data points may not be sufficient to establish a trend for IT payoff, especially when there are noticeable time lags between IT investment and discernable payoffs, as is the case in the context of e-Business and supply chain management (SCM) related projects.

Sircar et al. (2000) showed that there was a relationship between firm performance and both IT and corporate investments. The data used to validate their framework was more extensive in both quantity and quality than data used in previous analyzes. They addressed the following questions: (i) Can the relationship between sets of investment measures and firm performance be demonstrated? (ii) How are IT investments related to a firm's market value, market share, sales and assets? and (iii) Is there a difference in the effect of computer capital and non-computer capital? They concluded that both IT and corporate investments show strong positive relationships with sales, assets and equity, but not with net income.

Most researchers recognise the significance of costs and benefits and how to identify them, but many costs and benefits are interdependent, and it can be difficult to isolate the influence of each on IT/IS performance. A cause–effect relationship framework in IT/IS evaluation would be useful, but such a framework demands more research. Key performance indicators (KPI) based on core business processes would be very valuable to practitioners as they would allow practitioners to focus and on improved strategic and operational control to enhance organisational competitiveness.

Implications of IT/IS evaluation

Performance evaluation in general is a sensitive subject in any organisation and has to be handled cautiously. While developing performance measures and metrics to evaluate IT/IS investment, there is a need to develop an accurate and reflective evaluation system. The performance evaluation system must be clearly understood by employees to obtain their full cooperation in making IT/IS planning and implementation successful. Performance measures and metrics must support organisational goals and enhance or sustain competitiveness. Last, the evaluation system should not be counter-productive because it creates chaos in the organisation. Sethi et al. (1993) took a detailed and comprehensive look at the *Computerworld* (CW) index-ranking criteria and the overall index. They attempted to enhance understanding of how to measure the business value of IT. Ballantine and Stray (1999), on the other hand, focused on the process. They examined the following issues in IT/IS evaluation: the extent of evaluation; the extent to which the evaluation depends on organisational factors, such as project cost and level of organisational turnover; the existence of formal procedures for evaluation; the financial and other criteria used to evaluate investments, and their importance; and the problems organisations face when evaluating both types of investment.

The resource-based view of the firm attributes superior financial performance to organisational resources and capabilities. Bharadwaj (2000) developed the concept of IT as an organisational capability and empirically examined the association between IT capability and firm performance. The author classified the firm-specific IT resources as IT infrastructure, human IT resources and IT-enabled intangibles. The empirical findings showed that firms with high IT capability tended to outperform others without it on a variety of profit and cost-based performance measures.

Chircu and Kauffman (2000) explored market and process-level factors that impact value flows to firms that result from their IT investments, in particular their e-commerce-related IT investments. Their typology identified barriers specific to the valuation process (industry and organisational barriers), and to the conversion process (resource, knowledge and usage barriers). They developed an analytical framework from existing economic and organisational theories of IT valuation and technology adoption and diffusion. They found that justifying and demonstrating the effectiveness of IS was becoming more critical as firms looked to become more competitive and efficient.

To fully understand the implications of IT/IS evaluation, the following are important: (i) contribution to stakeholders such as employers and employees, customers, partnering firms, government agencies and the community, (ii) providing information for making more accurate and informed decisions, (iii) encouraging collaborative supported work, (iv) employee empowerment, (v) enhanced, motivating work environment, (vi) accountability and (vii) organisational competitiveness. Most companies fail to look at all of the implications of their IT/IS evaluation system on overall organisational operations and performance. The IT/IS evaluation system should take the above listed items into consideration, along with the cost and benefits, in order to encourage successful IT/IS planning and implementation.

Evaluation criteria emphasised for justifying IT/IS projects _____

Most studies of IT/IS project justification suggests that we should consider performance measures and metrics that can be categorised as financial, non-financial, tangible and intangible. First, however, one should identify the core business processes in a company and then determine which of the above four performance measures and metrics should be given due consideration. For example, if a company's business process effectiveness depends upon strategic alliances, then more emphasis should be placed on financial performance measures and perhaps some intangibles. On the other hand, a contract manufacturing company might lean more towards use of non-financial performance measures. This implies that there is a need for further research on which performance measures should be used and what weighting should be assigned to them, to best fit a particular business process/business need. Accordingly, suitable IT/IS evaluation and justification systems should be developed to support organisational IT/IS planning and implementation with the goal of improving organisational effectiveness.

Banker et al. (1993) argued that evaluating investments in IT poses a number of problems that investing in traditional assets does not. They asserted that the focus shifts from measuring hard and quantifiable dollar benefits that will appear on the firm's income statement, to measuring indirect, diffuse, qualitative and contingent impacts that are difficult to accurately quantify. Kazanjian and Green (2002) presented a comprehensive assessment framework as a conceptual tool for IT decision-making. The major framework dimensions were (i) population at risk, (ii) population impact, (iii) economic concerns, (iv) social context (including ethical, legal and political concerns) and (v) technology assessment information. This multidisciplinary approach provided guidelines on use of appropriate information in aligning 'stakeholder wants' and 'population needs'.

Strategic impact

The strategic significance of IT/IS in organisational performance plays a key role in determining whether a particular IT/IS is needed and how it should be implemented. In some cases, the nature of a business and major business thrusts, derived from corporate strategy and goals, drives the need for a particular system. Once the decision to implement a strategic IT/IS system is made, it drives decisions at the tactical and operational level, and thus the detailed planning and implementation of IT/IS at the lower levels. Strategic choices have a long-term impact on the planning and implementation of IT/IS, as well as the contribution of IT/IS to organisational performance. There is or should be a link between corporate strategy and IT/IS choices and activities. Powell (1993) discussed the nature and evaluation of strategy and related it to the literature on IT as a strategic tool. He noted that the relationship between IT and strategy had changed in recent years. The implementation process was investigated and evidence of IT investment activities and returns available to investing organisations were examined.

The advantage of enterprise information technologies (EIT) is that information is entered only once, and then available company-wide. A single entry into an EIT system triggers a whole set of processes that mirror the operations of the business in which the EIT is implemented; however, scrutiny of IT in general has been increasing along with the demands of IT departments for a greater share of the corporate budget. Sarkis and Sundarraj (2000) provided a conceptual framework, a compendium of factors, and an outline of evaluation tools and techniques to facilitate an EIT analysis that considered long-term and intangible benefits. They listed the following important factors to be considered in evaluating EIT: costs, intrafirm adaptability, interfirm adaptability, platform neutrality and interoperability, scalability, security, reliability, ease of use, customer support and perceived value. As systems become more encompassing and strategic, more elaborate techniques incorporating intangible factors and strategic measures should be utilised to fully determine the organisational impact of these systems. The authors noted that there is a balance between the complexity of the evaluation system and the support derived for making good decisions for IT/IS planning and implementation.

Strategic information systems (SIS) can support or even shape business strategy. Croteau and Bergeron (2001) conducted an empirical study to identify various profiles of technological deployment, including IT/IS specific to various types of business strategy that best support organisational performance. IT investment involves multiple risks, and there could be numerous ways to reconfigure the investment using a series of cascading (compound) options. Related to this perspective, Benaroch (2002) presented an approach for managing IT investment risk that helps to choose rationally which options to deliberately embed in an investment, so as to optimally control the balance between risk and reward. The author also illustrated how the approach could be applied to an IT investment that entailed establishing an Internet sales channel.

Wagner (2004) reviewed the landscape of SIS for enterprise strategy management (ESM), identifying their contributions, and deriving the requirements for the next generation of ESM systems. Wagner argued that companies could survive with new technologies subject to shorter planning and implementation cycles, frequent and rapid environmental changes, possible discontinuities, and organisation units that extended beyond a single company such as supply chains or virtual organisations. He made an interesting observation that a suitable IT/IS evaluation system should be agile and able to address changing organisational requirements. Strategic alliances will change as a consequence of the evolving virtual enterprise characteristics. As those business relationships change, so too will the IT/IS requirements, and hence the IT/IS justification system.

A framework for identifying major business processes in different enterprise environments, and then developing suitable criteria for evaluating the IT/IS for both planning and implementation of such technologies would be useful. Suitable weights should be assigned for tangibles and intangibles (including financial performance measures), when evaluating the impact of IT/IS at the strategic level, and thus some basis for assigning the weights would likewise be needed.

Tactical considerations

It is not enough to strategically plan for the selection and implementation of IT/IS in organisations. It is equally important to develop suitable programmes and actions for successfully implementing and using IT/IS, that in some way improve organisational competitiveness. IT/IS can play a key role in reengineering major business processes, and/or reengineering efforts might warrant IT/IS changes as part of the BPR effort. In either case, consideration should be given to how IT/IS might directly or indirectly affect organisational performance. This activity should help identify suitable measures and metrics for the planning and implementation of IT/IS. Tactical decisions involving major programmes and resource allocation can impact IT/IS and vice-versa. In either case, evaluation of IT/IS use at the tactical level is important and metrics and measures for doing so are important.

Innovation has been the key to success for a few progressive enterprises, but ultimately it influences the success of all. Lack of innovation can even lead to bankruptcy in some industries.

Innovative changes in management practice can assist in ensuring survival in an increasingly competitive world. Management IS are critical to exploiting technological process, and product innovations (Drury and Farhoomand, 1999), and thus their contributions should be evaluated. Drury and Farhoomand (1999) analyzed two principal types of impetus, technology-push and demand-pull. These two forces were found to produce different external and internal costs/benefits. Comparisons of organisation reactions to technology-push and demand-pull indicated that different management strategies and practices were required (Drury and Farhoomand, 1999). Technology-push and demand-pull are fundamentally different models of development and diffusion of technological innovations. Whereas technology-push requires the adopter to fit the technology to the organisation, demand-pull requires the technology fit the adopter – an organisational need drives adoption.

Many articles address, in some form or fashion, tactical considerations and to some extent criteria that could be useful in evaluating IT/IS contributions at the tactical level (Belcher and Watson, 1993; Kassicieh et al., 1993; Apostolopoulos and Pramataris, 1997; Cronk and Fitzgerald, 1999; Ezingeard et al., 1999; Lubbe and Remenyi, 1999; Bharadwaj, 2000; Larsen and Bloniarz, 2000; Gunasekaran et al., 2001; Irani and Love, 2001; Hitt et al., 2002; Alshawi et al., 2003). This review of the literature on tactical considerations revealed that additional research was needed in this area. There is a need for alignment of tactical planning and implementation of IT/IS with IT/IS and corporate strategy. Suitable measures and metrics are needed for linking/integrating strategic goals and tactical objectives in a way that enhances the success of IT/IS planning and implementation.

Operational performance

Operational performance tends to produce tangible, identifiable and measurable results; therefore, IT/IS impact on operational performance tends to be more easily measured. Performance measures should be considered from the IT/IS perspective and from the enterprise perspective. From the IT/IS perspective, the focus should be on if and how the systems can be implemented, maintained, updated and used. From the enterprise perspective, performance measurement should focus on how IT/IS contributes to operational performance in areas such as sales, production lead-time, inventory turnover and cost, utilisation of the available capacity, employee turnover, etc. (Clemons, 1991; Willcocks, 1992b; Sethi et al., 1993; Farbey et al., 1994; Small and Chen, 1995; Grover et al., 1998; Anandarajan and Wen, 1999; Ezingeard et al., 1999; Irani and Love, 2001; Love and Irani, 2001; Thatcher and Oliver, 2001; Hitt et al., 2002).[1]

While operational level performance measures are important, they present a greater challenge in the context of the virtual enterprise/strategic alliance. The challenging, rapidly changing environment of the virtual enterprise makes interoperability, maintenance and update of IT/IS systems particularly important. In those settings outsourcing, global outsourcing, in particular, may make it difficult to trace the activities of each cost object. In such cases, it will be difficult to determine the implications of IT/IS for operational performance. Tallon et al. (2000) introduced a process-level model of IT business value, defined as the contribution of IT to firm performance. Their model focused on how IT affected critical business activities within a corporation's value system in order to assess the payoffs from

---

[1] Only selected articles were reviewed in detail under each of the major and sub-classification criteria.

IT at the process level. Their primary concern was with the substance of the activities themselves, rather than their structure as chains, shops or networks.

Gunasekaran et al. (2001) presented a model for investment justification in IT projects. They looked at the key performance measurement areas including financial, non-financial, tangibles and intangibles. In operational justification, the existing IT infrastructure operation has to be considered as well as integration issues. Data migration, upgrades, host servers, database needs, the level of internal expertise, system administration, need for training, department users affected and type of licence required are just some of the issues included in the model (Gunasekaran et al., 2001). Further support for the importance of integration issues can be found in the work of Khoumbati et al. (2006) – they explored the evaluation and adoption of EAI systems in healthcare organisations, highlighting methods for evaluating the integration level, quality of services and integration costs.

Irani et al. (2002) identified a number of well-known project appraisal techniques used during the IT/IS investment justification process. They advocated the application of fuzzy cognitive mapping (FCM) to model IT/IS evaluation (integrating strategic, tactical, and operational and investment considerations). They pointed out that FCM should be a complementary tool to highlight interdependencies between contributory justification factors. The operational level indicators included inventory level, production throughput, scrap levels, work-in-process, adherence to schedule, machine downtime, etc. From the indicators one can see that they studied manufacturing. While Irani et al. (2002) proposed an interesting tool for IT/IS investment justification, the application of FCM would be more suitable for strategic level performance measures and metrics, rather than for tactical and operational performance measures of IT/IS.

While it would seem that mostly non-financial performance measures and metrics are employed to assess operational performance impact, especially in a manufacturing setting, both financial and non-financial measures and metrics can and probably should be used in the IT/IS justification process.

Financial measures

Although many researchers and practitioners emphasise non-financial performance measures and intangibles, in the final analysis, programmes, actions and projects should lead to improved financial performance, and hence the modelling of financial and non-financial performance measures would help companies to make more informed decisions about IT/IS planning and implementation. Financial performance measures of the tactical and strategic impact of IT/IS on firm performance are highly desirable, and financial measures can be useful in assessing operational IT/IS impact as well.

Ballantine and Stray (1999) conducted an empirical study of how investments in IT/IS were evaluated in order to ascertain whether IT/IS and other capital projects were in fact evaluated differently in terms of the criteria used during the decision-making process. Milis and Mercken (2004) studied an aspect of the evaluation and justification process that senior managers consider most important; the *feasibility* evaluation. The research strongly indicates that the feasibility study of capital investments in today's companies and organisations is mainly based on financial cost–benefit analysis, conducted using traditional capital investment appraisal techniques. Most commonly used for Information Communication

Technologies (ICT) appraisals are payback period (PP) and accounting rate of return/ return on investment (ROI). Techniques such as internal rate of return (IRR) and net present value (NPV) – which are perceived as being more difficult – are used to a lesser extent. The approach used should accurately measure IT/IS contributions at the strategic, tactical or operational level. If that means using the 'more difficult' approaches, then they should be used.

Love and Irani (2001) presented a comprehensive review of IT evaluation in construction from a benefits cost perspective. Since construction relies on subcontracting and outsourcing and construction, too, is project based, the framework provided by Love and Irani might be useful in evaluating IT/IS investments in the virtual enterprise and/or supply chain environments.

While assessing ROI has always been important in technology investment decisions (Cavusoglu et al., 2004), only recently has return on security investment (ROSI) attracted interest. Interest in ROSI is due to the immense growth in e-business. While calculating ROSI seems taxing, the increasing possibility and scope of IT security breaches, resulting from increased interconnectivity, makes it important. Cavusoglu et al. (2004) proposed a comprehensive analytical model to evaluate security investment decisions. This area of vulnerability certainly warrants careful consideration of the 'connectivity' risks involved in investing in IT/IS and its long-term influence on organisational performance. Some aspects of the model might be applicable more generally to IT/IS evaluation in other contexts.

Non-financial indicators

Economic conditions and competitive pressures are causing companies to closely scrutinise their IT/IS capital and operating expenditures. There are growing pressures to evaluate IT investments like any other, using traditional financial measures such as ROI, net discounted present value and benefit/cost analysis. Despite the pressure to use financial measures, the strategic and intangible nature of some IT benefits (and some costs) make it desirable to include non-financial performance measures in the analysis of IT investments. Decision-makers should always try to quantify where possible, but otherwise include in some way, relevant intangible benefits and costs, otherwise 'there may be an absence of disciplined analysis, no real basis of objective measurement, and limited awareness of the true costs and benefits of IT investments' (Belcher and Watson, 1993). Performance evaluation systems that focus on business processes, KPI and critical success factors should encourage incorporation of any relevant criteria into the IT/IS evaluation.

Advances in computer and communication technologies, standardisation, interoperability and connectivity pose a growing security threat to automatic data processing (ADP) and telecommunication systems that process sensitive or classified information. The activation of a threat could result in: disclosure, modification, or destruction of sensitive or classified information; modification to hardware or software; and/or non-availability of the system services (Chokhani, 1992). Embedded herein one can see some of the non-financial performance measures (primarily intangible costs) which could have a significant impact on long-term system performance and business health. Chokhani (1992) developed a comprehensive view of trusted computer system evaluation criteria with the following major components: security policy, accountability and documentation (all are areas related to security). The strategies and techniques to address these areas of concern include system architecture, system integrity, system testing, design specification and verification (which ensures security policy), as well as trusted facility management, trusted recovery, trusted distribution and configuration management.

The failure rate of IT projects/applications is high enough to be of concern to both organisational management and IS professionals. Davis et al. (1992) discussed the diagnosis of an information system failure. The basic premise underlying failure diagnosis was that IS are social systems that use IT. There are always social system elements and information technology elements to be considered in IS design, development and implementation. Many if not most social system elements are intangibles.

Social system benefits and costs can be crucial considerations in the implementation of IT/IS (Ryan and Harrison, 2000). The socio-technical systems approach is widely recognised for promoting the joint evaluation of both the social and technological subsystems of any overreaching organisational system. The social system consists of employees and the knowledge, skills, interrelationships, attitudes and needs they bring to the work environment. For example, increased role conflict, employee job satisfaction and greater employee empowerment are not typically addressed as costs/payoffs of IT/IS implementation, but who would deny their importance? Ryan and Harrison (2000) incorporated social subsystem costs and benefits in the IT investment evaluation process, which can give decision-makers a greater appreciation of hidden costs and benefits, thus helping them more accurately to anticipate IT payoffs. Ryan et al. (2002) included social subsystem costs and benefits in IT investment choices. They addressed the disparity between prescriptive theory and descriptive evidence. Their empirical results help researchers to understand (i) what kinds of IT decisions encourage stronger evaluation of social subsystem costs and benefits, (ii) what types of firms give the greatest consideration to these issues and (iii) which intangible social subsystem costs or benefits are seen as the most important. Performance measures and metrics may vary from industry to industry, and cultural aspects of the company environment will have significant influence on criteria and the approach to evaluation of IT/IS.

Tangibles

Tangibles have been widely used in evaluating IT/IS investments and projects. Numerous researchers have incorporated tangibles in operational and tactical level IT/IS evaluations (Some of them are: Anandarajan and Wen (1999); Clemons (1991); Ezingeard et al. (1999); Farbey et al. (1994); Grover et al. (1998); Irani and Love (2001); Hitt et al. (2002); Love and Irani (2001); Sethi et al. (1993); Small and Chen (1995); Thatcher and Oliver (2001); Willcocks (1992b)).[2] Tangibles such as unit sales per period, inventory level and turns, manufacturing cycle time, product defect rates, service system defect rate, dropped calls, etc. can easily be determined. However, one must identify the most important tangible performance measures and metrics, so that time will not be wasted in collecting unimportant data that will never be used in the IT/IS decision-making process, and that 'unimportant data' will not be redundant or misleading.

IT infrastructure consists primarily of physical assets, intellectual assets and standards. Whereas physical components include hardware and software related to computing,

[2]Only sample articles were reviewed in detail under each of the major and sub-classification criteria.

communications and database management, the intellectual and standard components of IT infrastructure refer to the human skill set and knowledge, policies and procedures required to combine the physical components to create shared IT services like network service, database management, video conferencing, electronic data interchange (EDI), hypertext publishing and electronic messaging. These services are then utilised to build specific business applications like order processing systems, package tracking systems and inventory control systems (Chatterjee et al., 2002). Incorporating the measurement of the costs and benefits associated with tangibles like these into the justification process is necessary, but not as easy as it might first appear. Just because they are tangible, that does not mean measurement is an easy task.

Intangibles

Intangibles such as good company image and reputation, teamwork, technological edge, etc. should be considered when evaluating the IT/IS. Quantifying intangibles is a real challenge and it can be aided by modelling (possibly mathematical models) and analysis. At times it is necessary to estimate the impact of intangibles on both tangibles and financial performance. Many authors have studied the importance of intangibles, but they have not succeeded in developing a widely adopted approach to evaluating the impact of the many intangibles on tangible and financial performance in planning and implementing IT/IS (Clemons, 1991; Willcocks, 1992b; Sethi et al., 1993; Farbey et al., 1994; Small and Chen, 1995; Grover et al., 1998; Anandarajan and Wen, 1999; Ezingeard et al., 1999; Irani and Love, 2001, Love and Irani, 2001; Thatcher and Oliver, 2001; Hitt et al., 2002).[3]

Kushniruk et al. (2001) presented a framework for conducting evaluations of healthcare information technologies that integrated a number of methods, ranging from deployment of online questionnaires (and Web-based forms) to remote video-based usability testing of user interactions with clinical IS. The evaluation criteria included: (i) the end-users' view of the system, (ii) changes in the users' interaction with the system over time, (iii) impact of systems on thought processes and (iv) technological and methodological issues. Just looking at the description of some of these intangibles should make it clear why measuring them presents a challenge. Challenge or no, measuring and including intangibles is nevertheless necessary if IT/IS justification is to be thorough and complete.

A rigorous evaluation of IT is recommended and of high importance for decision-makers and users. Ammenwerth et al. (2003) defined three main problem areas – the complexity of the evaluation object, the complexity of an evaluation project and the motivation for evaluation. When evaluating IT one must take into account that IT is only one part of the IS of an organisation. The human component cannot be overlooked. IS encompasses both key components of information processing in an organisation, the human players involved and the IT. The IT/IS evaluation should consider not only the technology itself, but also the interaction between IT and human players in their information processing role and the environment wherein that interaction takes place.

---

[3]Only selected articles were reviewed in detail under each of the major and sub-classification criteria.

Techniques and tools used for evaluating IT/IS performance _____

In the literature on IT/IS investment justification or project evaluation, one will find that in addition to criteria considered, tools and techniques play a major role in determining the best investment alternative for improving organisational competitiveness. Table 1.1 lists the references from which the tools and techniques included in this framework were selected. Table 1.2 lists the tools and the categories into which they were grouped. The proposed framework (see Figure 1.1) also contains the tools and techniques for evaluating IT investments. This framework is similar to, but more complete than the 'frame of reference' that Irani and Love (2002) proposed for navigation through the variety of appraisal methods available to decision-makers. The following paragraphs describe the many techniques and tools that are available for evaluating and justifying IT/IS projects.

Economic approaches

Many companies employ economic approaches to IT/IS justification like payback, ROI, cost/benefit analysis, NPV, IRR and cash flow; however, companies have problems in estimating the cost and benefits accurately in economic terms simply because they do not include the impact of intangibles and non-financial criteria. Intangibles and non-financial criteria influence economic outcomes and overall project outcomes.

IT outsourcing is a growing phenomenon in developed countries. In studies of IT outsourcing, assessment issues emerged as critical in the success or failure of IT outsourcing. According to the study by Willcocks (1995), the following are areas of weakness in current practice:

- Failure to establish adequate measurement of the pre-existing in-house performance.
- Limitations in the economic assessment of vendor bids.
- Failure to provide sufficient detail in contracts.
- Inadequate attention to measurement systems to monitor vendor performance.

To provide information assurance, the level of assurance attained must often be balanced with potential reductions in operational capability and the consumption of valuable resources such as time, money and people. Hamill et al. (2005) developed a methodology facilitating the generation of information assurance strategies and implementing measures to assess them. Having reviewed key factors and features of information assurance, value focused thinking was used to develop an information assurance analysis framework. Irani et al. (2002) discussed the evaluation of IT/IS economics (costs and benefits) from the perspective of financial performance measures and examined the level of IT/IS economic justification desirable. Irani (2002) offered detailed guidelines on the economic justification of investment in IT/IS projects. Kauffman and Wang (1994) used econometric analysis to study a specific kind of interorganisational system – shared electronic banking networks – and identified firm characteristics that are likely to influence the perceived business value of network membership, and thus lead to early adoption.

Strategic approaches

A strategic approach involves assessment of long-term implications of IT/IS investment. Among the strategic considerations are the following: technical significance, competitive advantage, research and development, management commitment, long-term outlook, intangibles and business strategy first (Irani et al., 2002).

No one would deny that there is, or should be, a link between corporate strategy and IT activities, but just how much attention do strategic considerations actually get? Powell (1993) argued that often mere lip service is paid to the strategic nature of IT. Furthermore, he believed that strategic justification had become a means for securing investment in IT by circumventing established organisational policy on investments. Moreover, he asserted that many IT investments labelled 'strategic' appeared to be operational in nature. Powell discussed the nature and evaluation of strategy and related it to the literature on IT as a strategic tool. The implementation process was investigated and evidence of IT investment activities and the returns available to investing organisations was reviewed. Powell (1993) argued that a number of alternative views on the IT strategy relationship exist, and that some of them were detrimental.

Sarkis and Sundarraj (2000) discussed the following EIT evaluation techniques and tools: the analytic hierarchy process (AHP), data envelopment analysis (DEA), expert systems, goal programming, multi-attribute utility theory (MAUT), outranking, simulation and scoring models. Lefley and Sarkis (1997) provided some insight into technique characteristics, as well as some representative references of their application to justification of strategic technologies.

Suwardy et al. (2003) explored the full IT experience: from its inception as an idea, through the evaluation and implementation process, and finally to outcomes. They identified the motivating factors in the investment, the benefits achieved and the impediments faced in the implementation of an IT project. While many other authors reported on the use of IT for competitive advantage in a variety of industry settings, Suwardy et al. (2003) concluded that, although most businesses had achieved operational benefits from their IT investments, very few had achieved significant strategic business benefits. Technical feasibility of projects and rapid technological change were found to be impediments in the most successful and in the least successful projects. Technical specifications were believed to dominate financial considerations in the evaluation of investment proposals.

Analytic approaches

Analytic approaches include non-numeric models, scoring models, computer-based techniques, risk analysis, value analysis, the analytic hierarchal process, expert systems and more. Numerous articles examine analytic approaches, but more work is needed to develop an integrated model that includes the strategic, tactical and operational impact of IT/IS.

Kassicieh et al. (1993) introduced a decision support system (DSS) to help strategic planners in evaluating the effect of advanced manufacturing technology (AMT) on the performance of an organisation and determine the parameters affecting the costs and benefits of such a system. The proposed DSS analyzed and quantified project costs and benefits through the use of interacting accounting, simulation and optimisation models.

Some methods are time consuming, heavily analytical and require precise quantification of risk, yet risk involves many subjective factors. Lichtenstein (1996) proposed a risk assessment method for examining an organisation's information security. The author discussed requirements for an ideal risk assessment method, and developed and evaluated factors to be considered. The method selected for risk assessment should operate at any desired level of granularity, be adaptable, and produce reliable and accurate results. His recommended method would not rely too heavily on mathematical quantification; it would be fast, inexpensive and easy to use; it would employ a standard risk model; and it would integrate with existing system development methods, models and case tools. The proposed risk assessment method should provide clear, precise and well-justified recommendations to management and should be automated to an acceptable level.

Thatcher and Oliver (2001) used a closed-form analytical model in challenging some contemporary assumptions about the impact of technology. They demonstrated that investment in technologies that reduced the firm's fixed overhead costs did not affect the firm's product quality and pricing decisions, but did increase profits and improve productivity. They also demonstrated that investments in technologies that reduce the variable costs of designing, developing and manufacturing a product encourage the firm to improve product quality and charge a higher price.

Phillips-Wren et al. (2004) proposed a framework for evaluating DSS that combined outcome- and process-oriented evaluation measures. The approach was demonstrated in the context of a real-time, threat-critical detection DSS. They found that the real-time DSS offered significant improvement in process-related characteristics and statistically significant improvement in outcome-related characteristics.

Evaluation of the implementation of IT/IS projects

Implementation of IT/IS, a critically important aspect of IT/IS projects, has been ignored in many IT/IS justification systems. This is a challenging area for performance evaluation in IT/IS, since there are many interdependent variables and outcomes which are difficult to quantify. While it may be challenging, decision-makers should attempt to identify and measure KPI during implementation – focus on measures that are most influential on outcomes. Love and Irani (2004) presented findings from a questionnaire survey that sought to examine the approaches used by 126 construction organisations to evaluate and justify their IT investments, as well as the benefits and costs that they experienced due to IT implementation.

Rackoff et al. (1985) developed and implemented a five-phase planning process to identify and evaluate SIS and win top management support. Underlying their approach was a conceptual framework that viewed enterprise suppliers, customers and competitors as the strategic targets of five strategic thrusts: differentiation, cost, innovation, growth and alliance. Strategic thrusts represent the fundamental link between the firm's strategy and its use of IT. SIS support and shape the organisation's strategic thrusts. Kumar (1990) argued that, contrary to the widely held view that post-implementation evaluations are performed to assess and improve the information system and system development practices, that in actual practice, the primary reason for such evaluation seems to be project closure rather than project improvement.

Fink and Shoeib (2003) examined the nature of IT outsourcing decision-making and developed a theoretical framework consisting of the following five decision-making phases; (i) intelligence phase, (ii) analysis and planning phase, (iii) strategy selection phase, (iv) action phase, and (v) evaluation and monitoring phase. Fink and Shoeib (2003) asserted that the action phase – that would be implementation – was the most critical activity and should include vendor evaluation, vendor selection, contract negotiation, contract management and post-contract management. They suggested that more research is needed on core contract issues. Love et al. (2005) presented the findings from an exploratory study that used a questionnaire survey to determine the benefits, costs and risks of IT investments from 130 small-to-medium-sized enterprises (SMEs) in Australia. This research highlights specific issues related to SMEs and IT investments.

Financial

Apostolopoulos and Pramataris (1997) proposed a methodology for evaluating investments in IT, with special emphasis on investments in telecommunications infrastructure. They took into account the cost involved in implementing IT, including development cost, transition cost, operational-maintenance cost and expansion cost. They used the following investment evaluation methods: (i) PP, (ii) accounting rate of return, (iii) NPV and (iv) IRR. The following were used in technical evaluation: reliability, security, availability, response time, capability to support special application (such as CAD/CAM), functionality and ease of use. Ballantine and Stray (1999) addressed the extent to which evaluation depends on organisational factors such as project cost, level of organisational turnover, the existence of formal procedures of evaluation, as well as financial and other criteria.

Gottschalk (1999) examined the existing knowledge on implementation by examining previous research in three areas: (i) empirical evaluation of the plan–implementation link in the theory of SIS planning; (ii) integration of research literature on organisational practices influencing implementation and (iii) application of validated instruments to measure potential predictors of the implementation. Love and Irani (2001) presented a review of IT evaluation in construction from a benefit and cost perspective and identified future challenges for IT cost evaluation research in construction.

Hitt et al. (2002) found that firms that invest in Enterprise Resource Planning (ERP) tend to show higher performance across a wide variety of financial metrics. Even though business performance and productivity suffer somewhat shortly after implementation, financial markets consistently reward the adopters with higher market valuation. These authors concluded that a lack of mid-term and long-term post-ERP implementation data created a void, thereby necessitating additional research on the long-run impact of ERP.

Milis and Mercken (2004) presented a balanced scorecard approach for the evaluation of information and communication technology projects. The proposed model had four dimensions (incorporated four perspectives): financial (ROI, productivity, costs, market share, sales), innovation and learning (time to adapt new system, percent cross-functional teamwork, rate of cost reduction for IT services, deviations from system architectures), internal process (efficiency, capacity utilisation, transaction cost-per-time rate and per employee) and customer (customer satisfaction, service reliability, on-time delivery, speed, and delays).

Non-financial

Non-financial factors have a significant impact on the implementation process for most IT/IS. Consequently, any assessment of the implementation process should consider non-financial criteria. Executive information systems (EIS) are a good example of systems in which non-financial considerations loom large. Most companies estimate the costs of the proposed EIS but do not attempt to quantify the possible returns. The executive sponsor simply provides the support and resources necessary to undertake the project (Watson et al., 1991). In short, he/she wants it, so he/she gets it. Belcher and Watson (1993) described an EIS evaluation methodology developed and successfully used at Conoco. Their investigation found that the EIS returned significant tangible benefits that exceeded costs, plus it produced important intangible benefits. Powell (1993) highlighted the importance of non-financial measures in strategic alliances from the perspective of business and IT strategy alignment. Hitt and Brynjolfsson (1997) examined the relationship between IT and the organisational structure of firms. They argued that firms using IT extensively tend to adopt complimentary organisational practices that include decentralisation of decision-making authority, emphasis on subjective incentives, and a greater reliance on skills and human capital.

Apostolopoulos and Pramataris (1997), in their study of investment in telecommunications infrastructure examined technical evaluation criteria such as reliability, security, availability, response time, flexibility to support other systems, functionality and ease of use. Huerta and Sanchez (1999) used cluster analysis in describing common behavioural characteristics of companies that distinguish them from others. In their study the criteria identified for use in evaluating IT/IS included: innovative technology, investment in IT, competitiveness, foreign collaboration and innovative products. Gunasekaran et al. (2001) and Irani et al. (2002) offered comprehensive frameworks for evaluating investment in IT/IS considering relevant performance measures and metrics that were financial, non-financial, tangible and intangible. Those frameworks considered strategic, tactical and operational perspectives.

Tangibles

Evaluation of investments in IT/IS is quite difficult from both a conceptual and functional perspective. Because the performance of an investment in IT/IS is very much dependent on the way it is implemented, the evaluation procedure is even more difficult.

Powell (1993) highlighted the importance of intangibles in strategic alliances from the perspective of business and IT strategy alignment. Sethi et al. (1993) took a detailed and comprehensive look at the CW ranking criteria and the overall index for IT/IS evaluation and organisational performance. Farbey et al. (1994) focused on the need for a comprehensive search for benefits of IT investment and advocated placing that activity firmly on management's agenda. They believed that the activity would be advantageous to organisations. They provided a comprehensive framework for evaluating strategic and operational performance implications of IT/IS investment.

Apostolopoulos and Pramataris (1997) proposed a methodology for evaluating investments in IT, placing special emphasis on investments in telecommunications infrastructure. Huerta and Sanchez (1999) examined various financial performance measures used in justifying investment in IT/IS. They provided a list of methods that could be used for evaluating the strategic implications of IT/IS for organisational performance and competitiveness. Sarkis and Sundarraj (2000) provided a conceptual evaluation of strategic information technologies from the standpoint of costs and benefits.

Intangibles

The main drawbacks of traditional methods using NPV and IRR, according to Anandarajan and Wen (1999), is that they do not (i) consider hidden costs of IT projects, (ii) quantify many intangible benefits or (iii) sensibly incorporate risk into the models. Davis and Venkatesh (1996) provided a critical assessment of potential measurement biases in the technology acceptance model using three experiments. Some of the factors considered include external variables, perceived usefulness and ease of use, behavioural intention, and actual usage. Croteau and Bergeron (2001) identified profiles of technological deployment (strategic impact, management style, architecture, scanning, source of IS development and IS performance evaluation) specific to various types of business strategy (prospector, analyzer, defender and reactor) that best support organisational performance (sales growth and profitability). Ryan et al. (2002) used empirical analysis to explain how costs and benefits of IT investment will influence the social system.

IT/IS is rapidly invading the healthcare industry, and healthcare workers and organisations are being exposed to many new technologies. Implementation and evaluation are intertwined at all stages. IT/IS changes often occur in a climate of organisational change such as restructuring, reengineering, merger/acquisition, down-sizing, to name a few areas of organisational change (Dixon, 1999). Dixon (1999) presented an information technology adoption model (ITAM) from a behavioural perspective. The following were the major behavioural (individual adoption behaviour) aspects of the adoption of IT they identified: perceived usefulness, perceived ease of use and end-user fit. Dixon (1999) discussed the resulting behavioural implications for IT/IS adoption.

Anandarajan and Wen (1999) used examples in highlighting tangibles and intangibles in different functional areas of an organisation. The measurement of those tangibles and intangibles should, however, be within the broad scope of achieving long-term goals and objectives. Gunasekaran et al. (2001) discussed the importance of intangibles in justifying investment in IT/IS with the help of a case analysis. They pointed out the challenge of quantifying intangibles and the challenge of convincing stakeholders to invest in IT/IS projects. Irani (2002) provided a comprehensive overview of IT/IS evaluation criteria, including intangibles, and tested his propositions with the aid of a case study.

A framework for IT/IS evaluation and justification

In this section, a framework is introduced to promote a better understanding of IT/IS evaluation and justification. This framework is based on the review of literature on IT/IS evaluation and justification (see Figure 1.1). Reviewing the literature has helped to identify the major concerns, approaches and strategies related to IT/IS justification, evaluation criteria and categories of the same, and tools and techniques used. In addition, the literature review provided insight into assessment of the implementation process. This framework helps to organise and classify topics and articles pertaining to IT/IS evaluation and justification, and provides some insight into how they all 'fit' into the broad area called IT/IS justification. The sub-classification scheme should assist researchers and practitioners in understanding the context of reviewed articles and content contained therein. The framework should be helpful to researchers in identifying fruitful areas for future research.

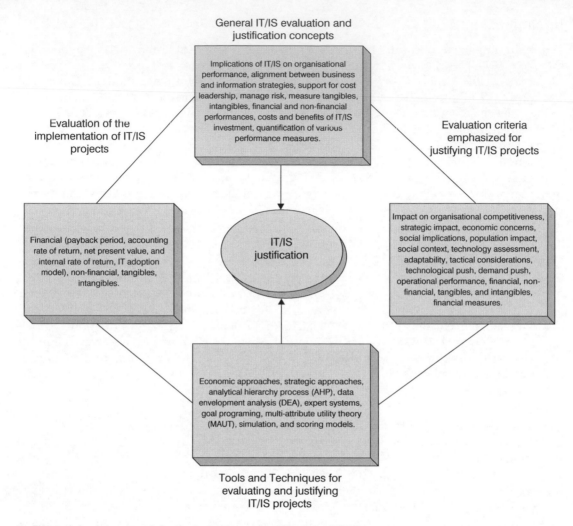

General IT/IS evaluation and
justification concepts

Implications of IT/IS on organisational
performance, alignment between business
and information strategies, support for cost
leadership, manage risk, measure tangibles,
intangibles, financial and non-financial
performances, costs and benefits of IT/IS
investment, quantification of various
performance measures.

Evaluation of the
implementation of IT/IS
projects

Evaluation criteria
emphasized for
justifying IT/IS projects

Financial (payback period, accounting
rate of return, net present value, and
internal rate of return, IT adoption
model), non-financial, tangibles,
intangibles.

IT/IS
justification

Impact on organisational competitiveness,
strategic impact, economic concerns,
social implications, population impact,
social context, technology assessment,
adaptability, tactical considerations,
technological push, demand push,
operational performance, financial, non-
financial, tangibles, and intangibles,
financial measures.

Economic approaches, strategic approaches,
analytical hierarchy process (AHP), data
envelopment analysis (DEA), expert systems,
goal programing, multi-attribute utility theory
(MAUT), simulation, and scoring models.

Tools and Techniques for
evaluating and justifying
IT/IS projects

Figure 1.1   A framework for the evaluation and justification of IT/IS

The major issues to be addressed when developing IT/IS evaluation are discussed in this section along with the criteria that have been used for literature classification and review including: (a) general IT/IS evaluation and justification concepts, (b) evaluation criteria emphasised in justifying IT/IS projects, (c) techniques and tools used for evaluating and justifying IT/IS projects, and (d) evaluation of the implementation of IT/IS projects.

General IT/IS evaluation and justification concepts

In evaluating IT/IS project investments, it is essential to define the objectives of such an evaluation with reference to organisational mission, strategy and goals. Some companies fail to understand the purpose of IT/IS justification. A fundamental reason for evaluating IT/IS projects before plunging into them, is to be sure that they in some way benefit the organisation. Projects must align with organisational goals and purpose. If it cannot be demonstrated that they do, then management must seriously question the need for the proposed

IT/IS. Those responsible for the selection and implementation of IT/IS should clearly define the purpose of IT/IS and it would help to answer the following questions as honestly as possible. Is the contribution of the proposed IT/IS strategic, tactical or operational in nature? Will it influence organisational competitiveness and if so, in what way? What tools and techniques will be used in the justification process and what criteria will be used? How will contributions be assessed post-implementation and what criteria will be used? Many companies fail to assess the outcome of the investment in IT/IS projects, and thus they have no sound basis for knowing whether or not the system was worth its cost. Accountants and IT/IS project managers should work with other managers (functional and other), perhaps using a steering committee approach, to examine IT/IS investments for suitability. See the framework in Figure 1.1 housing items identified in the literature that were included in the framework as general IS/IT evaluation and justification concepts. Table 1.1 shows all the literature contained in this category, and Table 1.2 highlights sub-areas within this broad area, and thus the organisation of this category and references in which related materials were found.

Evaluation criteria emphasised for justifying IT/IS projects

The evaluation criteria should be derived from a sound understanding of an organisation's vision, mission, strategy and goals. Suitable criteria for IT/IS evaluation must be consistent with the nature of the system – is its impact strategic, tactical or operational? Often companies just look at the operational benefits and miss important strategic benefits. They may fail to consider relevant costs because of a rush to achieve real or perceived strategic benefits. Candidate criteria used in the justification process may be economic, social, adaptability concerns, tactical considerations, financial and non-financial, tangible and intangible. A balanced scorecard approach might be desirable if it encourages due consideration be given to all relevant costs and benefits of the proposed IT/IS. In the past, social implications have often been ignored. A balanced scorecard approach might encourage more reasonable treatment of 'soft' considerations like social system impact. The framework in Figure 1.1 shows the individual criteria in the context of the framework. Table 1.1 shows all references for evaluation criteria, and Table 1.2 shows the organisation of evaluation criteria.

Techniques and tools used for evaluating and justifying IT/IS projects

The hard choices in IT/IS justification do not end with selection of suitable performance measures and metrics and criteria for use in justifying IT/IS projects or initiatives. Choices must be made regarding the tools and techniques to use in evaluating alternatives. Furthermore, the choice of tools is influenced by the criteria to be used. Tools and techniques may be applicable only to certain types of data, so it is important for decision-makers to understand their range of choices relative to selected criteria. Without the right tools, decision-makers cannot expect to accurately measure the implications of IT/IS, even though they are using the right criteria, measures and metrics. In the evaluation process, economic, strategic and analytic tools might be employed. Specific tools within these categories can be seen in the framework (see Figure 1.1) and they are listed in Table 1.2. Table 1.1 contains all articles falling within the category we have labelled *tools and techniques for evaluating and justifying IT/IS projects*.

Evaluation of the implementation of IT/IS projects _____

Companies sometimes fail in their IT/IS projects or initiatives, not in selecting suitable IT/IS alternatives, but rather in the implementation process. The implementation stage of the systems development life cycle (SDLC) should not be ignored. In fact, in the formal SDLC methodology, a justification takes place at each stage to determine whether to proceed to the next stage or abandon the project – they call it a feasibility study, but make no mistake about it, it is justification. It is important to justify before implementation and to continue justification into the implementation process. Suitable measures and metrics are needed for evaluating the progress of IT/IS implementation. The last area of our framework, labelled *evaluation of the implementation of IT/IS projects* (see Figure 1.1), includes measures possibly appropriate for evaluating implementation in progress, and that could assist in post-implementation review. Table 1.1 list all references for materials included in this portion of our framework, and Table 1.2 shows the breakdown of implementation into relevant sub-areas, as well as the contents of those sub-areas.

■ Concluding remarks

There are problems in IT/IS justification. Many organisations find themselves in a 'Catch-22' situation. For competitive reasons, decision-makers may believe they cannot afford not to invest in IT, but on the other hand, within the context of accepted organisational policy, they cannot present sufficient justification for making the investment. Willcocks (1992a, b) identified these common problems in justifying IT/IS: inappropriate measures, the budget practice conceals full cost, understanding knock-on costs, overstating costs, neglecting 'intangible' benefits, not fully investigating risk, failure to devote evaluation time and effort to major capital assets (IT assets in particular) and failure to take into account the time scale of likely benefits. Sadly, there has not been great progress since 1992 as the following questions posed by Doherty and McAulay (2002) show. They identified the following questions for future research:

1 How important is it for organisations to formally evaluate investment in IT?
2 Is a simple evaluation framework which typically addresses costs and benefits, appropriate for the evaluation of IT?
3 Should IT evaluation address wider issues, such as risks, implementability, flexibility, organisational impacts and links to strategy?
4 What are the specific tools, techniques or approaches that are particularly appropriate for evaluating investments in IT?
5 Is non-investment in IT/IS of itself a high risk strategy, particularly in the environments of e-commerce and SCM?

Examination of the two lists above would suggest that not much progress has been made in IS/IT justification. However, some progress has been made, and the literature review shows keen interest in this area and ongoing research to bring about improvement. The proposed framework is an attempt to make a further contribution. This manuscript addresses in some small way, all of the above five questions posed by Doherty and McAulay (2002), but most directly it attempts to answer question four. Much work remains to be done.

IT/IS evaluation/justification is critically important in IT/IS planning. Projects must be approved by someone, possibly by a group such as a steering committee or by a single individual, before they are implemented. Projects that are not approved and implemented cannot improve efficiency, effectiveness, or organisational competitiveness, and projects that are approved, and should not have been, may not improve conditions and could make things worse. During the past decade, numerous articles on IT/IS justification have appeared in academic journals, trade magazines and on the WWW. Most of them discuss IT/IS justification from both financial and non-financial perspectives (including tangibles and intangibles), but few directly address the need for a complete and integrated framework for IT/IS justification to guide researchers and help practitioners understand their full range of choices. In starting the development of such a framework, it is acknowledged that much work remains to be done to move it forward towards the aforementioned goal of a complete and integrated framework. The framework classified the literature into four areas pertaining to IT/IS justification: general IT/IS evaluation concepts, evaluation criteria emphasised for justifying IT/IS projects, techniques and tools used for IT/IS evaluation and justification, and evaluation of the implementation of IT/IS projects. The literature under these areas is further sub-classified with the objective of identifying areas of key importance in justifying and successfully implementing IT/IS projects. The following 'to do' list flows logically from this study and represents what are believed to be knowledge gaps that should be bridged. A 'to do' list can be summarised as follows:

- Develop a comprehensive methodology that is eclectic in nature, drawing from whatever areas of knowledge are appropriate to produce a complete, efficient and effective methodology for justifying IT/IS on a small or large scale.
- Develop a holistic and integrated approach to IT/IS justification capable of assessing large-scale IT/IS projects/initiatives (like e-business, m-commerce or systems to support virtual organisations and integrated SCM) within which are embedded many smaller projects, some of which might not stand on their own using traditional justification methods, but nevertheless are critical to the overall endeavour.
- Examine the concept of 'success' with IS/IT projects to see how organisations arrive at the conclusion that an undertaking is successful or unsuccessful.
- Develop a framework for IT/IS project risks evaluation in large-scale undertaking like e-Business, m-commerce, ERP, integrated SCM and partnering with others to create a virtual enterprise.
- Design and develop intelligent DSS (possibly incorporating fuzzy logic and/or neural networks) to support IT/IS evaluation.
- Utilise data mining technology to discover possible influences on, or impacts of, IT/IS that have been overlooked.

Researchers might consider tackling some of the projects on the above list, or they might consider extending the proposed framework. This framework should be examined critically to discover weaknesses, then assessed in terms of the remaining gaps in knowledge about how best to justify IT/IS projects. There is much to be done, and there is no time like the present to get started.

■ References

Alshawi, S., Irani, Z. and Baldwin, L. (2003). 'Benchmarking information technology investment and benefits extraction'. *Benchmarking: An International Journal*, 10(4), 414–423.

Ammenwerth, E., Graber, S., Herrmann, G., Burkle, T. and Konig, J. (2003). 'Evaluation of health information systems – Problems and challenges'. *International Journal of Medical Informatics*, 71, 125–135.

Anandarajan, A. and Wen, H. J. (1999). 'Evaluation of information technology investment'. *Management Decision*, 37(4), 329–337.

Apostolopoulos, T. K. and Pramataris, K. C. (1997). 'Information technology investment evaluation: Investments in telecommunication infrastructure'. *International Journal of Information Management*, 17(4), 296.

Bacon, C. J. (1992). 'The use of decision criteria in selecting information systems/technology investments'. *MIS Quarterly*, September, 335–353.

Ballantine, J. A. and Stray, S. (1999). 'Information systems and other capital investments: Evaluation practices compared'. *Logistics Information Management*, 12(1–2), 78–93.

Banker, R., Potter, G. and Schroeder, R. (1993). 'Reporting manufacturing performance measures to workers: An empirical study'. *Journal of Management Accounting Research*, 5, 33–55.

Belcher, L. W. and Watson, H. J. (1993). 'Assessing the value of Conoco's EIS'. *MIS Quarterly*, September, 239–253.

Benaroch, M. (2002). 'Managing information technology investment risk: A real options perspective'. *Journal of Management Information Systems*, 19(2), 43–84.

Bharadwaj, A. A. (2000). 'A Resource-based perspective on information technology capability and firm performance: An empirical investigation'. *MIS Quarterly*, 24(1), 169–196.

Cavusoglu, H., Mishra, B. and Raghunathan, S. (2004). 'A model for evaluating IT security investments'. *Communications of the ACM*, 47(7), 87–92.

Chatterjee, D., Pacini, C. and Sambamurthy, V. (2002). 'The shareholder-wealth and trading-volume effects of information-technology infrastructure investments'. *Journal of Management Information Systems*, 19(2), 7–42.

Chircu, A. M. and Kauffman, R. J. (2000). 'Limits to value in electronic commerce-related IT investments'. *Journal of Management Information Systems*, 17(2), 59–80.

Chokhani, S. (1992). 'Trusted products evaluation'. *Communication of the ACM*, 35(7), 64–76.

Clemons, E. K. (1991). 'Investments in information technology'. *Communications of the ACM*, 34(1), 23–36.

Connell, N. A. D. and Young, T. P. (2007). 'Evaluating healthcare information systems through an enterprise perspective'. *Information and Management*, 44, 433–440.

Cronk, M. C. and Fitzgerald, E. P. (1999). 'Understanding IS business value: Derivation of dimensions'. *Logistics Information Management*, 12(1–2), 40–49.

Croteau, A.-M. and Bergeron, F. (2001). 'An information technology trilogy: Business strategy, technological deployment and organizational performance'. *Journal of Strategic Information Systems*, 10, 77–99.

Davis, G. B., Lee, A. S., Nickles, K. R., Chatterjee, S., Hartung, R. and Wu, Y. (1992). 'Diagnosis of an information system failure'. *Information and Management*, 23, 293–318.

Devaraj, S. and Kohli, R. (2000). 'Information technology payoff in the health-care industry: A longitudinal study'. *Journal of Management Information Systems*, 16(4), 41–67.

Dixon, D. R. (1999). 'The behavioral side of information technology'. *International Journal of Medical Informatics*, 56, 117–123.

Doherty, N. F. and McAulay, L. (2002). 'Towards the formulation of a comprehensive framework for the evaluation of investments in sell-side e-commerce'. *Evaluation and Program Planning*, 25, 159–165.

Drury, D. H. and Farhoomand, A. (1999). 'Information technology push/pull reactions'. *The Journal of Systems and Software*, 47, 3–10.

Ezingeard, J.-N., Irani, A. and Race, P. (1999). 'Assessing the value and cost implications of manufacturing information data systems: An empirical study'. *European Journal of Information Systems*, 7(4), 252–260.

Farbey, B., Targett, D. and Land, F. (1994). 'The great IT benefit hunt'. *European Management Journal*, 12(3), 270–279.

Fink, D. and Shoeib, A. (2003). 'Action: The most critical phase in outsourcing information technology'. *Logistics Information Management*, 16(5), 302–311.

Gottschalk, P. (1999). 'Implementation predictors of strategic information systems plans'. *Information and Management*, 36, 77–91.

Grover, V., Teng, J. T. C. and Fiedler, K. D. (1998). 'IS investment priorities in contemporary organizations'. *Communications of the ACM*, 41(2), 40–48.

Gunasekaran, A., Love, P. E. D., Rahimi, F. and Miele, R. (2001). 'A model for investment justification in information technology projects'. *Informational Journal of Information Management*, 21, 349–364.

Hamill, J. T., Deckro, R. F. and Kloeber Jr., J. M. (2005). 'Evaluating information assurance strategies'. *Decision Support Systems*, 39, 463–484.

Hitt, L. M. and Brynjolfsson, E. (1996). 'Productivity, business profitability, and consumer surplus: Three different measures of information technology value'. *MIS Quarterly*, June, 121–142.

Hitt, L. M. and Brynjolfsson, E. (1997). 'Information technology and internal firm organization: An exploratory analysis'. *Journal of Management Information Systems*, 14(2), 81–101.

Hitt, L. M., Wu, D. J. and Zhou, X. (2002). 'Investment in enterprise resource planning: Business impact and productivity measures'. *Journal of Management Information Systems*, 19(1), 71–98.

Huerta, E. and Sanchez, P. (1999). 'Evaluation models of information technology in Spanish companies: A cluster analysis'. *Information and Management*, 36, 151–164.

Irani, Z. (2002). 'Information systems evaluation: Navigating through the problem domain'. *Information and Management*, 40, 11–24.

Irani, Z. and Love, P. E. D. (2001). 'The propagation of technology management taxonomies for evaluating investments in information systems'. *Journal of Management Information Systems*, 17(3), 161–177.

Irani, Z. and Love, P. E. D. (2002). 'Developing a frame of reference for ex-ante IT/IS investment evaluation'. *European Journal of Information Systems*, 11, 74–82.

Irani, Z., Ezingeard, J.-N. and Grieve, R. J. (1997). 'Integrating the costs of a manufacturing IT/IS infrastructure into the investment decision-making process'. *Technovation*, 17(11–12), 695–706.

Irani, Z., Sharif, A., Love, P. E. D. and Kahraman, C. (2002). 'Applying concepts of fuzzy logic cognitive mapping to model: The IT/IS investment evaluation process'. *International Journal of Production Economics*, 75, 199–211.

Kassicieh, S. K., Ravinder, H. V. and Yourstone, S. A. (1993). 'Proposed design of a DSS for the justification of advanced manufacturing technologies'. *IEEE Transactions on Engineering Management*, 40(4), 398–403.

Kauffman, R. J. and Wang, Y.-M. (1994). 'An exploratory econometric analysis of shared electronic banking network adoption'. *Journal of Strategic Information Systems*, 3(1), 61–76.

Kazanjian, A. and Green, C. J. (2002). 'Beyond effectiveness: The evaluation of information systems using a comprehensive health technology assessment framework'. *Computers in Biology and Medicine*, 32, 165–177.

Khoumbati, K., Themistocleous, M. and Irani, Z. (2006). 'Evaluating the adoption of enterprise application integration in health-care organizations'. *Journal of Management Information Systems*, 22(4), 69–108.

Kim, Y. J. and Sanders, G. L. (2002). 'Strategic actions in information technology investment based on real option theory'. *Decision Support Systems*, 33, 1–11.

Kumar, K. (1990). 'Post implementation evaluation of computer-based information systems: Current practices'. *Communications of the ACM*, 33(2), 203–212.

Kushniruk, A. W. and Patel, V. L. (1998). 'Cognitive evaluation of decision making processes and assessment of information technology in medicine'. *International Journal of Medical Informatics*, 51, 83–90.

Kushniruk, A. W., Patel, C., Patel, V. L. and Cimino, J. J. (2001). 'Televaluation of clinical information systems: An integrative approach to assessing web-based systems'. *International Journal of Medical Informatics*, 61, 45–70.

Larsen, K. R. T. and Bloniarz, P. A. (2000). 'A cost and performance model for web service investment'. *Communications of the ACM*, 43(2), 109–116.

Lee, J. W. and Kim, S. H. (2000). 'Using analytic network process and goal programming for interdependent information system project selection'. *Computers and Operations Research*, 27, 367–382.

Lefley, F. and Sarkis, J. (1997). 'Short-termism and the appraisal of AMT capital projects in the USA and UK'. *International Journal Production Research*, 35(2), 341–368.

Lichtenstein, S. (1996). 'Factors in the selection of a risk assessment method'. *Information Management and Computer Security*, 4(4), 20–25.

Lin, C. and Pervan, G. (2003). 'The practice of IS/IT benefits management in large Australian organizations'. *Information and Management*, 41, 13–24.

Love, P. E. D. and Irani, Z. (2001). 'Evaluation of IT costs in construction'. *Automation in Construction*, 10, 649–658.

Love, P. E. D. and Irani, Z. (2004). 'An exploratory study of information technology evaluation and benefits management practices of SMEs in the construction industry'. *Information and Management*, 42, 227–242.

Love, P. E. D., Irani, Z. and Edwards, D. J. (2004). 'Industry-benchmarking of information technology benefits, costs and risks for small-to-medium sized enterprises in construction'. *Automation in Construction*, 13, 507–524.

Love, P. E. D., Irani, Z., Standing, C., Lin, C. and Burn, J. M. (2005). 'The enigma of evaluation: Benefits, costs and risks of IT in Australian small–medium-sized enterprises'. *Information and Management*, 42, 947–964.

Lu, C.-S. and Yang, C.-C. (2007). 'An evaluation of the investment environment in international logistics zones: A Taiwanese manufacturer's perspective'. *International Journal of Production Economics*, 107, 279–300.

Lubbe, S. and Remenyi, D. (1999). 'Management of information technology evaluation – The development of a managerial thesis'. *Logistics Information Management*, 12(1–2), 145–156.

Massey, A. P. (2001). 'Reaping the benefits of innovative IT: The long and winding road'. *IEEE Transactions on Engineering Management*, 48(3), 348–357.

Milis, K. and Mercken, R. (2004). 'The use of the balanced scorecard for the evaluation of information and communication technology projects'. *International Journal of Project Management*, 22, 87–97.

Palvia, S. C., Sharma, R. S. and Conrath, D. W. (2001). 'A socio-technical framework for quality assessment of computer information systems'. *Industrial Management and Data Systems*, 101(5), 237–251.

Phillips-Wren, G. E., Hahn, E. D. and Forgionne, G. A. (2004). 'A multiple-criteria framework for evaluation of decision support systems'. *OMEGA*, 32, 323–332.

Powell, P. (1993). 'Causality in the alignment of information technology and business strategy'. *Journal of Strategic Information Systems*, 2(4), 320–334.

Rackoff, N., Wiseman, C. and Ullrich, W. A. (1985). 'Information systems for competitive advantage: Implementation of a planning process'. *MIS Quarterly*, December, 285–294.

Ryan, S. D. and Harrison, D. A. (2000). 'Considering social subsystem costs and benefits in information technology investment decisions: A view from the field on anticipated payoffs'. *Journal of Management Information Systems*, 16(4), 11–40.

Ryan, S. D., Harrison, D. A. and Schkade, L. L. (2002). 'Information-technology investment decisions: When do costs and benefits in the social subsystem matter?' *Journal of Management Information Systems*, 19(2), 85–127.

Sarkis, J. and Sundarraj, R. P. (2000). 'Factors for strategic evaluation of enterprise information technologies'. *International Journal of Physical Distribution and Logistics Management*, 30(3–4), 196–220.

Senn, J. (1989). 'Debunking the myths of strategic information systems'. *Business*, 39(4), 43–47.

Serafeimidis, V. and Smithson, S. (1999). 'Rethinking the approaches to information systems investment evaluation'. *Logistics Information Management*, 12(1–2), 94–107.

Sethi, V., Hwang, K. T. and Pegels, C. (1993). 'Information technology and organizational performance'. *Information and Management*, 25, 193–205.

Shank, J. K. and Govindarajan, V. (1992). 'Strategic cost analysis of technological investments'. *Sloan Management Review*, 34(1), 39–51.

Sircar, S., Turnbow, J. L. and Bordoloi, B. (2000). 'A framework for assessing the relationship between information technology investments and firm performance'. *Journal of Management Information Systems*, 16(4), 69–97.

Small, M. H. and Chen, J. (1995). 'Investment justification of advanced manufacturing technology: An empirical analysis'. *Journal of Engineering and Technology Management*, 12(1–2), 27–55.

Southon, G. (1999). 'IT, change and evaluation: An overview of the role of evaluation in health services'. *International Journal of Medical Informatics*, 56, 125–133.

Suwardy, T. and Ratnatunga and Sohal, A. S. (2003). 'IT projects: Evaluation, outcomes and impediments'. *Benchmarking: An International Journal*, 10(4), 325–342.

Tallon, P. P., Kraemer, K. L. and Gurbaxani, V. (2000). 'Executives' perceptions of the business value of information technology: A process-oriented approach'. *Journal of Management Information Systems*, 16(4), 145–173.

Thatcher, M. E. and Oliver, J. R. (2001). 'The impact of technology investments on a firm's production efficiency, product quality, and productivity'. *Journal of Management Information Systems*, 18(2), 17–45.

Wagner, C. (2004). 'Enterprise strategy management systems: Current and next generation'. *Journal of Strategic Information Systems*, 13, 105–128.

Watson, H. J., Rainer, R. K. and Koh, C. E. (1991). 'Executive information systems: A framework for development and a survey of current practices'. *MIS Quarterly*, 15(1(March)), 13–30.

Willcocks, L. (1992a). 'IT Evaluation: Managing the Catch 22'. *European Management Journal*, 10(2), 220–229.

Willcocks, L. (1992b). 'Evaluating information technology investments: Research findings and reappraisal'. *Journal of Information Systems*, 2(3), 243–268.

Willcocks, L. (1995). 'Information technology outsourcing in Europe and the USA: Assessment issues'. *International Journal of Information Management*, 15(5), 333–351.

Chapter 2 ■ ■ ■

Revisiting the content, context and process of IS evaluation

R. Stockdale, C. Standing, P. E. D. Love and Z. Irani

■ Introduction

An overview of the array of information systems (IS) tools, techniques and strategies that can be used by managers and decision-makers for making investment decisions has been described elsewhere. Yet, with the emergence and increasing pressure to adopt new technologies and requirement for process integration there is a need to revisit the way in which IS evaluation is undertaken. This reappraisal of IS evaluation has been influenced by a paradigm shift in the way evaluation is perceived in other disciplines (Irani and Love, 2001). Within the field of IS, the adoption of an interpretative view of evaluation has become important with the increasing use of electronically enabled interorganisational IS to improve supply chain operations (Irani et al., 2007). This is because the evaluation process should take into account both social and technical entities that an organisation is, or could possibly be, confronted with when adopting information technology (IT) (Hirschheim and Smithson, 1988; Symons, 1991; Walsham, 1993).

Treating IS evaluation as a technical problem can lead to meaningless conclusions that overlook the social activity inherent in the evaluation process and ignore the socio-political environment of an organisation (Hirschheim and Smithson, 1988). Symons (1991) has stated that the benefits associated with IT implementation tend to be qualitative and often intangible. Consequently, the evaluation process must look beyond 'a narrow quantification of costs and benefits to an analysis of the opportunities presented by IT, together with the potential constraints on its application' (Symons, 1991, p. 211). This broader perspective is echoed in Walsham's (1993) view that evaluation is a dynamic socio-political process within multi-level social contexts.

Recognition of the socio-political contexts and role of the stakeholders demands an interpretive approach to allow for the deepening of understanding and generation of motivation and commitment to an evaluation. While there are many methodologies for evaluating systems as noted in chapter 1, many of which have been summarised in substantial review papers (e.g. DeLone and McLean, 1992; Powell, 1992; Farbey et al., 1993; Seddon, 1997; Irani and Love, 2002; Klecun and Cornford, 2005), there are few examples of frameworks from which to build evaluation strategies that encompass the broader context demanded by interpretive arguments.

Irani (2002) has argued that generic IS evaluation is not an effective process and that there is a need for specific models. With this in mind, this chapter builds on the *context, content* and *process* (CCP) approach used by Pettigrew (1985) and Symons (1991) to develop a parsimonious framework for building individual IS evaluation models. The selection of the CCP approach has two advantages. Firstly, there is a widespread acceptance of CCP among leading contributions to IS evaluation theory that has led to recognition of the concepts in much of the normative literature (Lyytinen et al., 1991; Walsham, 1993; Serafeimidis and Smithson, 1998; Smithson and Hirschheim, 1998). Secondly, the concepts are broad enough to accommodate the myriad of ideas and arguments in this well-documented field, while still providing parameters for reviewing them.

A major challenge for IS evaluation is to develop frameworks that are sufficiently generic to be applicable to a wide range of circumstances, but also sufficiently detailed to provide effective guidance. The use of CCP as an overarching approach to evaluation allows for questions of what is being measured, by whom and for what purpose, to be asked. The interaction and linking between CCP allow for the complicated procedure of evaluation to be explored in multiple dimensions. For example, an exclusive focus on what is to be evaluated ignores the reasons for the evaluation and the stakeholders that impact on the IS. The context of the organisation, including its history, its relationships and its information flows supports the treating of evaluation as a longitudinal process through the life cycle of a system. This flexibility encourages deeper questions in regard to socio-technical-political aspects of evaluation to be asked. Such questions address the focus from the perspective of the technology and the people engaged in that technology. This requires an understanding of why the evaluation is being conducted, who is conducting it, what needs to be measured and for what audience. Recognition of the intended outcomes of the evaluation also require explanation if effectiveness is to be achieved.

Evaluating IS: CCP

The categorisation of relevant IS evaluation literature as presented by Symons (1991) is built upon to provide explanations of the significant constructs and alternatives for evaluation. The constructs of the CCP approach are examined to identify the elements that affect the conduct of an evaluation and to distinguish the interaction between them.

Content

A critical factor in any evaluation study is an understanding of *what* is being measured. Researchers in the socio-technological paradigm advocate a shift away from straightforward measures such as the narrow quantification of cost, to include such measures as intangible benefits, risk and an analysis of opportunities presented by the IS (e.g. Serafeimidis and Smithson, 2000; Love et al., 2006). The changing nature of IT and its uses suggest that the content elements have changed and new methods that account for the richness of more intangible benefits are needed (Irani, 2002; Love et al., 2006). This does not mean that all previous measurement tools can be discarded or that there is one single instrument that can capture all aspects of an evaluation (Mirani and Lederer, 1998). The adoption of an IS can significantly impact the functioning social, economic, organisational and management aspects of an organisation. Consequently, there is a need to consider measurements against an established set of criteria to manage its effective adoption and implementation (Smithson and Hirschheim, 1998). Yet, the choice of criteria determines the content, by what it excludes as well as includes. Frameworks such as the Benefits Evaluation Ladder (Farbey et al., 1995) identify the various levels of IS complexity and the approach of the evaluation process. Similarly, the model of effectiveness measures of Seddon et al. (1999) uses the level of system to be evaluated as one of two dimensions in their model. Their second dimension is based on the value judgement of five identified stakeholder groups and the different perspectives they may hold. The recognition of stakeholder perspective is an acknowledged facet of interpretive evaluation (Guba and Lincoln, 1989; Walsham, 1993) and does not confine the evaluation to one group. When examining *what* is to be measured, within the context of a CCP framework, more distinct, less complex taxonomies are required. The use of recognised success measures within a holistic interpretive model enables an evaluator to add flesh to the bones of the evaluation process, building on established IS research, thus contributing to a cumulative body of work within the discipline.

The most tried and tested model is DeLone and McLean's IS Success Model (1992, 2003). Within the concept of *what* is being measured, the metrics outlined in their model allow for detailed identification of categories that support evaluators in the identification of success in an IS. However, one area of metrics that is not included in the model is that of financial measures. Adherence to financial methods is understandable when organisations are faced with a range of seemingly unmeasurable intangibles and where a money value enables everything to be reduced to one recognised acceptable measure or value (Land, 2000). In many cases the dominance of financial executives in the political structure ensure that such measures, relevant to them, remain in use (Irani and Love, 2002; Mogollon and Raisinghani, 2003). A decision on what is to be evaluated is a more complex process than might first appear and is significantly influenced by the stakeholders and by the context of the organisation.

Context

Approaching IS as socio-technical entities in research requires consideration of the role of context (Avgerou, 2001; Trauth, 2001). Avgerou's (2001) advocacy of technical innovation is considered within the organisational and environmental context in which it is embedded supports the context element of the CCP approach to evaluation. External and internal influences identified from the literature are presented in Table 2.1.

The organisational context will determine the reason for an evaluation, influence the stakeholders and will also require the *why* and *who* of evaluation to be considered within the context section. The purpose of an evaluation tends to be for appraisal of value, a measure of success or recognition of benefits (House, 1980; Guba and Lincoln, 1989). However,

Table 2.1 External and internal influences on the context in an IS evaluation

Context	Influences on context	Source
Inner or organisational context	Organisational structure	Symons (1991); Willcocks (1992); Irani and Love (2002)
	Organisational goals and strategies	Willcocks and Lester (1996); Mirani and Lederer (1998)
	Organisational culture	Huerta and Sanchez (1999); Irani and Love (2001)
	Political structures Hierarchical structures (e.g. management structures) Social structures and processes	Willcocks (1992); Farbey et al. (1995); Ward et al. (1996); Huerta and Sanchez (1999); Remenyi and Sherwood-Smith (1999); Jones and Hughes (2001)
	Stakeholders	Symons (1991); Walsham (1993); Smithson and Hirschheim (1998); Remenyi and Sherwood-Smith (1999); Serafeimidis and Smithson (1999); Jones and Hughes (2001)
Outer or external context	Social, political, economic and technological factors including: ■ National economic situation ■ Government policy and legislation ■ Market structures and conditions ■ Competitive environment ■ Industry sector ■ Globalisation ■ Privatisation ■ Cultural influences ■ Technological developments	Symons (1991); Vetschera and Walterscheid (1995); Smithson and Hirschheim (1998); Huerta and Sanchez (1999); Remenyi and Sherwood-Smith (1999); Serafeimidis and Smithson (1999, 2000); Jones and Hughes (2001)

evaluation can be used to reinforce an existing organisational structure for political or social reasons and be a ritualistic rather than effective process. Table 2.2 identifies both ritualistic as well as value reasons for why an evaluation is carried out.

The complexity of an interpretive approach to evaluation owes much to the different perceptions and beliefs of the different stakeholders involved; an aspect that is being recognised from a pragmatic perspective in the literature (e.g. Boulmetis and Dutwin, 2000; Jones and Hughes, 2001; Irani et al., 2006). Stakeholder groups are identified in Table 2.3.

Process

Guidance on the process of evaluation requires information to explain the *how* it will be undertaken (Symons, 1991). There are a plethora of different methodologies and instruments that can be used to examine the *how* of evaluation; such as simulation modelling

Table 2.2 The why of evaluation

Why of evaluation	Comments	Source
Ritualistic reasons	Ritual evaluation reinforces existing organisational structures	Walsham (1993)
Budgetary process that gives 'a final *yes* or *no* – *pass* or *fail* verdict'	Especially manufacturing – focus on justification rather than constructive appraisal	Irani and Love (2002)
Systems to participate in current business processes	Justification outweighs need to evaluate	Powell (1992)
Hoop jumping exercise	Ritual rather than effective process	Farbey et al. (1999)
Project closure	Not an opportunity for improvement	Remenyi and Sherwood-Smith (1999)
Value reasons Appraisal of value Measure of success Recognition of benefits	Leading to:	House (1980); Guba and Lincoln (1989)
	▪ Improvement in business goals ▪ Organisational effectiveness ▪ Investment management ▪ Problem diagnosis	Symons (1991); Smithson and Hirschheim (1998); Remenyi and Sherwood-Smith (1999); Serafeimidis and Smithson (1999)
	▪ Consensus achievement ▪ Decision-making	Farbey et al. (1999); Remenyi and Sherwood-Smith (1999); Serafeimidis and Smithson (1999)
	▪ Understanding risk	Serafeimidis and Smithson (1998); Smithson and Hirschheim (1998); Remenyi and Sherwood-Smith (1999)
	▪ Gains in organisational and personal learning	Mirani and Lederer (1998); Serafeimidis and Smithson (1998); Smithson and Hirschheim (1998); Remenyi and Sherwood-Smith (1999)

(Giaglis et al., 1999), cost–benefit analysis, return on investment (Ballantine and Stray, 1999) and the traditional measure of user satisfaction (e.g. Bailey and Pearson, 1983; Ives and Olson, 1984; Goodhue, 1998). Although evidence suggests that organisations remain with these tried and tested methods (Smithson and Hirschheim, 1998; Love and Irani, 2004), they do not enable a holistic approach to evaluation to be achieved. Thus many factors that can significantly influence the conduct of the evaluation are ignored and the benefits of the interpretive approach lost. These include recognition of the role of evaluation in organisational learning, more examination of the strategic value of systems and exploration of the softer methods for determining benefits (Farbey et al., 1993). For example, there is some evidence that informal evaluation procedures are often ignored by senior management (Jones and Hughes, 2001), but that informal communication is an essential element in effective

■ Table 2.3 The who of evaluation: the stakeholders

Who of evaluation	Comment	Source
Initiators	Influence the evaluation process	Vetschera and Walterscheid (1996)
	Issues of accountability and dissemination of results	Guba and Lincoln (1989)
	Impact on the purpose and level of formality of evaluation process	
	Application of power – implications from senior management involvement	Farbey et al. (1995); Willcocks and Lester (1996); Serafeimidis and Smithson (1999); Jones and Hughes (2001)
Evaluators	Deep understanding of stakeholder perspectives	Serafeimidis and Smithson (1998)
	Human intuition	
	Understanding of politics	
	Moral agent – stakeholder conflict interpretation	Walsham (1993)
	Need to recognise different stakeholder perceptions of benefit	Smithson and Hirschheim (1998)
Users	Long recognition of use as a measure of success	Bailey and Pearson (1983); Goodhue et al. (2000)
	Major stakeholders in the evaluation	Mirani and Lederer (1998)
	Contributes information for evaluation process	Mirani and Lederer (1998)
	Different perspective from IT people	
	Close perception of benefit delivery	Remenyi and Sherwood-Smith (1999)
	Subjectivity – differences of opinion can be seen as rich source of data	Belcher and Watson (1993)
Interested parties	Identification of range of interested parties and effective analysis of their input can be problematic	Serafeimidis and Smithson (1998)
	Interested parties may include: ■ Trade union ■ Shareholders ■ IS personnel ■ Managers and workers affected by the changes ■ Government agencies	Gregory and Jackson (1992); Grover et al. (1996); Willcocks and Lester (1996); Willcocks et al. (1996); Mirani and Lederer (1998); Seddon et al. (1999)
	May use evaluation for own reasons and own political agenda – arena for organisational politics	Symons (1991); Jones and Hughes (2001)
	Stakeholder conflict can be used to inform the evaluation process	Guba and Lincoln (1989); Walsham (1993); Farbey et al. (1999)

evaluation (Serafeimidis and Smithson, 1994; Smithson and Hirschheim, 1998; Farbey et al., 1999; Jones and Hughes, 2001).

Symons (1991) describes the informal procedures and information flows around an IS as integral to the work done using the system and argues that evaluation should consider the diversity of official and unofficial information flows. Other *how* factors to be considered include the involvement and commitment of stakeholders and the conducting of both formative and summative evaluations. Remenyi and Sherwood-Smith (1999) assert that continuous formative evaluation helps to minimise cases of failure, whereas summative evaluation is aimed at assessing outcomes and impacts and is by nature more financial/statistical. This view is supported by Farbey et al. (1999) who see accounting and control as essentially a summative evaluation process.

The final element of the CCP approach is the *when* of evaluation. Symons (1991) argues for 'treating evaluation as continuing throughout the various stages of system development' (p. 211); an argument supported by Jones and Hughes (2001), and Irani et al. (2003) but neglected by Willcocks (1992). Extending the life cycle of evaluation from pre- to post-implementation can enable changes in organisational objectives, the system and learning processes to be incorporated in the evaluation (Ward et al., 1996; Remenyi and Sherwood-Smith, 1999; Serafeimidis and Smithson, 1999). Thus, the emphasis moves from evaluation as a summative process, that is aimed at assessing outcomes and impacts to formative evaluation where ongoing examination can reduce the risk of failure (Remenyi and Sherwood-Smith, 1999).

Integration of the CCP framework

In IS, the adoption of a broader view has become more important as systems have become more pervasive. IS are no longer confined to one department, but often interconnect an entire firm or cross into interorganisational roles (e.g. Enterprise Resource Planning and Customer Relationship Management). This is particularly true with the advent of e-commerce where systems connect firms and customers in new ways, and where the system is a competitive necessity rather than a competitive advantage.

In the rich field of IS evaluation literature, the single most important point that arises is the complexity of an effective evaluation process. The problems that surround an organisation in setting out to achieve an effective process are numerous. Systems are often purchased as an 'act of faith' (Powell, 1992) and the decision to evaluate can lead to perceptions of chaos and out-of-control costs (Irani, 2002), where CEOs fall back on informal 'gut feeling' methods of assessment (Irani and Love, 2002). There is also evidence that this lack of willingness to be rigorous and analytical in the evaluation process is more common in IS projects than with other capital projects (Ballantine and Stray, 1999). This raises serious questions at a time when IS are moving beyond internal, departmental systems and becoming capable of capturing benefits at strategic, tactical and operational levels (Weill, 1992; Irani and Love, 2002).

The IS evaluation literature follows two strongly identifiable themes; the development of instruments and tools to measure identifiable constructs, such as user satisfaction and system use, and at a meta-level, discussions on the paradigms that should be used to approach the evaluation process. These two themes are not mutually exclusive and can be drawn together within the concepts identified by Pettigrew (1985) and Symons (1991). The choice of the CCP approach is validated by a review of the IS literature where it is possible to identify the rich vein of work that considers the *what, why, who, how* and *when* factors of evaluation. Placed within an interpretive paradigm as advocated by many IS evaluation researchers, the CCP concepts allow for the recognition of a wide range of factors that need to be taken into account in an effective evaluation. These factors are interlinked and cannot be considered in isolation. For example, *how* the evaluation is to be carried out and *when* (the process) is closely informed by *what* is being evaluated (the content). These factors are affected by the different perceptions of the stakeholders involved, the *who*, and the reason for the evaluation (the context). Informing the entire evaluation are the internal and external contexts of the organisation in which the evaluation is being carried out.

The consideration of all the identified concepts within an evaluation demands an interpretive approach to capture the interlinking of factors and the richness of the data available. This can be far more demanding than the single instrument approach evident in the literature, but once the need for a more holistic approach is accepted, the outcomes from an evaluation process can change from a judgemental function to one of learning through understanding (House, 1980). This is only achievable if the results are widely disseminated and the learning cycle is taken through the organisation, leading to organisational change. This is clearly highlighted in Serafeimidis and Smithson's (2000) case study where changes in evaluation procedures were ineffective because of lack of organisational change, lack of senior management support and lack of formal dissemination of changes throughout the large organisation.

Figure 2.1 provides a framework for examining the key issues of IS evaluation. The concepts of CCP are divided into elements of *what, why, who, how* and *when* to enable the influences within an interpretive evaluation approach to be reflected upon. Figure 2.1 illustrates the interlinking of the three primary concepts and their smaller elements in this approach as discussed above. The concept of the external context encompasses the whole framework as the factors provide perspective for the organisation and its environment. The element of *who* is discussed within the concept of context, but its central relationship to the other elements is emphasised by placing it in the middle of the framework. Symons (1991) argues that a consideration of the interactions draws in the qualitative aspects of IS evaluation and prevents the narrowing of focus on the technical or quantifiable economic elements that have been a focus of the majority of IS evaluation to date. The CCP approach allows for the social, political and economic consequences of evaluation by examining the interplay of the elements, including the many stakeholder perspectives that can influence the outcome of an evaluation study. A parsimonious framework (Figure 2.1) enables it to be used in a wide variety of evaluation situations, but should not be underestimated in the complexity required to inform an effective evaluation process. The planning and conduct of the evaluation requires an appropriate methodology to encompass this complexity.

■ Methodological implications

Use of the proposed framework in Figure 2.1 requires an approach that supports understanding of the nuances, influences and perceptions of those involved in the evaluation, and the way they are, in turn, influenced by the context of the organisation. This provides justification for the use of an interpretive methodology that allows for the element of sense-making in a complex situation, taking into account multiple interpretations and drawing lessons from the evaluation process that can be used to improve future processes. Multiple interpretations enable

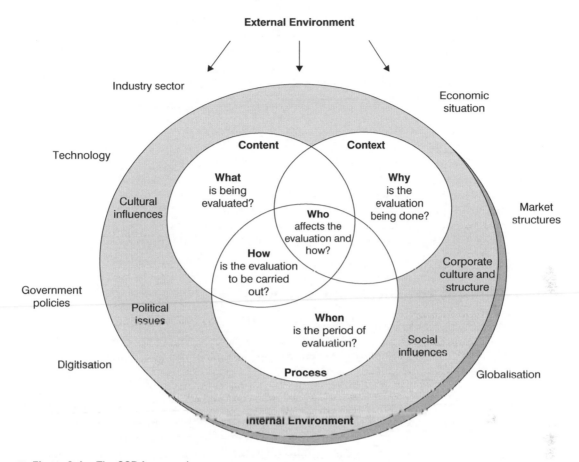

Figure 2.1   The CCP framework

the evaluation to be regarded as an encompassing activity that takes account of both the positive and the negative side of any IS, the informal and formal, and the subjective and objective.

The principles proposed by Klein and Myers (1999) for the conduct and evaluation of interpretive field studies inform such a research approach. Their fundamental principle of the hermeneutic circle echoes calls for the reiterative examination of 'contrasting divergent constructions' until a sense of coherence is achieved (Schwandt, 1994, p. 128). Hermeneutics is primarily concerned with the meaning of text and seeks to make sense of confused, incomplete or seemingly contradictory meanings to bring out the underlying coherence or sense (Myers, 1994). It allows the researcher to critically examine conflicts and contradictions within the complexity of social, cultural and political systems from many perspectives within the organisation. The requirement for meanings to be set in the context of the micro- and macro-environments accords with the CCP framework's acknowledgement of the need to examine context when evaluating a system. Thus, conducting the evaluation process through the methodology of an interpretive case study supports the richness and complexity demanded by the CCP approach.

The acceptability of case study research has suffered from a perceived lack of ability to generalise the findings, a clear outcome of positivist research studies. However, drawing on Yin (1994), Walsham (1995) argues that case studies are generalisable to theoretical propositions: an argument supported by Klein and Myers' (1999) observation that there is a philosophical basis for abstraction and generalisation in interpretive field studies. Unique instances can be related to ideas and concepts that apply to multiple situations. What differentiates anecdote from interpretive research is relating the latter to theory. Case study findings can be used to develop the concepts identified from the literature and where appropriate to draw implications from the data.

The influences of the case study method, together with those of the theoretical perspective of hermeneutics require adherence to the principles of dialogical reasoning, multiple interpretations and suspicion (Klein and Myers, 1999). Dialogical reasoning within a hermeneutic study allows for the inherent prejudices of the researcher to be recognised and used to improve understanding through the interpretation process. This process also needs to take account of the multiple interpretations, the sixth of Klein and Myers (1999) principles that will be evident among the participants. The reconsideration of the different interpretations within the context of all the data sources enables recognition of where and why views diverge.

Strengths and limitations of the framework

In reviewing the CCP framework (Figure 2.1), the importance of the elements of the constructs, rather than those constructs themselves, is suggested. The elements allow for more flexibility when indicating the interrelatedness of the different aspects of the evaluation. The *who* of evaluation is shown as central to the other elements since the stakeholders are seen to affect every aspect of the evaluation, from *why* the evaluation was being carried out, to the examination of *what* was to be evaluated and *how* it was to be done. The *what* of evaluation can include a range of measures as advocated by Mirani and Lederer (1998) who argue that any single instrument cannot capture the complexity of any evaluation. Using recognised IS measures can enable a cumulative tradition to be carried forward within the discipline, although this does not preclude new measures that can account for the richness of intangibles in the complex environment of interorganisational systems. These should, however, not ignore the need for a consideration of intangibles, which requires that an open approach be taken when contemplating *how* the evaluation measures are to be examined. The *how* also requires a consideration of the period of evaluation. The *when* is also influenced by the stakeholders as the different stages of e-marketplace participation involves different people from different perspectives, as well as changes in the views of stakeholders as participation progresses.

The evaluation framework reflects the connections observed between the decision on what is being evaluated, with the process of carrying out the evaluation and the time scale in which it takes place. The time element is particularly important in the evaluation of dynamic e-commerce systems where changes can occur rapidly and where stages of development can be observed. This supports the calls in the literature for more formative evaluation and also for more acceptance of informal evaluation findings, seen as an essential element in effective evaluation (Farbey et al., 1999; Jones and Hughes, 2001).

The internal and external environments have a significant influence on understanding the many factors affecting the realisation of benefits and this is indicated in the framework. The social, political, cultural and economic factors are actually inherent within these environments, and provide background to the framework because of their intrinsic importance to the evaluation process. The use of an interpretive case study approach to evaluation, based on the constructs of the CCP framework, necessarily imposes limitations on the generalisability of an evaluation study. The outcomes of individual evaluation studies can be used to inform other organisations of the concepts and conclusions that may be applicable to their own case. They cannot provide the quantitative application of statistical sampling procedures to a larger population, but rather enable an assessment of the 'fit' between the case and other firms where one might apply the concepts and conclusions from the evaluation study (Schofield, 2002). The CCP framework does not allow for generic solutions, but supports the ability of evaluators to apply the relevant questions to the constructs and to explore the range of influences from the social and political to the cultural.

In the same way, the framework does not reflect the outcomes from the conduct of an evaluation. Definitive outcomes from evaluation are the hallmark of the scientific paradigm. In the context of an interpretive approach these outcomes are ideally replaced with a consensus on the claims, concerns and issues of the stakeholders (Guba and Lincoln, 1989). The implications are that such evaluation is less definitive, often leading to ambiguous outcomes with attendant implications of less direct managerial control with an interplay of power and politics among the stakeholders. However, the gains from consideration of the concerns, claims and issues of the stakeholders leads to widespread involvement and consensus (Guba and Lincoln, 1989; Rossi and Freeman, 1989) and more learning and understanding (Serafeimidis and Smithson, 2000).

Conclusions

If IS are considered to be social as well as technical entities and stakeholders are key to every stage of their deployment, then the traditional methods of IS evaluation based on the use of technical measures are no longer sufficient. The CCP framework provides a parsimonious model that offers a structure against which individual evaluation studies can be planned and carried out. The structure incorporates the elements that will contribute to the rich, holistic studies advocated by current evaluation thinking to achieve an understanding of the contribution of an IS. However, the framework supports the use of existing measures within the evaluation design to contribute to a cumulative tradition of evaluation literature, but allows for new measures to be incorporated. This approach reflects the requirement for evaluations to be tailored to the needs of individual organisations based on their environment, the context of the evaluation, what is to be evaluated and recognition of stakeholders.

References

Avgerou, C. (2001). 'The significance of context in information systems and organisational change'. *Information Systems Journal*, 11, 43–63.
Bailey, J. and Pearson, S. W. (1983). 'Development of a tool for measuring and analyzing computer user satisfaction'. *Management Science*, 29(5), 530–545.
Ballantine, J. A. and Stray, S. (1999). 'Information systems and other capital investments: Evaluation practices compared'. *Logistics Information Management*, 12(1–2), 78–93.
Belcher, L. W. and Watson, H. J. (1993). 'Assessing the value of Conoco's EIS'. *MIS Quarterly*, 7(3), 239–253.

Boulmetis, J. and Dutwin, P. (2000). *The ABCs of Evaluation*. Jossey-Bass Publishers, San Francisco.

DeLone, W. H. and McLean, E. R. (1992). 'Information systems success: The quest for the dependent variable'. *Information Systems Research*, 3(1), 60–95.

DeLone, W. H. and McLean, E. R. (2003). 'The DeLone and McLean model of information systems success: A ten-year update'. *Journal of Management Information Systems*, 19(4), 9–30.

Farbey, B., Land, F. F. and Targett, D. (1993). *How to Evaluate your IT Investment*. Butterworth Heinemann, Oxford.

Farbey, B., Land, F. F. and Targett, D. (1995). 'A taxonomy of information systems applications: The benefits' evaluation ladder'. *European Journal of Information Systems*, 4, 41–50.

Farbey, B., Land, F. F. and Targett, D. (1999). 'Moving IS evaluation forward: Learning themes and research issues'. *Journal of Strategic Information Systems*, 8, 189–207.

Giaglis, G. M., Mylonopoulos, N. and Doukidis, G. I. (1999). 'The ISSUE methodology for quantifying benefits from information systems'. *Logistics Information Management*, 12(1–2), 50–62.

Goodhue, D. L. (1998). 'Development and measurement validity of a task-technology fit instrument for user evaluations of information systems'. *Decision Sciences*, 29(1), 105–138.

Goodhue, D., Klein, B. and March, S. (2000). 'User evaluations of IS as surrogates for objective performance'. *Information and Management*, 38, 87–101.

Gregory, A. J. and Jackson, M. C. (1992). 'Evaluation methodologies: A system for use'. *The Journal of the Operational Research Society*, 43(1), 19–28.

Grover, V., Jeong, S. R. and Segars, A. H. (1996). 'Information systems effectiveness: The construct space and patterns of application'. *Information and Management*, 31, 177–191.

Guba, E. G. and Lincoln, Y. S. (1989). *Fourth Generation Evaluation*. Sage Publications, London.

Hirschheim, R. and Smithson, S. (1988). 'A critical analysis of information systems evaluation'. In Bjorn-Andersen, N. and Davis, G. B. (Eds.), *Information Systems Assessment: Issues and challenges*. Elsevier Science, Amsterdam, pp. 17–37.

House, E. R. (1980). *Evaluating with Validity*. Sage Publications, London.

Huerta, E. and Sanchez, P. J. (1999). 'Evaluation of information technology: Strategies in Spanish firms'. *European Journal of Information Systems*, 8, 273–283.

Irani, Z. (2002). 'Information systems evaluation: Navigating through the problem domain'. *Information and Management*, 40, 11–24.

Irani, Z. and Love, P. E. D. (2001). 'Information systems evaluation: Past, present and future'. *European Journal of Information Systems*, 10, 183–188.

Irani, Z. and Love, P. E. D. (2002). 'Developing a frame of reference for ex-ante IT/IS investment evaluation'. *European Journal of Information Systems*, 11, 74–82.

Irani, Z., Themistocleous, M. and Love, P. E. D. (2003). 'The impact of enterprise application integration on information system lifecycles'. *Information and Management*, 41(2), 177–187.

Irani, Z., Gunasekaran, A. and Love, P. E. D. (2006). 'Qualitative and quantitative approaches to information systems evaluation'. *European Journal of Operational Research*, 173, 951–956.

Irani, Z., Sharif, A. and Love, P. E. D. (2007). 'Knowledge and information systems evaluation in manufacturing'. *International Journal of Production Research*, 45(11), 2435–2457.

Ives, B. and Olson, M. H. (1984). 'User involvement and MIS success: A review of research'. *Management Science*, 30(5), 586–603.

Jones, S. and Hughes, J. (2001). 'Understanding IS evaluation as a complex social process: A case study of a UK local authority'. *European Journal of Information Systems*, 10, 189–203.

Klecun, E. and Cornford, T. (2005). 'A critical approach to evaluation'. *European Journal of Information Systems*, 14, 229–243.

Klein, H. K. and Myers, M. D. (1999). 'A set of principles for conducting and evaluating interpretive field studies in information systems'. *MIS Quarterly*, 23(1), 67–93.

Land, F. F. (2000). 'Evaluation in a socio-technical context'. In Baskerville, R., Stage, J. and DeGross, J. I. (Eds.), *Organisational and Social Perspectives on Information Technology*. Kluwer Academic, Dordrecht, pp. 115–126.

Love, P. E. D. and Irani, Z. (2004). 'An exploratory study of information technology evaluation and benefits management of SMEs in construction'. *Information and Management*, 42(1), 227–242.

Love, P. E. D., Irani, Z., Ghoneim, A. and Themistocleous, M. (2006). 'An exploratory study of indirect IT costs using the structured case method'. *International Journal of Information Management*, 26(2), 167–177.

Lyytinen, K., Klein, H. and Hirschheim, R. (1991). 'The effectiveness of office information systems: A social action perspective'. *Journal of Information Systems*, 1(1), 41–60.

Mirani, R. and Lederer, A. L. (1998). 'An instrument for assessing the organisational benefits of IS projects'. *Decision Sciences*, 29(4), 803–838.

Mogollon, M. and Raisinghani, M. (2003). 'Measuring ROI in e-business: A practical approach'. *Information Systems Management*, 20(2), 63–81.

Myers, M. D. (1994). 'Dialectical hermeneutics: A theoretical framework for the implementation of information systems'. *Information Systems Journal*, 5, 51–70.

Pettigrew, A. (1985). *The Awakening Giant. Continuity and Change in ICI*. Blackwell, Oxford.

Powell, P. (1992). 'Information technology evaluation: Is it different?' *Journal of the Operational Research Society*, 43(1), 29–42.

Remenyi, D. and Sherwood-Smith, M. (1999). 'Maximise information systems value by continuous participative evaluation'. *Logistics Information Management*, 12(1–2), 14–31.

Rossi, P. H. and Freeman, H. E. (1989). *Evaluation. A Systematic Approach*, 4th ed. Sage Publications, Newbury Park, CA.

Schofield, J. W. (2002). 'Increasing the generalizability of qualitative research'. In Huberman, A. M. and Miles, M. B. (Eds.), *The Qualitative Researcher's Companion*. Sage Publications, Thousand Oaks, CA, pp. 171–203.

Schwandt, T. A. (1994). 'Constructivist, interpretivist approaches to human inquiry'. In Denzin, N. K. and Lincoln, Y. S. (Eds.), *Handbook of Qualitative Research*. Sage Publications, Thousand Oaks, CA, pp. 118–137.

Seddon, P. B. (1997). 'A respecification and extension of the DeLone and McLean model of IS success'. *Information Systems Research*, 8(3), 240–253.

Seddon, P. B., Staples, S., Patnayakuni, R. and Bowtell, M. (1999). 'Dimensions of information systems success'. *Communications of the Association for Information Success*, 2(20), 427–442.

Serafeimidis, V., and Smithson, S. (1994). 'Evaluation of IS/IT investments: Understanding and support'. Paper presented at the *First European Conference on Information Technology Investment Evaluation*. Henley on Thames, UK, 13–14 September.

Serafeimidis, V., and Smithson, S. (1998). 'Information systems evaluation: The interpretive paradigm'. Paper presented at the *6th European Conference on Information Systems*. Aix-en-Provence.

Serafeimidis, V. and Smithson, S. (1999). 'Rethinking the approaches to information systems investment evaluation'. *Logistics Information Management*, 12(1–2), 94–107.

Serafeimidis, V. and Smithson, S. (2000). 'Information systems evaluation in practice: A case study of organisational change'. *Journal of Information Technology*, 15, 93–105.

Smithson, S. and Hirschheim, R. (1998). 'Analysing information systems evaluation: Another look at an old problem'. *European Journal of Information Systems*, 7, 158–174.

Symons, V. J. (1991). 'A review of information systems evaluation: Content, context and process'. *European Journal of Information Systems*, 1(3), 205–212.

Trauth, E. M. (2001). 'The pursuit of information technology in context'. Keynote Address. Paper presented at the *ACIS 2001*. Coffs Harbour, NSW.

Vetschera, R. and Walterscheid, H. (1995). 'A process-orientated framework for the evaluation of managerial support systems'. *Information and Management*, 28, 197–213.

Vetschera, R. and Walterscheid, H. (1996). 'The evaluation of managerial support systems in German companies'. *European Journal of Information Systems*, 5, 182–195.

Walsham, G. (1993). *Interpreting Information Systems in Organisations*. John Wiley and Sons Ltd., Chichester.

Walsham, G. (1995). 'Interpretive case studies in IS research: Nature and method'. *European Journal of Information Systems*, 4, 74–81.

Ward, J., Taylor, P. and Bond, P. (1996). 'Evaluation and realisation of IS/IT benefits: An empirical study of current practice'. *European Journal of Information Systems*, 4, 214–225.

Weill, P. (1992). 'The relationship between investment in information technology and firm performance: A study of the valve manufacturing sector'. *Information Systems Research*, 3(4), 307–333.

Willcocks, L. (1992). 'Evaluating information technology investments: Research findings and reappraisal'. *Journal of Information Systems*, 2(4), 243–268.

Willcocks, L. and Lester, S. (1996). 'The evaluation and management of information systems investments: From feasibility to routine operations'. In Willcocks, L. (Ed.), *Investing in Information Systems. Evaluation and Management*. Chapman and Hall, London.

Willcocks, L., Fitzgerald, G. and Lacity, M. (1996). 'To outsource IT or not? Recent research on economics and evaluation practice'. *European Journal of Information Systems*, 5, 143–160.

Yin, R. K. (1994). *Case Study Research Design and Methods*, 2nd ed. Sage Publications, Thousand Oaks, CA.

How IT evaluation methods are used: Examining case research from an ANT perspective

M. Nijland and L. P. Willcocks

■ Introduction

The literature suggests that organisational managers as well as information systems (IS) professionals recognise information technology (IT) evaluation as one of the important unresolved concerns in IS management (Farbey et al., 1993; Grembergen and Bloemen, 1997; Seddon et al., 2004). Evaluation of IT investments is problematic not only because of the inherent difficulties of evaluation (such as making estimates for future situations), but also due to typical characteristics of such investments in comparison with other investments (Ballantine et al., 1995). IT projects frequently have numerous intangible costs and benefits, and significant impacts on many aspects within an organisation. IT projects often are innovative and involve (non-proven) technology. Moreover, IT investments are associated with shorter life cycles due to continuous technology development. Whether IT projects really are different from other business projects remains a topic of debate (e.g. Powell, 1999), but clearly IT projects pose several difficulties if managed from a cost–benefit perspective.

In the literature devoted to the evaluation of IT investments, there are many studies focusing on different methods to address the intangible benefits of the investments using various criteria for evaluation. Wolfsen and Lobry (1998) give a good overview of some of the techniques and methods developed for this purpose. Considering over 65 methods for IT evaluation, Renkema and Berghout (1997) conclude that the available non-financial evaluation methods are barely supported by theoretical foundations. Furthermore, the methods focus on the evaluation criteria rather than the evaluation process by which the evaluation takes place.

Despite the existence of a large number of enhanced methods especially geared to evaluating IT, research shows that the traditional discounted cash flow appraisal techniques, such as cost–benefit analysis, payback time and return on investment still dominate in IT evaluation

(Bacon, 1992; Yan Tam, 1992; Ballantine and Stray, 1998; Seddon et al., 2002). These general methods have been criticised for not allowing for specific IT characteristics (e.g. Earl, 1989; Willcocks, 1994; Farbey et al., 1999; Willcocks and Graeser, 2001). Moreover, although they are widely used, they are not always trusted (Farbey et al., 1993) or not considered an important factor in decision-making by the organisations that use them (Ballantine and Stray, 1998). This seems to suggest that frequently these techniques are being used in a more ritualistic manner – for example, as a means to gain project approval – rather than contributing directly to evaluation purposes. Ballantine and Stray (1998) surmise that the trend of using financial techniques for IT evaluation is likely to continue, contrary to their inappropriateness to the task of IT evaluation. They contend that 'more research needs to be undertaken, to ascertain what barriers, if any, discourage use [of more sophisticated techniques], so as to avoid potentially useful techniques being dismissed as inappropriate' (ibid., p. 13).

Hochstrasser (1994) concluded from his research that only 16% of companies used rigorous methods to evaluate and prioritise their IT investments. Kumar (1990) showed that only 30% of the organisations researched performed a post-implementation evaluation on a majority (75% or more) of their information systems. Nijland (2000) concludes from a study of the financial sector in the Netherlands that *ex ante* evaluations hardly display the use of formal evaluation methods, and *ex post* evaluations are almost never carried out. Reviewing the literature, Kleist (2003) reported indifferent use of IT evaluation methods, though also weaknesses in the evaluation methods themselves. Reporting a survey, Seddon et al. (2002) found 20% failing to carry out post-implementation evaluations, but also recorded few significant changes in actual practices when compared to those reported in studies going back to the early 1990s. Here, 30% reported new practices, mainly in the form of IT scorecards and benchmarking, but also recorded indifferent use of these. Only 5% of respondents rated their IT evaluation practices 'world-class'. While evaluation of IT operations and of (internal) customer satisfaction with IT service were rated highest, nevertheless all IT evaluation practices were rated between 3 and 4.5 (on a scale of 1 = 'unsuccessful', 7 = 'very successful'), suggesting considerable room for improvement.

Given the large and increasing number of evaluation methods, it seems unlikely that the reason such methods fall short of what one would expect, is due to evaluation methods not addressing the right characteristics (e.g. technical or economic criteria) for IT investments. Still, many new evaluation methods are being developed to improve certain characteristics, displaying minor revisions of already developed – but, it would seem, widely unused – methods. Such new developments are often justified by a reaction against conventional investment appraisal methods since 'these [traditional] methods simply do not work in today's sophisticated technology-led environments' (Irani and Love, 2001). Such arguments, however, seem to ignore the abundance of more advanced evaluation methods already available. They address the paradox of underutilisation of evaluation methods by suggesting a 'sharpen the tools' approach, for example, add more criteria (e.g. measure risk in addition to costs and benefits; also measure *intangibles* (Parker et al., 1988; Farbey et al., 1993)), define better what is meant by certain definitions (e.g. have a new definition on how the value of information can be measured (Parker et al., 1988)), extend the scope of the method (e.g. to include life-cycle evaluation (Willcocks, 1996a; Swinkels, 1997)), employ an IT scorecard approach (Willcocks and Graeser, 2001), blend qualitative and quantitative measures and use economic models for e-business projects (Kleist, 2003), and shape the tool to certain contexts or types of IS (e.g. use different criteria for different types of organisations or IS (Serafeimidis and Smithson, 1995; Gunasekaran et al., 2001)).

Organisations are aware of the shortcomings in their evaluation of IT, and through time they continue to demonstrate a major interest in this topic (Keen, 1991; Farbey et al., 1993; Willcocks, 1996b; Thorp, 1998; Seddon et al., 2004). Every year, consultancy enquiries (e.g. from Gartner Group, IDC) into the top issues on the agenda of CIOs typically show that the topic of evaluating costs and benefits of IT remains high on the list of management issues. This is reinforced by great attendance by managers at IT cost–benefit seminars and the abundance of publications on evaluating IT investments in both business journals and academic publications. The high interest in the topic of evaluation stands in contrast to the lack of use of those evaluation methods that address the shortcomings in actual management of IT costs and benefits. This suggests that that the use of advanced IT evaluation methods does not automatically happen simply because they exist and seem to serve a rational purpose. Powell (1999) asserts that investment evaluation techniques are successfully employed in other fields of application (such as in engineering, various social projects, and research and development). He argues that IT investments should be evaluated in a similarly rigorous manner, but 'getting organizations to apply and stick with techniques, rather than their existence, may be the more critical issue' (ibid., p. 163). To understand how organisations 'apply and stick with' such techniques and why this process seems to be so often unsuccessful, is the central aim of our research.

This study aims to develop a better understanding of the adoption and use *process* for IT evaluation methods in organisations. Though the importance of developing more advanced IT evaluation methods that better support IT cost–benefit improvement is not denied, there still is a considerable gap between *having* sophisticated IT evaluation methods and actually *employing* them in organisational practice. This gap needs to be bridged if difficulties in IT cost–benefit management are to be addressed. Therefore it seems relevant to ask the central question in this paper: 'Why do organisations generally seem to be unsuccessful in employing IT evaluation methods that help them in clarifying costs and benefits of IT, even when they express the need for more insight into the costs and benefits of IT?'

To tackle this question, the focus of this paper is on an organisation that has actually attempted to employ such a method. For deeper understanding a case study is researched and a theoretical perspective is employed already utilised in the IS literature – actor-network theory – as the analytical framework. The chapter first discusses the literature that can be related to the employment of evaluation methods and the promise and ability of actor-network theory to offer new insights. The research methodology used in this study is presented. This is followed by the in-depth case study and its analysis. Finally, a discussion of the analysis and conclusions are presented.

Issues in the use/non-use of IT evaluation methods

Though not a widely researched issue, several studies hint at why the employment of IT evaluation methods might be problematic. Studies on the employment of IS, system development methodologies, management techniques and accounting techniques offer a plethora of suggestions on the elements influencing the potential for success (Smith et al., 1989; Wilson, 1991; Kautz and McMaster, 1994; Gosselin, 1997; Miller, 1997; Premkumar et al., 1997; Ballantine et al., 1998; Plouffe et al., 2001; Aladwani, 2002). In these studies problematic evaluation employment is related to characteristics of the evaluation method itself, the organisation that is trying to adopt it, the people involved in the employment, the process of implementation and the external environmental context. Table 3.1 gives a general overview of emerging relevant influences on the employment, or otherwise of IT evaluation approaches.

Table 3.1 Examples of possible influences on the employment of IT evaluation methods

Topic	Examples of influences
Evaluation method	Evaluation criteria
	Object under evaluation
	Employed time frame
	Supporting tools
	Outputs it provides
	Compatibility with organisational and technical infrastructure
	Ease-of-use
Organisation	Culture
	Structure
	Management procedures
	Decision-making procedures
	Organisational procedures
	Other financial, budgeting and accounting methods
	Business strategy
	IT strategy
People	Management support
	Characteristics of the stakeholders
	People involved in method construction
	The project team members involved in the implementation project
	A project champion
Process	Project management
	Project planning
	Order of actions
	Available resources
Environment	External pressures (e.g. Y2K, millennium, euro currency change)
	Opportunities
	Organisational priorities with respect to other issues
	Impulse or reason to change
	Institutional context

Source: Literature review.

Studies based on Rogers' widely used theory of diffusion of innovations (Rogers, 1995), reveal other factors influencing adoption of IT evaluation method as an innovation. Thus the list presented in Table 3.1 undoubtedly can be expanded and viewed from different analytical levels (from micro- to macro-levels; from individual to organisational; to societal levels). However, that is not the aim of this research. Neither is the aim to test which reasons are influential and which not. Most likely, all of the reasons mentioned, plus a great number not yet identified, will affect use/non-use of an IT evaluation method. The degree to which they are relevant is highly situational and contextual. In a similar argument, diffusion research, based on functionalistic assumptions, has been critiqued to produce endless lists of factors which are 'inconclusive, inconsistent and characterised by low levels of explanation' (Wolfe, 1994, p. 405). An explanatory theory based on research aimed at finding such factors has been elusive because 'virtually every determinant employed has proved to be a highly and inexplicably erratic predictor of innovativeness with an impact that varies dramatically across studies' (Wolfe, 1994, p. 405). The influence of factors can be shown to be very dependent on the time, history, situation and context in which they are applied. Institutional arrangements, context and technological, and economic constraints reshape the diffusion space in which the innovation is diffused (Lyytinen and Damsgaard, 2001).

The literature shows that the IT evaluation process can be regarded as a social and political process (Walsham, 1993; Hirschheim and Smithson, 1999; Willcocks and Lester, 1999a). This supports the choice of an interpretive approach to this research. A new lens based on another theoretical framework than the diffusion and innovation theory may reveal more in an in-depth case study.

Given the special design of the evaluation methods it seems reasonable to assume they have gained some qualities to be easily employed by managers to address costs and benefits of IT. The low uptake of evaluation methods then seems to be a paradox (i.e. a situation that seems to be contradictory) but in fact is or may be true. It is argued here that it is neither the inherent *properties* of the evaluation method nor some properties of the (social) context (including potential adopters and other actors) that drives the employment of the method, but rather the *associations* that exist and that are created between the evaluation method and its surrounding actors. Such a perspective brings us to the choice of actor-network theory (ANT) for the analysis since it focuses on the associations between actors that can be both social and technical; both human and non-human. The initial assumption, from a close reading of ANT and its critics, is that ANT can offer an analytical language that can sensitise us to new ways of understanding needed for attempting to explain the seeming paradox of (a) the existence of many (often sophisticated) IT evaluation methods and (b) their indifferent usage, despite the demand. Therefore, ANT is used to gain deeper understanding of this paradox. ANT has already been utilised successfully in other studies of IT issues (e.g. Bijker and Law, 1994; Law and Hassard, 1999; Howcroft et al., 2004).

■ Adopting and applying a theoretical perspective: ANT

ANT, or the 'sociology of translations' (Callon, 1986a), is concerned with studying the construction and transformation of heterogeneous networks (Law, 1992) comprised of people, organisations, agents, machines and many other objects; studying the networks that constitute the world, existing of both humans and non-humans. It explores the ways that the networks of relations are composed, how they emerge and come into being, how they are constructed and maintained, how they compete with other networks and how they are made more durable over time (Tatnall and Gilding, 1999). ANT examines how actors (or actants) enlist other actors into their world and how they bestow qualities, desires, visions and motivations on these actors (Latour, 1996).

ANT presents a view of *translation*, which, in focusing on associations rather than proper-ties, is radically different from the ideas proposed by theories such as the diffusion of innov-ations theory. Translation is concerned with the alignment of interests of different actors, which is necessary for stability in the network. From the outset actors have a diverse set of interests (Monteiro, 2000). Aligning these interests causes a network to become stable and durable. Translation can be seen to create new relationships between actors to form an actor-network: 'translation is a process in which sets of relations [...] are proposed and brought into being' (Callon and Law, 1989). The goal of translation can be seen as to bring together complex entities into a single object or idea that can be mobilised and circulated like a branded commodity or a taken-for-granted fact (Clarke, 2001). When translation is successful, the different aligned actors together form a network, and at the same time this network is an actor in a greater network. In ANT terms, the actor (to other actors) becomes a *black-box*, obscuring embedded interests and constituent actors (note this term *black-box* has a distinctive usage in ANT, not to be confused with the normal meaning of the term in IS studies). In Appendix 3.1 of this paper an overview of some key concepts in ANT is given, based on Walsham (1997).

One important aspect of ANT is the denial of an *a priori* dichotomy between the social and the technical; they are considered to be intertwined. ANT argues for avoiding both techno-logical determinism and social reductionism and states that there is no reason to assume that either objects or people in general determine the character of social change or stabil-ity (Law, 1992). For example, when driving a car we are influenced not only by the tech-nical capabilities of the car, but also by traffic regulations and previous driving experience (Monteiro, 2000). If we want to understand the driving behaviour, we should take all of these into account where none of the elements is beforehand more influential than the others. As such, ANT supports *analytically* treating objects and people the same; non-humans and humans together form the heterogeneous networks. This view proves to be crucial to the aim of developing a deeper understanding of the use of an IT evaluation method that can be regarded as actor in an organisational actor-network. After presenting the case study, the authors will come back to this in the analysis.

ANT has been employed in many different cases to investigate the successes and failures of technological innovations, including research on IS. Callon (1986a) has used it to explain the failure of the domestication of the scallops of St Brieuc Bay and the development of the elec-tric vehicle by the Electricité de France (Callon, 1986b). Latour has used ANT to analyze the development of a revolutionary public transportation system known as Aramis (Latour, 1996) and to discuss the achievements of Louis Pasteur (Latour, 1999b).

In IS research, Monteiro and Hanseth (1995) studied the role of standards in electronic data interchange systems and information infrastructure (Hanseth and Braa, 1999). Vidgen and McMaster (1996) have applied it to the adoption of a particular car-parking system. Silva and Backhouse (1997) used the concepts of ANT to explain the failure to institutionalise the London Ambulance Service information system. Mitev (2000) has employed ANT to study the problematic introduction of an American computerised reservation system and yield management at French railways. Wagner (2003) draws on ANT to study the design and implementation of an Enterprise Resource Planning system in an academic environment.

Though ANT has been applied in many researches, it has also been criticised from differ-ent stances. Some of its major critiques are voiced by Walsham (1997) who criticises ANT's disregard for social structures, its lack of political analysis and its poor capacity for explanations. In addition, the equality of humans and non-humans and the explanatory power given to each is subject to debate. The critiques can be drawn together as a warning that ANT might be too 'flattening'. By perceiving actors equally, important social constructions and discourses may be lost. Relying solely on the configuration of actor-networks is not enough to explain why and how some actors are more empowered while others are disempowered; and why and how there may be pre-existing conflicts between actors which shape outcomes (Howcroft et al., 2004). Using ANT, the role of 'exogenous contingencies' such as economic crises, deregulation and IT-supported managerial principles may be underestimated. Mitev (2000) argues that conceptualisations, for example, of the market, economics, organisations, management or culture should be explored further. She argues that it is not sufficient to understand that actors hold particular beliefs or interests, but rather an analysis is needed to understand how and why this actor has taken these beliefs for granted – how they have shaped the actor's interests. And moreover, how this grants particular actors the status of being more empowered than others. For several critics, then, ANT does not directly contribute to such understanding.

However, Latour (1999a) states that ANT was never intended to be 'a theory of the social or even worse an explanation of what makes society exert pressure on actors [but a] very crude method to learn from the actors without imposing on them an a priori definition of their world-building capacities. [...] ANT does not claim to explain the actor's behaviours and reasons, but only to find the procedures which render actors able to negotiate their ways through one another's world-building activity' (ibid., p. 20). In other words, it never was intended to explain the behaviour of social actors, but in a much more ethnographic sense a way for researchers to study what, how and why actors behave the way they do – not claiming to explain this behaviour by all kinds of exterior forces unknown to the actors themselves. 'Explanation' in this sense is intended to describe in detail the events and actions that take place and how they interact, rather than to find (invisible) causes (e.g. contextual explanations) or linking perceived events to generalised social theories (e.g. explaining that actors acted the way they did because that is consistent with a particular social theory). Explanation thus should be understood as presenting the events from a research study in such a way that they become clear (make sense) to the researcher and the reader.

Though not having a history comparable to that of, for example, diffusion theory by Rogers, ANT has gained a firm ground within IS research. However, during this research little evidence was found of studies that have applied it rigorously to IT evaluation and its practice.

Research strategy and method

A number of alternative approaches to IS research include laboratory experiments, field experiments, surveys, case studies, phenomenological studies, longitudinal studies and action research (Galliers, 1985). According to Walsham (1993) case studies are perhaps the most appropriate strategy for conducting empirical research from an interpretive stance. It has been an accepted method for research in IS for sometime (Benbasat et al., 1987). Case studies are defined as an empirical enquiry that investigates a contemporary issue or event within its real-life context, especially where the boundary between such issues or events and its context is not clearly defined, and in which multiple sources of evidence are used

(Yin, 1989). The case study allows for 'thick description', which gives the researcher access to the subtleties of changing and multiple interpretations (Walsham, 1995) which otherwise would have been lost. The aim of case-study research is not to say that the account given is what 'really happened', rather it is to make an informed interpretation and analysis of the events available (Geertz, 1973).

Many of the criticisms raised against the case-study strategy relate to the fact that it is specific to only a small number of cases and hard to generalise (statistically) to a wider range of situations. However, as Yin (1989) argues, case studies are useful for analytical generalisations, where the researcher's aim is to generalise a particular set of results to some broader theoretical propositions. Walsham (1993) argues that from an interpretive stance, the validity of the results is derived from the plausibility and cogency of the logical reasoning in its analysis. From that perspective, validity does not come from a large number of cases, but the choice of a singular case study can as easily be justified (Lee, 1989). In fact, given limited time and resources, the interpretive approach gives more weight to an in-depth case study with a thick description, rather than multiple case studies, which are less detailed. To gain deeper understanding of the evaluation method employment therefore, a singular case was chosen for in-depth research.

The research was conducted at a large insurance company, employing approximately 5000 employees, situated in the Netherlands, but operating on a European and a global scale. The company will be referred to by the fictional name of 'International Insurance Company' (IIC). IIC was selected because of its experiences and ongoing efforts to employ an IT evaluation method. It has been involved in the employment process related to the IT evaluation method since 1996 and this continued during 2001, the period in which fieldwork was conducted. Actually being present during the employment proved to be beneficial, since the respondents could tell their stories vividly – their accounts had not yet been tarnished too much by the distancing effect of time. Moreover, documents and other sources of information (e.g. intranet sources) were ready to hand.

The case is particularly interesting due to the comprehensiveness of the IT evaluation method adopted by the organisation. This is not merely a financial accounting technique, but a methodology specifically constructed for the evaluation of IT investment proposals. As was discussed above, such cases are not widespread. Its uniqueness is strengthened when we consider the ongoing effort. This was not a one-shot attempt, but a genuine effort to employ the evaluation method. The method, as detailed below, has had a real impact on the organisation. The in-depth case therefore offers a source for insight into the dynamics, richness and complexity of the IT evaluation employment process.

Lastly, the insurance industry is considered information rich and one of the most progressive sectors in their use of IT. It is argued that much can be learned from organisations with relatively long experience with IT and IT investment decisions, making the research interesting for informing other cases of IT evaluation method employment.

Empirical evidence was gathered using multiple methods of data collection. The main source of data was 15 interviews that were carried out on site, typically lasting for about two hours. They were conducted between April and September 2001. Respondents were selected on the basis of their involvement in the design, implementation, use or assessment of the evaluation method. Consequently, the respondents worked in functional areas such as finance, strategy, system development, programme management (PM), while several managers of various business units were also included. All interviews were tape recorded, and extensive research notes were taken. The respondents were provided with an initial overview of questions, but interviews were not required to follow strict guidelines; they were more open and less structured. This flexibility gave the opportunity to focus on the particularities of the case. In addition, some additional informal (non-taped) discussions with IIC employees took place during the fieldwork. Other sources include over 50 public and confidential reports on IIC, the intranet of IIC, and its Internet site. The reports included public reports, consultancy reports, press reports, technical documentation and annual reports. In particular, 13 internal reports, the intranet and e-mail correspondence allowed for triangulation (Jick, 1979). Statements by respondents could be verified and triangulated with these documents, thereby allowing the researchers to construct a more informed account of events.

A heuristic approach was taken to determine the total number of interviews. Though it was possible to acquire more IIC respondents for the research, when no new insights were gained by interviewing and the gathered data was believed to be sufficient for a thorough analysis, it was agreed to stop adding respondents and acquiring more documents. All formal interviews were transcribed and analyzed qualitatively. Typical issues arising from the analysis were: the reasons and prior conditions for the IT evaluation method to appear; the notion of rationality of the evaluation method; the processes of justification, scoring, prioritising and decision-making; the quality of evaluation results; politics in IT evaluation; the messiness of the prioritisation rounds; and the appropriation and changing of the method. The issues were grouped for further analysis. The final case study centred on the events, the construction of the evaluation method and the two applications of the evaluation method. These are discussed below.

Case study: The construction of the IT evaluation method at IIC

Context

Though an economic climate of recession is often claimed to induce the adoption of new IT evaluation methods to get a grip on costs and benefits (e.g. Ballantine and Stray, 1998; Willcocks and Graeser, 2001), the case shows that an economic climate of growth, in this case in the Netherlands, can also lead to the perceived need for such control.

The heated insurance market was demanding more products, and with the marketers selling all kinds of innovative products, the clockwork – processes, skills and technologies – that produced the products was being put to the test. For these products, the insurance industry depends heavily on IT for collection, manipulation, storage, retrieval and updating of considerable amounts of data. At the base of insurance products lay complex IS developed and changed over many years, resulting in inflexible legacy systems. The lack of insight into numerous serious failures in running IT projects led at this critical time to a search for more control over IT projects and related costs and benefits.

Different contextual developments strengthened the demand for a new IT evaluation method. For example, during the period discussed in the case study IT evaluation (Parker et al., 1988; Oirsouw et al., 2001), cost control of IT projects (Acohen and Florijn, 1992), the productivity paradox (Strassmann, 1985; Seddon et al., 2004), IT balanced scorecard (Kaplan and Norton, 1996; Plant et al., 2003) and IT benefit management (Irsel and Swinkels, 1992) were key issues in the Dutch management and IT-related literature. These topics were especially being addressed in the general financial literature. Why? Because, for example, as Campbell (1992) lastingly observed, too many financial institutions blindly invest in the latest technology, hoping that it would improve efficiency and control costs. Consultancy organisations influential in the financial sector were also increasing awareness on this topic (e.g. GartnerGroup, 2000).

Moreover, several developments in the late 1990s had increased IT costs without directly improving benefits (Spangenberg et al., 1999). One reason for this was the shortage of IT resources at that time. At the end of the millennium, there was a high demand for IT professionals, but the supply was limited. Moreover, salaries of IT employees were higher and rose faster than other categories of employees. Also, a large turnover in IT staff led to losses in productivity which needed to be compensated by increasing investments in training. The training costs also increased due to the newness of the technology, which in turn brought with it a high initial cost. Finally, a large number of IT projects (e.g. euro, millennium and legacy substitution projects) had no or little obvious return on investment at this time. These projects were considered inescapable and vital to organisations even though they did not produce direct benefits, other than avoiding future problems.

At the same time, there was growing awareness that IT projects frequently last much longer and cost much more than initially planned (Genuchten et al., 1991; Willcocks and Graeser, 2001). IT projects, indeed, had gained some notoriety amongst Dutch businesses, due to advertised failures, for being too partial as solutions, or, in some cases, as completely wasteful (Siskens et al., 1989; Berghout, 2002). Thus these different sources raised awareness of IT evaluation in general, and specifically in the financial sector with its high and increasing IT costs.

Creation and contents of the IT evaluation method

Founded in the nineteenth century, IIC is well established in the insurance industry and has undergone several major mergers. It has grown to be one of the most influential companies as it helped to shape the insurance field, first in the Netherlands, and later on a European and worldwide scale. It can be considered a commercially healthy company experiencing throughout an almost continuous growth in profits. By 2005, IIC had representative offices in the insurance industry in 29 countries worldwide.

This case focuses on the developments at IIC in the Netherlands. Here, IIC currently (2001–2005) employ approximately 5000 people. Its primary distribution channel is based on intermediaries (agents). Secondary distribution channels include the Internet and bank offices. IIC's insurance products cover life, property and health insurance for private employer insurance such as collective health insurance, pension insurance, disablement insurance and other loss of income insurance. In addition, it offers organisational insurance, such as insurance for company cars, technical insurance and all kinds of liability insurance.

As with most leading insurance companies, IT developments have played a dominant role within IIC. In the early years IT played an important role in cost reductions and addressing a tight labour market. Today, insurance products are so complex that without computerised systems they cannot be provided. Moreover, IT plays a vital role in communication with IIC's intermediaries.

However, the economic management of IT prior to this case study was mainly limited to operations, where an IIC department looked after software development. It decided on a day-to-day basis how to allocate resources to the various IT project requests presented to them by business managers. Questions such as 'What does the project cost?' and 'What does it deliver?' had not been an issue to either business or IT managers, particularly as the business was doing well financially.

The developments described above led to the creation at IIC of a Project Management (PM) department in 1996, with the initial task of improving the management of IT projects. With the introduction of PM, a new way of controlling IT was introduced. It entailed a new formal approach towards IT. This approach meant that IT was no longer characterised by unplanned, *ad hoc* projects where high IT budget overruns were the norm rather than the exception. The first thing addressed by PM was to make a list of all projects running each year. Such an overview did not exist until this point.

The list of projects raised questions as to why these projects were being carried out and what did they contribute. In 1997/1998 this led to the creation of a first prioritising method, reducing the selection amongst alternative solutions to a problem of detailed calculation. It was, however, soon discarded by PM as being too mathematical and theoretical. It relied too much on quantifying benefits, which, according to PM, was not always possible. However, PM used some of its concepts such as 'criteria', 'critical success factors' and 'measurement' to construct internally a list of criteria by which projects could be assessed on merit. This, in turn, led to the construction of the so-called Project Characteristics Template (PCT), a template on which projects could be summarised in a few criteria. Not only did the PCT give a quick overview of all projects, it also made projects more comparable, establishing a like-for-like basis. A further comparison was wanted, whereby projects could be weighted against each other and prioritised. But to do that accurately, more information was needed than the PCT provided. An IT evaluation method (ITEM) was constructed out of the PCT, designed on what was generally known as IT Economics Principles. Furthermore, ITEM was based on concepts from Information Economics (Parker et al., 1988) and the Balanced Scorecard (Kaplan and Norton, 1992; Kaplan and Norton, 1996).

From this time, projects were to be recorded using an ITEM-report covering financial costs and benefits, impacts on different criteria based on Information Economics and the Balanced Scorecard, and possible risks in carrying out the project. Apart from the calculations on the financial return of the project, most of these items were in 'free format' – there was freedom in the issues people could address on each of the points, although there was also an instruction document (and an example filled-in ITEM-report) pointing to issues that might be relevant.

ITEM could be classified as a multi-criteria method as opposed to financial, ratio or portfolio methods (Renkema and Berghout, 1997). Such a method entailed much more than ITEM being just a format of a written report. It included a particular view on how projects and criteria should be *scored*, how the projects should be *prioritised* and how a *decision* on projects could be reached. PM described it like this in an internal document:

> 'Before an idea becomes a going project, a process of analysis, justification and prioritizing precedes. [...] Within this process ITEM is used to list project proposals, to score and to prioritize. In this, different people have different functions and responsibilities' (PM document).

Scoring was envisioned to take place by means of a broad group of people who would value the effects of each individual proposal. The participants in the scoring group assess the projects based on the score model of ITEM (e.g. –1 for a negative contribution and a score of 0 to 5 for a positive contribution). If necessary, scores could be discussed by participants and refined further. Scores of all participants were combined on each of the criteria in a database, and each project proposal thus had a set of final scores. Rather than having one final score for each project, the different scores on criteria were kept so that all projects could be viewed according to their contribution to each of the criteria. The database allowed various views of different criteria, for example, in different scenarios. This was intended to help those who wished to prioritise.

Prioritising was done initially by PM. They constructed advice on the optimal portfolio of projects for general management. In this, the directors of the three market groups assisted PM. Prioritisation was based on the fit between the scored project effects and the organisational strategic goals and bottlenecks, given the available budget. The prioritisation included a check on technical feasibility and practicability. The IT departments of Systems Development and Infrastructure were consulted for this check. PM then presented its final recommendation to general management.

In turn, general management would make the final *decision* on prioritisation. To selected proposals, they granted budgets, which by then had become projects.

ITEM is illustrated in Figure 3.1 Notice that ITEM entailed both a process (of scoring, prioritising and decision-making) and several artefacts, such as documents and an automated database. The complete ITEM comprised:

- The ITEM-report, with an assessment of the effect of a proposal in terms of costs, benefits (both financial and non-financial), risks and urgency that justifies the investment.
- An internal rate of return (IRR) report, a calculation sheet for calculating the financial rate of return for the proposal, where financial costs and benefits are analyzed based on a 6-year timeline.
- A scoring process for valuing project effect.
- An automated database used to generate and support prioritisation based on the scoring process and a statistical analysis.
- A prioritisation process for determining the ranking of project proposals.
- Advice to general management about which projects should receive a budget (the priorities proposal).
- A decision process by general management that decides which proposals will be granted a budget.

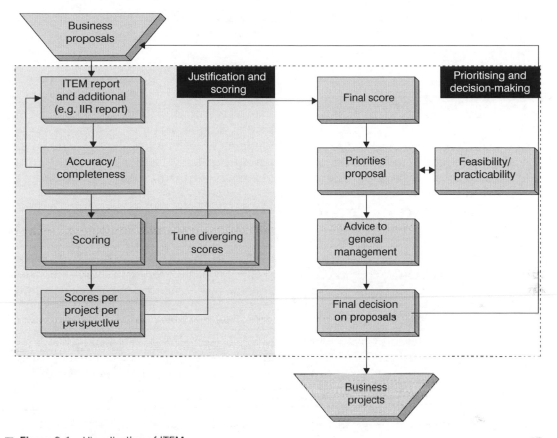

Figure 3.1   Visualisation of ITEM

The first ITEM-report was developed in 1998 and with it, ITEM was created. According to an internal report by PM describing the methodology:

> 'The method excels in simplicity, objectivity and uniformity. Its ultimate goal is to assist in making a right prioritization to improve the effectiveness and efficiency of the portfolio projects within IIC' (IIC intranet).

Employment of the ITEM

The introduction and use of ITEM

ITEM (and its predecessors) had already been developed in the period between 1996 and 1998, but it was not until the end of 1999 that it was widely spread throughout the organisation, and it has been used in the study organisation ever since for allocating the IT budget. By the end of 1999 PM agreed with general management that IT investment proposals should have an ITEM-report made up. 'Plans without the ITEM-report do not get a budget' was the message from PM. This resulted in 52 project proposals for the year 2000. However, the overall quality of the proposals was unsatisfactory to PM. In particular, the quantification of costs and benefits left room for improvement. Also in many cases, when asked for risks in carrying out the project, staff had written 'not applicable'. Risks of the project had not been made as explicit as PM had wanted.

The study revealed some reasons why the quality of the proposal was low in the eyes of PM. Firstly, the people involved in constructing the ITEM-report struggled with it. They all had different backgrounds, as diverse as technical specialists, project specialists, process specialists and business specialists. A small number of them were familiar with a broad view on investment proposals. Respondents report typical questions asked by users, such as 'What is an IRR?' and 'Effects on market share? How do I know?' Although ITEM supposedly had been constructed to be simple and plain, with good documentation, in practice it required both specific knowledge and experience to be able to cope with it. As a result, some ITEM-reports focused only on technical aspects, whereas others focused primarily on business benefits. In their focus on some aspects, they downplayed others.

Furthermore, managers required to use the method struggled with the criteria ITEM proposed. One anecdotal story tells of a manager trying to justify an investment in a new information system which would save a specialist employee about half his/her time:

> 'Being one of the few specialists with knowledge of a particular system, it would be a very welcome relief for the whole department involved. The idea was that he/she now could spend time addressing other issues with regard to that system, ones that urgently needed attention' (manager).

However, she received a response from the Finance Department (involved in checking financial estimations in ITEM-reports), that the proposed time savings were not actually a saving at all since the specialist was not losing 50% of his/her employment. Therefore, costs would remain the same and for the Finance Department, the project delivered no savings. The manager argued that:

> 'We did not know how to quantify the benefits of the project in another way. The specialist was not going to deliver more products – only address arrears work. To the Finance Department the benefits of the project were zero. But for people on the work floor it would have meant so much relief!' (manager).

Finally, the manager worked around the problem by viewing the additional criteria ITEM provided to show the benefits of the project. Benefits such as increased knowledge due to the specialist possibly training other people in his or her spare time and increases in professionalism were thus selected:

> 'You go about quite artificially, trying to fit the benefits somewhere. You think to yourself: at least I can get a positive score on those items, because on the other items there is no chance' (manager).

Since ITEM did not provide enough room for the manager to capture the perceived benefits, thereby threatening dismissal of the proposal, she took a detour. The example shows that the ITEM-report was used creatively to be able to justify the project proposal.

Secondly, PM noticed that the quantification of costs and benefits frequently were assessed in a way very favourable to the project proposal under review. Cost and benefit estimates were unrealistically positive, financial ratios were not properly calculated (e.g. proposals used different interest rates and thereby became incomparable), in a large number of cases risks were qualified as 'not appropriate for this project', and many projects were classified as 'strategic' or 'must-do', having been put under the label 'millennium project' (the Y2K problem). In addition, some managers noted high rising maintenance costs by some departments (as opposed to lowering project budgets), thereby insinuating that some projects were evading ITEM by qualifying themselves as maintenance costs (which do not require an ITEM-report and almost automatically get budget). Such expressions of politics in IT evaluation are very common (Willcocks and Lester, 1999a; Nijland et al., 2002).

This led PM at an early stage to ask the Finance Department to assist in calculating the financial returns of proposed projects. One manager of PM said:

> 'We decided to calculate the Internal Rate of Return ourselves, rather than let the managers involved do it. Because if they do it themselves, they change the different rates of interest. We have seen proposals that adjusted the profit margin from the standard 5% to 10%. Our financial controller said: "What's this nonsense? I have worked for 20 years at IIC and have never seen a margin of 10%! That is impossible!" But still the project leader simply puts his signature under the proposal!' (manager PM).

Some managers confessed that some costs and benefits were over-positive, rather than realistic. Superficial analysis of this behaviour would qualify it as political behaviour designed only to serve the self-interest of individuals. Politics in decision-making is often seen as disruptive and as something that should be suppressed. It is regarded as disrupting the 'rational model' deeply rooted within western, especially management, society (Morgan, 1986; Willcocks and Lester, 1999). The comments made by some PM managers on these expressions of politics demonstrate a similar viewpoint and show a rational discourse. Politics are blamed for the low quality of ITEM-reports, thereby failing to produce a proper justification for the project. On the IIC intranet, the page concerning ITEM states that the:

> 'Improper use and hiding behind these procedures and methods should be prevented and where observed, be corrected' (IIC intranet).

However, quite a different view comes from a director of one of the business units at IIC. He argues:

> 'Self-interest is the source for new initiatives. If everybody had the same interest, nothing would happen! Moreover, self-interests often are not just solely linked to the individual interests, but to the role one plays in the organization, the function you have' (BU director).

Being committed to those interests serves the interests of the organisation. Thus, such politics are healthy and taking them out of the organisation would be disastrous, he argues. Rather than marking a (too) positive view on project proposals as a 'bad thing', he sees it as a sign of support and motivation for the project. Such support is crucial to the success of any project. The director argued that when people are enthusiastic about an idea, who can blame them for not seeing all its negative sides? Such behaviour can thus be explained as a form of 'bounded rationality' (Simon, 1960) or cognitive dissonance, where people who are excited about a project see the positive sides more than the negative ones. Political actions can then be understood, not only to serve personal interest but as being committed to the interest of the department, business unit or even IIC as a whole.

Farbey et al. (1993) noticed the same paradox: on the one hand you need a project champion to lead the project enthusiastically, on the other hand you do not want him to 'cheat' to get the 'go ahead' for a project: 'If we praise the champion we diminish evaluation; if we promote the proper role of evaluation, we marginalize the champion' (ibid., p. 154).

Thirdly, the ITEM-report was regarded by some to be more of a checklist than supporting a justification, scoring, prioritisation and decision-making process. Rather than taking the time to think proposals through and consider thoroughly the costs, benefits and risks, ITEM-reports were filled in thoughtlessly by some, and within a short period of time. In addition the people responsible for delivering the ITEM-reports were also responsible for day-to-day operations, and thus faced the balancing of long-term- vs. short-term-focused decisions. In the long term, they were interested in getting budget for new investments and were required to develop ITEM-reports. By contrast, in the short term, their interest was to keep business operational. In the rush of the day to day and the focus on delivering practical results, rather than 'writing project descriptions', little time was available for drafting ITEM-reports.

Scoring and prioritising

In this case-study work, the focus was on two rounds of budget allocation. The first round included a round of scoring. Several directors and senior managers were asked by PM to give scores to all the proposals based on the criteria ITEM provided. All scores by each scoring member were put into a database. By statistical comparisons an analysis was made on the final scores of the proposed investments. From the database, PM created an overview of the projects from different perspectives (product variation, market segmentation, etc.). The priority list was presented to general management in March 2000. But rather than taking the advice to carry out the prioritised selection of the projects, general management decided to approve all 52 projects by granting more overall IT budget. The reason for this was the result of the many projects that had a 'must-do' status. Due to the large number of projects necessary because of the euro currency adjustments, millennium issues and mandatory changes by law and regulatory changes, only a small number of projects remained that were eligible for prioritisation of investment. Because those remaining constituted such a relatively small number of projects, general management decided to allow all projects that had a valid ITEM-report to carry on.

At the end of 2000, a new round of project prioritising had started to set up budgets for the year 2001. All business units had to hand in their new project proposals. This second round of prioritisation has been characterised by one of the PM employees as a 'black page'. Not only because the quality of the ITEM-reports was still unsatisfactory to PM, but, more importantly, because the process of scoring and prioritisation went differently than planned. Rather than having a time-consuming scoring procedure, PM decided to organise a discussion with several directors of IIC business units. The aim of the discussion was to select a number of proposals from the 80 proposals received. General management would be advised to grant budget to those selected. However, in a fierce discussion in which all directors pleaded for their own projects, no consensus was reached on a plan that could fit the available budget. As a result, PM handed over to general management a list of, according to PM, 'must-do' projects. General management, however, concluded that several projects without the 'must-do' status, but which were crucial in their own view, had to be carried out. In the end, general management spent two days at the beginning of 2001 prioritising all the projects on the list, resulting in the project list for that year.

At the end of the second prioritisation round, general management commented:

> 'This actually is crazy. [By prioritizing ourselves,] we are doing the work of our business directors. We do not want to do that' (general manager).

They asked PM to come up with a solution. PM came with a proposal to create a prioritisation platform, in which managers took time to discuss on a monthly basis IT projects and new IT proposals.

Situation as at 2001

During the year 2001, the time the research was conducted, all respondents regarded ITEM as being employed by the organisation. It had become common practice to fill in ITEM-reports when a new project was proposed. PM noticed that people came to them to request the ITEM-report form when they wanted to start a project, and information managers noticed business managers telling each other not to forget to use ITEM. ITEM was also considered to be the normal road one had to take in order to get project approval; without an ITEM-report, projects did not enter the project prioritisation and decision-making process. Moreover, the systems development department no longer worked on projects that had not been approved.

Not only had ITEM become regarded as integrated in the business, it was also regarded as an improvement on the (lack of) prior evaluation practices. The financial department argued that in making explicit assumptions, ITEM supported budget allocation and led to more disciplined use of budgets. This was regarded as a step in the right direction as opposed to previous practices where IT budget overruns were the norm. IIC had changed to become more cost-conscious in IT projects. Moreover, ITEM filtered away initial ideas that could not yet be worked out thoroughly. In the past these proposals slipped through, but now they were halted at the outset. They did not enter the process of prioritising at all. Business managers contended with regard to the overall success of ITEM that:

> 'Now we really make plans, make choices and follow projects. Everything is much more methodical and structured than it used to be' (BU manager).

In summary, since 1996, IIC had come a long way with regard to getting a grip on the economic aspects of IT. All respondents saw the introduction of ITEM as an improvement in handling IT projects. Although some noticed that the ultimate goal of an ideal, rationalised grip on IT may never be reached due to the flexibility to shape the ITEM-reports and difficulties in making valid estimates of all benefits, they came to regard ITEM as a major contribution to IT decision-making and communication.

Analysis and discussion

The primary reason for using ANT in the analysis is that by demonstrating how technology operates together with the social (which are a priori the same) we come to deeper understanding of the case. It is possible to see how ITEM both acts and is enacted in the organisational network. ANT attempts impartiality towards all actors, whether technical or social, whether human or non-human, and makes no distinction in approach between the social, the natural, technological or any other a priori distinction between actors. The analysis starts by demonstrating how ITEM can be considered an actor and then demonstrate how this actor interacts with others during the employment process. This section closes by discussing the results of the employment.

ITEM as an actor

From an actor-network perspective, ITEM can be considered to be a *heterogeneous network*, consisting both of physical artefacts (reports, written instructions and a database) and associations to ideas on evaluation. The method can be said to be inscribed by different backgrounds and discourses. The financial background provided the need for basic financial costs and benefits, including financial return ratios (e.g. the IRR calculation); the ITEMs in the literature, such as Information Economics and Balanced Scorecard, provided criteria for assessing qualitative and intangible costs, benefits and risks; and lastly the ideas of PM about decision-making, being able to judge and prioritise proposals (including scoring techniques) were inscribed in the method.

As an actor, ITEM comes in contact with many different actors in the organisational actor-network during the adoption and use. These actors include ITEM, PM, other departments at IIC (such as finance and software development), managers who have to evaluate their IT proposals (users of ITEM), the investment proposals themselves and decision-makers (business directors and general management) and employees who provide input for the ITEM-reports.

Through its inscriptions and interaction with different actors, ITEM displays particular behaviour. It can be considered not a passive artefact that can be shaped (within certain boundaries) at will by its surrounding actors, but rather as an *actor* that imposes worldviews and its inscriptions on its surrounding actors. ITEM brings with it a certain process: how IIC members should use it and what kind of behaviour is expected from them to suit its specific purpose. Illustrative is one internal document describing the process by which ITEM has to be carried out. It states that in this process 'different persons have different functions and responsibilities'. ITEM redefines responsibilities and roles of different people at IIC. In the process of ITEM employment, several changes occur or are attempted. Some notable changes are discussed below.

PM changed its role from initially being a project administrator to becoming an important player in decision-making at IIC. Business directors were moved from a position where they only had to consider their own business unit, to consider the impact of their IT projects on the whole of IIC. The perspective of general managers on IT project proposals changed from their own constructed view, to a view given to them by the ITEM. The decision-making at IIC in general moved towards a more rational perspective, rather than one based on intuition and gut-feeling. The department of Software Development was burdened no longer with making decisions on which projects they were to allocate their scarce resources, but now was transformed into a department that could focus on its core business: developing software. In sum, in ANT terms ITEM can be said to make an attempt to translate its surrounding actors towards its interests (stemming out of its inscriptions).

Moreover, ITEM can be argued to become a spokesperson for the different IT investment proposals. A critical perspective shows that in its representation ITEM does not capture an independent reality, as was initially envisioned by PM, but rather it can be seen to *create reality* (Power and Laughlin, 1992). It is not what the evaluation method says, but rather what it allows to be said that makes the difference (Smithson and Tsiavos, 2003). By choosing an evaluation process that emphasises financial elements, other elements, such as social ones (e.g. the quality of the work experience, a consideration of the impact on people and their working environment – Garrity and Sanders, 1998), may lack representation. In other words, ITEM as an actor, and with its inscriptions, influences how investment proposals are valued and how they enter the decision-making process. The criteria the method uses, specify which projects are the 'right' projects to be selected, and which projects will not be carried out (Bacon, 1992).

A dominant notion locked in many of the evaluation methods, including the one in this case study, is the notion of rational decision-making. Typically, rational decision-making is associated with terms such as measurable, calculated, based on logic and hard data, systematic, objective, factual, reasoned, etc. This view however results in a misconception that the value of information can somehow be measured objectively and captured by a neutral tool. This feeds the idea, for example, that a tool can measure the value of information and come up with the best investment proposals. Instead, we argue the value of information can only be discussed meaningfully *in casu* and can only be interpreted (socially), not measured. This relates to the notion of value described by Legge (1984) who states the following propositions about value (ibid., p. 149):

- 'Values derive from and are embedded in communities of people who share experience and attributed meanings.
- Values are ideas about what 'should be' to produce the kinds of consequences an individual or group desires.
- An entity, such as a change programme or IT investment, has value if those attributing value to it believe it has produced desirable consequences'.

Empirical research has found ample evidence of decision-making processes that appear 'irrational' by the normative standards (Brunsson, 1985). Irrational elements in decision-making are associated with personal preferences, (gut) feelings, subjectivity, politics, intuition, entrepreneurship, ambition, instincts, beliefs, etc.

Critiquing the objectivity of method's criteria, Legge (1984) argues that the selection of criteria will depend on the desirable consequences the investments should have. What count as 'desirable' and which projects are 'right' will depend on the developers of the evaluation criteria (or their sponsors); the overt and covert functions of the evaluation will undoubtedly shape the method, possibly to the detriment of other functions and consequences desired by others. Ultimately ITEM is inscribed with these criteria, which determine ITEM's own interests. The faithfulness of ITEM as a spokesperson for the investment proposals can be questioned. The actor may betray the interests of the proposals.

The employment of ITEM

The case shows that the roles ITEM would like to assume, aiding in justifying scoring, prioritising and deciding on proposals, seem not to be automatically appropriated through the employment of the ITEM-reports. In justification, users of ITEM have problems shaping their proposals into the format required, as is demonstrated by the example of the user artificially finding categories to demonstrate the benefits of a project, which could otherwise not be justified. Moreover, the way they use ITEM politically is contrary to the expectations of PM, which leads to a lower quality of ITEM-reports than PM had hoped for. Users only partially complete ITEM-reports, for example leaving out the risk assessment; users make their own (favourable and/or partial) estimates of benefits and costs and they make their own (favourable) return-on-investment calculations – leading to the Finance Department having to make these calculations afterwards. In scoring and prioritising, ITEM seems helpful at the first attempt, but the results are negated by general management. In the second round, scoring does not take place at all. The proposed scoring process is being replaced by a meeting with the aim of coming to agreement via discussion. Rather than trusting the outcomes of ITEM, general management makes its own interpretation of the projects, coming to a decision that differs from the one proposed by ITEM. Results of the evaluation process were instead used for other purposes than IT decision-making (e.g. for operational activities, such as planning and assigning IT capacity to projects). In sum, it appears that ITEM is not able to fully assume the roles PM had wanted it to have.

Thus, there seemed to be a mutual change going on. On the one hand, people change their work processes to write ITEM-reports, assuming new roles in the justification and IT decision-making process, ITEM becomes a spokesperson for the IT investment proposals, shaping their plea for budget and ITEM influencing decision-making. On the other hand, the way ITEM is used goes against its intentions and inscriptions: political behaviour influences the way ITEM-reports are written; discussion on investment proposals is a fierce debate rather than a neat scoring technique and the actual decision-making does not resemble the envisioned rational decision-making. Users use the method in an unanticipated way (follow an *anti-programme* – Latour, 1991) rather than following the assigned programme. In the end, the method is used in many different ways and for all kinds of different purposes that go against most of the ideas inscribed in the method itself.

Followed over time, ITEM is transformed under the influence of all (both human and non-human) actors. A transformation which is guided by different types of change (Orlikowski, 1996). Changes occur by planned actions (e.g. transforming ITEM from project-detailing instrument, to decision-making aid), by improvisations to unexpected events (e.g. strengthening the inscriptions of ITEM along the way, to get it adopted and PM scoring the projects themselves, when business failed to do it) and by emergent events (e.g. ITEM not being used in times of budget crisis). From an outside perspective, ITEM seems to 'drift' (Ciborra et al., 2000) away uncontrollably from its original ideas. It changed roles, varying from tool to listing investment proposals, to communicating them and even deciding on them.

As a result of different acts of translation, the final shape and position of the innovation is unlikely to be that of the original developers (Mitev, 2000). Actors adapt the evaluation method during the process, and the innovation often cannot fully persuade other actors to follow its initial goals. The employment process is a dynamic negotiation (Monteiro, 2000).

Moreover, unintended effects occur resulting in changes in the network. The resulting network is the (combined) translation that becomes irreversible; it becomes impossible for other (past or future) translations to develop and impose themselves.

Due to mutual translation, the result of the employment of IT evaluation becomes unpredictable. It is an emergent rather than blueprinted process (Orlikowski, 1996); a continuous process rather than one that ends (Law, 1992). Understanding the evaluation method as a black-box, which packs different interests and actors, can help describe how only some of the elements in the method become employed while others are rejected, modified or appropriated.

Employment of ITEM: success or failure?   Referring to the central question about the unsuccessfulness of the employment of ITEMs, what can be concluded from this case? ITEM ended up being part of a translation, though not the translation initially preferred by PM. Only part of the black-box ITEM was enrolled. While being enrolled, it acted in quite a different way than was intended. The actors enacted (Weick, 1990) ITEM to suit their needs but in ways that contradicted the (rational) inscriptions of ITEM. The different interests of the actors at IIC shaped the employment of ITEM, and the obtained results were quite different from the results initially envisioned by PM; both visible in the produced ITEM-report and in the decision-making process it was supposed to support.

But though the resulting employment, in terms of intent, may be classified as failure, it is regarded by many respondents as a success. The ITEM came to be the accepted way to get IT investment approval. ITEM can be seen to be mobilised (Callon and Law, 1989) since participants draw upon the information, rules and resources embodied in ITEM in their daily activity. In doing so, they reproduce and reaffirm its importance, form and content (Bloomfield et al., 1994). It is said to be helpful in structuring IT investment information, to have heightened the attention of the critical issue of IT in the organisation, to have triggered people to think about their ideas before starting them and to involve more people in the IT decision-making process, which has led to broader acceptance of decisions.

Concluding the discussion, it is possible to argue that two interesting findings have come out of this research. First, if ITEM is considered to be an actor, which is not neutral and objective but has inscribed interests, then it is possible to understand how the employment process is influenced by the evaluation method itself and how actors react to ITEM. Both ITEM and the other actors influence the process. Second, if the employment process is viewed as a dynamic process in which both ITEM as well as other actors are mutually changing each other, one can understand how the outcomes of the employment are quite different than intended.

■ Conclusions

Acknowledging that in general little of the specifically designed ITEMs can be found in practice, it was stated at the beginning of this paper that the following question seemed relevant: 'Why do organisations generally seem to be unsuccessful in employing ITEMs that help them in clarifying costs and benefits of IT, even when they express the need for more insight into the costs and benefits of IT?' Looking at the IIC case, the conclusion is that this question cannot be answered simply. When comparing the results to the intentions of PM, one would say the employment of ITEM was a failure. The outcomes differ so much, that ITEM cannot be considered a success. On the other hand, ITEM has had an undeniable impact, which has changed the organisation. Respondents overall agree that the introduction of ITEM was a success.

The understanding gained from the analysis of this case study can help to overcome the apparent paradox of the underutilisation of ITEMs. The central question is tackled by addressing the underlying assumptions about evaluation methods and their employment. The question displays two assumptions that can be critiqued from our understanding of the case. First, the assumption that the evaluation method is in someway a neutral tool that can objectively be used in an organisation. Evaluation methods are not neutral, value-free instruments that can be implemented in organisations through blueprints. Evaluation methods are inscribed with ideas about what the value of an IT investment is, how decision-making should take place and how different actors should perform different roles. They create reality, rather than (re)present reality; thus they have an active role as actors in the actor-network.

Second, the assumption that the adoption process is either successful or unsuccessful, depending on the difference between planned and resulting outcomes. The process of diffusion and adoption of such methods is instead guided by emergent transformation, both of the evaluation method itself and as the organisational actors. Looking at it from an actor-network perspective, one can see that the method changes over time. In a dynamic process (which cannot be reduced to a set of simple factors), it translates actors and is translated by actors; it acts and is enacted. In the process of employment, a metamorphosis (under the influence of planned, emergent and improvised change by different actors) shapes the method and in so doing allows it to transform in some way so that it can find its place in the network. But in addition, the method has a profound impact in the sense that it translates (the roles of) many organisational actors. In this way, it is not just an *improvisation* (Orlikowski, 1996) from one actor on another, but rather a mutually transformative improvisation: a *mutual translation*. Efforts to get a method employed thus can be argued not to be fruitless, but to have a more gradual, emergent impact instead of a dramatic impact (Legge, 1984). The results are not likely to resemble the intended outcomes, but can have a profound impact on the way costs and benefits are managed in organisations and on how managers tackle problems when faced with addressing this issue. In fact, it could be argued that translations of the method might be the reason for its employment altogether; the necessary ongoing alignment process leading to a stable network where the evaluation method is black-boxed. Instead of a process of transmission there is a process of translation where 'faithful acceptance involving no changes is a rarity requiring explanation' (Tatnall, 2000).

One reason, then, why organisations do not seem to be 'successful' in employing ITEMs is that success is defined too narrowly in terms of fulfilling initial, stated objectives. On another view, as informed by Ciborra (2002) and Avgerou et al. (2004), in a 'successful' employment process both the evaluation method and the organisation changes beyond recognition – most likely having a gradual rather than a dramatic effect. One could even argue that the employment is a success when the evaluation method eventually is abandoned, but it enticed an organisational change that improved organisational evaluation of IT – for example, when users from then on are inclined to think through costs and benefits of IT whenever they introduce a new IT proposal. A 'failed' employment occurs when the ITEM is not translated.

ANT has proven useful to come to the conclusions presented above. It helped to see that ITEM actually changes and is changed in a process of translation. In contrast to other analytical interpretive frameworks, ANT helped to look beyond explanations based on social agents reacting to ITEM or on a perspective of a technical implementation with unintended consequences. By demonstrating that in perceiving ITEM as an actor, one can see it struggles to make alliances (and thereby changing part of its interests) to involve PM, users, employees, general management and other (human) actors. ITEM rallies support by providing an ultimate answer to general management and PM, and promises to demonstrate *the* value of IT. It attempts to change the perception of the 'value of IT' from gut-feeling and intuition to a rational and calculated definition. In this respect there is no a priori difference between ITEM and other (human) actors: they both act, interpret, redefine meanings (such as value of IT and approaches to decision-making) and have equal substantial impact on the organisational dynamics. Thus ANT brings new understanding to this case and in the use of ITEMs in general.

Critiques on ANT suggest that it is a poor source on which to draw from when looking for psychological explanations. ANT does not uncover the origins of the interests of actors. It is also ahistorical and does not take into account institutionalised structures or the interpretive schemes by which actors make sense of the phenomenon. For example, many of the actors in the case can be seen to be influenced by a rational discourse. They hold a rational view of the problem and therefore seek a rational solution, and argue: 'To attain better insight in costs and benefits of IT, we have to develop a technique that shows us these things'. This shapes the way they interpret events (e.g. seeing evaluation results as having low quality) and the way they act (e.g. sharpen the tools). Understanding it would involve analyzing the rational discourse, the norms and values within the organisation of IIC (and society as a whole) and possibly applying some theories of psychology to explain the behaviour of the individuals involved; just as a theory of biology would be required to understand the behaviour of the scallops in the classic ANT study of their domestication (Callon, 1986a); and further enquiry would be needed to see if the interest of slowing-down motorists comes from a respect for law and life (following traffic signs and warnings) or from selfishness (avoiding car damage by the speed bump), an example given by Latour (1999b).

However, the strength of ANT in the case presented here was not to find explanations for the different types of behaviour, but rather come to a deeper understanding of the employment of ITEMs. The study presented in this paper supports the view that the application of ANT can lead to helpful new understandings of phenomena in IS study. From the experiences in the presented case study and its ANT analysis, two conclusions have been reached, which taken together provide a basis for a deeper understanding of evaluation in practice. This leads not only to the dissolving of the paradox as phrased in the research question, but also to new directions for research and practice. The new perspective should provide a better basis for academic research on the many topics yet open to research in IT evaluation (e.g. Farbey et al., 1999), and in practice guide the development of new evaluation methods and the processes by which evaluation methods are introduced in organisations. Moreover, it should lead to new suggestions to improve IT costs–benefit management in organisations other than to 'sharpen the tools'. And that, ultimately, will result in an increase in obtaining benefits from the use of ITEMs.

■ Appendix 3.1 Some Key Concepts in ANT

Concept	Description
Actor (or actant)	Both human beings and non-human actors such as technological artefacts
Actor-network	Heterogeneous network of aligned interests, including people, organisations and standards
Enrolment and translation	Creating a body of allies, human and non-human, through a process of translating their interests to be aligned with the actor-network
Delegates and inscription	Delegates are actors who 'stand in and speak for' particular viewpoints which have been inscribed in them (e.g. software as frozen organisational discourse)
Irreversibility	The degree to which it is subsequently impossible to go back to a point where alternative possibilities exist
Black-box	A frozen network element, often with properties of irreversibility
Immutable mobile	Network element with strong properties of irreversibility, and effects which transcend time and place (e.g. software standards)

Source: Adapted from Walsham (1997).

■ References

Acohen, J. and Florijn, R. (1992). 'Besturen en beheersen van de kosten van de informatievoorziening (Control and management of costs of information supply; in Dutch)'. *Informatie*, 34(themanummer), 730–741.

Aladwani, A. M. (2002). 'An empirical examination of the role of social integration in system development projects'. *Information Systems Journal*, 12, 321–338.

Avgerou, C., Ciborra, C. and Land, F. (Eds.), (2004). *The Social Study of Information and Communication Technologies*. Oxford University Press, Oxford.

Bacon, C. J. (1992). 'The use of decision criteria in selecting information systems/technology investments'. *MIS Quarterly*, September, 335–353.

Ballantine, J. and Stray, S. (1998). 'Financial appraisal and the IS/IT investment decision making process'. *Journal of Information Technology*, 13, 3–14.

Ballantine, J. A., Galliers, R. D. and Powell, P. L. (1995). 'Daring to be different: Capital appraisal and technology investments'. *3rd Conference on Information Systems*, Athens (Greece). 87–97.

Ballantine, J., Bonner, M., Levy, M., Marin, A., Munro, I. and Powell, P. L. (1998). 'Developing a 3-D model of information systems success'. In Garrity, E. and Sanders, G. L. (Eds.), *Information Systems Success Measurement*. Idea Group Publishing, Hershey, USA, pp. 46–59.

Benbasat, I., Goldstein, D. K. and Mead, M. (1987). 'The case research strategy in studies of information systems'. *MIS Quarterly*, 11(3), 369–386.

Berghout, E. W. (2002). Informatietechnologie, een bodemloze put? (Information technology, a bottomless pit? in Dutch). Unpublished inaugural lecture, University of Groningen.

Bijker, W. and Law, J. (Eds.), (1994). *Shaping Technology/Building Society: Studies in Sociotechnical Change*. The MIT Press, Cambridge, MA.

Bloomfield, B. P., Coombs, R. and Owen, J. (1994). 'The social construction of information systems: The implications for management control'. In Mansell, R. (Ed.), *The Management of Information and Communication Technologies: Emerging Patterns of Control*. Aslib, London, pp. 143–157.

Brunsson, N. (1985). *The Irrational Organization*. John Wiley and Sons Ltd., Chichester.

Callon, M. (1986a). 'Some elements of a sociology of translation: Domestication of the scallops and the fishermen of St Brieuc Bay'. In Law, J. (Ed.), *Power, Action and Belief*. Routledge and Kegan Paul, London and Newyou, pp. 196–233.

Callon, M. (1986b). 'The sociology of an actor-network: The case of the electric vehicle'. In Callon, M., Law, J. and Rip, A. (Eds.), *Mapping the Dynamics of Science and Technology*. Macmillan Press, London, pp. 19–34.

Callon, M. and Law, J. (1989). 'On the construction of sociotechnical networks: Content and context revisited'. *Knowledge and Society: Studies in the Sociology of Science Past and Present*, (8), 57–83.

Campbell, J. (1992). 'Does technology deliver?' *Bankers Monthly*, 17–21.

Ciborra, C. (2002). *The Labyrinths of Information*. Oxford University Press, Oxford.

Ciborra, C. U., Braa, K., Cordella, A., Dahlbom, B., Failla, A., Hanseth, O., Hepso, V., Ljungberg, J., Monteiro, E. et al. (2000). *From Control to Drift: The Dynamics of Corporate Information Infrastructure*. Oxford University Press, Oxford.

Clarke, J. (2001). 'Using actor-network theories for the study of literacy events and practices in global and local settings'. *International Literacy Conference*, Cape Town.

Earl, M. J. (1989). *Management Strategies for Information Technology*. Prentice-Hall, New York

Farbey, B., Land, F. and Targett, D. (1993). *How to Assess Your IT Investment: A Study of Methods and Practice*. Butterworth-Heinemann, Oxford, Boston.

Farbey, B., Land, F. and Targett, D. (1999a). 'Moving IS evaluation forward: Learning themes and research issues'. *Journal of Strategic Information Systems*, (8), 189–207.

Galliers, R. D. (1985). 'In search of a paradigm for information systems research'. In Mumford, E. (Ed.), *Research Methods in Information Systems*. Elsevier Science Publishers BV, pp. 281–297.

Garrity, E. and Sanders, G. L. (1998). 'Dimensions of information systems success'. In Garrity, E. and Sanders, G. L. (Eds.), *Information Systems Success Measurement*. Idea Group Publishing, Hershey, USA, pp. 13–45.

GartnerGroup (2000). *Using Measurement to Demonstrate the Business Value of IT*. GartnerGroup, Connecticut.

Geertz, C. (1973). *The Interpretation of Cultures*. Basic Books, New York.

Genuchten, M.v., Heemstra, F., Lierop, F.v. and Volkers, R. (1991). 'Heeft iemand de software al gezien? (Has anyone seen the software yet? in Dutch)'. *Informatie*, 33(3), 193–200.

Gosselin, M. (1997). 'The effect of strategy and organizational structure on the adoption and implementation of activity-based costing'. *Accounting, Organizations and Society*, 22(2), 105–122.

Grembergen, W.v. and Bloemen, I. (1997). 'Belangrijke en problematische thema's in de bedrijfsinformatica (Important and problematic topics in organisational informatics; in Dutch)'. *Informatie*, 39(6), 23–31.

Gunasekaran, A., Love, P. E. D., Rahimi, F. and Miele, R. (2001). 'A model for investment justification in information technology projects'. *International Journal of Information Management*, 21, 349–364.

Hanseth, O. and Braa, K. (1999). Hunting for the treasure at the end of the rainbow: standardizing corporate IT infrastructure. *New Information Technologies in Organizational*

Processes: Field Studies and Theoretical Reflections on the Future of Work. Kluwer Academic Publishers, St. Louis, Missouri.

Hirschheim, R. and Smithson, S. (1999). 'Evaluation of Information Systems'. In Willcocks, L. and Lester, S. (Eds.), *Beyond the IT Productivity Paradox*. John Wiley and Sons Ltd., West Sussex, UK, pp. 381–409.

Hochstrasser, B. (1994). 'Justifying IT investments'. In Willcocks, L. (Ed.), *Information Management: The Evaluation of Information Systems Investment*. Chapman and Hall, London, New York, pp. 272–300.

Howcroft, D., Mitev, N. and Wilson, M. (2004). 'What we may learn from the social shaping of technology approach'. In Mingers, J. and Willcocks, L. (Eds.), *Social Theory and Philosophy for Information Systems*. Wiley, Chichester.

Irani, Z. and Love, P. E. D. (2001). 'Editorial – Information systems evaluation: Past, present and future'. *European Journal of Information Systems*, 10(4), 183–188.

Irsel, H. G. P.v. and Swinkels, G. J. P. (1992). 'Investeren in informatietechnologie: Take IT or leave IT (Investing in information technology: Take IT or leave IT; in Dutch)'. *Informatie*, 34(themanummer), 624–636.

Jick, T. D. (1979). 'Mixing qualitative and quantitative methods: Triangulation in action'. *Administrative Science Quarterly*, 24, 602–611.

Kaplan, R. and Norton, D. P. (1992). 'The balanced scorecard-measures that drive performance'. *Harvard Business Review*, January/February, 71–79.

Kaplan, R. and Norton, D. P. (1996). *The Balanced Scorecard*. Harvard Business School Press, Boston.

Kautz, K. and McMaster, T. (1994). 'Introducing structured methods: An undelivered promise? – A case study'. *Scandinavian Journal of Information Systems*, 6(2), 59–78.

Keen, P. G. W. (1991). *Shaping the Future: Business Design through Information Technology*. Harvard Business School Press, Boston, MA.

Kleist, V. (2003). 'An approach to evaluating E-business information system projects'. *Information Systems Frontiers*, 5(3), 249–263.

Kumar, K. (1990). 'Post implementation evaluation of computer-based information systems: Current practices'. *Communcations of the ACM*, 33(2), 203–212.

Latour, B. (1991). 'Technology is society made durable'. In Law, J. (Ed.), *A Sociology of Monsters. Essays on Power, Technology and Domination*. Routledge, London, pp. 103–131.

Latour, B. (1996). *Aramis, or the Love of Technology*. Harvard University Press, Cambridge, MA.

Latour, B. (1999a). 'On recalling ANT'. In Law, J. and Hassard, J. (Eds.), *Actor Network Theory and After*. Blackwell Publishers, pp. 15–25.

Latour, B. (1999b). *Pandora's Hope: Essays on the Reality of Science Studies*. Harvard University Press, Cambridge, MA.

Law, J. (1992). 'Notes on the theory of the actor-network: Ordering, strategy and heterogeneity'. *Systems Practice*, 5(4), 379–393.

Law, J. and Hassard, J. (Eds.), (1999). *Actor Network Theory and After*. Blackwell Publishers, Oxford.

Lee, A. S. (1989). 'A scientific methodology for MIS case studies'. *MIS Quarterly*, March, 33–50.

Legge, K. (1984). *Evaluating Planned Organizational Change*. Academic Press, London.

Lyytinen, K. and Damsgaard, J. (2001). 'What's wrong with the diffusion of innovation theory?'*Diffusing Software Products and Process Innovations*, Kluwer Academic Publishers, Banff, Canada, pp. 173–190.

Miller, S. (1997). 'Implementing strategic decisions: Four key success factors'. *Organization Studies*, 18(4), 577–602.

Mitev, N. N. (2000). *Information Systems Failure, Politics and the Sociology of Translation: The Problematic Introduction of an American Computerised Reservation System and Yield Management at French Railways*. Unpublished PhD Thesis, University of Salford.

Mitev, N. N. (forthcoming). 'Constructivist and critical approaches to an IS failure case study: Symmetry, translation and power'. *Information and Organization*.

Monteiro, E. et al (2000). 'Actor-network theory and information infrastructure'. In Ciborra, C. U., Braa, K. and Cordella, A. (Eds.), *From Control to Drift: The Dynamics of Corporate Information Infrastructures*. Oxford University Press, Oxford, pp. 71–83.

Monteiro, E. and Hanseth, O. (1995). 'Social shaping of information infrastructure: On being specific about the technology'. In *Information Technology and Changes in Organisational Work*, Orlikowski, W. J. Walsham, G. Jones, M. R. and DeGross J. (Eds.), Chapman and Hall, Cambridge University. *Proceedings of the IFIP WG8.2 working conference*: 325–343.

Morgan, G. (1986). *Images of Organization*. Sage Publications, Beverly Hills; London.

Nijland, M. H. J. (2000). Grip op kosten en baten van informatietechnologie-toetsing van een quickscan methode (Grip on costs and benefits of IT-evaluation of a quick scan method; in Dutch). Unpublished MSc Thesis, University of Delft.

Nijland, M. H. J., Berghout, E. W. and Grant, K. (2002). 'Seven Ways to Get Your 'Pet' IT Project Accepted – Politics in IT Evaluation'.*7th United Academy of Information Systems Annual Conference*, Leeds Metropolitan University, 422–431.

Oirsouw, R. R.v., Spaanderman, J. and Arendonk, C.v. (2001). *Informatiseringseconomie*. Academic Service, Schoonhoven.

Orlikowski, W. J. (1996). 'Improvising organizational transformation over time: A situated change perspective'. *Information Systems Research*, 7(1), 63–91.

Parker, M. M., Benson, R. J. and Trainor, H. E. (1988). *Information Economics: Linking Business Performance to Information Technology*. Prentice Hall, Englewood Cliffs, NJ.

Plant, R., Willcocks, L. and Olson, N. (2003). 'Managing e-business performance: Towards a revised balanced scorecard approach'. *Information Systems and e-Business Management*, 1(3), 265–281.

Plouffe, C. R., Hulland, J. S. and Vandenbosch, M. (2001). 'Research report: richness versus parsimony in modeling technology adoption decisions-understanding merchant adoption of a smart card-based payment system'. *Information Systems Research*, 12(2), 208–222.

Powell, P. L. (1999). 'Evaluation of information technology investments: Business as usual?' In Willcocks, L. and Lester, S. (Eds.), *Beyond the IT Productivity Paradox*. John Wiley and Sons Ltd., West Sussex, UK, pp. 151–182.

Power, M. and Laughlin, R. (1992). 'Critical theory and accounting'. In Alvesson, M. and Willmott, H. (Eds.), *Critical Management Studies*. Sage Publications, London, pp. 1–20.

Premkumar, G., Ramamurthy, K. and Crum, M. (1997). 'Determinants of EDI adoption in the transportation industry'. *European Journal of Information Systems*, 6, 107–121.

Renkema, T. J. W. and Berghout, E. W. (1997). 'Methodologies for information systems investment evaluation at the proposal stage: A comparative review'. *Information and Software Technology – Elsevier Science B.V.* (39), 1–13.

Rogers, E. M. (1995). *Diffusion of Innovations*. Free Press, New York.

Seddon, P., Graeser, V. and Willcocks, L. (2002). 'Measuring organizational IS effectiveness: An overview and update of senior management perspectives'. *Database*, Spring.

Seddon, P., Goodhue, D., Mclean, E. and Willcocks, L. (2004). 'Perspectives on IS success'.*Communications of the AIS*.

Serafeimidis, V. and Smithson, S. (1995). 'Requirements for an IT investment appraisal framework for the 1990s: Towards a more rigorous solution'.*European Conference on Information Technology Investment Evaluation*, Greenlands, 146–160.

Silva, L. and Backhouse, J. (1997). 'Becoming part of the furniture: The institutionalization of information systems'. In Lee, A. S., Liebenau, J. and DeGross, J. I. (Eds.), *Information Systems and Qualitative Research*. Chapman and Hall, London, pp. 389–414.

Simon, H. A. (1960). *The New Science of Management Decision*. Hamilton, Harper.

Siskens, W., Heemstra, F. J. and Stelt, H.v.d. (1989). 'Kostenbeheersing bij automatisering-sprojecten: een empirisch onderzoek (Cost management of automatisation projects: An empirical research; in Dutch)'. *Informatie*, 31(1), 34–43.

Smith, G. N., Cohen, W. M., Hefley, W. E. and Levinthal, D. A. (1989). *Understanding the Adoption of Ada: A Field Study Report*. Carnegie Mellon University, Pittsburg.

Smithson, S. and Tsiavos, P. (2003). *Working Paper: Re-constructing Information Systems Evaluation*, Department of Information Systems, London, LSE.

Spangenberg, J. F. A., Peters, R. J. and Heijningen, E. P.v. (1999). 'Investeren in informati-etechnologie-rendement op onzekerheid? (Investing in information technology-return on uncertainty? in Dutch)'. *de Accountant*, 4, 242–246.

Strassmann, P. (1985). *Information Payoff: The Transformation of Work in the Electronic Age*. Free Press, New York.

Swinkels, F. G. J. P. (1997). 'Managing the life cycle of information and communication technology investments for added value'.*European Conference on the Evaluation of Information Technology*, Delft University Press, Delft, The Netherlands, 85–92.

Tatnall, A. (2000). *Working Paper: Information Systems Innovation – Two Different Models*, Victoria University, School of Information Systems, Victory, Australia.

Tatnall, A. and Gilding, A. (1999). 'Actor-Network Theory and Information Systems Research'.*Proceedings of the 10th Australasian Conference on Information Systems*, 955–966.

Thorp, J. (1998). *The Information Paradox: Realizing the Business Benefits of Information Technology*. McGraw-Hill Ryerson, Toronto.

Vidgen, R. and McMaster, T. (1996). 'Black boxes, non-human stakeholders and the translation of IT through mediation'. In Orlikowski, W. J., Walsham, G., Jones, M. R. and DeGross, J. (Eds.), *Information Technology and Changes in Organizational Work*. Chapman and Hall, London, pp. 250–271.

Wagner, E. (2003). *Narrating an Organisational Matter of Fact: Negotiating with Enterprise Resource Planning Technology to Achieve Order Within a Traditional Academic Administration*, Unpublished Doctoral Dissertation, The London School of Economics.

Walsham, G. (1993). *Interpreting Information Systems in Organizations*. Wiley, Chichester.

Walsham, G. (1995). 'Interpretive case studies in IS research: Nature and method'. *European Journal of Information Systems*, 4, 74–81.

Walsham, G. (1997). 'Actor-network theory and IS research: Current status and future prospects'. In Lee, Liebenau and DeGross, (Eds.), *Information Systems and Qualitative Research*. Chapman and Hall, London, pp. 466–480.

Weick, K. E. (1990). 'Technology as equivoque: Sensemaking in new technologies'. In Goodman, P. S. and Sproull, L. S. (Eds.), *Technology and Organizations*. Jossey-Bass Inc., San Francisco, pp. 1–44.

Willcocks, L. (1994). *Information Management: The Evaluation of Information Systems Investments*. Chapman and Hall, London; New York.

Willcocks, L. (1996a). 'The evaluation and management of information systems investments: From feasibility to routine operations'. In Willcocks, L. (Ed.), *Investing in Information Systems: Evaluation and Management*. Chapman and Hall, London; New York, pp. 15–34.

Willcocks, L. (1996b). *Investing in Information Systems: Evaluation and Management*. Chapman and Hall, London; New York.

Willcocks, L. and Lester, S. (1999). *Beyond the IT Productivity Paradox*. Wiley, Chichester, England/New York.

Willcocks, L. and Graeser, V. (2001). *Delivering IT and E-Business Value*. Butterworth, Oxford.

Wilson, T. (1991). 'Overcoming the barriers to the implementation of information system strategies'. *Journal of Information Technology*, 6, 39–44.

Wolfe, R. A. (1994). 'Organisational innovation: Review, critique and suggested research directions'. *Journal of Management Studies*, 31(3), 405–431.

Wolfsen, R. and Lobry, R. (1998). Automatiseren met rendement (To automate with return; in Dutch), Tilburg University, Tilburg.

Yan Tam, K. (1992). 'Capital budgeting in information systems development'. *Information and Management*, (23), 345–357.

Yin, R. K. (1989). *Case Study Research: Design and Methods*. Sage Publications, London.

Chapter 4

IT project evaluation: Why more formal evaluation is not necessarily better

G. Thomas, P. B. Seddon and W. Fernandez

■ Introduction

Given the high cost and strategic importance of many information technology (IT) projects, evaluation decisions about the feasibility, relative priority and impact of these projects are important (Smithson and Hirschheim, 1998; Irani et al., 2005). However, despite the extensive literature on IT evaluation (Irani and Love, 2001, 2002), organisations appear to be no nearer a solution to meaningful evaluation than they were over a decade ago (Ballantine and Stray, 1998). Longstanding difficulties with evaluating IT projects are also exacerbated by a rapidly changing business environment and a high degree of uncertainty regarding IT project outcomes (Patel and Irani, 1999; Melville et al., 2004). The result is that IT projects continue to experience high failure rates (Lubbe and Remenyi, 1999; Love et al., 2005).

In an effort to gain a better understanding of which IT evaluation methodologies and practices are being used today, their relative effectiveness, and what value they bring, a series of 36 case studies was conducted in three industries in Australia. The research question was as follows:

> What are the most effective IT project evaluation practices used by organisations in Australia and why do they work?

The study concludes that the key to more effective IT evaluation is not more formal and sophisticated methods, but rather, more effective governance structures and leadership behaviours. Six key drivers of effective IT evaluation practices, that lead, in turn, to more efficient use of resources and improved IT project outcomes, are presented and justified.

■ The current domain

Evaluation is 'the process of providing information designed to assist decision-making about the object being evaluated' (Owen, 1993, p. 3). Evaluation is a key part of effective IT governance (McKay and Marshall, 2004). Thus IT project evaluation is a technique or a set of techniques that facilitates decision-making across the project life cycle with the goal of achieving the best outcomes for the organisation (Smithson and Hirschheim, 1998; Remenyi and Sherwood-Smith, 1999; Irani et al., 2005). Since IT evaluations may be conducted either prior to investment, during project delivery, or after the project is complete, IT evaluation includes both *predictive* evaluations (*ex ante*) and *prescriptive* evaluations (*ex post*) (Remenyi and Sherwood-Smith, 1999).

Predictive evaluations are used to predict the feasibility, cost and impact of proposed IT investments. Typically, predictive evaluations are used to: inform IT investment decisions, compare the merit of different projects, provide a set of measures to inform improvement efforts and to obtain commitment for the project (Farbey et al., 1992; Remenyi and Sherwood-Smith, 1999). By contrast, prescriptive evaluations are typically conducted to assess the performance of the project, the impact of the system and to learn lessons for further process improvement. For example, post-implementation reviews are prescriptive evaluations conducted after the project has been finalised. The purpose of post-implementation reviews is to provide a comparison of planned with actual achievements, to learn how well resources have been used, and to improve the selection and management of future IT investments (Farbey et al., 1992). Also, the process of benefits realisation involves *both* predicting and planning for benefits from IT projects, and then actively tracking and managing them for improvement (Lubbe and Remenyi, 1999). While benefits realisation spans the life cycle of a project, it is most prominent after project implementation (Farbey et al., 1999).

Since the purpose of project evaluation is to inform action, enhance decision-making and apply knowledge to solve problems (Patton, 1990), it seems reasonable to expect a positive correlation between effective evaluation practices and project success. Thus the well publicised and continuing high rate of IT project failure (The Standish Group International, 2004) has been partly attributed to a lack of management tools for evaluating, prioritising, monitoring and controlling IT investments (Hochstrasser, 1992). This presumed causal connection has resulted in numerous studies on methods and criteria for IT evaluation, and in a myriad of tools and techniques for predictive evaluations (Irani and Love, 2001). Most of the prevailing research supports the view that the use of formal processes, more sophisticated methods and more points of evaluation are generally related to more effective evaluations (i.e. improved decision-making (Remenyi and Sherwood-Smith, 1999), greater consistency (Ward, 1990), greater accuracy (Love et al., 2004) and corporate learning (Farbey et al., 1992)).

Good decision-making regarding IT investment is particularly important for those organisations that use IT for strategic purposes. In such organisations, Tallon et al. (2000, p. 154) argue that 'there is an even greater need for these investments to undergo routine, systematic and recurring evaluation'. Further, based on an Australian survey of 81 senior executives, Sohal and Ng (1998) found that the potential of IT has not been met due in part to IT strategy not being aligned with business objectives, and inadequate and inappropriate evaluation of proposed IT investments. Alshawi et al. (2003) and Love et al. (2004) also conclude that organisations need to undertake more systematic and rigorous evaluation processes before implementing IT if they are to achieve improvements in business performance. Despite such evidence and strong academic arguments for a more systematic monitoring and more rigorous evaluation of IT projects, it appears that many companies do not collect much information concerning IT performance, and evaluation practices remain patchy (Willcocks and Lester, 1997).

While organisations normally carry out some form of predictive evaluation as part of a feasibility study, investment appraisal, or 'business case' (Smithson and Hirschheim, 1998; Irani and Love, 2001), it seems that post-implementation evaluations and benefits realisation are rarely carried out (Sohal and Ng, 1998; Seddon et al., 2002; Lin et al., 2005). For example, Remenyi and Sherwood-Smith (1999, p. 15) state that 'ongoing evaluation of information systems (IS) projects, once the projects are initiated, is generally not carried out with sufficient frequency or attention to detail'. Similarly, Lin and Pervan (2003, p. 14) state that 'much attention is paid to ways of justifying investments, with little effort being extended to ensuring that the benefits expected are realised'. Thus, empirical evidence of post-implementation evaluations seems to contrast with the perceived value of the practice as espoused in the literature, in terms of improved organisational learning and greater understanding of the required and existing IT infrastructure (Irani, 2002).

One reason that formal evaluation methods are not widely or consistently adopted by organisations may be the host of practical difficulties with IT evaluation. Studies have consistently found that the identification and quantification of relevant costs and benefits is a major problem for IT project evaluation (Willcocks, 1992; Ballantine et al., 1996; Seddon et al., 2002; Alshawi et al., 2003). This is because cost and benefits change and evolve over time (Remenyi et al., 2000); some IT benefits tend to be intangible (Seddon et al., 2002); and IT projects are often complex (Melville et al., 2004).

These difficulties in measuring benefits and costs are often the cause of uncertainty about the expected impact of IT, and result in a low perceived value of evaluation and poor evaluation practices (Irani and Love, 2001). Consequently, organisations may decide not to use formal evaluation methods, either *ex ante* or *ex post*, since they are considered as difficult or costly to implement (Lin et al., 2005), often involving many political agendas (Smithson and Hirschheim, 1998; Irani and Love, 2001). In other cases, managers simply do not understand the importance of the investment evaluation process or the concepts involved (Willcocks and Lester, 1997; Remenyi et al., 2000). Ballantine et al. (1996) also identify organisational problems that hinder the evaluation process – such as lack of time, management support and organisational structure.

In short, most of the literature supports the view that more formal and more sophisticated IT project evaluation methods are required (Irani and Love, 2002). However, focusing on solving evaluation problems through new methods is not necessarily the solution. Investment decisions depend not only on methods or techniques but also on management incentives and the organisational context in which such decisions are made (Keyes-Pearce, 2005). Moreover, there is very little research on what constitutes an *appropriate* level of formality or rigour, or what specific practices are necessary for evaluation to be effective. According to Ballantine et al. (1996, p. 139), for instance, 'the role of formal procedures in the IS/IT evaluation process needs to be more closely examined to identify whether their use results in any significant benefits'. To meet this challenge, this study takes an holistic and systemic view of IT project evaluation. Its goal is to identify effective practices and understand why they work. The next section describes the research method used to identify such practices.

Research strategy and method

Selection and justification of the research method

An embedded multiple case-study design with several units of analysis was used for exploring which practices are more effective than others. Case studies are considered to be a sound research strategy for examining 'a contemporary phenomenon within some real-life context' (Yin, 2003, p. 1). Multiple case studies provide more opportunities for generalisation than single case studies (Yin, 2003). A qualitative approach using interviews was adopted because it allowed a rich exploration of evaluation processes while remaining open to emergent issues. The primary unit of analysis in this study is the organisation. The higher, industry level and lower, project level were considered for context. Scheepers and Scheepers (2003, p. 26) argue that 'a failure to consider these interdependent levels of context runs the risk of partial or even incorrect conclusions being drawn'.

Three Australian industry sectors were selected: finance and insurance (F & I); mining (M); and electricity, gas and water supply (E, G & WS). These three sectors were chosen because they seemed likely to cover a range of IT evaluation practices. As evidence of the likely range of practices, the Australian National Office for the Information Economy (NOIE) reports:

> 'Australia has invested heavily in ICT, with expenditure on ICT now representing more than 8% of GDP. Sectors that have invested most heavily in ICT include finance, communications and utilities (electricity, gas, water), while ICT investment has been smallest in mining and agriculture' (NOIE, 2003, p. 6).

Data collection

A total of 78 in-depth interviews were conducted with 72 senior managers in 36 companies operating in these three industry sectors. The sample of companies was derived from a combination of opportunistic and snowball sampling (Sarantakos, 1998). The mix of participant companies is summarised in Table 4.1. It represents a diverse range of organisations by size, focus of operations and ownership.

Since interviews were the primary source of data, care was taken to ensure that the person(s) selected were the most appropriate for each part of the interview. This was done through an initial phone conversation. Those interviewed were either Chief Information Officers (or equivalents), Program Managers, Project Managers or other senior managers involved in the evaluation of IT projects. All interviews were conducted by the lead researcher. The time taken for each interview ranged from 45 minutes to 2 hours, averaging 1 hour.

The interview process explored IT evaluation at various stages of the project life cycle from opportunity identification, priority setting and project approval (predictive evaluation), through the stages of project delivery, then closure, post-implementation review and benefits realisation (prescriptive evaluation). The interview format had two parts. The first focused on IT project evaluation practices in the participant company in general. The second focused on the evaluation practices used in a recently completed IT or e-business project. The questions were mainly of an exploratory nature, such as 'What?', 'How?' and 'Why?' In addition to the interviews, sample documents relating to project management and evaluation

■ **Table 4.1** Mix of case-study companies, by industry sector

Sector	Size (annual revenue)			Focus of operations			Primary ownership			
	<A$500 million	≥A$0.5 ≤A$2b	>$A2b	AU State	AU National	International	AU Public	AU Private	Government	International
F & I	9	7	4	7	8	5	6	9	1	4
M	2	5	4	1	2	8	7	1	0	3
E, G & WS	0	4	1	4	1	0	0	0	5	0
Total	11	16	9	12	11	13	13	10	6	7

Key: F&I = Finance and Insurance; M = Mining; E, G & WS = Electricity, Gas and Water Supply.

practices were collected to validate the interviews. A total of 362 such documents were provided to the researcher. The use of multiple types of evidence to triangulate and cross-check different views is advocated by Patton (1990) and Yin (2003).

Data analysis

This study applied Eisenhardt's (1989) suggested steps for analyzing data: (a) within-case analysis, (b) cross-case search for patterns, (c) shaping propositions and (d) proposition verification. The interview notes (over 540 pages) and other supporting documents were examined for themes and coded (labelled) using *open coding* techniques borrowed from the grounded theory method (Glaser and Strauss, 1967). Responses to questions on *Satisfaction with IT evaluation processes* and *Confidence that IT projects are producing business benefits* were used to assess both effective and ineffective practices. Interview notes were analyzed based on participant descriptions of the strengths and weaknesses of their company's evaluation practices, to determine effective IT project evaluation outcomes. For example, selection of the right projects, consistent and timely decision-making, focused project delivery, corporate learning, timely stopping of projects, accurate estimation and measurement, and reduced politics.

The 36 case-study companies were first analyzed individually, then divided into three categories based on the effectiveness of their evaluation practices. The intent of the categorisation was not to be definitive, but to provide a means for understanding and comparing practices across companies. Effective practices were contrasted with ineffective practices. In addition, all practices were examined for their ability to address the significant evaluation challenges identified by the participants. While the general approach was to look for patterns in practices across companies, it was also recognised that effective practices may come from a single participant. Finally, to ensure the participants' anonymity, each company has been given an identifier: F1 to F20 for the 20 F & I companies; M1 to M11 for the 11 M companies and U1 to U5 for the 5 E, G & WS Utilities.

Results

Participants were asked to rate overall *satisfaction with IT evaluation processes* in their company. Average responses from the 36 companies are shown in Table 4.2. The results show that most companies in the study perceived a need to improve evaluation practices.

While 58% (21) of the companies rated satisfaction with their 'Approach' as 4 or higher (on a Likert scale from 1 = 'not at all' to 5 = 'very satisfied'), only 36% (13) rated 'Deployment' as 4 or higher. This suggests that, for most companies, the gap in evaluation practices extends beyond the actual approach taken in terms of the processes and methods used, to issues of implementation. Supporting this view, in one-third of companies (12), interviewees identified the 'consistency of processes and their application' as a key area for improvement.

> 'Competitive advantage is not in the processes and templates but how you use them' (Chief Information Officer, F10).

■ **Table 4.2** Mean overall satisfaction with evaluation practices, by industry sector

Evaluation dimension	Description	Mean satisfaction score (1 = not at all, 5 = very)		
		F & I	M	E, G & WS
Approach	What the organisation plans to do	3.8	3.4	3.2
Deployment	How well the approach is actually implemented and adopted	3.5	3.1	3.0
Results	How evaluation results are monitored and used	2.8	2.2	1.8
Improvement	How evaluation processes are reviewed and improved	3.2	2.9	2.2

Participants were also asked to rate their *Confidence that IT projects are producing business benefits* for their company, using a scale of high, medium and low. Three companies rated confidence as low, 18 companies as medium and 15 as high. The main reasons for high levels of confidence were related to project selection and approval processes, and reviews of benefits post-implementation. The main reason for lack of confidence was the lack of measurement of benefits post-implementation. Although confidence was also related to other factors, there appeared to be a relationship between *Satisfaction with IT evaluation processes*, in particular project appraisal, and *Confidence that IT projects were producing business benefits.*

Consistent with the literature cited earlier, most companies placed a higher level of importance on predictive rather than prescriptive evaluations. Table 4.3 summarises the use and effectiveness of portfolio selection and project approval processes among participant companies. All 36 companies had a process for identifying potential IT projects and for project approval, although the formality of these processes varied widely. Less than half of these

■ **Table 4.3** Portfolio-selection and project-approval processes, by industry sector

	Identification/selection			Priority setting			Project approval		
	F & I	M	E, G & WS	F & I	M	E, G & WS	F & I	M	E, G & WS
Effective process	13	3	1	12	3	1	11	2	3
Have process	20	11	5	20	8	5	20	11	5
No process	0	0	0	0	3	0	0	0	0

processes were considered effective. The main issues identified were consistent application and adherence to processes; ownership and understanding of the processes; the time taken for approval; distortions of the budget cycle; alignment with strategy; politics in decision-making; and the appropriate level of rigour. Priority setting and portfolio management was considered by 25% (9) of companies as a key area for improvement and by 47% (17) of companies as a major challenge. Not surprisingly, only 44% (16) of companies described their priority-setting processes as effective. While roughly one-third of companies (13) had no formal criteria for priority setting, nearly half of these (5) considered their practices effective.

Table 4.4 summarises the use and effectiveness of post-implementation review and benefits-realisation processes in the case-study companies. Only 22% (8) of the companies had a process in place to track benefits from individual projects, and only half of those (4) were considered effective. A further 7 companies used their one-off post-implementation review process to measure benefits and none of these were considered effective. Instead of benefits realisation, many companies relied on the accuracy of their project appraisal processes. Post-implementation reviews were often only conducted for larger projects or when 'things went wrong'. The reasons for not conducting post-implementation reviews and benefits realisation included lack of management support, unclear ownership of processes, limited accountability, resource constraints, difficulties with measurement and attribution, and non-use of evaluation results.

Table 4.4 Post-implementation review and benefits realisation processes, by industry sector

	Post-implementation review/closure			Benefits realisation		
	F & I	M	E, G & WS	F & I	M	E, G & WS
Effective process	7	2	0	4	0	0
Have process	19	8	4	7	1	0
No process	1	3	1	13	10	5

Overall, those companies with high levels of satisfaction and confidence tended to conduct evaluation across the whole project life cycle and shared the following key characteristics.

Characteristics of effective IT project evaluation practice

Across the 36 companies, eight characteristics of effective IT evaluation practice were found to be related to effective IT project evaluation outcomes leading to more efficient use of resources and improved IT project outcomes (see Figure 4.1). In particular, it was when simple and flexible evaluation processes (top left of Figure 4.1) *were combined with* the six key organisational drivers (bottom left of Figure 4.1) that positive behaviours were reinforced, actions were aligned and evaluation processes had the best outcomes. Most of the effective

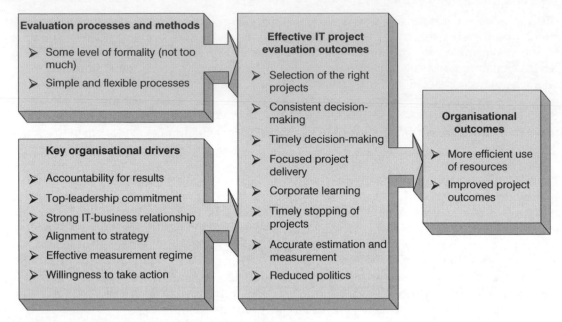

practices were found within five companies, F2, F4, F5, F10 and M6, with four being from the finance and insurance sector. By contrast, companies F12, M1, M2, M3, M4, M5, M9 and U2 were found to have the least effective practices. The majority of these companies were from the mining sector.

Each of the eight key characteristics of effective IT evaluation practice on the left of Figure 4.1 is now discussed in turn.

Evaluation processes and methods

In terms of evaluation processes and methods, this study found that some level of formality was required but not too much, and that simple and flexible processes were most effective.

Some level of formality (not too much)

Formality, in this study, refers to use of official and prescribed rules for evaluation in the form of procedures, review points, reporting, documentation and meetings/workshops. Formality was not irrelevant. Some level of formality was needed for consistency and to avoid excessive political activity. In addition, too much formality reduced the effectiveness of evaluation processes, due to delays in decision-making. However, there was a wide band of companies where formality of IT evaluation processes, methods and techniques did not distinguish those companies with effective practices from those without.

At one extreme, those companies without formal project governance had low levels of satisfaction and low confidence that IT projects were producing benefits. In such companies, decision-making tended to be subjective and there appeared to be greater opportunity for political interference.

> 'All IT projects are not formally evaluated. IT budgets are distributed, not central-ised, and Business Units have a fair degree of autonomy about how they spend this money. Project sponsors can initiate a project without any formal documentation no matter what the value is. It is not clear what constitutes an IT project. There are no consistent, controlled, uniform procedures and no centralised governance' (Project Management Office Manager, M9).

At the other extreme, too much formality slowed decision-making and, in some cases, resulted in behaviours to avoid formal approvals such as the splitting of projects. Several companies, such as U5, M8 and F7, described their processes as 'bureaucratic'. Others described processes that attempted to be too 'scientific' and were manipulated.

> 'It takes months to get projects approved and this time could have been spent get-ting things done. To get around this people segment projects to be <$100K and put them through as three work requests rather than one big project' (IT Program Manager, F7).

Companies that were most satisfied with their priority-setting processes used formal cri-teria but balanced these with management judgement. There was a view that formal tech-niques could only go so far, and that the management team 'knew things that criteria could not account for'. The following company found formal evaluation practices helped:

> 'Before the introduction of the Project Management Framework we used to work on projects for people who "shouted loudest", there was no real respect for IT resources, projects were done three times because no processes were in place, and the business did not know how to facilitate a good return' (IT Manager, F19).

However, having formal processes did not mean that these processes were necessarily used or applied consistently:

> 'In general, we have processes documented but they are not strongly enforced. Projects run over the original Application for Expenditure but no supplementary request for funding is put in. For example, one mining project ran $180m over the authorised expenditure limit. They knew this was going to happen but did not sub-mit anything formal. This is just the mining way' (Manager Accounting, M3).

Finally, the levels of governance and the formality of the processes applied to a given project were commonly tiered, based on the financial value of the project. In a few cases other criteria were used such as effort, risk, complexity and business impact.

Simple and flexible processes

In terms of the processes and methods used, simplicity and flexibility were key character-istics underlying effective IT evaluation practices. Those companies with flexible processes, such as F2, F4, F5 and F10, had more effective evaluation practices than companies with rigid processes. While flexibility was related to more timely decision-making, simplicity was related to the consistent application of processes. In addition, companies with flexible processes were most able to cope with the challenges of a dynamic environment.

Flexible processes included use of 'lite' versions of evaluation processes with clear minimum requirements; the ability to start work before all approvals are complete; flexibility in the use of stage gates, dependant on project size and the certainty of requirements; flexible budget provisions for pilot projects and scoping studies; contingency in budgets adjusted for risk; identification of sufficient benefits rather than all benefits and a focus on continual review rather than full analysis up front. For example, company F10 completes the initial analysis quickly but then continually reviews projects and has a high willingness to stop them.

> '[Our parent company] looks at more detail than we would look at before approval. Therefore, the "burn rate" starts early in the project and a lot of work goes into the business case up front. A business case can take several months to put up and then may not get approved. In [our company] we continually review and the initial approval may not be the most accurate but every time there is a change we go back for approval' (Head of Projects Office, F10).

Simple processes included a clear focus on what was important for decision-making, and a minimum of paperwork. Although tiered levels of governance were found to be an effective practice, too many different levels, procedures and methods were not. Simplicity was particularly important given the environment of time pressure, rapid change and limited access to business resources described by participants.

> 'It is a very quick process and the standard presentation is 2-3 slides. If the CEO cannot be convinced in three minutes the manager gets knocked back and that is not good. Therefore, only the good proposals get to the top' (Head of IT Department, F2).

On the other hand, a 'one size fits all' approach to governance did not appear to be the solution. This practice was inflexible and inefficient, particularly for smaller projects. In the mining sector, in particular, a common complaint was that the evaluation process was the same as that 'required to buy a truck'. In company M4, for example, any expenditure greater than 'one dollar' required the completion of a standard capital-expenditure request.

Well-defined simple and flexible processes were effective because they were more likely to be consistently applied. By contrast, when processes or methods were complicated, decisions were often not made on a consistent basis, and resources were not put to best use. Other practices that enhanced consistency were a single point of IT funding approval, employment of IT relationship managers, clearly defined evaluation criteria aligned to strategy and independent verification of project benefits (*ex ante* and *ex post*).

Key organisational drivers

Six key organisational drivers of effective IT evaluation practices were identified: accountability for results, top-leadership commitment, a strong IT-business relationship, alignment to strategy, an effective measurement regime and a willingness to take action. These are discussed next.

Accountability for results

Companies that held business managers accountable for results had the most effective evaluation practices. Accountability for results drove positive behaviours, improving the accuracy of business cases and providing the motivation to measure results after implementation. Further, it appeared that accountability addressed many of the significant evaluation challenges identified by companies, in particular, business engagement, and the accurate estimation of costs and benefits. The fundamental principle was that if managers were held accountable then evaluation got done.

> 'There is accountability for hard financial measures and if a project declares that it will reduce costs then this is reflected in the budget. They are tough on this. This is a good discipline and drives positive behaviours. I have worked in other organisations where they sign off on huge revenue increases, for example, but there is no consequence if they do not deliver. In these organisations there is no incentive to question the benefits claimed' (Head of IT Architecture, F1).

When managers were accountable for results, there was no incentive to overstate benefits. Sixty-one per cent (22) of the companies did not overstate benefits in order to get approval. In such companies, the main reason given was accountability, though other reasons included rigour in the justification process, independent checks of benefits claimed and cultural conservatism.

Different companies achieved accountability in different ways. Methods included reporting to an executive committee, and use of budgets and/or personal scorecards/remuneration. In all companies with effective practices, success was clearly defined 'up front' then measured later. Some companies even had means for ensuring that benefits were not understated, such as using incentive payments capped at 120% of performance targets.

> 'Because of the governance processes they need to go to Program Promise. It is called this because they are making a promise to deliver and are held to it' (Head of IT Department, F2).

In contrast, those companies without accountability for results tended to have more issues with the accuracy of business cases and, in particular, with the overstating of benefits. Eleven of the 14 companies who said that benefits were overstated in order to get approval had no form of accountability for results.

> 'Benefits do get overstated and this is linked to lack of accountability for project benefits' (Global Manager IT Services, M5).

In relation to the appropriate level of accountability, those companies who measured results against performance targets at both the project and company level tended to have more effective practices than those companies who tied accountability to only one of these levels.

Top-leadership commitment

Another characteristic of those companies with effective evaluation practices was commitment from the top. If leadership does not think evaluation is important it will not get done.

Companies such as F2, F5 and F10 spoke of cohesive top management buy-in and support, resulting in more consistent and timely decision-making. This was enacted through the involvement of the leadership team in the evaluation process, in both decision-making roles and ensuring a culture of accountability.

> 'The business is totally engaged in this and it is driven from the CEO down' (IT Program Manager, F2).

Ownership and commitment from management was identified as a key desired improvement by 11 companies. Those companies without top-leadership commitment had less effective evaluation outcomes. For example, a previous attempt by company U3 to introduce benefits realisation stalled due to lack of management commitment. Other companies also gave examples where evaluation processes became ineffective without top management support.

> 'The IT aspects of the budget get lost; say $30m in terms of billions. There is no IT Steering committee or other structures because they became ineffective. Managers would not turn up and would send replacements who could not make decisions' (Project Management Office Manager, M9).

Strong IT-business relationship

A strong IT-business relationship based on trust and shared responsibility provides the basis for effective IT investment decisions. Most companies said that evaluation processes worked best when the business drove the processes rather than the IT department. For companies where a strong relationship existed, such as F10, this resulted in ownership by the business and more effective evaluation outcomes in terms of selecting the right projects, focused project delivery, accurate estimation and reduced politics.

> 'The engagement process with business is sound and it is not just what IT thinks is a good idea' (IS Program Office Manager, M6).

In contrast, the IT department in companies such as F12 said that they were viewed as a 'service department' rather than a critical 'business enabler'. They described an ineffective IT-business relationship in terms of lack of communication, IT being bypassed or not consulted during decision-making, and the business being unwilling to provide subject-matter experts for evaluation. Access to and engagement of the business was identified by 58% (21) of companies as a significant challenge.

Notably, there was a distinct difference in terminology used by companies depending on the relationship between IT and the business. When projects were driven by the business they were seen as 'business' projects or 'IT-enabled' projects and not 'IT' projects. The relationship between IT and the business was one of shared responsibility and the IT function were not 'order takers'. However, in the mining sector, in particular, IT was often considered as 'a commodity'. This resulted in greater challenges in terms of obtaining access and information from the business and had a serious negative impact on the effectiveness of IT project evaluation.

> 'A weakness is the tension between process 'parochialism' and IT 'centricity'. This often results in: Business Units buying proposed solutions that do not meet corporate

requirements or corporate IT infrastructure, and IT approaches unrelated to the Business Unit need, respectively' (Assurance Manager, M9).

Alignment to strategy

It is necessary to align IT investment decisions to a corporate strategy in order to provide a consistent basis of comparison and select the right projects, thereby balancing both long- and short-term goals.

> 'We deal with about 100 projects per year. The annual planning process starts from the Corporate Strategy and cascades to Business Strategies for each Functional Unit. Targets are set and each Functional Unit develops Business Strategies from Issues and Responses to those issues. Each Functional Unit submits bids for funding in a ranked order. The Program Management Office interacts with the management team and determines a cut-off. The projects are discussed relative to strategy, high level cost estimates and a view of the benefits' (Workstream Driver, F5).

There were two levels of positive strategic alignment. At the highest level, those companies with effective evaluation practices *drove* IT-related investments from the strategic plan. In other words, the strategy drove the projects not vice versa. To do this first required a clearly articulated strategy, which for companies like U4, was not always in place. A lower level of still-positive alignment occurred if a project came up out of the planning cycle and was evaluated against strategic fit or the existing strategies. In such cases the project was not driven by the strategy, but was identified and then was tested against the strategy. The use of consistent evaluation criteria tied to the strategic intent of the company for both project selection and priority setting was an effective practice. In some cases these criteria were also weighted to reflect relative strategic priorities or projected growth areas.

In other companies there was no attempt to align IT investments to strategy. In such cases, decision-making was not tied to the direction of the company, decision-making was incon- sistent and resources were often not used effectively.

> 'There is not a consistent corporate approach to business planning. We have just started strategically evaluating what the company is trying to do. Before this there were just IT delivery people, and IT projects were centrally controlled and approved' (IT Superintendent, M4).

Effective measurement regime

An effective measurement regime or system is necessary for accountability. Such regimes were often associated with consistent decision-making, focused project delivery, accurate estimation and corporate learning. Identification and measurement of costs and benefits was identified as a major challenge by 44% (16) of companies. In terms of benefits, only 55% (20) of the companies said that they identify all benefits, and 28% (10) said that they adequately measure them. For costs, the picture was slightly better. Sixty-nine per cent (25) of companies said that they identify all costs, and 75% (27) said that they adequately measure costs.

The key for those companies that were effective at establishing a baseline and then meas-uring the results was a robust company performance-measurement system. In companies such as F2 and F5, measurement was part of 'business as usual'. For these companies the use of specific evaluation techniques also became more effective. For example, the use of results chains by companies F3 and F5 allowed them to overcome issues of attribution, by understanding and measuring interim outcomes. These measures acted as lead indicators for higher-level outcomes such as sales and profit.

> 'Benefits realisation is across three levels. Benefits are monitored at a project level by key performance indicators, the portfolio level by dashboards and then rolled up to the business level. There is a strong connection between project outcomes, the portfolio and the business' (Workstream Driver, F5).

Where a performance-measurement regime was in place, the accuracy of estimates was also improved by an independent review of the benefits claimed, both 'up front' and after imple-mentation. Companies without any verification often mentioned inaccuracy of estimates.

> 'The project Business Case justified savings of $31.7m over three years. As the Project Manager I did not see this as credible but my role was project delivery' (Project Manager, M1).

When measurement was an add-on, because an effective performance-measurement regime was not in place, it was more difficult to establish links to strategy and overall performance. Also, due to the additional effort involved, the measurement of benefits both to establish a baseline, and measure results, was unlikely to be done consistently or at all.

Willingness to take action

An evaluation process, even one built on a solid foundation of measurement, means very little if the results are not acted upon. Evaluation was most effective when it formed the basis for action. In particular, effective practices were associated with a willingness to stop projects and redirect projects during delivery, to act on the findings of post-implementation reviews and to enforce accountability for results through both incentives and sanctions. The effective use of evaluation results was not only associated with the continuous improve-ment of evaluation processes, but also reinforced their use.

Companies that were not willing to act on evaluation results did not learn lessons and wasted valuable resources.

> 'My experience in this organisation is that they do not stop a lot of projects. There would be few projects that are shut down even if they are "off the rails". We tend to "throw good money after bad". I do not see a lot of projects shut down, but I have seen a lot that should have been' (Head IT Architecture, F1).

Significantly, only 14% (5) of the companies were satisfied with their overall use of evalu-ation results. In particular, most companies that had post-implementation review proc-esses made very little use of the findings from these reviews to improve processes or learn corporately. Stage gates (where funds are released in stages) and periodic reviews or health checks for larger projects were effective practices. Both processes provided the opportunity to stop projects if circumstances changed or there were significant over-runs in cost and schedule. However, a key finding of this study was that periodic reviews are not effective by themselves; they must be combined with a willingness to act. Companies that had both periodic check points and a willingness to stop projects and redirect resources were most effective. Trials of projects (or 'pilot' studies) also provided a similar opportunity to test assumptions and stop projects before too many resources were committed.

Linking characteristics of effective IT evaluation practice to evaluation outcomes

Table 4.5 summarises the preceding discussion by showing which of the eight characteristics of effective IT evaluation practice on the left of Figure 4.1 affect the eight IT project evaluation outcomes in the middle of Figure 4.1. The lower half of Table 4.5 also summarises links between these characteristics and the key challenges they address.

The judgements behind the Xs in Table 4.5 were based on both direct statements by the participants and patterns between IT evaluation practices and evaluation outcomes across companies. There is no space to justify all the Xs in the table, but three examples will help. First, a clear relationship was evident between simple and flexible evaluation practices in companies F1, F2, F4, F5, F10, F16, F17, F19 and M2 and timely decision-making. In contrast, companies F7, F8, F13, F20, M8 and U5 described evaluation practices which were more formal or complex and which slowed decision-making. This is the justification for X_1 in Table 4.5. Second, where an appropriate strategy was in place, alignment to strategy helped select the right projects on a consistent basis. For example, project selection and approval processes were closely aligned to strategy in companies such as F2, F5, F8, F13, F18, F20 and U5. Their practices contrasted with companies such as F12, M3 and U2, which had issues with consistent decision-making and selection of the right projects. This is the justification for X_2 in Table 4.5. Third, the data suggested that the challenge of business engagement was best addressed where processes were simple and flexible (F19), there was accountability for results (F1), top-leadership commitment (F2), a strong IT-business relationship (F10), alignment to strategy (F8) and a willingness to take action (F5). These findings are the basis for X_3–X_8 in Table 4.5. Similar lines of reasoning to these examples were used in deciding whether to include Xs in each of the other cells in Table 4.5.

While Table 4.5 shows pairwise relationships, it was the *combination* of the eight characteristics of effective IT evaluation practice which resulted in the most effective outcomes. For example, column 2 of Table 4.5 shows that some level of formality was related to 7 out of 8 of the effective IT project evaluation outcomes. However, it was only when simple and flexible evaluation processes were combined with *all* of the six key organisational drivers that IT project evaluation was *most* effective and the key challenges of evaluation were *best* addressed. In addition, the six key organisational drivers did not operate independently of each other but were also closely interrelated. For example, top-leadership commitment and an effective measurement regime were both considered necessary for accountability. A feedback loop was also evident in the data. Achieving effective IT project evaluation outcomes

Table 4.5 Relationships summarising why effective evaluation practices work

Effective IT project evaluation outcomes	Evaluation processes and methods			Key organisational drivers				
	Some level of formality	Simple and flexible processes	Accountability for results	Top-leadership commitment	Strong IT-business relationship	Alignment to strategy	Effective measurement regime	Willingness to take action
Selection of the right projects	X	X	X	X	X	X_2	X	X
Consistent decision-making	X	X	X	X	X	X	X	
Timely decision-making		X_1		X				X
Focused project delivery	X		X		X	X	X	
Corporate learning	X						X	X
Timely stopping of projects	X		X					X
Accurate estimation and measurement	X		X	X	X		X	
Reduced politics	X			X	X	X	X	

Key evaluation challenges addressed

Key evaluation challenges addressed	X_3	X_4	X_5	X_6	X_7	X_8
Business engagement	X				X	X
Estimation and measurement		X	X	X	X	
Setting priorities	X				X	
Consistent application of processes	X	X	X	X		
Accurate scoping and justification	X	X	X	X		
Changing scope and requirements	X			X		X
Objectivity of evaluation	X			X		
Resource constraints	X		X	X		

Note: The meanings of X_1–X_8 are explained in the associated text.

and improved IT project outcomes appeared to reinforce drivers such as top-leadership commitment and a strong IT-business relationship.

Discussion

Researchers have wondered over several decades why so few of the IT evaluation methods described in the literature are used in practice. The key finding of this study is that the real problem of IT evaluation is *not* the choice of methods, nor formality of evaluation processes, but rather the need to ensure that effective decision-making is reinforced through account-ability, leadership, relationships, strategy, measurement and action. As discussed earlier, in the 36 case-study companies, some level of formality helped improve evaluation and, ulti-mately, IT project outcomes. However, evaluation processes that were too formal were inef-fective, resulting in dysfunctional behaviours. While regular evaluation across the project life cycle was the goal of most companies, the key issue was one of implementation of that intention. Many companies had well-documented processes and methods, but they were not applied consistently. Thus formal processes and methods alone were not enough. It was only when combined with the six organisational drivers shown in Figure 4.5 that those processes were *used* and so became effective.

How generalisable are the results summarised in Figure 4.5? It may be argued is that since the 36 companies are a diverse range of organisations by size, focus of operations and owner-ship, and since the drivers identified are related to management issues such as 'accountabil-ity for results', known to be important in organisations the world over, something like the model in Figure 4.5 probably applies to most organisations in the developed world.

Conclusion

This chapter set out to identify the most effective IT project evaluation practices used by organisations in Australia, and to understand why they work. Based on interviews with 72 senior managers in 36 companies, effective evaluation outcomes such as selection of the right projects, consistent and timely decision-making, corporate learning, and thus, improved IT project outcomes, were found to be closely related to the six key drivers pre-sented in Figure 4.1. The contribution of this chapter is the finding that effective evaluation outcomes are more closely related to evaluation *behaviours* in organisations than the use of specific methods and techniques. Simplicity and flexibility were also found to be key char-acteristics underpinning effective IT evaluation practice. These conclusions provide impor-tant insights for improving IT evaluation practices, and ultimately, improving IT project outcomes, both in Australia and around the world.

Acknowledgement

An earlier version of this chapter was presented at the 11th Pacific Asia Conference on Information Systems, Auckland, NZ, 2007.

■ References

Alshawi, S., Irani, Z. and Baldwin, L. (2003). 'Benchmarking information technology investment and benefits extraction'. *Benchmarking: An International Journal*, 10(4), 414–423.

Ballantine, J. and Stray, S. (1998). 'Financial appraisal and the IS/IT investment decision making process'. *Journal of Information Technology*, 13(1), 3–14.

Ballantine, J., Galliers, R. and Stray, S. (1996). 'Information systems/technology evaluation practices: Evidence from UK organizations'. *Journal of Information Technology*, 11, 129–141.

Eisenhardt, K. (1989). 'Building theories from case study research'. *Academy of Management Review*, 14(4), 532–550.

Farbey, B., Land, F. and Targett, D. (1992). 'Evaluating investments in IT'. *Journal of Information Technology*, 7, 109–122.

Farbey, B., Land, F. and Targett, D. (1999). 'The moving staircase: Problems of appraisal and evaluation in a turbulent environment'. *Information Technology and People*, 12(3), 238–252.

Glaser, B. and Strauss, A. (1967). *The Discovery of Grounded Theory*. Aldine, New York.

Hochstrasser, B. (1992). 'Justifying IT Investments', *Proceedings of the Advanced Information Systems Conference*, London, pp. 17–28.

Irani, Z. (2002). 'Information systems evaluation: Navigating through the problem domain'. *Information and Management*, 40, 11–24.

Irani, Z. and Love, P. (2001). 'Information systems evaluation: Past, present and future'. *European Journal of Information Systems*, 10, 183–188.

Irani, Z. and Love, P. (2002). 'Developing a frame of reference for ex-ante IT/IS evaluation'. *European Journal of Information Systems*, 11, 74–82.

Irani, Z., Shariff, A. and Love, P. (2005). 'Linking knowledge transformation to information systems evaluation'. *European Journal of Information Systems*, 14, 213–228.

Keyes-Pearce, S. (2005). *IT Value Management in Leading Firms: The Fit Between Theory and Practice*, PhD Thesis, University of Sydney.

Lin, C. and Pervan, G. (2003). 'The practice of IS/IT benefits management in large Australian organisations'. *Information and Management*, 41, 13–24.

Lin, C., Pervan, G. and McDermid, D. (2005). 'IS/IT investment evaluation and benefits realisation issues in Australia'. *Journal of Research and Practice in Information Technology*, 37(3), 33–49.

Love, P., Ghoneim, A. and Irani, Z. (2004). 'Information technology evaluation: Classifying indirect costs using the structured case method'. *The Journal of Enterprise Information Management*, 17(4), 312–325.

Love, P., Irani, Z., Standing, C., Lin, C. and Burn, J. (2005). 'The enigma of evaluation: Benefits, costs and risks of IT in Australian small–medium-sized enterprises'. *Information and Management*, 42, 947–964.

Lubbe, S. and Remenyi, D. (1999). 'Management of information technology evaluation – The development of a managerial thesis'. *Logistics Information Management*, 12(1), 145–156.

McKay, J. and Marshall, P. (2004). *Strategic Management of E-business*. Wiley, Australia.

Melville, N., Kraemer, K. and Gurbaxani, V. (2004). 'Information technology and organisational performance: An integrative model of business value'. *MIS Quarterly*, 28(2), 283–322.

National Office for the Information Economy (NOIE) (2003). *Productivity and Organisational Transformation: Optimising Investment in ICT*, Consultancy Study NCON/02/38.

Owen, J. (1993). *Program Evaluation: Forms and Approaches*. Allen and Unwin, Australia.

Patel, N. and Irani, Z. (1999). 'Evaluating information technology in dynamic environments: A focus on tailorable information systems'. *Logistics Information Management*, 12(1), 32–62.

Patton, M. (1990). *Qualitative Evaluation and Research Methods*, 2nd ed. Sage Publications, Thousand Oaks, CA.

Remenyi, D. and Sherwood-Smith, M. (1999). 'Maximise information systems value by continuous participative evaluation'. *Logistics Information Management*, 12(1), 14–31.

Remenyi, D., Money, A. and Sherwood-Smith, M. (2000). *The Effective Measurement and Management of IT Costs and Benefits*, 2nd ed. Butterworth-Heinemann, UK.

Sarantakos, S. (1998). *Social Research*, 2nd ed. MacMillan Education, Australia.

Scheepers, R. and Scheepers, H. (2003). 'Contexts of Relevance in Exploratory Case Studies in Information Systems: Ubiquitous Information Technology Implementation in Organisations'. *Proceedings of the 24th International Conference on Information Systems*, pp. 25–35.

Seddon, P., Graeser, V. and Willcocks, L. (2002). 'Measuring organisational IS effectiveness: An overview and update of senior management perspectives'. *Database for Advances in Information Systems*, 33(2), 11–28.

Smithson, S. and Hirschheim, R. (1998). 'Analysing information systems evaluation: Another look at an old problem'. *European Journal of Information Systems*, 7, 158–174.

Sohal, A. and Ng, L. (1998). 'The role and impact of information technology in Australian business'. *Journal of Information Technology*, 13, 201–217.

Tallon, P., Kraemer, K. and Gurbaxani, V. (2000). 'Executives' perceptions of the business value of information technology: A process orientated approach'. *Journal of Management Information Systems*, 16(4), 145–173.

The Standish Group International (2004). *Chaos Report*, 3rd Quarter, The Standish Group International, USA, http://www.standishgroup.com.

Ward, J. (1990). 'A portfolio approach to evaluating information systems investments and setting priorities'. *Journal of Information Technology*, 5, 222–231.

Willcocks, L. (1992). 'Evaluating information technology investments: Research findings and reappraisal'. *Journal of Information Systems*, 2, 243–268.

Willcocks, L. and Lester, S. (1997). 'Assessing IT productivity: Any way out of the labyrinth?' In Willcocks, L., Feeney, D. and Islei, G. (Eds.), *Managing IT as a Strategic Resource*. McGraw-Hill, Maidenhead, pp. 64–93.

Yin, R. (2003). *Case Study Research: Design and Methods*, 3rd ed. Sage Publications, Thousand Oaks, CA.

Chapter 5 ▪▪▪

Don't mention the war: Managing disbenefits

F. Bannister

Introduction

Articles, papers and books on information systems (IS) evaluation often open with either a reference to the amount currently spent on information and communications technology (ICT) and/or on the amount of expenditure on ICT that is wasted. While it is probably fair to say that nobody really knows how much is spent each year on ICT, never mind IS, it is certainly a large sum of money. Research firm IDC estimates that the global information technology (IT) spend in 2006 was $1.16 trillion and forecast this to rise to nearly $1.5 trillion by 2010 (Kelly, 2007).

Whatever their accuracy, it is not unreasonable to ask what these numbers represent (presumably IDC has a solid basis for these numbers; at a cost of $15 000 for its report, one would expect reasonable accuracy)? Arriving at total global hardware expenditure is challenging enough. Even defining what constitutes 'hardware' in contemporary ICT is becoming increasingly difficult with devices which would formerly have been classified as consumer entertainment, such as televisions or digital cameras, now becoming fully fledged members of the wider ICT family. Software is even more elusive. It might be possible, with some effort, to come up with a credible figure for global expenditure on packaged software. But what about embedded software – the type of software that runs iPods or computer-controlled furnaces? And what of software that is developed in-house? The UK government is currently revising the method of computing gross national product (GDP) to take into account, *inter alia*, the economic value of in-house software developments. This is expected to add about 0.7% to UK GDP (Duncan, 2007). UK GDP in 2005 was estimated to be in excess of £1 trillion (Economic History Services, 2007). All this before one even starts to consider the cost of operations, management and overheads.

And then there are disbenefits: the unwanted, often unexpected and almost invariably unmeasured side effects or consequences of ICT projects and investments. A survey of the extensive literature on IS evaluation will throw up many references to disbenefits, but little by way of exploration of the concept. As might be expected, the benefits management literature discusses how to avoid waste and minimise or eliminate certain types of disbenefit (Willcocks and Renkema, 1999; Ward and Daniel, 2005; Remenyi et al., 2007). However the latter tend to be what will be classified below as *anticipated disbenefits*, problems that can, with planning, be headed off at the pass or at least reduced in impact. Unfortunately, a substantial number of disbenefits come in the shape of unpleasant surprises, often in the form of changes in personal or organisational behaviour unforeseen by project managers, system designers, analysts or sponsors. Disbenefits can cause sizeable problems, many, though not all, of which can be readily translated into a bottom-line financial cost to the organisation. This chapter is an attempt to address this neglected topic.

Defining disbenefits

A disbenefit can be defined as an impact, direct or indirect, of ICT, which has an unwanted and negative effect on the performance of an individual or organisation. The definition begs at least two questions:

- What constitutes 'negative'?
- What is meant by 'performance'?

A pragmatic approach is to take a negative impact on performance as something that those making the investment in the IS, and/or the stakeholders whose interests they represent, would regard as undesirable. Why such a convoluted definition? One reason is that what constitutes a disbenefit can be a matter of opinion and/or of perspective. To take a trivial example, if installing external Web access in a company enables staff to book their holidays online from their desks, many junior staff might regard this as a distinct benefit; most middle and senior managers, not to mention the shareholders, almost certainly will not. An even more subtle problem is the related phenomenon of benefits leakage. This occurs where the entity making the investment loses some of the benefit to a third party, usually a customer, but sometimes a supplier or other external party. While the problem of benefits leakage is really a topic for another chapter, some aspects of it are discussed below. For the purpose of this chapter, the discussion of disbenefits will primarily be in terms of business organisations although many of the ideas and concepts considered can be applied or adapted to other types of organisations, the public sector and even to individuals.

Some further dissection can be performed on this concept. As noted above, one key differentiation in disbenefits is between *anticipated* and *unanticipated* disbenefits. Anticipated disbenefits can and should be managed. Examples of these include the disruption caused by ICT projects, learning curves, possible user or customer resistance to technology enabled change and so on. Unanticipated disbenefits are much more problematic. By definition, these have to be managed in a reactive manner. Furthermore, because they are unforeseen, they may not be detected for some time. In such circumstances, a crisis may only be identified when a cumulative problem suddenly becomes visible and in extreme cases, this may only happen when a crisis occurs. One example of the latter is the legal exposure from an internal e-mail uncovered during legal discovery. Another is the business risk from records of search engine queries (Webpronews.com, 2006). If, for example, an employee uses his office machine to search for pornography on the Internet, the result can be embarrassing for the company concerned. A particularly high profile case of this occurred in the Bank of Ireland in 2004 when the recently appointed CEO was alleged to have been accessing call girl sites via his office PC and had to resign (Creadon, 2004). On the assumption that he was an executive with the capability to lead the bank to greater business success, the loss to the bank was not only reputational, it also lost its leader and potentially somebody that could have increased shareholder wealth. This is a disbenefit of giving Web access to staff that was almost certainly not considered when such access was given to senior managers. It is likely that the generic risk of staff accessing pornographic sites might have been considered, but probably not a situation where this would lead to the loss of a key executive. In another incident in 2006, a leading multinational bank operation in Ireland fired 13 staff because of alleged misuse of the Internet for accessing pornography. These were relatively junior staff, but the leaking of the event to the media caused the bank some embarrassment (Millman, 2006).

Other frequently unanticipated disbenefits are less dramatic. An example of hidden cost which gradually becomes visible is the cost of managing storage as more and more data of doubtful value accumulates in corporate data banks. The cost of periodic data clean-ups of such data can be considerable. The cost of the ever more storage required to hold data of doubtful value is more obscure, but can be measured in additional disk space, time spent in database tuning and slower searches through cluttered files.

Unanticipated disbenefits occur for a number of reasons which can be classified under three broad headings:

- The first of these can be loosely described as arising from the so-called *law of unintended consequences*. This type of disbenefit arises where appropriate use of the system leads to unexpected and unwanted side effects (strictly speaking, it refers to any unforeseen knock-on effect of a technology, be it either good or bad, arising from normal activities). Unforeseen impacts can range from repetitive strain injury to undermining product profitability.
- The second type of problem is *unforeseen use*, which may or may not qualify as 'misuse', of the technology. Again, such activities are not necessarily malicious, but here we are concerned with uses which reduce productivity, divert effort or give rise to an increase in cost or loss of profit. There are many examples of this. One of the earliest and most common is misuse of word processing. Modern office tools positively encourage users to indulge in quasi desktop publishing, sometimes at the expense of efficiency, content and effective communication.
- Thirdly, problems can arise from the *creation of new risks*. New types of risk created by ICT include business, personnel or legal risks, some examples of which were given above. New forms of fraud are another example of this phenomenon. Cybercrime is itself an important sub-class of disbenefit which is discussed in more detail below.

The phenomenon of unanticipated disbenefits is analogous to the well-known saying in military circles that no plan of battle ever survives the first contact with the enemy. It is in the nature of ICT that it changes organisations and the way people do things. Such changes may be subtle and take time to emerge or become evident (Orlikowski and Yates, 2006). Consequently, when a system designed to deal with situation X is implemented in human environment Y, it may result in unpredictable, or at least unforeseen, forms of behaviour. Any ICT project manager will tell you that no sooner is a new system implemented than users are demanding changes, often in the form of new features unstated at the specification stage. It is not uncommon for requests to start long before the system is even implemented.

This phenomenon can lead to interesting disbenefits. An example of this occurred in an organisation with a large key-punching operation that replaced a legacy mainframe computer system with a new client/server architecture. Keying staff, of whom there were about 90, were given green (in actuality they were orange) screen dumb terminals with which to work, similar to those that they had used for many years on the previous system. Others, including clerical staff and managers (of whom there were only a few) were given PCs with colour screens to replace their green screens. Hearing of this, one of the unions demanded that the keying staff be given 'parity', by which he meant that keypunch staff too should have colour screen PCs. This led to a triple disbenefit. First, it added a large additional capital cost to the project. Secondly, it laid the foundations for a future of increased maintenance problems from PCs which were more complex and prone to breakdowns than dumb terminals and thirdly, the lower resolution and higher screen surface temperature of the PCs (these were CRT screens) were more likely cause eye strain and eye irritation to the operators. The result was likely to be a fall in productivity, somewhat offsetting the advantages, if indeed there were any beyond keeping the industrial peace, of the new system.

Disbenefits are endemic; they come with all systems. They are also expensive leading to loss of productivity, unproductive, and suboptimal behaviour and increased business risk – all leading to real costs. There is therefore need to manage them. Three questions should be of considerable interest to ICT and other managers:

- What disbenefits are we incurring?
- How much are these costing us (in whatever metric we use)?
- How do we reduce this cost?

If a business does not understand the disbenefits of its ICT systems, then its evaluation of its ICT investments will not only overestimate the net benefit, but it will also not be getting the full potential return on those investments. To understand the dimensions of this problem, it is helpful to consider some examples. In the following section, several quite distinct examples of disbenefits are presented and analyzed. Following this, a proposed approach to managing these will be discussed.

Exploring disbenefits: some examples

Example one: The mixed blessing of e-mail

e-Mail is a particularly good example of mixed benefits. e-Mail is now so ubiquitous that it is hard to appreciate that, while it was available internally in some organisations as far back as the 1970s, it was only in the 1990s that it really took off on a significant scale and it was only with the large-scale expansion of Internet usage in the mid-1990s that it became a global phenomenon. There are many benefits of e-mail which will not be rehearsed here. An interesting example of them can be found in Hewill (2006). There are also many disbenefits of which the following are some:

- spam,
- time wasting,
- storage costs,

- harassment,
- impact on quality of thinking,
- impact on quality of writing,
- cost of mail management,
- legal exposures,
- accidents,
- stress induction,
- impatience.

For example, Borstorff and Graham (2006) report several cases of major lawsuits against companies arising from harassment via e-mail. According to the *British Journal of Administrative Management*, 38% of UK companies admit that their e-mail management systems are in 'complete chaos' (Anonymous, 2006). Swartz (2007) cites a 2006 AIIM survey of 741 companies which found that 63% of them had not analyzed the risks they faced from e-mail. Spam is worth special consideration and is discussed separately below. However, all of the headings listed above are a potential source of significant cost, even without lawsuits, spam or viruses. Two simple examples will be used to illustrate the potential scale of this. Consider an organisation with 500 employees at various grades, all of whom have access to e-mail. Furthermore, assume that:

- this organisation has simply installed this facility and that there are no internal protocols on its use (a common situation);
- no training has been provided on how to use e-mail effectively, but that some training in the basics of the technology has been provided (again, a common situation) and
- assume that there is no spam (a rather heroic assumption).

Taking the above hypothetical company, for illustrative purposes (and to take some more fairly conservative assumptions) if:

- each employee receives 50 e-mails a day;
- one in five of those e-mails is not relevant to his/her work;
- each non-relevant e-mail takes, on average, 60 seconds to open, read and discard;
- each employee works a 220 out of 250, 7.5 hour working days each year;
- the average full cost per employee per annum is €50 000.

Then the cost, in lost work time, of irrelevant e-mails is:

$$= 500 \times 10 \times 220 \times (60/3600) \times (50\,000/250*7.5)$$

$$= €488\,889.$$

Put another way, irrelevant e-mails are costing the company about 2% of its annual wage bill, in 'lost' productivity each year.

Some caveats must be added. An implicit assumption of computations such as these is that the wasted time could have been more productively spent. It could well be argued that if staff were not wasting time on e-mail, they would be wasting it on something else. On the other hand, this is only one modest negative impact of e-mail. Problems such as spam, time wasted in copying the world, and the simple disruption to output and concentration from the constant beep of incoming mail are ignored. In practice, therefore, in most organisations, the productivity loss of e-mail per employee is likely to be significantly greater than that shown above.

Another disbenefit arises from the fact that the very speed of e-mail encourages fast response. Such responses are often not thought through, generating follow-up enquiries. This can result in a discussion, which might take a minute to resolve by telephone, taking a much greater amount of employee time to resolve via e-mail. It is curious indeed that people continue to use e-mail rather than the telephone when the latter might be much more efficient. There are at least four possible reasons why this is so: the possibility that the person might not be there, the desirability of having a record, the fact that e-mail gives more time to think and the avoidance of having to deal with somebody in real time. Such is the scale of this problem that the phenomenon of e-mail addiction is now a matter of concern (Grodzinsky and Gumbus, 2005).

Now, of course, as stated above, e-mail delivers enormous benefits; most modern organisations could not survive for long without it. But the important thing is to recognise the disbenefits, because once they are recognised, they can be managed. To extend the above example, this is a disbenefit that, while it can probably never entirely be eliminated, can certainly be reduced by the simple expedient of putting in place proper mailing protocols such as only copying e-mails to those who really need to know and encouraging staff to desist from unthinkingly hitting the 'reply to all' button when responding to mail. The 'copy-the-world' syndrome, common in many organisations, is a material drain on productivity, organisational effectiveness and output. Good training may never exterminate this plague, but it can certainly reduce it. Even a 50% reduction in the above example is 'worth' €250 000.

As noted above, a more subtle disbenefit of e-mail is increased business risk. In addition to the example already cited, there are plenty of stories of companies and public bodies (and government ministers!) finding themselves in trouble or even in court over e-mails (e.g. see Brannigan, 2006). In the public sector, there is the added jeopardy of Freedom of Information Acts under which careless comments or simply jokes in bad taste can cause serious problems for an organisation. A recent incident in Ireland concerned a racist joke which was propagated via the Internet. The press got hold of the story and several reputable organisations, including one leading law firm, found themselves pilloried in the tabloids. In the case of the law firm, the mail had only been received. It had not been sent on, even internally. Nonetheless, the firm had to launch an expensive internal investigation to establish this and even though they found no evidence of inappropriate behaviour, there was still some residual reputational damage. Such damage is notoriously hard to quantify, but there is little doubt that the stakeholders, in this case the partners and employees of the firm, would regard this as a negative effect. In contrast, the type of problem encountered by Prudential Equity Group (Swartz, 2007), where e-mails became central to a settlement with regulators which cost the company $600 million, are distinctly measurable. E-mails can be leaked, sent to the wrong person, contain errors due to absence of proofreading and can cause internal arguments to escalate and occasionally run out of control. The latter can happens all too easily when a dispute between two people starts to be copied to third parties.

Example two: Management misinformation

The term 'management misinformation systems' was first coined by Ackoff (1967) and has been much debated since. Disbenefits arise from IS that delivers information to managers that is either not relevant to their needs or causes them to focus on the wrong questions. (Note that incorrect information is excluded from this discussion as the concern is with disbenefits of properly functioning systems. The case of bad information is discussed below.) Managerial information needs to vary according to manager level, role and function. Despite evidence from many years of business research, software companies continue to deliver products with marginal added value and significant disbenefit risk. Over the past three decades we have had:

- management information systems;
- decision support systems;
- executive information systems;
- online analytical processing;
- business analytics;
- data mining;
- business intelligence and, most recently,
- digital dashboards.

to name the main contenders. Some of these, notably executive information systems, have been expensive failures (Bussen and Myers, 1997; McBride, 1997), but all have the potential to distract managers from the real information that they need and use with the consequent misapplication of effort.

The problem here is a subtle one and is fuelled not just by the software industry – which needs to sell product – but by myths about management. One of the most provocative critiques of the rational manager model is from Mintzberg (1990), who suggests that managers play many roles, not all of which are helped by more information. This too is Ackoff's argument. Managers focus on the information, not the problem. The old saying, what gets measured is what get managed, means that what the system reports is where management attention is drawn. If this is the wrong place, then the business suffers. Thus badly designed IS create a lose–lose situation for the organisation. First, organisations waste much of the money spent in acquiring the system; second they lose money by using it!

A particularly dangerous form of disbenefit is when a system gives incorrect or misleading information. This is a particular risk with decision support systems and models and nowhere more so than with spreadsheets. There is actually a minor research field dedicated to spreadsheet errors and their impact on companies and governments (Eusprig, 2007). To take just two examples:

- Nevada City was embarrassed to find a $5 million deficit in its annual budget due to a spreadsheet error (Pokorny, 2006).
- Kodak was forced to restate its financial results resulting in a drop in its share price, after an $11 million severance error was traced to a faulty spreadsheet (Jelter, 2005).

These, of course, are only examples of problems that have come into the public domain. It is probable that such public problems are only the tip of a large iceberg.

Example three: Undermining product profitability _____

A particularly toxic form of disbenefit is when an ICT investment actually undermines the profitability of a company's product. This can occur when the adoption of a technology by an industry reduces real prices in the market and/or product profitability. From a detached point of view, this is a good thing. Lower prices for the same product has been the way of economic progress since the first industrial revolution (Chandler, 1990). However sustaining ICT-dependent competitive advantage is much harder than sustaining an advantage based on, say a patent or generations of embedded knowledge. While ICT can deliver competitive advantage, it does not always do so and in that case a company's last circumstance could be worse than its first. It is not unknown for competitive advantage, rather than taking the form of improved margins or market share, to translate instead into price reductions which benefit customers more than shareholders. Theoretically, in these circumstances, the vendor should be able to add value to the product and increase margins accordingly. If it cannot, then there is a disbenefit. This can be a particular problem in knowledge-based industries.

To see this, consider a number of competing firms offering legal advice. In the way of law firms, advice is charged for by the hour. Much of the time involved in this work is preparatory and consumed in researching legal texts and cases and in searching for precedents in court records. A software firm now enters the market offering an online searching service for an annual fee. The first legal firm to take this technology on board will have a first-mover competitive advantage. It can charge the same price in the market, but as the work required for a given deliverable is now less, so its profit margin increases. Alternatively, it could do the work in less time and therefore for a lower price with a view to gaining market share. As other firms acquire this service, the temporary advantage enjoyed by the first firm will be eroded. For the first mover, the key to extracting maximum value from the investment is to hold on to the additional market share that is has acquired even after competitors tool up. This is not easy to do. Critics have claimed that even early winners in the competitive advantage game such as the much cited cases of American Airlines and American Hospital Supply were unable to sustain that advantage for a long period (Carr, 2003; 2004).

The impact of such failure is a disbenefit. To get a sense of the scale of this, suppose that the law firm has 100 fee-earning staff, each working an 1800-hour year and that it has just acquired this new search technology. Assume 40% of staff time is chargeable at €1000 per hour (an optimistic figure for a lawyer, but it keeps the arithmetic simple) and that each member of staff earns €200 000. Finally, assume overheads including support staff of €40 million. Profit is therefore:

$$= 100 \times 1800 \times 40\% \times 1000 - (200\,000 \times 100) - 40\,000\,000$$

$$= \text{€}12 \text{ million.}$$

The critical point is that if, after acquiring the new service, the firm can fill the additional hours free with productive work but no more than that, then the above figure remains unchanged. However there is now an additional cost, namely the online service. If, say, this costs €250 000 per annum, it reduces the gross profit by approximately 2%. To gain a return on this investment therefore, the firm must either be able to charge more, either by raising its rate per hour, or by moving to a system of fixed fees, or it has to be able to increase its chargeable time above 40%. Its ability to do any of these will be largely determined by the behaviour of its competitors.

There is a critical difference here between a production- and a time-based service industry that is worth a moment's examination. If a manufacturing company can use technology to reduce the unit cost of production, then, *ceteris paribus*, the additional profit goes straight to the bottom line. This is not true when an organisation's income is based on charging out people's time and the primary cost is those people's time. In such organisations, technology will only have a significant impact on profit where it reduces non-productive time. In the above example, if, say, a new back office system enables the firm to raise chargeable hours from 40% to 45%, the effect is immediate and significant. Making staff more productive in their existing chargeable time is only more profitable if prices can be raised.

Cui bono? The answer in the case of the above example is the clients who are receiving more for the fees they pay for this service. Leakage of benefits of this type is a specialised form of disbenefit. It is a price of technological progress and of staying in business. A firm which did not invest in the new technology might be more profitable in the short term, but it would soon be out of business. Unfortunately, there may be nothing by way of financial return on the investment. As noted, in this instance, the return on the technology may be negative unless the firm can raise the value of its output and therefore its prices.

More subtle long-term effects of disbenefits can be seen in the banking industry. Clearly the banks need IT and have made substantial returns from investments in such technology. Modern modes of banking would be inconceivable without ICT. However, there are downsides. One impact of technology in banking has been the commoditisation of banking as a product. Technology has facilitated the emergence of banks that are purely online, and without physical branches, such as Egg and Rabo Direct. Use of first ATMs, then telephone and Internet banking has progressively reduced the cost of dealing with customers. But it has had some less desirable side effects. Two downsides are customer switching and loss of business opportunities. Because technology reduces switching costs for the consumer both technically and psychologically, customers can shop around for the best deal. The worst offenders are referred to in banking circles as 'serial switchers'. Ability to switch with minimal effort makes the banking market more competitive: good for consumers, but not for the owners of bank shares.

Secondly, for many modern consumers of banking services, the idea that they have a 'relationship' with their bank is foreign to them. One ATM is much like another. This loss of relationship with customers has implications for cross-selling. In particular, banks can lose contact with their wealthier clients and, most importantly, with customers who may not be profitable high net worth individuals today, but who may be in the future. The response of almost all banks has been to develop specialised services, such as private banking, to meet the needs of those customers. The latter's needs are often for more face time with the bank and less electronic interfacing. Gimmicks such as personalised Web portals may limit the problem a little, but not that much. It is ironic that in an electronic age, old-fashioned banking has re-emerged, if only for the select few.

The computation of the disbenefit here is complex and depends on a number of factors which have to be estimated. One approach is to use the concept of lifetime customer value (i.e. What is the total value to a bank of a customer over his or her life?). Services which the bank might like to sell to its retail customers such as life assurance, mortgages, stock trading, commercial loans, etc. are now harder to sell because there is a loss of personal relationship. Fifty years ago, even modest retail customers might have expected to be on first name terms with their bank managers. Today, it is unlikely that they would even know who their bank manager is. Factors such as inertia (or to use a more trendy word, stickability) also come into play. Of course, banks may pick up customers from competitors for precisely the same reasons, but it would be better not to lose customers in the first place.

Example four: The curse of PowerPoint

Does PowerPoint improve communication? The answer is only sometimes. With all PC-based presentation tools (not just PowerPoint, but since it is ubiquitous, it will be used as a signifier for all such systems), there are several potential disbenefits. These can be divided into two types: additional costs incurred and the risk of poor communication.

There are several sources of additional cost including:

- preparation time,
- costs of poor quality presentation,
- the substitution of production value for content,
- the cost of set-up.

and so on. Tuft (2003) has been particularly critical of PowerPoint and of the use of electronic presentation systems. Preparing a basic presentation on PowerPoint may or may not be more efficient than writing the same points on a piece of acetate. However, such tools provide a whole range of distractions such as:

- different fonts,
- style templates,
- customised animation,
- linkage to the Web,
- hot embedding of other documents,
- clip art galleries,
- screen grabbed images,
- video.

All of these encourage users to indulge their inner child when it comes to creating presentations. As the great majority of PowerPoint users have never been on a presentation course, the results are often badly designed slides which take a long time to prepare and fail to communicate effectively. The cost of this can be enormous. The most egregious incidents of this type are found in internal presentations. While it is understandable that a great deal of production design effort would be put into (say) a major sales pitch or a presentation to potential investors, this is rarely required for routine department meetings. Unfortunately, presenters often believe, sometimes with reason, that they are presenting not just information, but a personal image and that for this reason their slide set must be duly impressive.

Even more subtle damage is done when a poorly designed presentation does active harm to the objectives of the presenter.

Example five: Spam

For the purposes of discussion spam is here defined as unwanted mass e-mail. Strictly speaking, other forms of e-mail including some of those discussed above, could also be considered spam (see Keaney and Remenyi (2004) for a discussion of definitions). A great deal of e-mail might not be wanted, for example, somebody sending a query about something that is nothing to do with the recipient or the modern copy-the-world problems of office e-mail. However, most spam is e-mail sent to a large group of people who have not requested it and most, if not all, of whom do not want to receive it.

According to some estimates, spam now comprises over 78% of all of the e-mail traffic on the Internet (MessageLabs, 2007). Many organisations and individuals regard spam with a resigned irritation, a price one has to pay for the convenience and advantages of using the Internet and the Web. There is now a substantial industry in spam filtering which uses increasingly sophisticated tools such as Bayesian statistics to try to detect and stop or divert unwanted incoming traffic. Needless to say, spammers are continually finding new ways to bypass these defences and the spam-filtering world has become a game of cat and mouse as poachers and gamekeepers try to outmanoeuvre each other. Every so often a 'spam storm' breaks out (one occurred in the week of 11th April 2007 when a massive Trojan horse spam attack was launched worldwide (Keizer, 2007)). As the Internet Service Provider route has been closed down, botnets have taken over. People are often surprised when they receive a stream of mail rejection notices from people to whom they have never knowingly sent an e-mail. As image analysis software improves, so ways of producing images designed to foil scanners proliferate. From the perspective of the spammer, the economics of spam are such as to make all this effort worthwhile. A percentage success rate only measurable in the second place of decimals will more than cover the costs and even in the case of what might be loosely termed higher risk forms of spamming, such as 'pump and dump' where the spammer has to buy the stock first, it takes only a very modest response to make a tidy return.

The cost of this to companies is enormous. In 2003, Ferris Research estimated that spam was costing US business over $10 billion (Krim, 2003) each year. By 2005 *InfoWorld Tech Watch* estimated that this figure had risen to $22 billion. While such figures need to be treated with caution, not least because there is no agreed methodology for computing the cost of spam to a given business, there is no disputing the scale of the problem. Spam is an example of an almost pure disbenefit. For most businesses, apart from those in the filtering industry, there is no value in spam whatsoever.

The risks of spam are more than simply the waste of staff time or even the direct cost. Some other disbenefits and risks are as follows:

- Exposure of enterprise systems to malware (viruses, spyware, Trojan horse, worms, etc.).
- Storage (much spam contain disk-consuming image attachments or embedded text).
- The risk of missing genuine mail which is inadvertently deleted by the user or stopped by the filter.
- Risks to employees from frauds such as phishing or the Nigerian 419 scam.
- Potential security breaches.
- Cluttering up the e-mail system.
- Denial of service attacks.

Most of these can readily be translated to a bottom-line cost. As noted above, accurate current figures for the cost of spam are hard to come by. To add to the above US figures, in 2003, it was estimated that spam cost organisations $13 billion each year (Swartz, 2003a, b). The Radicati Group (cited by Keaney and Remenyi) estimated the total cost in 2003 to companies, including extra servers, additional storage and network capacity, to be $20 billion and research by Nucleus Research Inc. (2007) put the annual cost per e-mail user at $712. Whatever the true figure, spam is a disbenefit with a capital D.

Some caveats

The above examples are by no means all of the disbenefits of ICT. Others include:

- Workplace injury such as repetitive strain injury (RSI).
- Time wasting.
- Impact of user errors.
- Disruption of other activities.
- The interrupt-driven organisation.
- Risks from powerful end-user computing tools.
- Increased worker stress and consequent health problems.
- Other forms of business risk (of which there are many).
- Increased risk of public liability.

It is worth concluding with a semantic point. Is the figure of the $712 annual cost of spam quoted above just a cost of running e-mail? The answer is no. This cost is neither planned nor budgeted for when installing e-mail systems. It delivers no benefit to any stakeholder in the organisation. It is not part of any contract or agreed set of terms. In other words, it is a pure disbenefit. Furthermore, at this stage, it is also a well-established disbenefit and therefore it can be managed. The management of this, and other types of disbenefit, will now be considered.

Disbenefit management

Like benefits, disbenefits need to be managed; the difference is that in the case of disbenefits the objective is minimisation. The following is a strategy for disbenefit management. A disbenefit management strategy is pre-emptive as well as reactive. It comprises six steps which are set out in the following paragraphs.

Step one: Disbenefit identification

It was noted at the outset that not all disbenefits are foreseeable, but many are. One of the main reasons that they are not foreseen is that when considering computer systems, people tend to consider the technical and financial rather than the human and organisational risks. This is despite a large industry dedicated to change management. The following are some techniques which can be used to try to spot disbenefits before they occur:

- *Organised workshops to brainstorm disbenefits*: In ICT projects, when it comes to putting together the business case, one technique used is brainstorming the benefits that are expected. Often considerable effort will be put into preparing estimates of the positive impact of the technology–reduced inventories, better customer retention, fewer defective products, reduced administration costs, etc. What is suggested is that there should be a separate workshop which asks the following questions:

- What could go wrong here?
- What negative impact *will* this have on:
  - people?
  - the organisation?
  - systems?
  - products?
  - processes?
  - stakeholders?
- What negative impacts *might* it have on:
  - people?
  - the organisation?
  - systems?
  - products?
  - processes?
  - stakeholders?
  - How might the behaviour of staff change for the worse when we introduce this new system?

- *Appoint a devil's advocate*: A useful tactic is to ask somebody to play the role of the devil's advocate. This entails trying to come up with as negative a view of a proposed system's impact as possible. The person who does this must be chosen with care. (S)he needs not only enough business and technical knowledge and experience to foresee possible problems, (s)he also needs to be imaginative and diplomatic. An important point to remember is that this person may end up torpedoing somebody's pet project. If this occurs, it needs to be handled with care.

- *Research the problem*: Many disbenefits of ICT are well documented in the business press and academic literature. Despite this, organisations are adept at repeating the same mistakes made by many other organisations before them that have learned the hard way. Most professional ICT staff, including top managers, tend to pay little attention to the academic literature, if indeed they are aware of it at all. Only when research findings find their way into the professional or popular press do they tend to be widely read by practitioners.

- *Observe what is going on*: Observing existing/ongoing disbenefits is harder. With regard to work practices, it is tempting to suggest that what is needed here is a good, old-fashioned, time-and-motion expert to look at how people use the technology at their disposal. A more constructive approach is to get people to look critically at their own behaviour and to share knowledge. To take a trivial example, there are many helpful shortcuts in office software. Typically most staff are aware of only a subset of these. Again observation of how people actually use basic tools like Word and Excel often reveals that there are many small ways in which they could speed up their work.

- *Survey stakeholders*: The survey can be a useful weapon in surfacing disbenefits. Surveys can be used with different stakeholder groups – critically customers, staff and suppliers, to find out what problems they have with the organisation's technology. To take a depressingly common example, many firms unthinkingly install telephone systems which are almost designed to lose them customers ('To hear this message repeated, press 1. To hear the opening bars of *Eine Kleine Nachtmusik* repeated played out of tune press 2.

For 3 press 4. Your custom is important to us, please wait until the next customer service representative is available'...). Many customers and potential customers may be being lost through such systems. One way to find out if this is happening out is to ask.

■ *Monitor relevant indicators*: Another approach is to monitor events in suspect areas. For example, to keep an eye on data storage on the e-mail system. One IT manager (in conversation with the author) described the bane of his life to be users using the internal e-mail system to distribute photographs, typically family or holiday snapshots. These were often copied to several people at a few megabytes a time and accounted for an alarming amount of his storage. Care is required here. There may be ethical considerations to be taken into account before, for example, monitoring user behaviour. Monitoring should always be done with the knowledge and consent of users.

■ *Prepare a report*: A sobering action is to put these findings into a report. This has the advantage of giving at least an initial sense of the scale of the problem and will help in assessing the degree of effort justified in managing it. This question is further discussed below.

Step two: Establishing metrics _____

How to measure the impact of disbenefits is the next problem. There is a strong temptation to bring everything back to money. Money is useful in many cases, but it should not be used as the only metric for a couple of reasons. One is that it is sometimes quite difficult to translate things to money terms without making many assumptions which undermine the credibility of the exercise. This was discussed above in the hypothetical example of the law firm. Bear in mind that it is often possible to judge something to be of value in its own right, without having to convert it to cash. A second reason is that some things are more meaningfully measured in non-monetary terms. With this in mind, and starting with money, the following are useful metrics:

■ *Money*: It is always possible, although the process is sometimes questionable, to convert a disbenefit to a profit and sometimes to a cash impact. This is akin to doing a cost benefit analysis without the benefit. Caution is needed because many assumptions can find their way into this process. It is also important to be clear that all costs are tracked (in the case of employees, e.g. this includes all pay overheads).

■ *Time*: Time is sometimes a better measure than money. It is possible to measure return on time in the same way as return on money. In other words, if I must invest X hours in order to save Y, is the ratio Y/X greater than 1? The important difference here is that if Y is a continuing saving, then it is not discounted with time. For example, if with 100 work hours of effort, I can reduce time wasted by 200 work hours a year, then the return is, if not infinite, certainly very large.

■ *Risk*: Risk is measured in terms of undesirable events and the probability of those happening. This is a complex topic and beyond the scope of this chapter, but standard risk management techniques can be used to reduce or eliminate disbenefits. One such model is:
  ■ identify an undesirable event,
  ■ estimate the probability of its occurring,
  ■ assess impact if it does occur,
  ■ identify possible preventative actions,
  ■ identify possible remedial actions,
  ■ choose best option.

To take a simple example, employees, especially those new to the Internet, may be vulnerable to frauds via the Internet. If an employee were to lose a large amount of money, it could affect their work performance adversely in a number of ways. A good employer will, of course, think of more than just the company's interest, but even a less humane organisation should think of its self-interest.

■ *Health*: For some disbenefits, it may be appropriate to use health-related proxy variables. Sick leave, complaints about work-related health problems, etc. can be used for assessing and monitoring certain types of disbenefit.

■ *Direct metrics*: In some cases, it is appropriate to measure something directly. For example, the amount of storage used for e-mail or the type of traffic on the Web. An organisation may tolerate employee use of the Web for personal purposes subject to certain controls. In such cases, a system to monitor breaches of those controls will be necessary.

Step three: Set targets

The third stage of the disbenefits management process is to set targets for disbenefit reduction. There is a temptation just to take some appropriate actions (see below) and assume that things will improve. Undoubtedly, if the proper steps are taken there will be improvements, but to get the most of the good work, it should be followed up. Specific targets should therefore be set and measured. The appropriate yardstick will vary with the problem and will be in terms of the metrics determined in stage two. Examples of specific targets might be:

■ Reduce volume of e-mail storage by 50%.
■ Ensure that all staff have typing training by end of year.
■ Reduce non-productive internal e-mail by 10%.
■ Prepare assessment of legal risks from data on company machines.

Step four: Develop an action plan

The point of unearthing disbenefits is to eliminate them if possible and, if not, to reduce them. This needs an action plan tailored to the specific circumstances prevailing in the organisation. In many cases, the actions will be obvious and it would take too long to document all the possibilities here, but the following are some ideas that might be considered:

■ *Training in little things*: There are few people in modern organisations that do not use some combination of word processors, spreadsheets or graphics. In most such office products, an enormous amount of time is wasted for two reasons. First, the system defaults are not what the user wants, so hours are spent on trivial things like changing fonts, margins, print settings, etc. in the same way time and time again. Secondly, there are many shortcuts and ways to do things quickly in these products of which many users are unaware. By the simple expedient of showing users how to sort these problems once and for all, each user can save tens of hours per year. Even more effective is a basic typing course. This has a triple benefit: faster typing, fewer errors and less fatigue.

■ *Training in bigger things*: Staff need special training when using ICT tools that are potentially dangerous. At the top of this list is the spreadsheet (other contenders are query tools and high powered end-user development products). How many people who use spreadsheets have been properly trained in model building, design and testing? The spreadsheet is, from one perspective, just a specialised type of high-level programming tool, especially if macros are employed, and yet many businesses allow employees with no training or background in programming to develop models which may be used for important business decisions. For a litany of horror stories, the reader is referred to www .eusprig.com. Organisations should look at what end-user tools are in use and make sure that those who use them are properly trained and using them in a disciplined way.

- *Deploying templates*: Another common problem is re-inventing the wheel. One way to reduce unproductive effort is to provide templates for office documents and to enforce compliance with those templates. Users should be strongly discouraged from deviating from standard formats and layouts. Artistic licence should be banned.
- *Creating awareness*: It is important that users are aware of various causes of disbenefit. Such things can be divided into two classes; things they do and things that may happen to them. So users need to be aware of poor or unproductive behaviour on their own parts. A simple example is how they sit when working at their PCs. Some firms provide charts to employees to encourage them to do simple stretching and movement exercises during the day. They also need to be aware of potential risks they face in using systems, in particular from e-mail and the Web. Other areas where users need guidance is in how to update their PC system software sensibly and do's and don'ts of dealing with suspicious e-mail.
- *Implement process protocols*: These are a key weapon in the war against disbenefits. Protocols cover a range of behaviours with regard to ICT systems. An area where protocols are particularly useful is e-mail. For example, some organisations enforce a discipline whereby users only open their e-mails at certain items of day (many more self-disciplined individuals do this as well). There is an expectation, if not a presumption in e-mail of instant response. Why should this be so? By only switching on the e-mail at a point when they are ready to address the in-box, employees will be more productive. Furthermore, house rules covering who and what can and should be sent by e-mail should be determined and communicated to all users. Other areas where protocols can be useful are in Web usage, personal storage and dealing with information overload.
- *Implement good ethical standards*: Although this may seem like a rather odd technique to include, establishing and enforcing good ethical standards of behaviour throughout the organisation is an important part of good disbenefit management. The case of the bank CEO and the call girl site quoted above and the many reported cases of e-mail harassment with subsequent lawsuits are examples of the results of unethical behaviour. These can lead to reputational damage and financial loss. Good ethics is one way to reduce certain types of disbenefit.
- *Use good ergonomics*: One of the disbenefits of ICT is illnesses related to PC use. These range from eye problems to back strain. There are many sets of guidelines available on how to design an ergonomic workplace (see www.ergonomics.org.uk). Simple things like making sure each employee has a proper chair, that keyboards are at the appropriate height, checking lighting conditions and so on can make a significant contribution to employee comfort and productivity. Cheap furniture and poor seating are a false economy. The problem is, as noted elsewhere, that good ergonomics costs money and the results are not easy to discern. Nonetheless they are there.
- *Make virtue of necessity*: It is worth a note about benefit leakage. Often it is not possible, and sometimes it is not even desirable, to prevent benefit leakage. Where leakage occurs, organisations should try to capitalise on it. For example, marketing improved service to customers, using it as a bargaining chip with suppliers or promoting it in a way that will raise employee morale or make the organisation more attractive to potential recruits. Since it has to be paid for, one might as well exploit it.

Step five: Measure progress

It is important to measure progress. The impact of these changes on, for example, productivity and profitability may be subtle. Sometimes the results will be obvious, but often they will be mixed up with other factors. It is therefore important to go back to the metrics and targets set and see to what extent they have been achieved. This also has the effect of reminding everybody that this is not a one-off exercise. Eliminating disbenefits is, like painting the Forth bridge, a continuing process.

Step six: Review

The final step in disbenefits management is a periodic review. This does not have to be a full value for money audit or health check, but it should have some of the same characteristics. Technology does not stand still and neither do disbenefits. There will inevitably be new challenges in the future. The price of low disbenefits is eternal vigilance.

Conclusion

There is a story, probably apocryphal, about the CEO of a large US food company who was, one day, standing beside the bottling line for his company's best selling sauce product. He asked the production manager why there was a label on both the front and back of each bottle and was told that the front label contained the name, brand and logo while the label on the back contained nutrition and other information required by government regulation. The CEO suggested that they redesign the label on the front to contain the required information and eliminate the label on the back. The annualised saving that resulted was about $1 million – a figure that went straight to the bottom line.

Whether or not the story is true, it illustrates an important principle in mass production – when you are manufacturing by the million, savings of even a small fraction of a cent per unit can amount to a large sum at the end of the year. The same is true in areas far from the production line. Whether it is keystrokes, e-mails received per day, time spent finding information or loss of productivity due to fatigue caused by poor ergonomics, the potential loss of output, when summed over many employees over many years mounts up.

This chapter has set out an approach to disbenefits management which is systematic and which, if properly applied, will result in material productivity improvements and cost savings. The problem with disbenefit management is that many disbenefits are hidden. They are often harder to find than benefits, and the link between their elimination and better organisational performance is not always immediately obvious or simple to trace. It is not, therefore, surprising that books on benefits management tend to be more prominent. Benefits are generally easier to observe and quantify and what is easier to observe is, as is well known, easier to manage. Nonetheless, disbenefits cost organisations untold millions of euros, pounds and dollars each year. Just because the impacts of disbenefits are not always as visible, does not make them any the less real.

References

Ackoff, R. (1967). 'Management misinformation systems'. *Management Sciences*, 14(4), 147–156.

Anonymous (2006). 'Companies admit to email management system chaos'. *The British Journal of Administrative Management*, December 2006/January 2007, pp. 7–10.

Borstorff, P. and Graham, G. (2006). 'E-harassment: Employee perceptions of E-technology as a source of harassment'. *Journal of Applied Management and Entrepreneurship*, 11(3), 51–67.

Brannigan, T. (2006). Email leak fuels clamour to scrap ID cards scheme. *Guardian On-Line*, Monday, 10 July. Available at: http://www.guardian.co.uk/idcards/story/0,,1816799,00. html (accessed 27th April 2007).

Bussen, W. and Myers, M. (1997). 'Executive information system failure: A New Zealand case study'. *Journal of Information Technology*, 12(2), 145–153.

Carr, N. (2003). 'IT doesn't matter'. *Harvard Business Review*, May, 41–49.

Carr, N. (2004). *Does IT Matter?* Harvard Business School Press, Boston, MA.

Chandler, A. (1990). 'The enduring logic of industrial success'. *Harvard Business Review*, March–April, pp. 131–140.

Creadon, S. (2004). 'It was a silly incident. I am paying a very high price for it'. *The Irish Times*, 31st May 2004.

Duncan, G. (2007). 'GDP overhaul set to boost data for next Chancellor'. *The Times* (London), 26th February 2007.

Economic History Services (2007). What was the GDP then? Available at: http://eh.net/hmit/ukgdp/ukgdp_answer.php (accessed 27th April 2007).

Eusprig (European Spreadsheet Risks Interest Group). Available at: http://www.eusprig.org/stories.htm (accessed 27th April 2007).

Grodzinsky, F. and Gumbus, A. (2005). 'Internet and production: Ethical perspective on workplace behaviour'. *Journal of Information Ethics and Communications in Society*, 3(supp), S5–S12.

Hewill, P. (2006). 'Electronic mail and internal communication: A three-factor model'. *Corporate Communications*, 11(1), 78–92.

InfoWorld Tech Watch (2005). Cost of spam soars toward $22 billion. *InfoWorld*, 3rd February 2005. Available at: http://weblog.infoworld.com/techwatch/archives/001056. html (accessed 27th April 2007).

Jelter, J. (2005). Kodak restates, adds $9 million to loss. MarketWatch, 9th November 2005. Available at: http://www.marketwatch.com/News/Story/Story.aspx?guid=%7B276F D56F%2D00CA%2D42AE%2DAD70%2DC66DF571FC77%7D&dist=rss&siteid=mktw (accessed 27th April 2007).

Keaney, A. and Remenyi, D. (2004). 'Spamming and scamming: The real picture!'. *Irish Journal of Management*, 25(1), 23–40.

Keizer, G. (2007). Massive spam shot of 'Storm Trojan' reaches record proportions. It's the biggest spam blast in the last year. *ComputerWorld*, 7th April 2007. Available at: http://www.computerworld.com/action/article.do?command=viewArticleBasic&articleId=901 6420 (accessed 27th April 2007).

Kelly, M. (2007). IT spend to hit USD1.5 trillion in three years. *Electric News*, 10th January, 2007. Available at: http://www.electricnews.net/frontpage/news-9866074.html (accessed 27th April 2007).

Krim, J. (2003). Bulk e-Mail threatens communication arteries. *The Washington Post*, Thursday, 13th March 2003, p. A01. Available at: http://www.washingtonpost.com/ac2/wp-dyn/A17754-2003Mar12 (accessed 27th April 2007).

McBride, N. (1997). 'The rise and fall of an executive information system: A case study'. *Information Systems Journal*, 7(4), 277–287.

Messagelabs (2007). Global trends and contents analysis. *MessageLabs*. Available at: http://www.messagelabs.com/publishedcontent/publish/threat_watch_dotcom_en/intelligence_reports/february_2007/DA_181260.chp.html (accessed 26th April 2007).

Millman, R. (2006). Unlucky 13 sacked by Merrill Lynch over porn. *SCMagazine*, 27th June 2006. Available at: www.scmagazine.com/us/news/article/566397/unlucky+13+sacked+merrill+lynch+porn/ (accessed 27th April, 2007).

Mintzberg, H. (1990). 'The manager's job: Folklore and fact'. *Harvard Business Review*, March–April, 163–176.

Nucleus Research (2007). Research Note; Spam: The repeat offender. *Nucleus Research*. Available at: http://www.nucleusresearch.com/research/h22.pdf (accessed 27th April 2007).

Orlikowski, W. and Yates, J. (2006). 'ICT and organizational change: A commentary'. *The Journal of Applied Behavioral Science*, 42(1), 127–134.

Pokorny, R. (2006). Budget discrepancies attributed to computer error. *Nevada Daily Mail*, Friday, 6th January 2006. Available at: http://www.nevadadailymail.com/story/1135458.html (accessed 27th April 2007).

Remenyi, D., Bannister, F. and Money, A. (2007). *The Effective Measurement and Management of ICT Costs and Benefits*, 3rd ed. Elsevier/CIMA Publishing, London.

Swartz, N. (2003a). 'The international war on spam'. *Information Management Journal*, 37(5), 18–24.

Swartz, N. (2003b). 'Spam costs businesses $13 billion annually'. *Information Management Journal*, 37(2), p. 9.

Swartz, N. (2007). 'Playing with electronic fire'. *Information Management Journal*, 41(1), 22–25.

Tuft, E. (2003). *The Cognitive Style of PowerPoint*. Graphics Press, Cheshire, CT.

Ward, J. and Daniel, E. (2005). *Benefits Management: Delivering Value from IS & IT Investments*. John Wiley and Sons Ltd., London.

Webpronews.com (2006). AOL forks itself, leaks user search data. *Webpronews* 7th August 2006. Available at: http://www.webpronews.com/topnews/2006/08/07/aol-forks-itself-leaks-user-search-data (accessed 28th April 2007).

Willcocks, L. and Renkema, T. (1999). *The IT Value Quest: How to Capture the Business Value of IT-Based Infrastructure*. John Wiley and Sons Ltd., London.

Chapter 6 ■■■

Spot the difference: Evaluation of custom and package applications

I. Entwistle and B. Light

■ Introduction

In terms of a genealogy of packaged software, many trace their roots to the United States' (US) Justice Department's decision to force International Business Machines (IBM) to unbundle hardware and software (Carmel, 1997). In the late 1970s and early 1980s packages were primarily viewed as a way to 'deal' with the applications backlog synonymous with custom development (Gremillion, 1982) and since then, people in organisations have used packages to varying extents although this has mostly been in smaller organisations (Markus and Tanis, 2000). In the mid-1990s, Enterprise Resource Planning (ERP) packages became a popular choice for larger organisations and today packages are pervasive (Light and Holland, 2000; OECD, 2002; Houghton and Vickery, 2004). Yet despite this, until around 1998 such technologies had received scant attention, in contrast to custom developments, from the information systems (IS) research community. Even now, most of the research in the area is still concerned with packaged software application types rather than packaged software *per se* (Esteves and Pastor, 2001; Westrup, 2002). For example, it has been reported that during the period 1997–2000, 189 papers related to the subject of ERP were published (Esteves and Pastor, 2001). Panels on the topic were held at key IS conferences such as the Americas Conference on Information Systems, the European Conference on Information Systems, the International Conference on Information Systems and the Australian Conference on Information Systems. However, it is again interesting to note that the focus was upon a particular application type rather than packaged software *per se*.

Moreover, the IS community still primarily focuses upon custom software, despite shifts in development strategies in work organisations. Very few courses on packaged software run on undergraduate and postgraduate degree programmes, and where they do, these centre on application types, usually with the sponsorship of the vendor. ERP vendors such as SAP and Oracle have been relatively quick to approach universities to set up joint initiatives. Certainly, ERP as an area of research has expanded dramatically since 1997 and it appears that a preoccupation with this application type has led to distinct neglect of the development of theory about packaged software. Such theorising would generally have more longevity than that specific to an application type. As a result of 'passing over' packaged software in favour of the 'glamour' of application types, valuable lessons that will enable the furtherance of theory in IS are being ignored. This is because packages, and particularly application types, have been sensationalised and held up as remarkably different from what has gone before. Instead, it would be preferable to view packages as technologies that may share similarities and differences when compared with those that are custom developed. Recognition of prior work in the area, rather than attempts to jump on the latest bandwagon are incredibly important if the field of IS is to avoid labels such as 'a fragmented adhocracy'. Banville and Landry (1992) afford IS this label on a number of fronts, but particularly because they perceive research as personal and weakly coordinated in the field and where researchers can gain a reputation by contributing to specific groups – ERP packages, for example. Of course there are aspects of applications such as ERP packages that are worthy of study, as is true of other package application types such as Customer Relationship Management (CRM) and groupware. Yet, the theoretical issues that may have broader consequences are, generally being ignored. This grounds the motivation for this paper – which is in locating process of package evaluation more squarely within IS research.

Packaged software evaluation

Package evaluation is usually conceptualised as part of the process of software selection. Like early approaches to IS evaluation in general, these theories of selection assume evaluation only happens in the early stages of a package software project. Evaluation is set to happen after requirements for a package have been identified and thus is seen as a process solely for deciding if a package meets those requirements and, consequently, it forms part of the final selection decision (see Table 6.1). The following sections, drawing upon insights from packaged software studies and commercial literature, will point to some of the problems with this thinking. The discussion considers issues with the objectivity/subjectivity of criteria, the incomplete and shifting nature of requirements, and links with the need to 'evaluate the future' of an application's development trajectory.

Package evaluation criteria

Package evaluation may be based upon a number of sources. Word of mouth, for example, has been highlighted as invaluable in identifying available packages (Kunda and Brooks, 2000). Others may include publications, market surveys, the Internet and mailing lists. However, it has been suggested that these sources may put purchasers at the risk of being enticed by the vendors' marketing people or being locked into a certain way of thinking by looking only at the available packages (Bansler and Havn, 1994). A further alternative

■ Table 6.1 A summary of packaged software selection processes

	Definition of user requirements	Package evaluation	Final selection
Stefanou (2001)	Organisations should clarify their business vision, requirements and capabilities.	The requirements should be used to evaluate various packages. Packages should be evaluated against each other.	Packages should be selected in the light of the evaluation activity.
Bansler and Havn (1994)	The organisation should know its requirements well enough to compare alternatives.	Packages should be evaluated on the basis of organisational and technical requirements and vendor capabilities.	Packages should be selected in the light of evaluation activity.
Chau (1995)	Study existing organisational needs and interview some of the future users.	Assess the available packages through vendor representations and comparison with the defined requirements.	Packages should be selected on the basis of maximising the fit between the application and the organisation.
KPMG (1998)	Consider 'as is' and 'to be'.		Select the package.
Lynch (1987)	Enough information is required to make the right choice.	Packages should be evaluated on the basis of their functionality.	Packages should be selected that fit with organisational requirements.
Martin and McClure (1983)	Identify current and future requirements of the package.	Survey all available packages for the application.	Select the package that most readily fits with organisational requirements.
Sharland (1991)	Define requirements.	Evaluate each candidate package using the requirements.	Select the package.
Nelson et al. (1996)	Identify the company's information processing requirements.	Evaluate packages in respect of their characteristics, company requirements and the capabilities of the company relative to the package characteristics.	Packages should be selected that most readily fit the organisational situation.
Welke (1981)	This process is not described in any great detail. The paper suggests that when a requirement for an application arises the best thing to do is to categorise the types of software you can buy.	Assess the available packages.	Select a package that most readily meets organisational requirements.

might be experimentation. Indeed, it is suggested that the best way of evaluating packages, is through experimentation with the operating environment in which the product will be used (Martin and McClure, 1983; Kunda and Brooks, 2000). Indeed, as Hecht (1997) points out, however package evaluation is performed, it is a difficult process because; searching for products is resource intensive, requiring personnel, travel, the development of requests for proposals, gathering and analyzing data, development of selection criteria and vendor interviews for instance; it may be difficult to find independent guidance. Purchasers may be forced to rely on vendor proposals, presentations and marketing materials; and given a lack of a selection methodology political agendas and/or gut feelings may well dominate rather than well thought out requirements.

Reputation, capability, training and support offered, product reputation and whether it is a market leader are further related indicators of the significance of organisational perception of vendor and implementation partner (Kunda and Brooks, 2000). At Siemens, consultants were chosen based on a recommendation from within the company (Hirt and Swanson, 1999) and at Mitek and DMC prints, SAP was chosen as it was perceived as the market leader in ERP packages (Dolmetsch et al., 1998). The whole idea of deciding if a vendor is good or bad is an interpretive act. Despite checklists such as those provided by Sharland (1991) and Welke (1981), the choice of a vendor – as shown above – may be based upon very personal criteria and very little rigour (Howcroft and Light, 2002).

What this shows is the wide-ranging scope for the process to be shaped by different view points and actions. Marketing documentation, for example, however ethical the vendor, will be populated with arguments as to why its product should be chosen. Moreover, even Hecht's advice of having selection criteria in place is no guarantee of objectivity – the criteria themselves are the results of interpretation as is their application. Selection criteria will be specific to organisational context and even individuals. In general, however, the major criteria for the evaluation of packaged software centre on the themes of the functionality of the software – currently and in the future and the capabilities of the vendor – currently and in the future. Indeed some of the theories of packaged software selection explicitly incorporate these criteria – see Welke (1981); Martin and McClure (1983) and Sharland (1991). Much of the reasoning behind the importance of these themes is concerned with taking a long-term view of living with the outcome of the selection process. That is, selecting a product and vendor that meets and will continue to meet the requirements of those in the organisation.

Evaluating the 'unknown'

It would be expected that those in organisations would usually need to have some idea of their functional requirements before they begin to assess whether a particular package will fit with these. This is because some required functionality might only be partially met and in others, missing entirely (Butler, 1999). Moreover, the significance of this is increased in the light of the various selling acts that may occur in the process of selection and procurement, for example, the blurring of packaged software capabilities by vendors as alluded to below:

> 'with the huge explosion in the CRM market it is not surprising that the ERP vendors are quick to jump on the bandwagon, touting the benefits of an extended product' (August, 1999: 38).

However, it is widely reported that software purchasers often do not understand their own requirements and that they may choose a package on the basis of a few sales pitches (Butler, 1999; Howcroft and Light, 2002). Furthermore, as the software and the systems architecture will be new to an organisation, the practices that the software supports may also be new and therefore it is suggested that organisations must engage in a process of organisational learning (Lee and Lee, 2000; Scott and Vessey, 2000). The idea that people in organisations may have to learn about the packages they have adopted is touched upon in the literature. Interestingly though, this is usually during implementation. For example, at Dow Corning, team members who requested modifications to the SAP package they were implementing were often unsure if the need for this had arisen from a deficiency in the package or their ability to learn how the package allowed a process to be performed (Ross, 1999). Adam and O'Doherty (2000) also report that in a few cases the packages adopted led to the development of managerial expectations – they learnt what was possible and became more ambitious in terms of their objectives for the system.

It is argued that a better fit between the packaged software functionality and user requirements leads to successful implementation and usage (Janson and Subramanian, 1995). At a simple level, this seems logical. However, as illustrated in the last section, those in organisations are often uncertain about their precise requirements and therefore it may prove difficult to evaluate a package upon the basis of these 'incomplete' or 'inadequate' requirements. Moreover, even where requirements are fairly well articulated, evaluation can still be problematic as packages may well meet the requirements in an unfamiliar or unacceptable way (Gremillion, 1982). It has been suggested, for example, that most package purchasers find that at least 20% of their requirements are missing from the functionality of packages (Scott and Kaindl, 2000). At the University of Nebraska, for example, the average fit between the implemented SAP packaged was 60% and as low as 30% in some areas yet they had bought the package with the expectation of it providing enterprise support (Sieber et al., 2000). This discussion implies that even though it has been argued that those in an organisation purchasing a package must determine its functional requirements and weigh these against various products, this may not happen as expectations are fuelled by a combination of selling acts and organisational learning. Moreover, as a result, expectations of package functionality may also shift when the realities of implementation and usage are experienced, that is, when *in-situ* evaluation occurs.

Evaluating 'the future': customisation, maintenance and upgrades

Packaged software is generally tailored to the specific requirements of an organisation (Klaus et al., 2000). For the purposes of this study, configuration (sometimes called tailoring) and customisation (sometimes called modification, custom fitting and tailoring!) are used. Configuration refers to the 'switching on and off' of functionality that is part of the blueprint of the software, customisation is used to describe changes or additions to the functionality pre-built into a package (Light and Wagner, 2006).

Several studies highlight the importance of consumer organisation views of the vendors of, and implementation partners associated with, particular packaged software products. First, purchase is often motivated by expectations of the direction of vendor products as much as by specific internal needs (Butler, 1999; Sawyer, 2001). That is, a consumer organisation will be interested in the development trajectory of a vendor. Furthermore, the vendor's perceived strength and stability is also a significant consideration (Chau, 1994) and trust from a customer is reportedly often gained through vendor responsiveness and dependability (Gefen, 2002). In one study it is suggested that:

> 'universities are not likely to make an investment in an ERP system that is intended to provide institutional support for many years unless they are convinced that the vendor is totally reliable. Continued enhancement of the ERP product is less likely to be achieved by a supplier of dubious stability' (Oliver and Romm, 2000: 1042).

In order to avoid problems of invalidating packaged software support, those in an organisation may attempt to minimise customisation and rely upon the vendor to develop the package in an appropriate fashion. A number of early studies of packaged software indicate that there was an intention to customise products as a short cut to development – and thereby deal with the applications backlog (Weing, 1984; Trauth and Cole, 1992). Indeed, in one study, a whole category of analysis is devoted to problems with product customisation (Gross and Ginzberg, 1984). To clarify this, the subject's problem was that it was unable to customise the software easily, rather than it had difficulty following the customisation activity. However, from this point, and more strongly in the 2000s, packaged software is linked with the minimisation of customisation activity (Dolmetsch et al., 1998; Brehm et al., 2001) even though this still occurs (Light, 2001). This means that those in the consumer organisation may have to live with the vendor's decisions about maintaining and upgrading its software products (Bansler and Havn, 1994). Usually, because of the desire for vendors to maintain economies of scale and a generic product, they will determine who gets involved in this. As shown by Scott and Kaindl (2000), SAP chose customers that suited their product development objectives for their R/3 3.1 and 4.0 releases, rather than aiming to satisfy the requirements of their user base.

In sum, the evaluation of package applications is complex because it is difficult to set up, and deploy criteria in the face of shifting, incomplete requirements and the absence of knowledge about the potentialities of product evolution. This seems similar to custom development evaluation. A demonstration of such resonances throughout this case now follows.

Research strategy and method

The following case study is a representation of a software procurement process followed by a large European organisation, and is intended to be a interpretive explanation of the sequence of events from which we may be able to shed rich insight (Walsham, 1995) into how custom and packaged software evaluations are enacted in practice. Materials supporting this qualitative evaluation of the process were supplied by the independent selection organisation and HallConsult, mentioned in the case. This data was supported by explanations of the decision-making process by the ultimate clients, those on the steering group at Transport Plc and the organisation responsible for authoring the functional requirements specification, UniSoft. In particular, the artefacts evaluated in the data collection process included: structured and unstructured discussion with all parties; participant and non-participant observation of the evaluation process; documents including the functional requirements specification and use cases; and documented evidence of the results of each stage of the evaluation process. Rather than speculate as to how large organisations, such as Transport Plc, position themselves in terms of their preconceptions of their need, it seemed more relevant to follow the timeline of an actual selection process, from which it is possible to draw conclusions. This would not be possible without observations and access to the materials and individuals involved in the process, and results in a study grounded in the real world environment. Each participant was given the option to opt out of the research entirely but in each case quite the opposite was found to be the case, with each participant volunteering their documentation and opinions where confidentiality allowed. Interviews were open and friendly with no one declining to be interviewed. Perhaps this may be due in part to the successful outcome of the project; no participant feeling that they needed to defend their decisions. Nevertheless, to respect the privacy of individuals, the case of the research participants has been anonymised.

Case study: Transport Plc

Transport Plc operates as a natural gas transport company across Belgium, and as such is responsible for the infrastructure and control systems required for transporting gas at pressure from a number of suppliers to their customers via a network of pipelines and storage installations. It has over 800 employees and a balance sheet total of €2 billion. Its gas infrastructure comprises some 3730 km of pipeline and has 14 connection points to neighbouring countries and sea ports.

Transport Plc suffered in 2004 from a significant accident at one of the large installations on its gas network, resulting in the tragic loss of lives. During the investigation carried out by the government in conjunction with Transport Plc's own accident investigators, one area of concern cited was the lack of connectivity between the gas installation's control panel, which displays the current status of all gas pressures being measured at various points around the installation, and the contact management software. As the gas pressure at one point dropped to a critical level an alarm sounded, but the guard on duty needed to go to a different terminal in order to bring up the emergency contact list and their telephone numbers. This led to an important delay which could have been avoided if more interconnected software systems had been in place. In response to this event Transport Plc's senior IT personnel to board level carried out a thorough review of its gas network's guard management systems and emergency response procedures, then began the search for a software vendor who could work with them to improve visibility, tracking, cohesion and response. It was key to the operating procedures that the guard role management software, which is used to control which security guards are on duty and when across the entire gas network was operating as a natural extension to the gas network monitoring software.

The initial review of systems

The review of guard role management and emergency response was initiated at board level, and delegated to the Software Projects Manager at Transport Plc headquarters in

Brussels. After consultation with the Gas Flow Management Team it was decided that the current, internally developed and maintained, guard role management software was out of step with the changing requirements of the business as it was not directly integrated into the gas network monitoring software. However, rather than simply revising the specification of the existing system and carrying out alterations to the current software, the Software Projects Manager took a more holistic view of the business and decided to evaluate whether the scope of the application should be broadened. Emergency contacts and their communication details; telephone, fax, mobile, are simply one category of a broader class of object namely, contacts. The scope of the project was therefore extended to absorb the contacts in use by the commercial and business development departments of Transport Plc.

Over several years, Transport Plc have built up software applications development capability, and developers are assigned to projects for a particular department. Without the guidance of a steering group to ensure that no two pieces of software were addressing the same problem this led to silo-development, where contact management information, for example, was being held in more than one database in the organisation. The resulting problems from silo-development included, but were not limited to:

- Duplicated software effort.
- Different object definitions, for example one team may store a contact's name, address and telephone number, the other might include these but also fax and e-mail. No two data definitions will be identical, resulting in data reconciliation problems later.
- Duplicated data storage.
- Unnecessary hardware procurement for database and application servers.
- Mismatched data, where the telephone number for a given contact may be different in one system than in another, making the information unreliable.

In order to address this fragmentation and consolidate the information across their contact management systems, the Software Projects Manager decided to invite additional departments, specifically the Commercial and Business Development departments in to talk about their requirements. As a result, it was decided to broaden the scope of the new software system to include contact management as a whole, rather than just contact management for guards and emergency services.

The introduction of the steering committee

Assigning a project of this scope to a single responsible individual was considered too risky by the IT Director of the Transport Plc organisation because (s)he may not be equipped to consider the full implications of a new software system across the entire organisation at all levels. To mitigate this risk, a steering committee was assigned to the project, and the Software Projects Manager presents their progress to the steering committee on a regular basis. This allowed for some regulation of the project life cycle by a range of interested parties. In all, 10 people from across the organisation were assigned to the steering committee as shown in Table 6.2.

Table 6.2 The steering committee

Actor	Role
IT Director	Responsible for chairing the steering committee meetings and a key decision-maker on the direction of the project based on input from the other team members.
Principle IT Systems Architect	Responsible for ensuring that any chosen software system fits with the IT infrastructure, procedures and policies.
Software Projects Manager	Responsible for day-to-day management of the project reporting to the steering committee.
Representatives of the Gas Flow Management Team	Responsible for ensuring that the needs of those employees directly involved in the management of the gas network are represented in the steering meetings.
Representatives of the Commercial Team	Responsible for ensuring that the needs of those employees who manage existing customers and suppliers of gas are represented in the steering meetings.
Representatives of the Business Development Team	Responsible for ensuring that the needs of those employees who seek new contracts or develop existing lines of business are represented in the steering meetings.

The requirements specification process

The first task of the steering committee, having decided to proceed with broadening the scope of the new software application, was to decide how best to gather requirements. Assigning an internal person to the task was fraught with political sensitivities and potential personal bias as (s)he would undoubtedly be drawn from a department which would otherwise be neutrally represented in the steering committee, so the decision was made by the director of IT to look for an independent software development house, with a proven track record of requirements specification and successful project delivery. Unisoft, a Belgian software consultancy and development organisation based near Brussels Airport, had been involved with software projects at Transport Plc in the past and had been responsible for the specification and implementation of the Transport Plc intranet, an extensive content management project delivered in three languages to 800 users across Belgium. As Unisoft had no experience of contact management or any off-the-shelf offerings in this area, it was also felt by the steering committee that it was unlikely to try and influence the requirements with its own preferences, capabilities or technologies as its implementation preferences in the past had been aligned more with the outgoing system's implementation than any potential new system. Unisoft was employed by the steering committee to begin the requirements-gathering process in the summer of 2004.

While the requirements gathering and use-case analysis was being carried out, it was deemed important to start to investigate potential software providers, with experience not only of CRM and contact management, but also, importantly, with experience of the other primary requirement: emergency incident management. In this task Transport Plc's steering committee chose to consider both custom and packaged software suppliers rather than restrict itself to one or the other. Even with only the broad requirements known, the steering committee felt that it had defined the scope enough for an initial shortlist to be drawn up of potential suppliers.

The shortlisting process

In order to accelerate the project's progress, the steering committee asked Unisoft to remain focused on the requirements gathering and use-case scenario development, and subcontract out the search for potential suppliers. Transport Plc had previously worked with a Belgian business performance specialist company called HallConsult who also provide technical consultancy. The steering committee decided that a parallel path would be to ask HallConsult to begin the search for software vendors with security guard management and contact management experience. The consultant assigned began with a two-pronged approach, firstly through a series of searches of the Internet, and secondly through contacting organisations who operated in similar markets to Transport Plc, to ask if they had already sourced similar systems and, if so, who from. This first pass resulted in a list of 38 potential suppliers. Each of the suppliers was then contacted and asked to supply detailed information on their products and capabilities. This information was summarised into a table and presented to the Transport Plc steering committee along with recommendations for a shortlist of just six companies, who would then be invited in to give a demonstration. An excerpt from the shortlist evaluation spreadsheet they produced is shown in Table 6.3. Real company names are not shown.

Table 6.3 Excerpt of shortlisting evaluation criteria

Vendor	Comments on the application	Reason for withdrawal
Simply Safety Ltd.	Package for managing people, training and safety.	Developed for small- to medium-sized enterprises. No European experience. Probably poor customisation possibilities.
SecureTime Ltd.	Focused on security guard scheduling, payroll and billing.	Too focused on scheduling. No incident management or sufficient contact management detail.

In addition to a simple product-fit evaluation, a Dunn and Bradstreet report was requested for each shortlisted company to evaluate their accounts. The stability and long-term viability of the supplier was felt by the Director of IT to be important if they were to provide ongoing maintenance and support of a business-critical application with more than 180 users across the country. With this in mind, during the later evaluations, the smaller vendors were asked if they would consider placing the source code with an independent party in case their company failed, or whether they would consider being subcontractor to a main contractor.

The vendor demonstrations

The first draft of the use cases and requirements specification became available 48 hours prior to the demonstrations and was delivered electronically to the shortlisted companies. Each of the companies was then invited to the Unisoft offices in Brussels to present their products and/or capability to a panel consisting of project representatives from Transport Plc, UniSoft and HallConsult. The shortlist was focused on the suppliers of custom and packaged products which roughly met the anticipated requirements. However, product fit varied, and reservations were expressed in a few cases as to whether certain product/supplier combinations were going to be flexible enough to meet the requirements. On receipt of the requirements it soon became evident to the suppliers that they requested a specific database layout of tables and fields, far removed from the fields in use by products such as ACT! or Microsoft Outlook. It was realised by custom suppliers that this limitation on the structure of the underlying database was likely to cause problems for suppliers of most packaged products because their solutions were based on tables and fields which were felt to be quite rigid. The team knew that minor configuration changes and add-ins were normally acceptable, but that fundamental underlying schema changes were unlikely to be accommodated without significant development effort. Thus, primarily due to the database restrictions, the requirements favoured companies who were custom providers. Two packaged software suppliers, on receipt of the draft requirements, backed out and explained that they could not address the requirements with their products. Moreover, the team reported that, during the demonstrations, packaged software suppliers came across

Table 6.4 Details of the vendors and products

Vendor	Summary of outcome

Respond BV (Package)	■ Application not selected
	  – No XP support
	  – No integrated reporting engine
	  – Difficult to add custom functionality

SCI (Custom)	■ Application not selected
	  – No support for Oracle
	  – Poor security model
	  – Dated user interface design
	  – Doubtful extensibility

PDR (Custom)	■ Application not selected
	  – Significant redundancy in terms of irrelevant features
	  – No support for Oracle

Cabis (Custom)	■ Application selected
	  – Open extensible design
	  – Modern user interface
	  – Built-in reporting engine

as inflexible, whereas the custom developers had time to develop new database schemas and overlay their technologies on top to produce convincing, if early, prototypes which closely matched the intent of the specification if not all of the functionality. It was to one of these solution providers that the contract was awarded (see Table 6.4).

Conclusion

It is important to note that although this case ends with a piece of custom-developed software being selected, up to the demonstration point, three package and three custom applications were being simultaneously evaluated using the same processes. Even at demonstration point, one package provider was still included in the process. This alone provides empirical evidence to support the argument that package evaluation should be located more squarely within IS evaluation thinking.

As with custom development, at Transport Plc the evaluation process begins well before typical views of the packaged software selection process would imply – after requirements gathering. Before this process is enacted, there has to be a reason for this (whether or not this is a sensible reason is another matter). In this case, a key influence was the industrial accident and the repercussions of this. This process of reasoning is very similar to the processes of alignment, prioritisation and feasibility study – the early stages of traditional IS evaluation (Willcocks and Lester, 1999). Moreover, the experimentation with packages as a form of evaluation, also closely emulates prototyping approaches in custom development. This idea is more readily achievable as 'custom' components can be trialled where custom software reuse takes place, as the vendors did in this case. Indeed, their ability to incorporate desired functionality within a very short period of time actually won one of the custom vendors the contract.

There are also similarities in respect of vendor reputation in packaged software environments. In custom development, the reputation of a particular programming language or platform may act as a surrogate for this; even software houses will fall under this banner. At Transport Plc, package and custom providers were both investigated in terms of their commercial viability and customer satisfaction. We have to remember that custom development is not always performed in-house, and thus it can also be market oriented in nature. This point shown in Natovich's (2003) case where risks associated with working with a commercial custom development provider were identified as adversarial relationships between custom vendors and those in consumer organisations and custom vendor commitment. Thus, there will still be jockeying for position in custom development environments where requirements gathering and their evaluation is politicised at the market level, as well as the organisational level, as traditionally recounted (Markus, 1983; Kling and Iacono, 1984; Markus and Bjørn-Andersen, 1987; Smithson and Hirschheim, 1998; Farbey et al., 1999; Walsham, 1999; Wilson and Howcroft, 2000; Howcroft and Light, 2006). For packages, this is really no different to custom development where various users at the organisational level deal with the development team in various ways with various outcomes (Quintas, 1994; Flynn and Davarpanah Jazi, 1998). Yet, with packaged software the stakes are higher as this negotiation is undertaken in a market environment where the user base is more diverse and diffuse. Clearly, the evaluation of packages and custom development for many of those in organisations is about 'backing the right horse' – which technology and developer is going to stand the test of time.

In terms of what is being evaluated, much of the extant packaged software literature would have us believe that requirements can be known 'up front' (see Table 6.1). However, in the case of Transport Plc we see requirements shifting over time. Again, these issues do not vary widely from those encountered for some time in custom development. For example, Flynn (1998) states that users often only have a vague notion of requirements at the beginning of a project, there may be changes in external environments and initial requirements may have unfeasible implications that are not realised until implementation. What this case also shows is that evaluation processes may get 'clouded' by various forms of commercially and non-commercially fuelled salesmanship (Friedman and Cornford, 1989), as noted by Howcroft and Light (2002). In this case we see this happening in respect of custom and packaged software products simultaneously. The successful custom vendor influenced the sale by giving the customer a taste of what they could do for them. Like custom development, package evaluation is a moving target where the 'right' product can become the 'wrong' one (and potentially vice versa), because of shifting objectives for the technology in question, and indeed as will be argued, the dependability and responsiveness of the vendor. In some cases the vendor may even influence the requirements. In the case of the study one demonstration illustrated a comprehensive audit trail; the customer immediately showed significant interest in the possibilities leading from this and embraced it as a new 'must-have' requirement. Thus, as shown at Transport Plc, package evaluation is shown to be a process not an event, as typified by traditional theories of IS evaluation (cf. Willcocks and Lester, 1999) and neglected in typical views of package evaluations. Thus, in both the case of custom and package applications, users might 'learn' through the process of evaluation and beyond. Clearly then, users will have to learn about packages, but from whom? The 'teachers' (vendors) are biased so evaluation is done within their parameters (as discussed above). Interestingly at Transport Plc, we can see this point applies to commercial custom developers too. Also those doing the evaluation might not be the most appropriate. Business managers are often cited as being the primary decision-makers in packaged software project decision-making (Hirt and Swanson, 1999; Brown and Vessey, 2001; Sawyer, 2001) and the parallel here is the longstanding call for cross-organisational user participation (and lack of this) in custom development (even though this does not necessarily lead to success (Wilson and Howcroft, 2002)).

The aim here has been to illustrate the similarities between the packaged software evaluation process and more 'traditional' custom development approaches. This has been done with the motivation of spurring the location of packaged software studies (such as those concerned with enterprise systems), more squarely within the field of IS. Underpinning this is the need to move the field of IS forward and away from 'pockets of thinking' that has lead to IS being characterised as a fragmented adhocracy. In summary then, there are many parallels between packaged software and custom development evaluation processes. Indeed, although this argument is that packaged software research has much to draw on from prior work on custom development, the reverse is also arguable.

■ References

Adam, F. and O'Doherty, P. (2000). 'Lessons from Enterprise Resource Planning implementations in Ireland – towards smaller and shorter ERP projects'. *Journal of Information Technology*, 14(4), 305–316.

August, V. (1999). 'Escape modules'. *Information Week*, 31 March, 36–38.

Bansler, J. and Havn, E. C. (1994). 'Information Systems Development with Generic Systems'. In Baets, W. R. J. (Ed.), *Proceedings of the 2nd European Conference on Information Systems*. Nijenrode University Press, Breukelen, pp. 707–715.

Banville, C. and Landry, M. (1992). 'Can the field of MIS be disciplined'. In Galliers, R. (Ed.), *Information Systems Research: Issues, Methods and Practical Guidelines*. Blackwell Scientific Publications, Oxford, pp. 61–88.

Brehm, L., Heinzl, A., and Markus, M. L. (2001). 'Tailoring ERP Systems: A Spectrum of Choices and their Implications'. *Proceedings of the 34th Hawaii International Conference on System Sciences*. IEEE Press, Maui, Hawaii, CD-ROM.

Brown, C. V. and Vessey, I. (2001). 'NIBCO'S "Big Bang"'. *Communications of the Association for Information Systems*, 5(1), 1–42.

Butler, J. (1999). 'Risk management skills needed in a packaged software environment'. *Information Systems Management*, 16(3), 15–20.

Carmel, E. (1997). 'American hegemony in packaged software trade and the "culture of software"'. *The Information Society*, 13(1), 125–142.

Chau, P. Y. K. (1994). 'Selection of packaged software in small businesses'. *European Journal of Information Systems*, 3(4), 292–302.

Chau, P. Y. K. (1995). 'Factors used in the selection of packaged software in small businesses: Views of owners and managers'. *Information and Management*, 29(2), 71–78.

Dolmetsch, R., Huber, T., Fleisch, E. and Osterle, H. (1998). *Accelerated SAP: 4 Case Studies*. IWI-HSG – Universitat St. Gallen, St. Gallen.

Esteves, J. and Pastor, J. (2001). 'Enterprise resource planning systems research: An annotated bibliography'. *Communications of the Association for Information Systems*, 7(8), 1–52.

Farbey, B., Land, F. and Targett, D. (1999). 'Moving IS evaluation forward: Learning themes and research issues'. *Journal of Strategic Information Systems*, 8, 189–207.

Flynn, D. (1998). *Information Systems Requirements: Determination and Analysis*. The McGraw-Hill Companies, London.

Flynn, D. and Davarpanah Jazi, M. (1998). 'Constructing user requirements: A social process for a social context'. *Information Systems Journal*, 8(1), 53–83.

Friedman, A. L. and Cornford, D. S. (1989). *Computer Systems Development: History, Organization and Implementation*. John Wiley and Sons Ltd., Chichester.

Gefen, D. (2002). 'Nurturing clients' trust to encourage engagement success during the customization of ERP systems'. *Omega – The International Journal of Management Science*, 30(4), 287–299.

Gremillion, L. L. (1982). 'Improving productivity with application software packages'. *Business Horizons*, 25(2), 51–54.

Gross, P. H. B. and Ginzberg, M. J. (1984). 'Barriers to the adoption of application software packages'. *Systems, Objectives, Solutions*, 4(4), 211–226.

Hecht, B. (1997). 'Choosing the right ERP software'. *Datamation*, March, 56–58.

Hirt, S. G. and Swanson, E. B. (1999). 'Adopting SAP at Siemens Power Corporation'. *Journal of Information Technology*, 14(3), 243–251.

Houghton, J. W. and Vickery, G. (2004). *Digital Delivery of Business Services*. Organisation for Economic Co-operation and Development, Paris.

Howcroft, D. and Light, B. (2002). 'A study of user involvement in packaged software selection'. In Applegate, L., Galliers, R. D. and De Gross, J. I. (Eds.), *Proceedings of the 23rd International Conference on Information Systems*. Association for Information Systems, Barcelona, Spain, pp. 69–77.

Howcroft, D. and Light, B. (2006). 'Reflections on issues of power in packaged software selection'. *Information Systems Journal*, 16(3), 215–235.

Janson, M. A. and Subramanian, A. (1995). 'Packaged software: Selection and implementation policies'. *Infor*, 34(2), 133–151.

Klaus, H., Rosemann, M. and Gable, G. G. (2000). 'What is ERP?' *Information Systems Frontiers*, 2(2), 141–162.

Kling, R. and Iacono, S. (1984). 'The control of information systems developments after implementation'. *Communications of the Association for Computing Machinery*, 27(12), 1218–1226.

KPMG (1998). *Exploiting Packaged Software*. KPMG, London.

Kunda, D. and Brooks, L. (2000). 'Identifying and classifying processes (traditional and soft factors) that support COTS component selection: A case study'. *European Journal of Information Systems*, 9(4), 226–234.

Lee, Z. and Lee, J. (2000). 'An ERP implementation case study from a knowledge transfer perspective'. *Journal of Information Technology*, 15(4), 281–288.

Light, B. (2001). 'The maintenance implications of the customization of ERP software'. *The Journal of Software Maintenance: Research and Practice*, 13(6), 415–430.

Light, B. and Holland, C. (2000). 'Enterprise Resource Planning systems: Impacts and future directions'. In Henderson, P. (Ed.), *Systems Engineering for Business Process Change: Collected Papers from the EPSRC Research Programme*. Springer, London, pp. 117–126.

Light, B. and Wagner, E. L. (2006). 'Integration in ERP environments: Rhetoric, realities and organisational possibilities'. *New Technology, Work and Employment*, 21(3), 215–228.

Lynch, R. K. (1987). 'The Impact of packaged software on user/vendor life cycle concepts'. *Journal of Information Systems Management*, 4(2), 34–40.

Markus, M. L. (1983). 'Power, politics, and MIS implementation'. *Communications of the Association for Computing Machinery*, 26(6), 430–444.

Markus, M. L. and Bjørn-Andersen, N. (1987). 'Power over users: Its exercise by system professionals'. *Communications of the Association for Computing Machinery*, 30(6), 498–504.

Markus, M. L. and Tanis, C. (2000). 'The enterprise system experience – From adoption to success'. In Zmud, R. W. (Ed.), *Framing the Domains of IT Research: Glimpsing the Future Through the Past*. Pinnaflex Educational Resources, Cincinnati, pp. 173–207.

Martin, J. and McClure, C. (1983). 'Buying software off the rack'. *Harvard Business Review*, 61(6), 32–62.

Natovich, J. (2003). 'Vendor related risks in IT development: A chronology of an outsourced project failure'. *Technology Analysis and Strategic Management*, 15(4), 409–419.

Nelson, P., Richmond, W. and Seidmann, A. (1996). 'Two dimensions of software acquisition'. *Communications of the Association for Computing Machinery*, 39(7), 29–35.

OECD (2002). *OECD Information Technology Outlook (Highlights)*. OECD, Paris.

Oliver, D. and Romm, C. (2000). 'ERP systems: The route to adoption'. In Chung, H. M. (Ed.), *Proceedings of the 6th Americas Conference on Information Systems*. Association for Information Systems, Long Beach, USA, pp. 1039–1044.

Quintas, P. (1994). 'Programmed innovation? Trajectories of change in software development'. *Information Technology and People*, 7(1), 25–47.

Ross, J. W. (1999). 'Dow Corning Corporation: Business processes and information technology'. *Journal of Information Technology*, 14(3), 253–266.

Sawyer, S. (2001). 'A market-based perspective on information systems development'. *Communications of the Association for Computing Machinery*, 44(11), 97–102.

Scott, J. E. and Kaindl, L. (2000). 'Enhancing functionality in an enterprise software package'. *Information and Management*, 37(3), 111–122.

Scott, J. E. and Vessey, I. (2000). 'Implementing Enterprise Resource Planning systems: The role of learning from failure'. *Information Systems Frontiers*, 2(2), 213–232.

Sharland, R. (1991). *Package Evaluation: A Practical Guide to Selecting Application and Systems Software*. Avebury Technical, Aldershot.

Sieber, T., Siau, K., Nah, F. and Sieber, M. (2000). 'SAP implementation at the University of Nebraska'. *Journal of Information Technology Cases and Applications*, 2(1), 41–72.

Smithson, S. and Hirschheim, R. (1998). 'Analysing information systems evaluation: Another look at an old problem'. *European Journal of Information Systems*, 7(3), 158–174.

Stefanou, C. J. (2001). 'A framework for the ex-ante evaluation of ERP software'. *European Journal of Information Systems*, 10(4), 204–215.

Trauth, E. M. and Cole, E. (1992). 'The organizational interface: A method for supporting end users of packaged software'. *Management Information Systems Quarterly*, 16(1), 35–53.

Walsham, G. (1995). 'Interpretive case studies in IS research: Nature and method'. *European Journal of Information Systems*, 4(2), 74–81.

Walsham, G. (1999). 'Interpretive evaluation design for information systems'. In Wills, K. and Lester, S. (Eds.), *Beyond the IT Productivity Paradox*. John Wiley and Sons Ltd., Chichester, pp. 363–380.

Weing, R. P. (1984). 'Finding the right software package'. *Journal of Information Systems Management*, 8(3), 63–70.

Welke, L. A. (1981). 'Buying software'. In Cotterman, W. W., Enger, N. L. and Harold, F. (Eds.), *Systems Analysis and Design: A Foundation for the 1980s. An Invitational Conference and Workshop*. North Holland, Atlanta, pp. 400–416.

Westrup, C. (2002). 'Discourse, management fashions and ERP systems'. In Wynn, E. H., Whitley, E. A., Myers, M. D. and De Gross, J. I. (Eds.), *Global and Organisational Discourse about Information Technology*. Kluwer Academic Publishers, Boston, pp. 401–418.

Willcocks, L. and Lester, S. (1999). 'In search of information technology productivity: Assessment issues'. In Willcocks, L. and Lester, S. (Eds.), *Beyond the IT Productivity Paradox*. John Wiley and Sons Ltd., Chichester.

Wilson, M. and Howcroft, D. (2000). 'The politics of IS evaluation: A social shaping perspective'. In Orlikowski, W. J., Ang, S., Weill, P., Kramar, H. C. and DeGross, J. I. (Eds.), *Proceedings of 21st International Conference on Information Systems*. Associated for Information Systems, Atlanta, Brisbane, pp. 94–103.

Wilson, M. and Howcroft, D. (2002). 'Re-conceptualising failure: Social shaping meets IS research'. *European Journal of Information Systems*, 11(4), 236–250.

Chapter 7

Post-implementation evaluation of IT systems: A close review of practice

H. Al-Yaseen, T. Eldabi, R. J. Paul and R. El-Haddadeh

■ Introduction

Information technology (IT) investment within the UK and other countries continues to grow at an accelerating pace. This is particularly fuelled by the ever increasing reliance by businesses on IT. Consequently the issue of IT evaluation is increasingly a concern for all decision-makers. IT share of investment is taking up a large proportion of organisational spending while – since the early 1990s – justification of such investments has become a major issue for decision-makers (Farbey et al., 1993). Justifying expenditure on IT is a long standing problem, and managers for the past few decades have expressed concerns about the value they are getting from IT investments; moreover they have been searching for ways to evaluate and justify the use of IT. 'Many conduct cost–benefit evaluation on projects, but most of them have an element of fiction. The saddest part is that it is not just the benefits that are fictional, but the costs are as well' (Farbey et al., 1993). Such a continuous increase in investment coupled with continuous need for justification presents a challenge to the information systems (IS) community.

Many authors agree that evaluation of investment is a key issue for such IT projects and their management (Kumar, 1990; Dabrowska and Cornford, 2001; Irani et al., 2002). Investment justification and evaluation of effectiveness is traditionally – within fields other than IT – a complex process. However, analysts usually manage to get an answer which they can feel confident as a valid representation of the real value. But in IT confidence in measures has never reached a level similar to traditional products. Many organisations report that they are uncertain about how to measure the impact and the outcomes of their IT investments. This is mainly attributable to the fact that IT returns-on-investment are mostly intangible which makes it difficult to measure using traditional accounting practice.

IT evaluation has been a widely explored issue in order to resolve the above issues and in search of reliable measurement drivers. Most of the theoretical literature in IT evaluation;

such as Bradford and Florin (2003); Gunasekaran et al. (2001); Lin and Pervan (2003); Liu et al. (2003); Remenyi et al. (2000) and Irani and Love (2002) tend to depart from the traditional accounting-based evaluation methods by appreciating the intangible aspects of IT benefits as well as the tangible ones. Authors are more inclined to view evaluation as part of the planning activity only or, in some cases, as part of the development process. There are also a number of empirical studies – such as those reviewed by Ballantine et al. (1996) – which examined *ex ante* evaluation, yet only a few (e.g. Kumar (1990) and to some extent Beynon-Davies et al. (2004)) that have explored the *ex post* evaluation.

Generally speaking, most empirical and theoretical articles (with very few exceptions) tend to classify IT evaluation as a planning activity or take a temporal view along the development life cycle only to stop short of the operational phase. Although a number of the above authors have touched upon this phase, evaluation activities are still not represented as integral parts of the evaluation process. The extent to which organisations adopt rigorous evaluation at the operational phase is unknown.

In this chapter, the aim is to explore the evaluation process by extending the temporal view – with more concentration on the operational phase – in order to understand issues related to IT evaluation after project completion. The following section starts by taking a temporal view of the process of IT evaluation. This is then used as the platform for defining the main research problem tackled in this chapter. The next section draws the theoretical basis for the research which is based on two phases for collecting information from major companies regarding their approaches and processes for IT evaluation. The section after that synthesises the findings from the two phases and discusses the results. In the final section the lessons learned from this research are presented.

Temporal view of evaluation of IT investment

The stance is taken that evaluation is a process that takes place at different points in time, or continuously, explicitly searching for (quantitatively or qualitatively) the impact of IT projects (Al-Yaseen et al., 2006). This definition recognises the different stages in the full life cycle of an IS in which evaluation is performed, and provides the opportunity to discriminate between two decidedly different views of the evaluation process, each serving different aims.

The first view of evaluation is as a means to gain direction in the IS project. Here, 'predictive' evaluation is performed to forecast the impact of the project. Using financial and other quantitative estimates, the evaluation process provides support and justification for the investment through the forecasting of projected baseline indicators such as payback, net present value (NPV) or internal rate of return (IRR) (Farbey et al., 1993; Liu et al., 2003; Yeo and Qiu, 2003). It is known variously as '*ex ante*' evaluation (Remenyi et al., 2000), 'formative' evaluation (Brown and Kiernan, 2001), or as referred to here, 'prior operational use' (POU) evaluation. This form of evaluation guides the project, and may lead to changes in the way the system is structured and carried out. It does not however give any feedback beyond the design, implementation and delivery of the project outcomes.

In contrast, evaluation can also be considered in terms of the effectiveness of the IT system *in situ* – what a system actually accomplishes in relation to its stated goals (Eldabi et al., 2003;

Al-Yaseen et al., 2006). This form of evaluation draws on real rather than projected data, and can be used to justify adoption (Love and Irani, 2001; Irani, 2002); estimates the direct cost of the system; estimates the tangible benefits of the system (Liu et al., 2003); ensures that the system meets requirements (Irani, 2002); measures the system effectiveness and efficiency (Poon and Wagner, 2001); measures the quality of programs and estimates indirect costs and other costs (Love and Irani, 2001) or to measure the quality of programs (Eldabi et al., 2003). This type of evaluation should be performed during the operational phase of the project. This is referred to as 'post-implementation' evaluation (PIE). Figure 7.1 shows these forms of evaluation with respect to the life cycle from a system's inception to the end of its useful life.

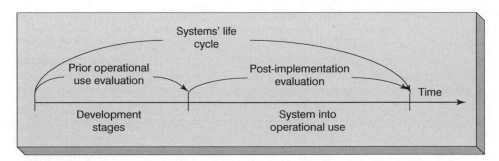

Figure 7.1   IS/IT evaluation types in the systems' life cycle

The problem and the research opportunity

Most of the current research on IT evaluation has focused on the early stages of development. In contrast, only rarely has PIE evaluation been studied. The most recent and comprehensive empirical study in this category was conducted by Kumar (1990). The main problem is that there is no body of knowledge in the area to help improve the techniques used in evaluation at this stage, which causes decision-makers to refrain from employing it altogether. This is the motivation for researching practitioners' perceptions of the evaluation process and the practices associated with the evaluation adopted within large organisations. So in this chapter an attempt is made to obtain insights into PIE in order to identify the real extent to which PIE is practised and what lessons could be learned to improve knowledge about it. To do that the following questions need to be answered:

- What is the balance between POU and PIE?
- Who are the stakeholder groups involved in conducting PIE?
- What are the main reasons for adopting each of the evaluation types?
- What criteria are currently being used for evaluating IT investment in each type of evaluation?

Research approach

This chapter follows a phased approach to the empirical study – namely two phases. By using different sources and methods at various points throughout the research, the team can build on the strength of each type of data collection and minimise the weaknesses of any single approach. A multi-method approach to evaluation research can increase both the validity and reliability of evaluation data. The validity of results can be strengthened by using more than one method to study the same phenomenon. The main purpose of the second phase is to capture the remaining issues that were missed in the first phase (Tashakkori and Teddlie, 2003).

The typology of the research purpose can be categorised into two main groups. Firstly, add to the knowledge base: to review the current state of practice of IT evaluation process and its types (prior implementation and post-implementation evaluation) in business organisations. Secondly, understand complex phenomena: to explain and understand the findings of this research to gain a comprehensive picture of IT evaluation.

The first phase of the research requires a certain type of data to be gathered to answer the research questions (e.g. how prevalent are POU and OU (operational use) evaluations of IT). This kind of research question needs a high rate of respondents in order to generalise the finding. According to Tashakkori and Teddlie (2003), a quantitative research implemented by questionnaire is the most appropriate method of research for the first part of the research purpose (add to the knowledge base) typology.

The second phase of the research is an in-depth data generation process where evidence of research findings that can be used to explain and understand the phenomena (e.g. how organisations carry out evaluation of their IT systems). According to Tashakkori and Teddlie (2003), a qualitative research implemented through in-depth interviews can answer the second part of the research purpose (understand complex phenomena where there are soft human and organisational interactions).

For the purpose of this research a questionnaire will be used as the mechanism for data capture. However, to support the findings and explore further complexities it was decided to follow it up with a set of structured interviews. *Phase one* (questionnaire) contains four stages: designing and testing the questionnaire; followed by data collection and then data analysis; and finally the preliminary findings of the questionnaire. *Phase two* (structured interviews) also contains four stages: designing a multi-site study; data collection followed by data analysis from the different organisations. Finally, the results and the conclusions from phase two will be integrated and synthesised with the results from phase one. The following two sections describe in more detail phase one and two, respectively, including results and initial analysis.

Phase one (questionnaire)

There are two main purposes for this part of the research: firstly, to review and document the current state of practice of the two types of evaluation: POU evaluation and PIE in order to better understand what is required for the evaluation process and its associated benefits; secondly, to collect information about how organisations carry out the evaluation process. In doing so this phase attempts to answer specific questions, such as: How prevalent is PIE? Who is involved in it? What criteria are being used? What methods are currently being used for it? What are its main benefits and uses? And what are the most important barriers to adopting it? The following section describes the processes of questionnaire design, deployment and analysis used, and summarises the participant characteristics.

Stages of phase one

Stage one of phase one reviews both types of evaluations (POU and PIE). The main issues identified in the literature were used to develop a questionnaire that focuses on how organisations carry out evaluation of their IT systems. The main components of the questionnaire are as follows: organisational background (general information about the organisation under investigation), IT infrastructure information, IT business information, POU evaluation (feasibility, development, implementation and testing stage), PIE stage of IT and the last stage of the questionnaire was other information related to the latter phase.

In *stage two*, the questionnaire was sent to the top 500 organisations in the UK (based on the FTSE 500). Table 7.1 shows the distribution of the different organisations approached. The final number of usable responses was 123, giving a response rate of 24.6%. This rate was considered to be above expectation given that the generally accepted average response to non-incentive-based questionnaires is around 20%.

Table 7.1 Organisations in the sample

Organisation	Percentage
Financial services	19
Manufacturing	15
Information technology	14
Retail/wholesaling	9
Computer manufacturing	7
Central government	6
Consultancy	6
Transport	5
Publishing	3
Others	16

In *stage three*, the data from the responses to the questionnaire was analyzed using a combination of the parametric statistical methods, descriptive analysis and factor analysis (Pett et al., 2003). Each of these variables (POU (codename: POUeR); PIE (codename: OUeR) and the PIE criteria (codename: OUeC)) were measured using a five-point Likert scales (1 = *not important* and 5 = *very important*). Factor analysis technique was employed in order to identify possible categories following Berthold and Hand (2003):

1 A matrix of correlation coefficients for all possible pairings of the variables was generated.
2 Factors were then extracted from the correlation matrix using principal factors analysis.
3 The factors were rotated to maximise the relationships between the variables and some of the factors and minimise association with others using Varimax Kaiser Normalisation,

which maintained independence among the mathematical factors. The Eigenvalues determined which factors remained in the analysis. Following Kaiser's criterion, factors with an Eigenvalue of less than 1 were excluded. A screen plot provides a graphic image of the Eigenvalue for each component extracted (see Figures 7.2 and 7.3).

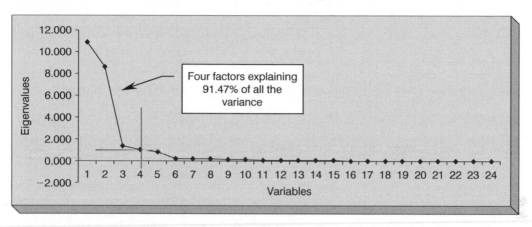

Figure 7.2   Eigenvalue of the reasons for adopting POU evaluation

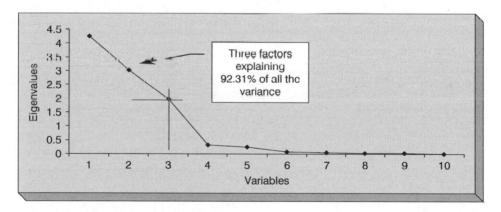

Figure 7.3   Eigenvalue of the reasons for adopting PIE

Data analysis and preliminary findings

This section presents aggregated results from direct answers to the research questions mentioned above. The basic issues considered here are: reasons for adopting either types of evaluation, criteria for evaluations, reasons for comparisons between the two types and reasons for any gaps.

Reasons for adopting POU evaluation

Using a factor analysis cut-off level of 0.5, four factors were considered the main reasons of adopting POU evaluation (explaining 91.47% of the variance – see Figure 7.2), which is defined as 'system completion and justification', 'system costs', 'system benefits' and 'other reasons'.

The first factor 'system completion and justification' is highly correlated with ten variables, the second factor 'system costs' is highly correlated with ten variables and the third factor 'system benefits' are highly correlated with three factors, whilst the fourth factor 'other reasons' is highly correlated with one variable barrier for adopting the system which was also found to be the least evaluated reason in practice.

Reasons for adopting PIE

Three factors were considered as the main reasons of adopting PIE (explaining 92.31% of the variance – see Figure 7.3), which we call 'system costs', 'system benefits' and 'other reasons'.

PIE criteria

PIE criteria were resulted in four factors explaining 87.03% of the variance (Figure 7.4), which are termed 'system completion', 'system information', 'system impact' and 'other criteria'. The first factor 'system completion' is highly correlated to seven criteria, the second factor 'system information' is highly correlated to five criteria, the third factor 'system impact' is highly correlated to four criteria while 'other criteria' is correlated to one criterion – net operating costs, which was also found to be the least evaluated criteria in practice.

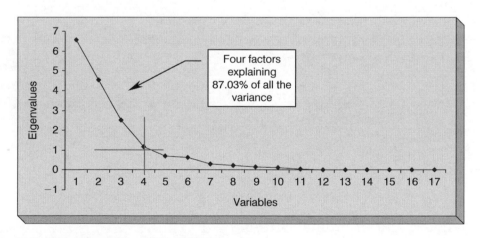

Figure 7.4   Eigenvalue of OU evaluation criteria

Reasons for adopting a comparison between PIE and POU evaluation

Most of the organisations (77.7%) that carried out a formal PIE conducted it in comparison with the outcomes of POU evaluation, and found that there was an important 'gap' or inconsistency between the evaluations. This gap comprised three major dimensions – gaps in estimating the systems' economic lifespan, cost and benefits.

The two most important reasons were to check that the planned benefits were achieved and to compare planned and actual costs. The least two important reasons for the comparison were to record lessons for the future and to improve the evaluation process for future systems.

Findings from phase one

All of the responding organisations have and do carry out formal POU evaluation, but only about a third (36.5%) currently perform a formal PIE. This means that about two-thirds (63.5%) of the organisations do not gather any evidence to establish how successful their IT projects were, therefore cannot use such information from PIE to improve their evaluation techniques. The most popular reasons for adopting PIE were related to formal aspects of signing off the project (based around traditional measures such as meeting requirements, and achieving agreed metrics for effectiveness, usage, efficiency, security, performance, etc.), and system costs. Two factors – systems' benefits and adoption barriers – were found to be less important. On the other hand, amongst the 45 organisations, the most frequent reason for adopting PIE was to do with systems' benefits (both tangible and intangible). Most of the sampled organisations attach greater importance to the measurement of benefits rather than the measurement of costs. The most frequently cited criterion for PIE was system information (accuracy of information, timeliness and currency of information, adequacy of information and quality of programs). System cost was found to be an important reason for adopting PIE (system cost includes: operational cost, training cost, maintenance cost, upgrade cost, reduction in other staff cost, reduction in salaries and other expenses saved).

Results suggest that most decision-makers do not place much importance on PIE of their IT systems. Most managers tend to think of it only as a formality rather than a proper evaluation process. It can be postulated that such a perception plays an important role in hindering the adoption of PIE. Results also provide evidence that PIE is useful if it is perceived as more than just a formality. For example, among the 45 who considered adopting PIE, those companies who undertake it seriously tend to gain considerable benefits, including the validation of their original POU evolutional estimates. But more importantly PIE helps those organisations to better appreciate and capture the intangible benefits associated with IT. Evidently, if IT evaluation is starting to capture the benefit side more than the cost side, then PIE – given the above results – should play an important role in gauging such benefits.

■ Phase two (structured interviews)

Findings of phase one gave some insight into the *proportion* of organisations that adopt PIE and for *what* purposes. The aim of phase two is to explore in further detail within those organisation that carry out PIE, *why* and *how* such organisations go about it in order to better understand what is required for the evaluation process. In doing so there is an attempt to answer specific questions: Who is involved in evaluation process? What criteria are being used for PIE? What are the main benefits and uses of PIE? What are the most important barriers hindering the adopting PIE? This phase will also attempt to elucidate the gap between the outcomes of POU evaluation and PIE and its causes.

Based on the findings from the previous phase it was evident that not many organisations conduct PIE. In fact some of the organisations do not know much about it. This has led to the assumption that there is no standard code of practice or a generalised set of rules for conducting PIE. For this reason it was decided to conduct in-depth interviews with fewer companies to capture more focused information about how these organisations conduct PIE. In order to avoid inconsistencies for highly structured interviews were adopted to provide answers to a set of common questions from the participating organisations.

Phase two: Data collection and analysis

A number of issues were considered and analyzed when designing this study, such as: organisation background (general information); IT infrastructure information; IT business information; POU evaluation (feasibility, development, implementation, testing evaluation of IT); PIE and other information related to PIE. The following two sub-sections provide an overview of the data collection and analysis of phase two which was conducted within the three companies.

Data collection

In this phase a series of structured interviews were conducted with IT system developers, user managers, IT systems department managers, internal audit department and external audit team, all of these participants have been directly involved in PIE as well as through the IT system development process, therefore it was considered important to select a cross-section of roles in PIE to obtain the views of participants at different levels within the organisation. The availability of interviewees was a problem during the study, since they were busy and therefore, there was limited time for interviews. One benefit of conducting structured interviews was to enable participants to provide succinct answers.

The data capture process was based on presenting each of the participants within the three companies with a list of criteria, which were commonly mentioned in IS literature as candidates for the evaluation process. These criteria were divided into separate categories in relation to each of the questions mentioned at the beginning for this section (namely: reasons for adopting PIE, what criteria were used and reasons for adopting POU evaluation). Participants were then asked to indicate the frequency and importance of these criteria as they perceived them. A 10-point scale ranging from 'not important (0)' to 'very important (9)' was used to determine the extent to which these criteria were being evaluated in practice.

Data analysis

Each interview started with questions relating to the role of individuals, background of the organisation and general facts about the IT system; these questions were open ended, as the aim was to obtain as much information as possible that might support our research. In addition to the above, new technologies were used, such as online databases and the Internet. Having multiple sources helped to confirm reliability of data, and furthermore, to successfully confirm the results and thus overcome most concerns while giving greater support to the conclusions. The following discussion provides brief descriptions of three companies used in phase two coupled with findings from the interviews conducted in these companies. The results are aggregated and presented in table format in descending order.

Company one: Abank.   For the purpose of this research 'Abank' will be used to refer to the organisation being studied. Abank is a multinational organisation that mainly operates in the financial services sector. It has 62 000 employees in 30 countries and has an annual net income of £444 000 000. Abank was established in 1930, as a public shareholding company. It is a leading international financial institution in terms of equity, earnings and assets. It is engaged in providing a wide variety of financial services, which include corporate, retail banking, private banking, trade financing, commercial real estate lending and other banking services. Abank has 400 subsidiaries and affiliated companies. Each of the subsidiary companies has its own IT infrastructure, every region has a main IT department, and it has one main IT department which organises and manages all sub-companies world wide. Results of the interviews are given in Tables 7.2–7.5.

Table 7.2 Reasons for adopting POU evaluation in Abank

Reasons	Rank (0–9)	Reasons	Rank (0–9)
Justify adoption	9	Maintenance costs	7
System effectiveness	9	Operational costs	7
System efficiency	9	Other costs	7
System meets requirements	9	Other expenses saved	7
System performance	9	Quality of programs	7
Tangible benefits	9	Other benefits	6
Direct costs	8	Quality of documentation	6
Indirect costs	8	Reduction in clerical salaries	6
System security	8	Reduction in other staff costs	6
System usage	8	Training costs	6
Hardware performance	7	Upgrade costs	6
Intangible benefits	7	Barriers of adopting the system	4

Table 7.3 OU evaluation criteria in Abank

Factors	Rank (0–9)	Factors	Rank (0–9)
System's impacts on users	9	User friendliness of system–user interface	7
System's fit with organisation	9	Timeliness of information	7
Performance vs. specifications	9	Security and disaster protection	7
Quality of programs	9	Quality documentation	7
Project schedule compliance	9	Net operating costs	7
Internal control	9	Appropriateness of information	7
Accuracy of information	9	Adequacy of information	7
User satisfaction and attitude	8	Hardware performance	6
System usage	8		

■ **Table 7.4** Reasons for adopting OU evaluation in Abank

Factors	Rank (0–9)
Tangible benefits	9
Justify system adoption	9
Other benefits	8
Indirect costs	8
Estimating of system life	8
Direct costs	8
Other costs	7
Risks	6
Barriers	6
Intangible benefits	5

■ **Table 7.5** Reasons for the gap in OU evaluation in Abank

Reasons	Rank (0–9)
Changing of the market's requirements	9
Changing of users' requirements	8
The lack of agreement on evaluation criteria	8
The lack of an appropriate evaluation method	7
Availability of qualified evaluator	6
Intangible benefits of the system	6
Changing of system's requirements	5
Indirect costs of the system	5
Operational costs of the system	4
Maintenance costs of the system	3

Company two: ArOil company. For the purpose of this research 'ArOil' will be used to refer to the organisation being studied. ArOil was established in 1937, as a public shareholding company. ArOil is a multinational organisation that produces oil for refining, supply or export. ArOil employs 54 000 employees. ArOil has 158 subsidiary companies in many countries. Similar to the above company, each of these companies has its own IT infrastructure, every region has a main IT department, furthermore, it has one main IT department that organises and manages IT in all of the subsidiary companies. Results of the interviews are given in Tables 7.6–7.9.

Company three: Agrco company. 'Agrco' will be used to refer to the organisation being studied. Agrco was established in 1971, as a public shareholding company. Agrco is a general investment organisation with operating divisions in tropical agriculture, trading and manufacturing, with a turnover of around £41 600 000. The major activities are landscaping and irrigation works and projects; gardening (construction and maintenance); farm management

Table 7.6 Reasons for adopting POU evaluation in ArOil

Reasons	Rank (0–9)	Reasons	Rank (0–9)
Tangible benefits	9	Hardware performance	7
System performance	9	Direct costs	7
System meets requirements	9	Reduction in clerical salaries	6
System efficiency	9	Quality of documentation	6
System effectiveness	9	Other benefits	6
System usage	8	Barriers of adopting the system	6
System security	8	Upgrade costs	5
Justify adoption	8	Operational costs	5
Indirect costs	8	Maintenance costs	5
Quality of programs	7	Reduction in other staff costs	4
Other costs	7	Other expenses saved	3
Intangible benefits	7	Training costs	2

Table 7.7 OU evaluation criteria in ArOil

Factors	Rank (0–9)
System's impacts on users and their jobs	9
System performance vs. specifications	9
Quality of programs	9
System's fit with the impact upon organisation	8
System usage	8
Project schedule compliance	8
Internal control	8
Appropriateness of information	8
Timeliness and currency of information	7
System security and disaster protection	7
Adequacy of information	7
User satisfaction and attitude towards system	6
User friendliness of system–user interface	6
Quality and completeness of system documentation	6
Net operating costs (saving of system)	6
Hardware performance	6
Accuracy of information	6

and consulting service; distribution of all agricultural products (seeds, fertilizers, soil, pesticides, garden tools, plants, farm supplies); veterinary clinics (treatment of animals, vaccines, surgery, special pet boarding facilities for vacationers); pest control and global trading (exporters of agricultural products i.e. dates, vegetables, fodder and landscaping plant materials to many countries in the world). Results of the interviews are given in Tables 7.10–7.13.

Table 7.8 Reasons for adopting OU evaluation in ArOil

Reasons	Rank (0–9)
Justify system adoption	9
Intangible benefits	9
Other benefits	8
Estimating of system life	8
Tangible benefits	7
Risks	7
Barriers	7
Indirect costs	6
Direct costs	6
Other costs	5

Table 7.9 Reasons for the gap in OU evaluation in ArOil

Reasons	Rank (0–9)
Changing of the market's requirements	8
The lack of agreement on evaluation criteria	7
Changing of users' requirements	7
The lack of an appropriate evaluation method	6
Availability of qualified evaluator	6
Intangible benefits of the system	5
Changing of system's requirements	5
Operational costs of the system	4
Indirect costs of the system	4
Maintenance costs of the system	2

Findings from phase two

Findings from phase two indicate that participating organisations are currently performing POU evaluation of their systems. The most frequent reasons for adopting POU evaluation include: to justify adoption of the system, system performance measure and estimating the systems' benefits. However, systems' cost factor was found to be less important than was expected. Both the IT department and project team are usually the main drivers in performing POU evaluation; also, they determine the evaluation criteria and the evaluation method, which is similar to the findings from the qualitative part. According to the participants, most of the evaluation is performed and managed by the system developers; who have control in determining evaluation criteria and evaluation method. Findings also confirmed that participating organisations are currently performing a formal PIE of their systems. Usually these organisations perform PIE just after the system becoming operational (6–9 months). The most frequent reason for adopting PIE included: justify system adoption, estimating systems' benefits and estimating systems' cost.

Table 7.10 Reasons for adopting POU evaluation in Agrco

Reasons	Rank (0–9)	Reasons	Rank (0–9)
Tangible benefits	9	Other benefits	7
System meets requirements	9	Operational costs	7
Justify adoption	9	Maintenance costs	7
Direct costs	9	Hardware performance	7
System performance	8	Reduction in clerical salaries	6
System efficiency	8	Quality of documentation	6
System effectiveness	8	Other expenses saved	6
Upgrade costs	7	Intangible benefits	6
Training costs	7	Indirect costs	6
System usage	7	Barriers to adoption	6
Quality of programs	7	System security	5
Other costs	7	Reduction in staff costs	5

Table 7.11 OU evaluation criteria (factors) in Agrco

Factors	Rank (0–9)
System's impacts on users and their jobs	8
System performance vs. specifications	8
Quality of programs	8
System's fit with the impact upon organisation	7
System usage	7
Project schedule compliance	7
Internal control	7
Appropriateness of information	7
Timeliness and currency of information	6
System security and disaster protection	6
Adequacy of information	6
User satisfaction and attitude towards system	5
User friendliness of system–user interface	5
Quality and completeness of system documentation	5
Net operating costs (saving of system)	5
Hardware performance	5
Accuracy of information	5

It can also be concluded that IT departments and project teams are the major participants in PIE. Barriers that are most likely to inhibit PIE were found to be the lack of agreement on evaluation criteria, the lack of an appropriate evaluation method, quantifying intangible benefits and availability of qualified evaluator; availability of users to spend time on evaluation activities; evaluation costs too much and is too difficult.

■ **Table 7.12** Reasons for adopting OU evaluation in Agrco

Factors	Rank (0–9)
Tangible benefits	9
Justify system adoption	9
Direct costs	9
Other costs	8
Other benefits	8
Indirect costs	8
Estimating of system life	8
Intangible benefits	7
Risks	6
Barriers	6

■ **Table 7.13** Reasons for the gap in OU evaluation in Agrco

Reasons	Rank (0–9)
Operational costs of the system	7
Intangible benefits of the system	7
Indirect costs of the system	7
Changing of the markets requirements	7
The lack of an appropriate evaluation method	6
The lack of agreement on evaluation criteria	6
Maintenance costs of the system	6
Changing of user's requirements	6
Availability of qualified evaluator	6
Changing of system's requirements	4

It is evident that the lack of structured evaluation methods is the most important reason for any gaps between POU and PIE results. Other reasons were found to be: the lack of an appropriate evaluation method, the lack of agreement on evaluation criteria, the stakeholders who involved in the evaluation process and changing of (users and systems) requirements, were found to be the main reasons for the gap between the expected performance and the observed performance of the system.

From the above discussion, there are many limitations in POU evaluation and PIE techniques. Furthermore, it may not be surprising to discover a gap between the outcomes of POU evaluation and the outcomes of PIE in both the questionnaire and the interviews. The lack of structured evaluation model was the most important reason for the gap between the estimated performance and the observed performance of the systems in the case studies.

Synthesis of findings from phase one and two

So far in this chapter several factors have been identified that affect the evaluation process, such as: timing of evaluation types; stakeholders and their role in the evaluation process; evaluation criteria; and the gap between POU evaluation and PIE outcomes. This section attempts to synthesise the findings of both phases to help provide a better understanding of the prevalence of PIE, who is involved in both evaluations and their respective uses as perceived by practitioners.

Prevalence of PIE

The results of the research indicated that all the participating organisations have carried out a formal POU evaluation, but that only 36.5% currently perform a formal PIE of their IT systems. That suggests only 36.5% of the participating organisations justified their investment in IT and if their IT systems achieved the anticipated benefits. There is a clear indication that PIE is not as prevalent as POU evaluation. What is also evident is that there is no consensus amongst practitioners about the use and necessity of PIE. Findings from both phases suggest that those organisations that adopt PIE are split, in terms of justification, between formal signing off the project and appreciation of lessons learned. Unfortunately, those who follow the latter justification seem in the minority.

Stakeholders involved

Results from phase one indicate that the main stakeholder groups, who are involved in the evaluation process are: IT department, project team, internal audit and external audits, while customer and user departments are sometimes involved in the evaluation process. In terms of determining the evaluation method and the evaluation criteria, questionnaire results indicate that (customer and user departments) are never involved in determining the evaluation method and/or the evaluation criteria. Furthermore, results suggest that one of the reasons for the gap between the estimated outcomes and the actual outcomes is the continuous change of requirements; hence, it may be not surprising to discover a gap between the expected performance and the observed performance of the system.

Results from phase two indicate the main groups who are managing and organising the evaluation process: IT department and project team. Other groups (internal audit and external audit) may be involved in managing and determining evaluation method and evaluation criteria depending on the systems' size, while user and customer departments are involved in the evaluation process and determining the evaluation criteria. These findings were also supported by findings from phase one.

It was evident from both phases that the same people who designed and developed the systems also managed the evaluation process, and for this reason, it is unlikely that an evaluation which is managed and performed by the developers will discover any fault in the systems' design. If users and customers are the main stakeholders who use the system when it becomes operational, it is necessary for them to be involved in the evaluation process.

Uses and benefits of PIE

Findings from phase two show that the seven most important uses of adopting PIE, in the order of importance, are justify adoption, continuity, termination of installed system, verification of whether new system meets system requirements, report on system effectiveness to management, transfer of responsibility from developers to users, and evaluation and refinement of system controls. The five least important uses are to provide feedback for modification to development methods, clarify and set priorities for necessary modifications to new system, to provide feedback to system development personnel, to provide feedback for modification to project management methods and verification of economic payoff of system.

Overall, results seem to suggest that most decision-makers do not place much importance on PIE. This may be due to the fact that most managers tend to think of it only as a formality rather than a proper evaluation process. It can be postulated that such a perception plays an important role in hindering the adoption of PIE. Results also provide evidence that PIE is useful if it is perceived as more than just a formality. For example, organisations that consider adopting PIE and seriously perform it tend to gain considerable benefits, including the validation of their original POU evaluation estimates. But more importantly PIE helps those organisations to better appreciate and capture intangible benefits associated with IT. Evidently, if IT evaluation is starting to capture the benefit side more than the cost side, then PIE – given the above results – should play an important role in gauging such benefits.

Conclusions

The main aim of this research was to understand the whole picture about PIE in contrast to POU evaluation as practiced within today's organisations in order to understand the obstacles hindering the full implementation of PIE and its potential benefits. In a survey (phase one) of the FTSE 500 companies we found out that around two-thirds of the 123 respondent organisations gave less importance to the PIE than POU evaluation. Of those organisations who did use PIE, some thought of it as a completion formality for signing off the project. Further findings from the research (phase two) suggest that within a structured approach, PIE could be more beneficial to organisations when acquiring new systems. This matches the expectation that whatever is learned from current evaluation ought to be useful when evaluating new systems. Currently there is no agreement concerning the timing of the evaluation types POU and PIE. Also there is a lack of agreement on the evaluation criteria (What is being evaluated?).

Having considered the results from both phases that companies appear to perform PIE as a formality rather than to reflect on (and improve) the appreciation of benefits. It is suggested that the reason for this is that while the potential benefits of engaging with a process of PIE exists, the organisational structure within which it must operate does not generally cater for it. A clear contrast between PIE and POU evaluation is evident when considering modern project management approaches such as PRINCE2, which usually incorporates frequent cycles of POU evaluation (OGC, 2002) as a fundamental component of the method. The fixed time horizon inherent in project-based work can be the precursor to a considerable organisational omission in full project evaluation. This omission occurs because no interest group is charged with assessing the value of the IT project over its entire life cycle (from inception to decommissioning) which would therefore include PIE. In other words, project completion is taken to mean exactly that – so evaluation ceases when the system becomes operational because the self-contained and budgeted project has then ended. After completion there is nothing else to do.

A further finding that can be attributed to this study is that when organisations carry out both types of evaluation the deviation from original estimates became a focal point for further analysis. This research shows that the reasons for adopting the OU–POU comparison were to enable the auditing of the planned benefits and to learn lessons appropriate for future projects. The results, regarding obstacles to PIE, were found to be mutually supported by the study by Owens and Beynon-Davies (1999) on mission-critical systems. Currently, only organisations who perform *serious* PIE understand the benefits of it. And there are not many of these, so very little analysis exists on planned costs and actual costs (or benefits).

To conclude the findings, it is clear that the practitioners do not appreciate the full benefits of PIE and need to be aware of such benefits. Such lack of appreciation is evidently behind the apparent scarcity of implementation of PIE, which negatively feeds back into perceptions and so forth.

References

Al-Yaseen, H., Eldabi, T., Lees, D. Y. and Paul, R. J. (2006). 'Empirical post-implementation evaluation of IT investment appraisals: Prior operational use and operational use'. *European Journal of Operational Research*, 173, 1000–1011.

Ballantine, J. A., Galliers, R. D. and Stray, S. J. (1996). 'Information systems/technology evaluation practices: Evidence from UK organizations'. *Journal of Information Technology*, 11, 129–141.

Berthold, M. and Hand, D. J. (2003). *Intelligent Data Analysis*, 2nd ed. Springer-Verlag, Berlin.

Beynon-Davies, P., Owens, I. and Williams, M. D. (2004). 'Information systems evaluation and the information systems development process'. *Enterprise Information Management*, 17, 276–282.

Bradford, M. and Florin, J. (2003). 'Examining the role of innovation diffusion factors on the implementation success of enterprise resources planning systems'. *International Journal of Accounting Information systems*, 4, 205–225.

Brown, J. L. and Kiernan, N. E. (2001). 'Assessing the subsequent effect of a formative evaluation on a program'. *Journal of Evaluation and Program Planning*, 24, 129–143.

Dabrowska, E. K. and Cornford, T. (2001). 'Evaluation and Telehealth – An Interpretative Study'. *Proceedings of the 34th Annual Hawaii International Conference on System Sciences (HICSS)-34*. January 2001, Maui, Hawaii, Computer Society Press of the IEEE. Piscataway, NJ (CD-ROM) p. 10,.

Eldabi, T., Paul, R. J. and Sbeih, H. (2003). Operational use evaluation/post implementation evaluation of IT, UKAIS, Warwick.

Farbey, B., Land, F. and Targett, D. (1993). *How to Assess Your IT Investment: A Study of Methods and Practice*. Butterworth-Heinemann, London.

Gunasekaran, A., Love, P. E. D., Rahimi, F. and Miele, R. (2001). 'A model for investment justification in information technology projects'. *International Journal of Information and Management*, 21, 349–364.

Irani, Z. (2002). 'Information systems evaluation: Navigating through the problem domain'. *International Journal of Information and Management*, 22, 11–24.

Irani, Z. and Love, P. E. D. (2002). 'Developing a frame of reference for ex-ante IT/IS investment evaluation'. *European Journal of Information Systems*, 11, 74–82.

Irani, Z., Sharif, A., Love, P. E. D. and Kahraman, C. (2002). 'Applying concepts of fuzzy cognitive mapping to model: The IT/IS investment evaluation process'. *International Journal of Production Economics*, 75, 199–211.

Kumar, K. (1990). 'Post implementation evaluation of computer information systems: Current practices'. *Communications of the Association for Computer Machinery (ACM)*, 33, 203–212.

Lin, C. and Pervan, G. (2003). 'The practice of IS/IT benefits management in large Australian organizations'. *International Journal of Information and Management*, 41, 13–24.

Liu, Y., Yu, F., Su, S. Y. W. and Lam, H. (2003). 'A cost–benefit evaluation server for decision support in e-business'. *Journal of Decision Support Systems*, 36, 81–97.

Love, P. E. D. and Irani, Z. (2001). 'Evaluation of IT costs in construction'. *Journal of Automation in Construction*, 10, 649–658.

OGC (2002). *Managing Successful Projects with PRINCE2*. Office of Government Commerce, London.

Owens, I. and Beynon-Davies, P. (1999). 'The Post Implementation Evaluation of Mission-Critical Information Systems and Organisational Learning'. *Proceedings of the 7th European Conference of Information Systems*. Copenhagen Business School, Copenhagen, 806–813.

Pett, M. A., Lackey, N. R. and Sullivan, J. J. (2003). *Making Sense of Factor Analysis*. Sage Publications, Thousand Oaks, CA.

Poon, P. and Wagner, C. (2001). 'Critical success factors revisited: Success and failure cases of information systems for senior executives'. *Journal of Decision Support Systems*, 30, 393–418.

Remenyi, D., Money, A., Sherwood-Smith, M. and Irani, Z. (2000). *The Effective Management and Management of IT Costs and Benefits*. Butterworth-Heinemann, London.

Tashakkori, A. and Teddlie, C. (2003). *Mixed Methods in the Social and Behavioural Sciences*. Sage Publications, Thousands Oaks, CA.

Yeo, K. T. and Qiu, F. (2003). 'The value of management flexibility – A real option approach to investment evaluation'. *International Journal of Project Management*, 21, 243–250.

Chapter 8 ■■■

■
■ Evaluation of information service
■ providers in support of the
■ fixed-income market

A. R. Montazemi, A. Esfahanipour and J. J. Siam

■ Introduction

Information systems' (IS) acceptance and use is an issue that has attracted the attention of the researchers and practitioners. With the increasing investment in IS, the evaluation of these systems is becoming an important issue for optimal information technology governance. Information systems that are not used are of little value. Therefore, it is important to find out why end-users elect to use or not use an information system when they have a choice. This enables developers to assess why end-users avoid existing IS and to ameliorate the possible problems towards enhanced system usage. To this end, usefulness and ease of use as determinants of acceptance, based on the technology acceptance model (Davis, 1989; Davis et al., 1989), are considered to be the major determinants of system usage through the mediating variables of attitude and intention (Venkatesh, 2000).

According to social exchange theory (SET), human behaviour is the product of a rational cost–benefit analysis. When confronted with a behaviour-related decision, individuals assess the various costs and benefits associated with different possible courses of action and then choose the most beneficial behaviour based on the expected costs and outcomes of each (Kelley and Thibaut, 1978). End-user attitudes are formed on the basis of their beliefs (Fishbein and Ajzen, 1975). In their attitude formation, end-users holding the beliefs that a system is both important and personally relevant are therefore likely to develop a positive attitude concerning the system. To this end, the objective of this chapter is to evaluate three different information systems. These information systems, considered global information service providers to fixed income (FI) market actors, are: Bloomberg, Reuters and Action Economics. The question raised in this chapter is: How valuable are these three systems to FI market actors? To this end, the functionality of each system is compared and contrasted to highlight their advantages/disadvantages towards usage.

Fixed-income market environment

A fixed-income security is defined as one whose income stream is fixed for the duration of the loan and where the maturity and face value are known. It is estimated that the global fixed-income market is about $45 trillion with the US having the lion's share of $19 trillion. Unlike equities that are traded on exchanges and are subject to the exchange rules, fixed-income securities trade over the counter. The term 'over the counter' (OTC) stems from the traditional method of selling securities literally over the counter before the establishment of exchanges. Fixed-income securities did not go via the exchange and continued to be an OTC operation.

In a typical fixed-income market there are four major players: securities issuers, dealers, inter-dealers brokers and investors. Fixed-income securities are issued by the borrower (governments or corporations) and purchased by a dealer or a group of dealers for resale. The dealers are the brokerage houses and the banks known in market parlance as the 'sell side'. A typical fixed-income transaction involves a considerable sum of capital and is mainly oriented towards institutional investors who constitute more than 80% of the market. Institutional investors are professional money managers who invest for third parties such as insurance companies, mutual funds, pension funds and deposit-taking institutions. These are referred to as the 'buy side'.

The supply of new fixed-income products comes from borrowers known as issuers. This is accomplished through the primary market, where borrowers issue paper (e.g. bonds) to raise funds. Dealers assist issuers with design, marketing and sale of the new securities. Dealers form a 'banking syndicate' consisting of a number of dealers and bankers whose job is to value the new issue, buy it and sell it to investors. The process is known as underwriting. Actual trading takes place in the secondary market. Secondary markets list and trade primary issues once they are sold. Market quotes (benchmark prices) to the fixed-income market are provided through information vendors such as Reuters and Bloomberg who are connected electronically to dealers' market. Investors (buy side) are usually blind to the 'real' and 'live' market and the prices (quotes) provided to them serve as a benchmark and are the first step in a process that may lead to a trade. The 'real' or 'live' dealers' markets are normally given over the phone and represent a binding commitment by the dealer either to buy or sell.

Need for information and knowledge

FI security trading is an ill-structured decision problem, where prices are not determined by auction but by bargaining among sellers–buyers. Information is critical to profitable trade in the FI market (Moulton et al., 1998; Chakraborty and Yilmaz, 2004) that include type of securities and their issuers, general market conditions, economic events and the analytic models used to analyze the profit margin of particular securities. FI market actors have access to a wealth of private and public information (Montazemi and Siam, 2005). Private information is communicated by phone/squawk box and e-mail between FI actors within each firm as well as outside contacts (e.g. market-makers, portfolio managers and sales reps). Public information is provided through media such as alternative trading systems

(ATSs such as TradeWeb, CBID), Bloomberg, Reuters and boutique research services (e.g. Action Economics, Gartman Letter). Figure 8.1 depicts an overview of the information flow in the sell side.

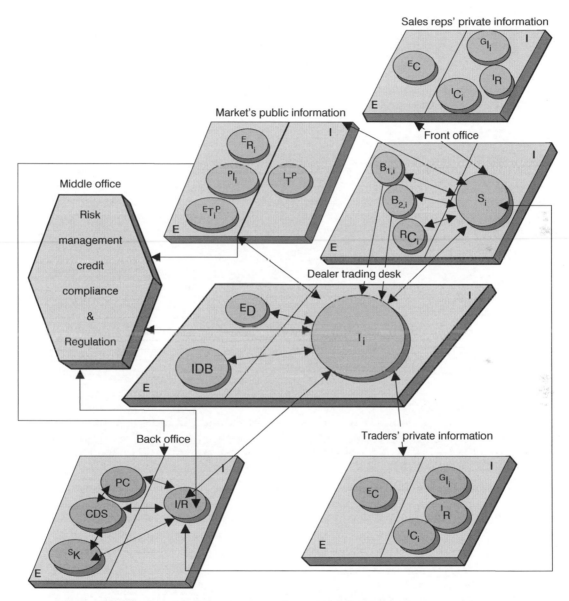

■ **Figure 8.1**   Information flow and network ties among actors in sell-side FI market (I stand for internal and E for external; see Table 8.1 for details). Adopted from Montazemi and Siam (2006)

The question arises as to the significance of different information sources in support of different stages of FI actors' decision-making processes (i.e. information categories). Information categories consist of three parts: (1) quoted benchmark price, (2) info/news release and (3) market research. Traders post the price of their products on ATSs, Bloomberg

Table 8.1 Legend for Figure 8.1

Description	Internal	External
Sales Office (front office)	S_i: Fixed-income sales force, including the retail sales force (sales/traders)	$B_{1,i}$: Large buy-side institutional firms $B_{2,i}$: Small buy-side institutional firms ^RC_i: Retail clients
Dealer trading desk	T_i: Sell-side market-makers or traders, including the senior trader/manager (VP trading)	IDB_i: Inter-dealers brokers ^ED_i: Other dealers C_i: Contacts
Sales reps' and traders' private information	^IR: Internal research ^IC_i: Internal contacts ^GI_i: Internal news, order flow and market intelligence	^EC_i: External contacts
Market's public information	$^IT^P$: Proprietary automated trading platform	^PI_i: Public information from vendors ^ER_i: External research boutiques $^ET_i^P$: External automated trading platforms
Clearing and settlement (back office)	I/R: Inventory	CDS: Canadian depository for securities ^SK: Sell-side custodian PC: Private clearing firm
Middle office	Risk management and trade policy credit compliance regulations	

and Reuters (i.e. quoted market price) that can be viewed by the buy-side portfolio managers. Albeit, for large and/or liquid products (e.g. corporate bonds), a more favourable price can be negotiated between buy side and sell side (i.e. traders and portfolio managers) through phone/squawk box. Pricing a bond is a complex task. There are more than 170 variables that can affect a bond price (Esfahanipour et al., 2007). Therefore, info/news release information category pertains to this notion that, access to the state of these variables at will is of utmost importance to the FI actors. Furthermore, market research related to these variables as well as commentary of the specialists regarding political and social events adds value to the traders/portfolio managers' decision processes towards a profitable trade.

Explicit knowledge sources used by the actors in the FI market

Actors in the FI market pursue information for decision-making as a result of the desire to reduce the uncertainty for optimal profitable transactions. The decision as to what kind of information will aid in reducing uncertainty, where to look for information and what the information is worth are made under uncertainty. One rarely knows in advance what kind of information one will find, what the quality of that information will be and to what extent it will actually reduce uncertainty. Some prior indication of the information may be available, such as quotation benchmark price of bonds through TradeWeb. However, such indications are partial, may be biased, and may not provide a true representation of the full information available. All of this stems from the fact that information is an experience, the value of which is revealed only after consumption. Therefore, actors in the FI market use a variety of information sources aiming to complete deals at the best prices and at low cost, with minimum delay or maximum discretion that affect trading decisions.

We can categorise FI market variables into two major groups as fundamental variables and market microstructure dynamics, depicted in Figure 8.2. Fundamental analysis is a method of evaluating a security by attempting to measure its intrinsic value by examining related macroeconomic, financial and other qualitative and quantitative factors. In the case of the bond market, macroeconomic analysis is relevant to analysis of international and domestic macroeconomic news that could be applied for evaluation of all types of bonds such as governmental, provincial, municipal and corporate bonds. Regional/industry analysis relates to economic events in each region and could be used for provincial, municipal and corporate bonds while company analysis is more relevant to corporate bonds. Therefore, fundamental variables have been categorised as macroeconomic, regional and corporate levels as depicted in Figure 8.2.

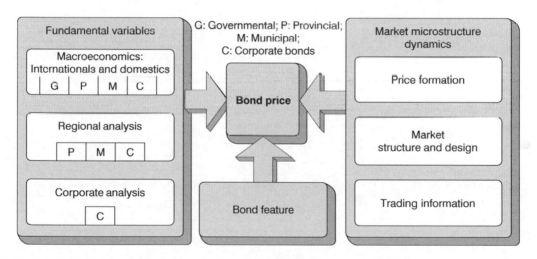

Figure 8.2   Structure of variables affecting bond price (Esfahanipour et al., 2007)

Madhavan (2000) published a comprehensive literature survey on market microstructure with a special focus on informational issues relating to four major areas: (1) price formation and price discovery, including both static issues such as the determinants of trading costs and dynamic issues such the process by which prices come to impound information over time, (2) market structure and design, including the effect of trading protocols on various dimensions of market quality, (3) market transparency (i.e. the ability of market participants to observe information about the trading process) and (4) interface of market microstructure with other areas of finance including asset pricing, international finance and corporate finance (see Figure 8.3).

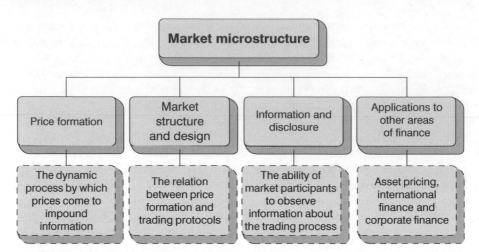

■ **Figure 8.3** Classification of market microstructure studies based on Madhavan (2000)

Macroeconomic variables can be grouped as inflation expectation and economic activity (see Figure 8.4). Market actors follow these variables to decide on the bond pricing. Therefore, any changes in macroeconomic variables can have an influence on the bond market.

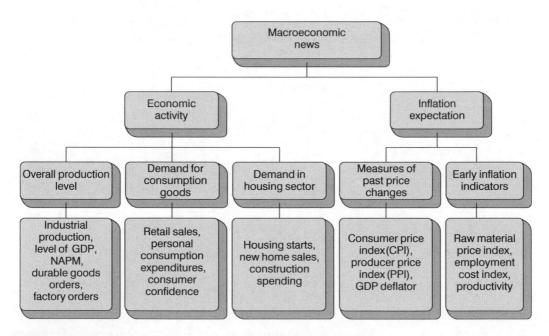

■ **Figure 8.4** Classification of macroeconomic news based on Hess (2004)

Our interest here is to investigate the value of information sources to actors in the FI market for pre-trade that may lead to an execution of trade and post-trade to assess the quality of their previous transactions. To this end, 44 traders and sales reps from seven major sell-side firms were asked to assess the significance of different information sources for each category for pricing a bond, using a nine-point Likert-type scale. Tables 8.2 and 8.3 depict

Table 8.2 Ranking of cluster of pre-trade information sources used by sell side in the FI market

Information category	Cluster of information source	Cluster ranking
Quoted benchmark price	Bloomberg (without e-mail)	1
	Other ATS	
	Phone	
	E-mail/instant message	2
	Reuters	
	TradeWeb	
	CBID	
Info/news release	Bloomberg (without e-mail)	1
	Reuters	2
	Newspapers	
	Government publications	3
	TV	
	research boutiques	
Market research	Internal research	1
	External contacts	2
	Bloomberg (without e-mail)	
	research boutiques	3
	Brokerage research	
	Reuters	

Table 8.3 Ranking of cluster of post-trade information sources used by sell side in the FI market

Information category	Cluster of information source	Cluster ranking
Quoted benchmark price	Bloomberg (without e-mail)	1
	Phone	
	Other ATS	2
	E-mail/instant message	
	TradeWeb	
	Reuters	
	CBID	

clusters of importance of different types of information sources in regard to 'quoted bench-mark price', 'info/news release' and 'market research'. Degree of importance ranking of each of these information sources is based on the statistical cluster analysis of data collected from traders/sales reps. These findings signify the fact that sell-side actors use a variety of information sources in support of their decision processes. Each information source provides a variety of data that are updated routinely, sometimes by seconds (e.g. quoted price in a volatile market). The most important source of information for FI market actors comes from their contacts in the business. This is mainly done by phone/squawk box.

Three information sources that are predominately accessible electronically to all the FI actors are Bloomberg, Reuters and research boutiques. Others, such as ATSs (e.g. TradeWeb), are used by a small number of the actors (about 10% of the FI transactions, see Montazemi and Siam, 2006). The question arises as to why Bloomberg is ranked higher than Reuters and research boutiques. What is it that Bloomberg offers that others don't? After all, Reuters has been in the market much longer than others. To this end, the director of IT at a major financial organisation was asked to reflect on this question. This is what he had to say:

> 'Reuters seems to have avoided investing on new developments for the past ten years in the FI market. Initially, Bloomberg was a new kid on the block. Bloomberg used to be called 'a glorified email system'. You had to have Reuters on your desk if you were in FI market. However, Bloomberg kept spending millions in developing their analytics, portfolio evaluation systems, data warehouse, and a nice user-friendly interface. In contrast, Reuter did little upgrades to its systems. Bloomberg kept attracting new clients and Reuters lost its clients. As of this year, we have pulled off Reuters from our bond sales desk completely. We only use Bloomberg instead.'

The aforementioned comments and our statistical analysis of the traders/sales reps show that end-users perceive Bloomberg to be more useful than other information providers. Next, a detailed analysis is provided of Bloomberg, Reuters and Action Economics (a research boutique) information systems to better understand the capabilities of each system in support of actors in the FI market. These analyses reveal how Bloomberg is better able to satisfy the information needs of the FI actors than Reuters and Action Economics.

Human computer interaction

In this section, the FI information providers based on a human computer interaction (HCI) framework is examined. HCI attempts to understand the way people interact with computers in terms of the processes they engage in, the resources they use and the task that they intend to accomplish. Thus, HCI should be designed to achieve a fit between the human (user), computer and task, and it should do so within a given context.

HCI can be examined as a multilayered activity: user activity that is conceptually viewed at multiple and distinct levels of interaction. Here, we adopt a framework called TSSL model with four levels of interaction as follows (Te'eni et al., 2006):

- Task level pertains to the information requirements that have to be met. It relates to the user's goals most closely.
- Semantic level pertains to the set of objects and operations through which the computer becomes meaningful to the user. It relates to the user's world of meaning but also to the information system's logical structure.

- Syntax level dictates the rules of combining the semantic objects and operations into correct instructions. This level directs the user how to manipulate the computer system.
- Lexical level describes the way specific computer devices are used to implement the syntactic level.

According to the above framework, four levels of interaction within the context of FI information providers are as follows.

Task level

FI actors need information in support of their decision-making processes. Three main information categories used by FI actors are as follows: quoted benchmark price, info/news release and market research. Due to a large volume of quantitative data, analysis is used to gain better insight to the problem at hand. These analyses are technical analysis, portfolio strategy analysis and benchmarking, among others.

Semantic level

The semantic level of FI information providers includes information-related operations such as retrieval of desired information at the right time in an appropriate format, as the main focus of the task level is to provide related information to the users. Other required operations are ability to search, compare, sort and organise information based on different criteria such as date, activity sectors, bond characteristics and economic indicators.

Syntax level

FI actors are dealing with different types of information format in support of the semantic level of interaction including numeric information that is mostly organised in table format, a collection of texts for news and commentaries, and different types of charts for visualisation of trends and changes in the numeric information. FI actors may need to follow a sequence of instructions to perform the required analysis. These are the syntax level of interactions between FI actors and information systems.

Lexical level

To implement the syntax level, some user interface features are used at the lexical level such as top-down menus, tree menu, tabbed forms, links to pages, list selection, top-down and/ or left-right navigations, command buttons and keystrokes.

The TSSL model is applied here as a conceptual framework to a selected sample of interfaces of the three FI market information service providers to assess their ease of use and usefulness. To this end, the first step is to identify a specific task to be accomplished, followed by the required semantics, syntactic and lexical levels of interaction.

Action Economics

The sample interface of Action Economics selected for this analysis is related to extracting information about the Canadian CPI (see Figure 8.5). Please note that the sample user interfaces depicted in Figures 8.5–8.8 are not in their original colour due to typesetting. Instead the are shown in shades of gray. The task level, in this case, is straightforward – the user's goal is to assess the state of the Canadian CPI as an economic indicator and to assess its variation relative to the historical data. The interface also provides other CPI-related information such as overall CPI, core CPI, CPI components, past trend of CPI, commentary remarks and CPI estimation. The semantic level of this user interface relates to information-related operations and access to the historical CPI report. The syntax level of this interface focuses on different ways of representing information such as: (a) charts to visualise the changes in CPI on an annual and monthly basis, (b) a table to display overall, core and componential CPI and their changes over the time periods and (c) textual commentary remarks.

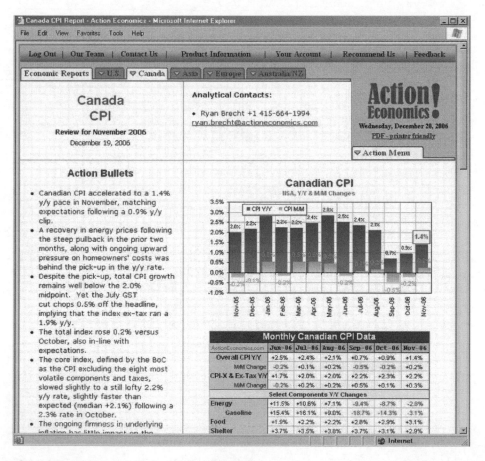

■ **Figure 8.5**   A sample user interface of Action Economics

The lexical level includes mouse-clicks of a sequence of top-down menus as follows: Action Menu -> Economic Report -> Canada -> CPI. The final page, containing information about Canadian CPI, highlights the menus selection in different colours (i.e. light gray menus against dark gray menus). The title of the page also shows that the current page includes information about Canadian CPI. Therefore, the user doesn't need to memorise the selected menus through this lexical feature. Top-down navigation of the screen is also available to read different parts of the interface.

The screen also displays the analyst's contact information which is useful for users who have questions and comments regarding the displayed information. Users' feedbacks can also be received through this contact. Trust in the system and its information can be increased through an efficient communication with users. This screen also provides related links to lead users to more detailed pertinent statistics as well as historical reports.

Different parts of the screen have been divided by thin lines consistent with the main colour of the system menu. For example, commentary texts are located beside the relevant chart or table which leads to ease of use. The main focus of the interface is graphical visualisation rather than text description, since the chart area is wider than the text area. This helps FI actors to extract pertinent information with ease. Use of different colours to draw charts and tables, and functionality for top-down navigation are other features that make the screen easy to read.

Reuters

Economic review screen is a sample user interface of Reuters which is selected to analyze it from an HCI point of view (see Figure 8.6). The interface provides information about an economic indicator for a specific country that the FI actor is interested in. The user can select one country and one indicator at a time to see the desired information. The task level of this

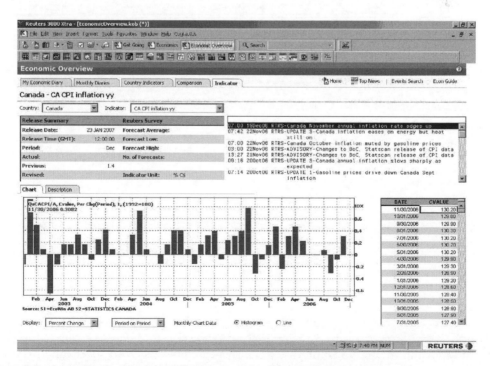

■ **Figure 8.6**   A sample user interface of Reuters for an economic indicator-chart tab

interface is to provide an economic indicator for a country (e.g. Canada in this case) along with historical values and related news about the indicator. The semantic level of the interface relates to operations such as selecting country, indicator and settings to display charts including display types of values in the chart (i.e. percent change, absolute change, absolute value), display period (i.e. period on period and year on year) and chart type (i.e. histogram, line). Although the task level of this interface and the Action Economics are almost similar, however, the two chart-related operations are not available in the Action Economics interface.

The syntax level of this interface includes numeric information for the indicator and its historical values, texts for related news as well as a customisable chart to visualise the changes of the indicator. The lexical level of the interface focuses on tabbed forms, list selection, command buttons and top-down navigations in different parts of the screen. The last lexical feature makes the screen easy to read.

The menu path is specified in this interface as Economic Overview button and Indicator tab. This helps the user to find the present screen easily for future use without memorising the menu path. The description tab of this interface (see Figure 8.7) provides the source of the indicator together with a contact to receive further information about the indicator. This tab also presents a short definition of the indicator which is useful for novice users.

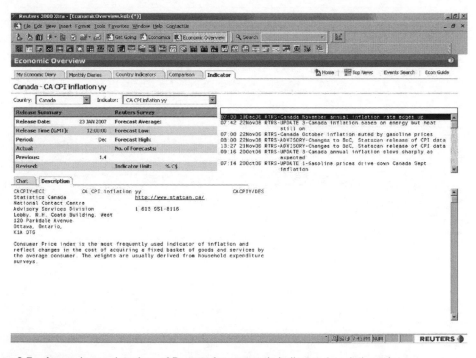

■ **Figure 8.7**   A sample user interface of Reuters for economic indicator-description tab

Bloomberg

Global economic matrix (see Figure 8.8) is a sample user interface of Bloomberg which is analyzed from an HCI point of view. This interface provides up-to-date top economic indicators on any country that the trader is interested in. This customisable worksheet can also provide special indicators. The task level of this interface relates to extracting the top economic indicator according to user's interest. The semantic level of the interface relates to indicator and country-related operations: the navigation consist of select country, select indicators and select the time period for the indicators. The syntax level is the sequence of operations that a user should do to extract economic indicators. For example, countries and indicators must be selected before retrieving desired economic indicators. Although there is a limitation of selecting only five indicators, all countries available in the system can be selected to extract economic indicators. The lexical level of this interface focuses on click-mouse and command buttons.

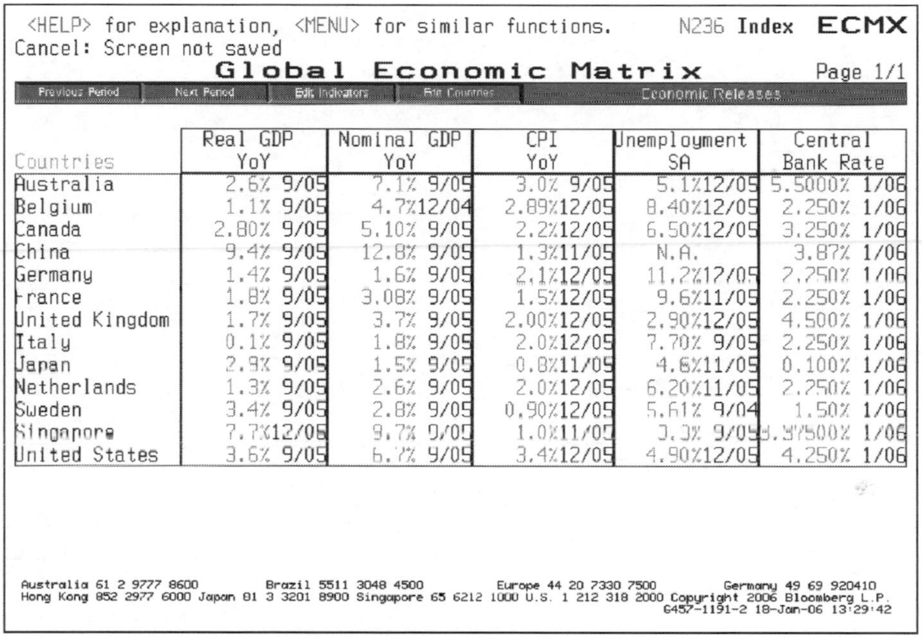

Countries	Real GDP YoY	Nominal GDP YoY	CPI YoY	Unemployment SA	Central Bank Rate
Australia	2.6% 9/05	7.1% 9/05	3.0% 9/05	5.1%12/05	5.5000% 1/06
Belgium	1.1% 9/05	4.7%12/04	2.89%12/05	8.40%12/05	2.250% 1/06
Canada	2.80% 9/05	5.10% 9/05	2.2%12/05	6.50%12/05	3.250% 1/06
China	9.4% 9/05	12.8% 9/05	1.3%11/05	N.A.	3.87% 1/06
Germany	1.4% 9/05	1.6% 9/05	2.1%12/05	11.2%12/05	2.250% 1/06
France	1.8% 9/05	3.08% 9/05	1.5%12/05	9.6%11/05	2.250% 1/06
United Kingdom	1.7% 9/05	3.7% 9/05	2.00%12/05	2.90%12/05	4.500% 1/06
Italy	0.1% 9/05	1.8% 9/05	2.0%12/05	7.70% 9/05	2.250% 1/06
Japan	2.9% 9/05	1.5% 9/05	0.8%11/05	4.6%11/05	0.100% 1/06
Netherlands	1.3% 9/05	2.6% 9/05	2.0%12/05	6.20%11/05	2.250% 1/06
Sweden	3.4% 9/05	2.8% 9/05	0.90%12/05	5.61% 9/04	1.50% 1/06
Singapore	7.7%12/05	9.7% 9/05	1.0%11/05	3.3% 9/05	3.37500% 1/06
United States	3.6% 9/05	6.7% 9/05	3.4%12/05	4.90%12/05	4.250% 1/06

Figure 8.8 A sample user interface of Bloomberg

The combination of colours has been used in a pleasant and meaningful manner where indicators' figures are displayed in yellow and dates are displayed in black (note: here they are displaced in light grey and dates are displaced in dark gray). This interface does not provide any sequence of menus – users can search the name of the screen to find it, and there is no need to memorise the path to reach the screen.

The interface provides contact information of Bloomberg offices around the world. Furthermore, Live Help is available on the screen that enables the user to chat with Bloomberg's staff to ask questions and receive answers immediately. This is a unique feature which is available only in Bloomberg.

Table 8.4 depicts a summary of this HCI analysis of the three information service providers. Comparisons of the functionality of the three systems show that Bloomberg provides better support than the other two systems.

Table 8.4 Comparison of the three FI information systems HCI capabilities

	Action Economics	Reuters	Bloomberg
Task level			
Information provided	Canadian CPI-commentary remarks	Economic indicator for one country and news	Economic indicators for different countries
Semantic level			
Customisable information	None	Can select different country, indicators and types of information in form of chart	Can select different countries and indicators, in different time period
Information format	Tables of numbers, charts and text for commentary remarks	Table of numbers, charts and text for news	Table of numbers
Syntax level			
Providing help for users	Contact information of the related analyst	Contact information for the source of information	Live Help through chat-line with Bloomberg's experts
Training needs	None	Minor	Minor
Need to memorise the menu path	None	None	There is a search option to find the desired screen
Lexical level			
Use of colours	Colourful and pleasant	Simple two colours	Different colours represent specific information
Main focus of the screen	Charts and tables	Chart	Table
Navigation	Top-down with a long screen	Top-down for different part of the screen	Use of different pages

Detailed assessment of the FI market public information providers

This section provides details of the significance of information provided to FI actors through Bloomberg, Reuters and a research boutique (Action Economics). We use the framework that consists of three well-known dimensions of information systems – time, content and form as follows.

Time dimension

Timeliness	Information should be provided when it is needed.
Currency	Information should be up to date when it is provided.
Frequency	Information should be provided as often as needed.
Time period	Information can be provided about past, present and future time period.

Content dimension

Accuracy	Information should be free from error.
Relevance	Information should be related to the information needs of a specific recipient for the specific situation.
Completeness	All of the information that is needed should be provided.
Conciseness	Only the information that is needed should be provided.
Scope	Information can have a broad or narrow scope, or an internal or external focus.
Performance	Information can reveal performance by measuring activities accomplished, progress made or resources accumulated.

Form dimension

Clarity	Information should be provided in a form that is easy to understand.
Detail	Information can be provided in detail or in summary form.
Order	Information can be arranged in a predetermined sequence.
Presentation	Information can be presented in narratives, numeric, graphic, video or animation.
Media	Information can be provided in the form of printed paper documents, video displays or other media.

Next, we use the above framework to identify attributes that are necessary to assess information systems in support of FI market actors. These attributes are as follows.

Time

- News
  - Time and date of publishing
  - Time and date of event covered
- Trades
  - Time/date of issuance
- Access to information
  - Speed of access to pages
- Speed guides (pre-set pages built for fixed income market indicators)
  - Pre-set economic models
  - Pre-set top news/stats pages

Content

- Economic matrix
  - Real GDP
  - Nominal GDP
  - Central Bank rate
  - Unemployment rate
- Yield curve analysis
  - Multiple region
  - Cross-region
  - Technical/fundamental analysis links

- Market microstructure information
  - High price
  - Low price
  - Last price
  - LIBOR
  - Cross-rates
- Treasury activities
  - Bills
  - 2–10-year notes
  - 30-year bonds
  - Curve trades (this allows traders to isolate the yield curve slope with just one trade)
- Individual market watch
  - Public finance model
  - Economic plans
  - Economic forecasts
  - Economic snapshot
  - Economic indicator releases (unemployment, inflation, currency fluctuation, etc.)
- Bond detail
  - Name of issuer
  - Date of issuance
  - Maturity of issuance
  - Price of issuance
  - Coupon rate
  - Amount outstanding
  - Book manager(s)
- Credit analysis
  - Debt ratings
  - Historic debt rating
  - Current debt rating
  - Forecasted debt rating
  - Credit spread
  - Benchmarking
- Calculation models
  - PV analysis
  - Sensitivity analysis
  - Value of bond vs. swap market
  - Price of bonds according to self-set spreads
  - Trade/hedge analysis
- Price performance
  - Graph historical prices
  - Analysis of weighted total returns
  - Correlation analysis between indices, stats and bonds
- Intelligence reports
  - Information and analytics provided beyond the normal provided to non-specialist traders

Form

- Video coverage
  - Conference calls with companies
  - Highlights of Central Banks Governors' addresses
  - Special announcement regarding the markets

- Viewing capability
  - Multiple screen capability
  - Drag-and-drop functions
  - Sizing of selected graphs/information
- Link ability
  - Excel feed function
  - Word document capability
  - PDF documents
- Ease of use
  - Search functions
  - Customisable templates
  - Save/open options
- Detail
  - In-depth news coverage
  - Links between particular events

Analysis of three modes of public information in regards to time

In this section an analysis is made of the time aspect of the three technological platforms. Table 8.5 provides definitions for each criterion that we will be looking to compare the three platforms.

Table 8.5 Criteria definition for the *time* aspect of the technological platform

Criteria	Definition
News	
Time and date of publishing	The time and date the article was written and placed on system.
Time and date of event covered	The time and date the economic indicator was updated.
Trades	
Time/date of issuance	The time and date of the last trade put through on the market.
Speed guides (pre-set pages for fixed income traders)	
Pre-set economic models	Set pages that already have all the main economic indicators listed for fixed-income traders.
Pre-set top news/stats pages	Set pages that have latest news regarding topics affecting the fixed-income markets, as well as statistics.

Bloomberg vs. Reuters

- Information provided is real time in both platforms
- Search capability
  - Bloomberg provides easier access by simple entry of query followed by the 'HELP' command
    - For example, Nikkei HELP

- Reuters doesn't provide the same level of ease of access. The query for accessing information in Reuters is longer and less efficient because the user has to open a separate search window under which filter system must be filled out
  - For example, if searching for Nikkei Index
    - click on search icon in toolbar
    - click on indices
    - type in Nikkei
    - double click on search results
- Bloomberg uses separate screens which are individually linked to all information that enable the end-user quick access to other pertinent information
  - For example, if one screen has the graph of Microsoft's equity performance then one may simply click on another monitor and enter HAL US EQUITY NEWS for updated news on the equity Halliburton. The same query in Reuters requires separate screens to be opened to create a NEWS box to extract news on Halliburton.

Action Economics

- Information is not as current as other platforms.
- There are no search functions, making it difficult to perform one's own analysis.
- Access to information is straightforward: a click on the hyperlinks provides the desired information.
- Screen switching capability is faster than Bloomberg/Reuters.

Analysis of three modes of public information in regards to content

Refer Tables 8.6 and 8.7 for the analysis of three modes of public information in regards to content.

Table 8.6 Criteria definition for the *content* aspect of the technological platforms

Criteria	Definition
Economic matrix	
Real GDP	The number reached by valuing all the productive activities within the country at a specific time of the year.
Nominal GDP	Gross domestic product not adjusted for inflation.
Central Bank rate	Interest rate set by the monetary authority of a nation.
Unemployment rate	The percentage of the population that is unemployed at a specific time interval.
Yield curve analysis (analysis of interest rates)	
Multiple region	Analysis of interest rates from different countries.
Cross-region	Analysis of interest rates between two countries.

(*Continued*)

■ **Table 8.6** (Continued)

Criteria	Definition
Technical/fundamental analysis links	*Technical analysis*: A method of evaluating securities by relying on the assumption that market data, such as charts of price, volume and open interest, can help predict future (usually short term) market trends. *Fundamental analysis*: A method of security valuation that involves examining the company's financials and operations: sales, earnings, growth potential, assets, debt, management, products and competition.
Market microstructure	
High price	The highest level the interest rate future has reached of the day and year.
Low price	The lowest level the interest rate future has reached of the day and year.
Last price	Last rate the interest rate was traded at.
LIBOR	London Inter-Bank Offer Rate. The interest rate that the banks charge each other for loans (usually in Eurodollars).
Cross-rates	Two interest rates placed against each other.
Treasury activities	
Bills	A negotiable debt obligation issued by the US government and backed by its full faith and credit, having a maturity of 1 year or less.
2–10-year notes	A negotiable debt obligation issued by the US government and backed by its full faith and credit, having a maturity of between 2 and 10 years.
30-year bonds	A registered, non-callable, non-transferable bond issued by the US Government, and backed by its full faith and credit.
Curve trades	This allows traders to isolate the yield curve slope with just one trade.
Individual market watch	
Public finance model	View all financials at the government level, such as total assets and liabilities.
Economic plans	Statements by government officials in terms of strategic outlook and decisions regarding future state of economy.
Economic forecasts	Predictions on how economy will perform.
Economic snapshot	Simple overview of how economy is performing currently.
Economic indicator releases (unemployment, inflation)	Latest statistics on economic performance of the nation.
Bond detail	
Name of issuer	Name of corporation or government who issued bond.
Date of issuance	When the bond was issued.
Maturity of issuance	Date when the bond will expire.

(*Continued*)

■ **Table 8.6** (Continued)

Criteria	Definition
Price of issuance	Price of the bond when first issued.
Coupon rate	The interest rate stated on a bond, note or other fixed-income security, expressed as a percentage of the principal (face value). Also called coupon yield.
Amount outstanding	The amount, in dollar value, that is left to be issued.
Book manager(s)	The person(s) responsible for the overall strategy and the specific buying and selling decisions for a mutual fund or other financial institution (called a money manager).
Credit analysis	
Debt ratings	A measure of the quality and safety of a bond, based on the issuer's financial condition.
Historic debt rating	Past ratings on bond.
Forecasted debt rating	Predication of future rating on bond.
Calculation models	
PV analysis	The current value of one or more future cash payments, discounted at some appropriate interest rate.
Sensitivity analysis	Investigation into how projected performance varies along with changes in the key assumptions on which the projections are based.
Value of bond vs. swap market	The simultaneous sale of one bond issue and the purchase of another, to stretch out maturities or for tax reasons.
Price of bonds according to self-set spreads	Pricing a bond according to what the trader is predicting factors of influence will be at, such as interest rates.
Trade/hedge analysis	Analysis on what returns would be when a strategy of hedging is used (an investment made in order to reduce the risk of adverse price movements in a security, by taking an offsetting position in a related security, such as an option or a short sale).
Price performance	
Graph historical prices	A graph that puts all historic and current prices in a linear fashion.
Analysis of weighted total returns	The total return on investment(s).
Correlation analysis between indices, stats and bonds	Tools to assess if certain indicators affect each other.
Delta analysis	The ratio comparing the change in the price of the underlying asset to the corresponding change in the price of a derivative.
Intelligence reports	
Information and analytics provided beyond the normal available to non-specialist traders	Information that puts traders ahead of retail traders with access to information that others do not have.

Table 8.7 Criteria checklist

	Reuters	Bloomberg	Action Economics
Economic matrix	☑	☑	☑
Yield curve analysis	☑	☑	
Interest rate futures	☑	☑	☑
Treasury activities	☑	☑	☑
Individual market watch	☑	☑	
Bond detail	☑	☑	
Credit analysis	☑	☑	
Calculation models	☑	☑	
Price performance	☑	☑	☑
Market intelligence		☑	☑

Summary of findings

The platform that seemed to serve a fixed-income trader best was Bloomberg followed by Reuters and then Action Economics. Reuters and Bloomberg serve the essential information that fixed-income traders require for their daily involvement in the markets, while Action Economics is used as a supplemental source. Action Economics provides certain intelligence reports that the other platforms do not have. Detailed analysis of the three platforms in support of the above assessment is provided next.

Reuters: positive aspects

- It has 40 analytic platforms readily available to be used by the traders for pertinent analysis of the market.
- All markets are accessible.
- Ability to customise almost all aspects of the platform regarding:
  - currency of choice,
  - market of choice,
  - time period of choice,
  - technical analysis tools of choice.
- Has the largest news source globally. Thus, it can offer timely and in-depth information. In particular, its in-depth analysis and access to the large database of past news on the topic of choice are of particular interest to the fixed-income traders.

■ The matrices, which are both pre-defined as well as customisable, provide traders with a lot of statistics that are essential in the calculation of forecasting methodology.
■ The scenario forecasting capabilities are very useful as well as detailed:
– They provide movement in the yield curve according to information inputted by trader.
– They also provide revised estimates and forecasts on the state of economic factors.
■ All calculations are shown in detail so that the trader can assess which aspects of his/her portfolio can be modified for a new result.

Reuters: negative aspects

■ There are no intelligence reports provided through this platform:
– Simply a good use for analytic information and static information.
■ There is no analysis on data that is provided:
– Raw data can be delivered from any source, but the analysis and opinions on results according to analysts and economists is what matters for traders in the fixed-income markets.

Action Economics: positive aspects

■ A very good source of market intelligence for traders.
■ Provides analysis of the large picture of the market. This is pivotal in the fixed-income markets, due to being analyzed predominantly in a top-down analytic approach.
■ Analytics that are openly available are not only provided but also analyzed to give the trader the 'So what?' aspect of data.
■ Allows the trader to read up on certain aspects of the markets in the post-market time frame:
– Conclusions and links analysts have made on quirks in market performance that the trader would not be able to come up with due to being busy trading.
– Another credible opinion on why markets went the way they did.
■ Analysts who wrote the reports are available to explain their analysis further.
■ Provides estimates on future performance of economies and fixed-income constituents.
■ Further analysis on the static data is provided:
– The 'Tail' – which exemplifies the prices traders are willing to pay on certain constituents.
– Bid to cover ratio – which allows trader to see the true demand on a constituent, thus the higher the ratio the higher the demand.
■ The auction demand breakdown is excellent for traders as a source of market intelligence. For instance, whether the buyers are speculating or are sound investors.

Action Economics: negative aspects

■ There are no calculation models for traders to verify numbers that have been provided in forecasts.
■ There are no calculation methodologies for any of the numbers provided.

- There are a minimal number of graphs, which is required in an industry where graphing is essential to analyzing the market.
- Nations are not able to be singled out, thus trader can only stick to a region unless it is the US or Canada (e.g. Asia is all under one heading, without any distinction between nations).

Bloomberg: positive aspects

- This platform provides the best of both worlds scenario (i.e. Reuters and Action Economics offerings together):
  - Provides substantial amount of statistical analysis and information which are needed by the traders.
  - Provides market intelligence that is needed to keep traders ahead in the market.
- Meets all basic requirements of fixed-income traders and goes beyond:
  - Provides statistics but allows for linking them for scenario forecasting.
  - Provides access to all markets globally with one common subscription.
- Ability to isolate markets and have all scrolling information on the market within one screen:
  - For example, you can isolate India with three separate graphs analyzing three separate fixed-income constituents, which automatically link to the scrolling news at the bottom of the page, along with key economic indicators that is required to analyze those constituents on the left-hand side of the monitor.
- Provides access to intelligence reports by the Bloomberg's in-house analysts as well as other analysts from large institutions such as Merrill Lynch, JP Morgan, Lehman Brothers and Goldman Sachs.
- Provides over 30 analytic platforms.
- Enables customisation on almost any aspect of information provided and graphs to be displayed.

Bloomberg: negative aspects

- Does not provide as many analytic platforms as Reuters.

Analysis of three modes of public information in regards to form

This section addresses the final aspect of the criteria: form of presentation. Simply put, form is the way the information is presented to the end-user as well as available functionality that allows the user to customise, download or view the information. Table 8.8 depicts the criteria used for assessing the form of presentation for the three platforms.

Reuters: positive aspects

- Has the ability to export data to Microsoft Excel.
- Has the ability to set parameters on all analytic models.

Table 8.8 Criteria definition for the *form* aspect of the technological platform

Criteria	Definition
Video coverage	
Conference calls with companies	Companies' financial directors, CEO's, inside and outside analysts, present their view on certain aspects of the market.
Highlights on Central Banks Governors' addresses	Speeches delivered regarding the monetary policy of the nations.
Special announcement regarding the markets	Any out of the calendar statements made regarding the economies.
Viewing capability	
Multiple Screen capability	Ability to view more than one screen with more than just one set of information.
Drag-and-drop functions	Ability to pull information out of one window and place it in another, such as price to graph.
Sizing of selected graphs/information	Ability to customise the size of the graph as well as the parameters it can display.
Link ability	
Excel feed function	Ability to download a matrix of information in Microsoft Excel.
PDF documents	Ability to view information provided on the screen in a PDF format for print.
Word document capability	Ability to display information on Microsoft Word.
Ease of use	
Search functions	Function that allows user to find any information on specific topics.
Customisable templates	Ability to change the view, parameters, analytics of certain screens.
Save/open options	Ability to save information on system for access at a later date.
Detail	
In-depth news coverage	Ability to provide beyond simple scrolling news.
Links between particular events	Explanation on certain background information needed in order to understand the screen that user is viewing.

- It is the only platform with drag-and-drop function.
- Enables the end-user to view as many screens required.
- Has the largest news source with historic linking capability.
- Enables the end-user to save templates.
- Enables linking between programs that Reuters offers (e.g. Reuters Bridge Station).

Reuters: negative aspects

- Doesn't have capability to create PDF documents.
- Doesn't offer video footage.
- It has limited search function.
- Is cumbersome to use, thus requires end-user training.

Action Economics: positive aspects

- Provides PDF documents for all information presented.
- It has a user-friendly interface that doesn't require any end-user training.

Action Economics: negative aspects

- It doesn't allow the end-user to save available templates.
- Information cannot be customised by the end-user.
- Doesn't allow data to be exported to Excel spreadsheet.
- Doesn't provide video coverage.
- Doesn't provide any search function.
- Doesn't provide drag-and-drop capability.
- Doesn't enable the end-user to customise analysis.

Bloomberg: positive aspects

- Provides a very user friendly interface that doesn't require any training to use.
- Provides a powerful search function that is easy to use.
- Enables simultaneous four-screen viewing ability.
- Provides video coverage on:
  - company calls,
  - analyst sessions,
  - speeches by government officials.
- Enabled to capture data with Excel spreadsheet.
- Provides an e-mail system that is secure and used by the traders and sales reps significantly.
- Enables the end-user to easily customise graphs and analytic models.
- Enables the end-user to save the information on the main screen to smaller windows to save each independently for future analysis.
- It enables historic news coverage together with background linking capability to the analysis.

Bloomberg: negative aspects

- Doesn't provide the information in a PDF format.
- Doesn't provide any drag-and-drop function.

■ References

Chakraborty, A. and Yilmaz, B. (2004). 'Manipulation in market order models'. *Journal of Financial Markets*, 7(2), 187–206.

Davis, F. D. (1989). 'Perceived usefulness, perceived ease of use, and user acceptance of information technology'. *MIS Quarterly*, 13(3), 319–339.

Davis, F. D., Bagozzi, P. R. and Warshaw (1989). 'User acceptance of information technology: A comparison of two theoretical models'. *Management Science*, 35(8), 982–1002.

Esfahanipour, A., Montazemi, A. R. and Siam, J. J. (2007). 'Information analysis in fixed-income markets', McMaster eBusiness Research Centre Working Paper #19.

Fishbein, M. and Ajzen, I. (1975). *Belief, Attention and Behavior: An Introduction to Theory and Research*. Addison Wesley, Reading, MA.

Hess, D. (2004). 'Determinants of the relative price impact of unanticipated information in U.S. macroeconomic releases'. *Journal of Futures Markets*, 24(7), 609–629.

Kelley, H. H. and Thibaut, J. W. (1978). *Interpersonal Relations: A Theory of Interdependence*. John Wiley and Sons Ltd., New York.

Madhavan, A. (2000). 'Market microstructure: A survey'. *Journal of Financial Markets*, 3, 205–258.

Montazemi, A. R. and Siam, J. (2005). 'State of Information Technology Support for Traders in Fixed-Income Market'. *Proceedings of the 11th Americas Conference on Information Systems*. August 11–14, Omaha, NE.

Montazemi, A. R. and Siam, J. (2006). 'Information Flow and Network of Interpersonal Ties in the Fixed-Income Market'. *International Conference on Information Systems*, December 10–13. Milwaukee, WI, USA.

Moulton, A., Bressan, S., Madnick, S. and Siegel, M. (1998). 'Using an active conceptual model for mediating analytic information interchange in the fixed income securities industry', MIT Sloan School of Management Working Paper Sloan WP#4023.

Te'eni, D., Carey, J. and Zhang, P. (2006). *Human Computer Interaction: Developing Effective Organizational Information Systems*. John Wiley and Sons Ltd.

Venkatesh, V. (2000). 'Determinants of perceived ease of use: Integrating control, intrinsic motivation, and emotion into the technology acceptance model'. *Information Systems Research*, 11(4), 342–365.

Chapter 9 ■■■

Evaluating actors and factors associated with healthcare information systems

V. Mantzana, M. Themistocleous, V. Morabito and K. Soulioutis

■ Introduction

Enterprise Application Integration (EAI) has emerged to support organisations overcoming their integration problems and it has been adopted by many organisations in various sectors. Despite its importance, the healthcare domain develops EAI solutions at a slower pace compared to other sectors. The small number of EAI applications in healthcare has resulted in limited research in this area with many issues requiring further investigation. The normative literature analyzes the factors that influence EAI adoption in healthcare (MAESTRO model) but it has not yet explored the role of actors during the adoption process. This chapter takes a step forward and contributes to the body of knowledge as it: (a) highlights the role of healthcare actors and attitudes towards EAI adoption, (b) identifies those actors involved in this process, by using the proposed IGOHcaps method and (c) combines the actor-oriented approach with the factors influencing EAI adoption. The authors believe that such an approach is significant and novel as it: (a) enhances existing EAI adoption models (MAESTRO) by incorporating an actor-oriented analysis and (b) facilitates healthcare organisations in making robust decisions for EAI adoption.

The authors aim to contribute in this area by presenting and validating a model that incorporates human actors (IGOHcaps method) (Mantzana et al., 2007) to an existing model on EAI adoption (MAESTRO) (Khoumbati et al., 2006). Accordingly the first and the second sections describe Healthcare Information Systems (HIS), their potential and challenges. In the third section, the need for HIS integration is presented. In the following sections, the adoption of EAI is analyzed and the authors derive and propose a conceptual model that incorporates human, organisational and technical factors. Thereafter, the research methodology and the case study used to evaluate the conceptual model are described. The findings and their analysis are presented and explained in the case analysis section before conclusions are drawn.

The HIS

Information systems (IS) play an increasingly crucial role in the healthcare sector, by providing an infrastructure to integrate people, processes and technologies (Ragupathi, 1997; Wanless et al., 2002). Information technology (IT) applications such as Internet-based telemedicine (Menachemi et al., 2004), personal health records (Lafky et al., 2006), asynchronous healthcare communication systems (Wilson, 2003) and picture archiving communication systems (Menachemi et al., 2004) have been applied in healthcare to improve the capabilities of physicians and clinical staff and provided increased services to patients, caregivers and citizens in general.

Rodrigues et al. (1999) defined HIS as:

> 'Computerized systems designed to facilitate the management and operation of all technical (biomedical) and administrative data for the entire healthcare system, for a number of its functional units, for a single healthcare institution, or even for an institutional department or unit' (Rodrigues et al., 1999, p. 2).

HIS are a key enabler, as they have the potential to improve healthcare services, by providing rapid and widespread access to information at the point of care (Lenz and Kuhn, 2004). In the early stages of implementing IT in the healthcare sector (e.g. 1960s), IS were dealing with simple transaction processing tasks (Siau et al., 2002). In the 1970s, HIS that support the management processes began to evolve and in 1980s, the traditional decision support systems started being developed and used. Network applications (e.g. Internet, intranet and extranet) and information warehousing integrated with data mining tools to support the identification of customer needs and hidden business challenges had been implemented in the healthcare sector in the 1990s. Recently, the need for implementing electronic patient records (EPR) and to integrate medical systems became apparent, as healthcare organisations have the vision to develop a patient-centric integrated system. Therefore, IT is not perceived as a supporting tool, but a strategic necessity for the development of an integrated healthcare IT infrastructure that will significantly improve services and reduce medical errors.

HIS: potential and current challenges

IS implementations have been reported to provide significant benefits to healthcare organisations, such as better data quality, availability, accessibility, connectivity, exchange and sharing (Trimmer et al., 2002; Stefanou and Revanoglou, 2006). Moreover, it has been reported that through minimum levels of automation, the percentage of human life loss would reduce by 50–80% in USA (Sutherland and Willem, 2002).

Despite the potential benefits of HIS, it has been reported that healthcare systems have a low success rate (Westrup, 1998; Heeks et al., 1999). In the UK, hundreds of millions of pounds and countless hours of peoples' time have been spent on IS implementations. However, the quality of the healthcare systems suffers as a result of medical errors, clinical employees' resistance to change and fragmented care (Leape et al., 1995; Stefanou and Revanoglou, 2006).

It appears that healthcare actors have a significant role in the introduction and use of IT and should be involved in the decision-making process (Chau and Hu, 2002). This literature finding emphasises the need to consider healthcare actors during the EAI adoption process.

The authors review the normative literature, identify the potential of HIS, as well as the challenges faced by healthcare organisations. The potential and current challenges are categorised in four main thematic areas, namely: (a) information quality, (b) information availability, (c) medical errors and (d) HIS integration. In addition, the HIS potential and current challenges are summarised according to the thematic areas, presented (Table 9.1) and discussed in the following paragraphs.

Table 9.1 HIS potential and challenges

Thematic areas	HIS potential	HIS current challenges
1 Information quality	Improve quality of information (Wanless et al., 2002)	The weak communication infrastructure delays the exchange and transfer of health information (Mundy and Chadwick, 2004)
2 Information availability	Improve availability of information (Neri et al., 1998; Trimmer et al., 2002)	Health information is partially available (Leonard, 2004) Clinical employees resistance to the adoption and use of HIS (Stefanou and Revanoglou, 2006) Privacy, security and confidentiality of data (Mundy and Chadwick, 2004)
3 Medical errors	Reduce medical errors (Sutherland and Willem, 2002)	Three out of four preventable errors in care hospitals are caused by systems failure (Leape et al., 1995) The healthcare system still suffers, as a result of medical errors occurring (Khoumbati, 2005; Stefanou and Revanoglou, 2006)
4 HIS integration	Improve integration of health information (Donlon, 2003)	HIS are fragmented (Lee et al., 2003) High integration cost (Khoumbati, 2005)

Thematic area one: information quality

Stefanou and Revanoglou (2006) reported that HIS have the potential to improve the visibility and quality of health data, information and knowledge. However, health data, information and knowledge are delayed, as a result of the weak communication infrastructure. Thus, health information is randomly exchanged and accessed (Mundy and Chadwick, 2004). Moreover, it has been reported that HIS improve the availability, accessibility, connectivity, exchange and sharing of information, data and knowledge (Neri et al., 1998; Trimmer et al., 2002).

Thematic area two: information availability

Despite the technological advancement, healthcare information is partially available, of poor quality and is displayed in non-correct/standardised format (Leonard, 2004). The clinical employees' resistance to adopt HIS has been reported to affect the quality of information provided (Stefanou and Revanoglou, 2006). In addition, the privacy, security and confidentiality of data is a major concern in the field of HIS (Mundy and Chadwick, 2004).

Thematic area three: medical errors

Sutherland and Willem (2002) pointed out that HIS have the potential to reduce the medical errors that occur and increase patients' safety. However, the medical errors that occur through the non-integrated nature of HIS are estimated to have resulted in the loss of 64 persons per day in the UK (Khoumbati, 2005).

Thematic area four: HIS integration

Despite the potential of the HIS to improve the integration of health information (Donlon, 2003), the systems are still heterogeneous and the care provided is fragmented (Lee et al., 2003). It appears that the requirement for integration has been raised as: (a) effective information sharing among systems is vital for the management of organisations, (b) data is mainly electronically transferred between the HIS (Spyrou et al., 2002) and (c) the healthcare system is becoming a 'virtual system' as a result of connectivity and telehealth projects (Mercer, 2001). Nonetheless, the need for the development of an information integrated infrastructure that will be cost effective, flexible and adaptive has become apparent.

HIS integration

Pink (1996) reported that the integration of HIS and the acceptance by the multiple actors are important requirements that can support timely, accurate and comprehensive information sharing (e.g. information related to health status, costs, quality, utilisation, workload outcomes and satisfaction). However, the implementation of a fully integrated system is a complex process that needs to be carefully planned and the actors involved have to be carefully coordinated (Rodrigues et al., 1999).

Various integration approaches have been adopted by healthcare organisations to overcome the fragmentation of HIS. The multiple integration approaches are characterised either as integration standards, as integration projects or as internally integrated systems. The field of integration standards include the following: (a) Health Level 7 (HL7), (b) Electronic Data Interchange (EDI), (c) CEN/TC251 and (d) Digital Imaging Communications in Medicine and Common Object Broker Architecture in Medicine (DICOM). Some integration projects that have been developed include the following: (a) Synergy Extranet (SynEx), (b) Synapses and (c) Healthcare Advanced Networked System Architecture Project (HANSA). Moreover, internally integrated systems like Enterprise Recourse Planning Systems have been used in the healthcare sector.

The implementation of these approaches has provided significant benefits to healthcare organisations. However, there are still many problems relating to their adoption. Among other problems the cost of the development of healthcare integration approaches is high and the level of interoperability remains low (Carr and Moore, 2003). Khoumbati (2005) has recognised, analyzed and identified the benefits and barriers of these integration technologies. From the evaluation of the barriers and the benefits of the integration approaches, it appears that each approach has been developed to provide specific solutions and there is a need for the use of more than one approach to get satisfactory integration outcomes.

Nonetheless, EAI is a relatively new integration technology that is used to incorporate custom applications, packaged systems and e-business solutions into a flexible and manageable business infrastructure. Both the private and public sectors have implemented and evaluated EAI solutions, which have been proved to provide satisfactory integration solutions. EAI offers multiple benefits to organisations such as: (a) reduced operational costs, (b) increased productivity, (c) improved planning in supply chain management and (d) increased collaboration among trading partners. Despite the significant benefits that EAI has provided to other sectors, healthcare organisations remain laggards in EAI implementations, thus, giving scope for timeliness and novel research. In particular, the normative literature has tended to focus on the identification of parameters affecting the EAI adoption process in the private sector (Puschman and Alt, 2001). Khoumbati (2005) was among the first to study the EAI adoption by healthcare organisations and among others, identified and analyzed the factors that motivate the adoption process (MAESTRO model). According to this classification, these factors include: (a) technical, (b) cost, (c) medical errors, (d) decision support systems, (e) collaboration, (f) access of patients' data and (g) confidentiality of patients' data. Nonetheless, further work should be carried out in this field as: (a) the adoption and (b) the integration of health services and IT infrastructures were the most frequently cited priorities in UK (HIMSS, 2004). Thus, this chapter focuses on the EAI adoption in healthcare organisations.

EAI adoption in healthcare organisations

The role of actors is considered to be of high importance during the EAI adoption process in healthcare organisations. As a result, the authors propose that when exploring EAI adoption in healthcare, the mapping of actors against the factors (MAESTRO model) provides a deeper understanding of such interrelationships. Thus, an actor-oriented approach might be considered during the EAI adoption process to (a) overcome the main limitation of the current research in EAI adoption, (b) improve the level of analysis and (c) support healthcare decision-makers when adopting EAI. To this end, the authors propose that to study the EAI adoption in healthcare organisations, the two approaches (factors and actors) should be integrated. In an attempt to piece together the factor- and actor-oriented approaches, there are numerous issues to be investigated. Among the first to be explored, is the identification of the healthcare actors that affect and are affected by the EAI adoption (actor-oriented approach). Thus, the IGOHcaps method proposed by Mantzana et al. (2006) was employed in this study, as it refers specifically to healthcare actors' identification (Figure 9.1).

As Figure 9.1 depicts, the IGOHcaps method for actors' identification indicates that healthcare actors involved in the adoption process can be defined as any human and/or organisation that accepts, provides, supports and controls healthcare services (static step) (Mantzana et al.,

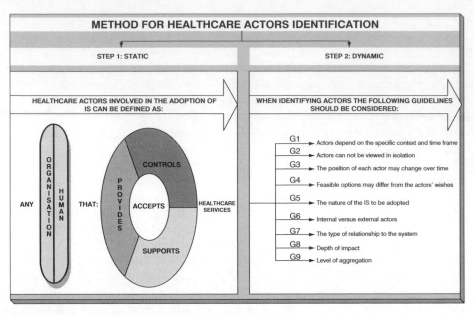

Figure 9.1 IGOHcaps method for healthcare actors' identification (*Source*: Mantzana et al., 2006)

2006). This static step should be combined with the dynamic one to enhance the actors' identification process. The dynamic step consists of a set of guidelines that can be used to identify a full range of actors. According to Mantzana et al. (2006), to apply IGOHcaps method in the practical arena, initially the static step (definition) should be understood. Then each of the guidelines should be applied to each of the proposed human and/or organisational categories (static step) individually (e.g. human acceptors, human supporters, etc.). In doing this, a list of healthcare actors will be identified and then evaluated in the case study, as the full actors' list depends on the specific context and time-frame. To this end, the authors propose that to study EAI adoption in healthcare organisations, and to enhance the understanding of EAI adoption process, the influential factors of MAESTRO model Khoumbati (2005), as well as the IGOHcaps method for healthcare actors' identification (Figure 9.1) should be combined. This is illustrated in Figure 9.2.

To use this method in the practical arena, initially the IGOHcaps method should be applied, as presented in Figure 9.1. In doing this, the following instructions should be followed:

- The static step (definition) should be considered before the dynamic.
- Each of the nine guidelines should be applied to each of the proposed human and/ or organisational categories (static step) individually (e.g. human acceptors, human supporters, etc.).
- Thus, a list of healthcare actors will be generated and then evaluated in the practical arena.
- Finally, the list of healthcare actors should be mapped with the factors affecting the EAI adoption (MAESTRO model).

In following the aforementioned instructions, it is expected to identify which actors are related to the factors. The proposed model in Figure 9.2 incorporates influential factors

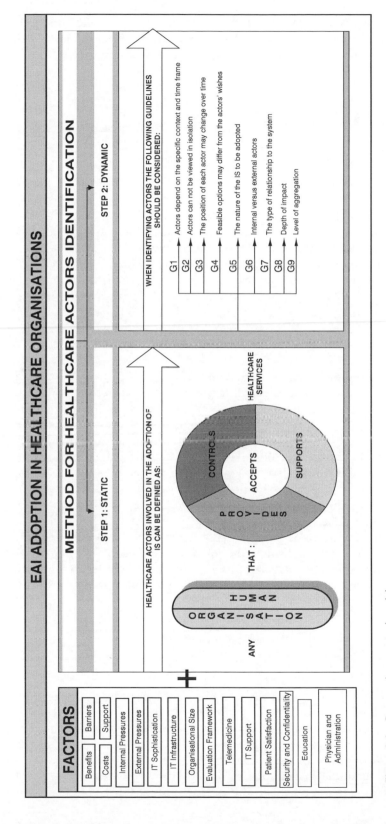

Figure 9.2 Proposed conceptual model

reported in previous studies (MAESTRO) and combines them with the method for health-care actors' identification (IGOHcaps). Moreover, the conceptual model contributes towards a better understanding of the EAI adoption in healthcare organisations.

Research strategy and methods

Considering the aim of this chapter (map actors and factors that affect the EAI adoption in healthcare organisations), a qualitative single-case study strategy was adopted (Yin, 1994). Such an approach can be used to (a) investigate little-known phenomena as if understanding and analyzing actors and factors affect and affected by EAI adoption in healthcare, (b) examine in-depth complex processes (EAI decision-making), (c) examine the phenomenon in its natural setting and (d) learn from practice. A single case study strategy was employed to explore and understand the EAI adoption. In doing so, various data collection methods such as interviews and observation were used. The bias that is considered a danger in using a qualitative research approach was overcome in this research through data triangulation. The use of multiple data collection methods makes the triangulation possible which provides stronger substantiation of theory (Eisenhardt, 1989). For the purpose of this chapter, three types of triangulation were used namely (a) data (Denzin, 1978), (b) methodological and (c) interdisciplinary triangulation (Janesick, 2000).

Interviews were the main data source that the authors used to collect data and to capture the verbatim. According to Lee (1991) interviews are described as verbal confirmation or disconfirmation of an observation or any formal, informal or causal answers to a question constituting the interview (Lee, 1991). Multiple actors were interviewed during the interviews. These interviews lasted for 45 minutes or more. The actors who were interviewed are the following: (a) Citizen A, (b) Citizen B, (c) Citizen C, (d) Clinician A, (e) Clinician B, (f) Clinician C, (g) Clinician D, (h) Non-Clinician A, (i) Non-Clinician B, (j) Non-Clinician C, (k) Administrator A, (l) Administrator B, (m) Departmental Director A, (n) Departmental Director B, (o) Office Director A and (p) Office Director B. The availability of interviewees was a problem during the case study, since they had demanding schedules. All interviews were tape recorded and transcripts prepared as soon as possible after each individual interview. Tape recording supported the authors in collecting accurate data and for its analysis. Taking notes during the interviews simply reduces the time of interviews since note-taking requires more time, thus, the authors considered tape recording as a more effective way of conducting interviews.

The case of HOSP

HOSP is based in Greece and operates as a non-profit institution, under the supervision of the Ministry of Health. It provides the complete spectrum of services to the local and international community, including preventive medicine, diagnosis and treatment for heart diseases. The hospital supports research related to the prevention, diagnosis and treatment of diseases, by providing considerable scientific resources. In doing so, HOSP cooperates with distinguished educational institutions, and specialised research centres. In terms of services provided, HOSP is organised in the following departments (a) Medical and Nursing

Services Department, (b) Financial Services Department and (c) Managerial Services Department.

Since the beginning of its operation, HOSP realised the catalytic role of IS and developed its first integrated healthcare IT Infrastructure. The latter comprised a set of Information Systems and Applications. Initially, the HIS communicated online with the Laboratory Information System (LIS). The HIS transmits to the LIS electronic orders of laboratorial examinations (with complete use of bar-codes for speed and safety). After the execution of the examination, the latter is checked either automatically from the laboratory analysts from LIS, or manually by the laboratory doctors. The examination results are collected by the LIS and the laboratory doctor verifies, approves and dispatches it to the HIS. Then, the electronic medical record of the patient is updated automatically and dispatched to the medical/ nursing personnel for review or printing. This communication was based on a proprietary protocol of communication, which was similar to HL7. The system proved to be a viable, effective and efficient integrated solution that provided significant benefits to the healthcare organisation. However, in 2000, due to the increasing needs and demands of HOSP, the management team decided to advance the existing healthcare IT infrastructure. Thus, they implemented an integrated healthcare IT infrastructure. The purpose of this integrated healthcare IT infrastructure is to provide reliable and functional access and sharing of information. This should be both on time and on place. To this end, the IS manager reported that:

> '…Since the beginning of its operation, HOSP realised that information has no meaning, if the IT Infrastructure is not integrated. Thus, all the implementation of the updated IS was based on this concept. Thus, by realising the need for integrated systems from the beginning, HOSP saved time and money….'

During the interviews, it was highlighted that the changes associated with the EAI adoption should be communicated to the multiple actors. The actors are not passive acceptors of an innovation, but they are actively involved in the adoption process by seeking for innovations, trying to understand and use them, developing feelings about them, complaining and trying to improve them (Greenhalgh et al., 2004). The actors' beliefs, reaction and attitude towards EAI adoption is crucial and it therefore forms a risk for the project. To this end, the IS manager reported that:

> 'Multiple actors are playing a critical role during the adoption of EAI … the successful implementation of the new system is based on these actors….'

It was revealed that the actors have a critical role and can affect the outcome, if they don't adopt the EAI technology. In support of this, the Director of Management mentioned that:

> '…Since the beginning of the HOSP operation, employers had been trained on the Information Systems developed. In 2000, when the new integrated system was implemented, HOSP realised that without training and education of users, the system will fail. Thus, as the users' adoption is the most critical part (regarding the successful implementation), the adoption of EAI was a well-planned process … the users and staff had been trained on the new system for approximately 6 months.'

These concerns indicate that it is of high importance to study and analyze the actors' views since their actions can have a great impact on IS adoption. These comments are in line with the normative literature which highlights that actors' reactions might lead to IS failure

(Fitzgerald and Russo, 2005). These views further support the aim of this research and demonstrate that there is scope for timeliness and novel research in this area. Thus, it is important to identify the actors and understand their stances towards EAI adoption.

This case study lasted for six months and during this period, the authors conducted interviews, to test and evaluate the proposed conceptual model. In doing so, the authors initially applied the IGOHcaps method to identify actors (as explained in the following paragraphs) and then interviewed the following actors: (a) Citizen A, (b) Citizen B, (c) Citizen C, (d) Clinician A, (e) Clinician B, (f) Clinician C, (g) Clinician D, (h) Non-Clinician A, (i) Non-Clinician B, (j) Non-Clinician C, (k) Administrator A, (l) Administrator B, (m) Departmental Director A, (n) Departmental Directors B, (o) Office Director A and (p) Office Director B.

Application of IGOHcaps method to HOSP

To identify the actors, the authors applied the IGOHcaps method (Figure 9.1). In doing this, the static step should be considered before the dynamic. Then each of the guidelines should be applied to each of the proposed human and/or organisational categories (static step) individually (e.g. human acceptors, human supporters, etc.). In doing this, a list of healthcare actors was generated and then evaluated in the HOSP, as the full actors' list depends on the specific context and time frame. The process for healthcare actors' identification is explained and displayed in Figure 9.1.

For instance, the authors applied the fifth guideline (related to the nature of IS) to the organisational providers (sub-category). The type of IS to be adopted is an EAI solution that will be used to integrate inter- and intra-organisational systems. Therefore, the organisational providers identified are the Hospital and the Hospital Departments and Hospital Office (sub-departments). In addition, the actor 'Citizen' was identified mainly through the application of the first guideline (G1) to the human acceptors category, as different European Union (EU) plans mention that the focus of healthcare should not be on *how* to provide treatment to patients but on minimising the percentages of people that need treatment. Thus, as the healthcare organisations should improve citizens' quality of life, the Citizen is considered as an actor.

Therefore, using the proposed guidelines within the specific case context and time frame the following healthcare actors were identified (Table 9.2). Table 9.2 shows how the guidelines were applied to support healthcare actors' identification. The first column refers to the guidelines and the rest to the actors being identified using these guidelines. The symbol tick (✓) indicates that the specific actor is identified by the specific proposed guideline, where the symbol (✗) shows the opposite.

After identifying the list of healthcare actors, *the list of healthcare actors should be validated.*

Case analysis

To test the *actors' list identified through the application of IGOHcaps method*, the interviewees were asked to comment on the proposed list of healthcare actors, presented in Table 9.2. The empirical data revealed that the various actors should be analyzed in more detail.

Table 9.2 Actors identification through the IGOHcaps method in HOSP

			Proposed guidelines								
			G1	G2	G3	G4	G5	G6	G7	G8	G9
Acceptor	H	Patients	✓	✓	✓	✓	✓	✓	✓	✓	✓
		Next of Kin	✓	✓	✓	✗	✗	✗	✗	✓	✓
		Citizens	✓	✗	✗	✗	✓	✗	✓	✗	✓
Provider	H	Clinicians	✓	✓	✓	✓	✓	✓	✓	✓	✓
		Non-Clinicians	✓	✓	✓	✓	✓	✓	✓	✓	✓
	O	Hospital	✓	✓	✗	✓	✓	✓	✓	✓	✓
		Hospital Department	✗	✓	✗	✓	✓	✓	✓	✓	✓
		Hospital Office (sub-departments)	✗	✓	✗	✓	✓	✓	✓	✓	✓
Supporter	H	Administrators	✓	✓	✓	✗	✓	✓	✓	✓	✓
		Legal Professionals	✓	✓	✓	✗	✓	✓	✓	✓	✓
		Researchers	✓	✗	✓	✗	✓	✓	✓	✓	✓
	O	Suppliers	✓	✓	✓	✓	✓	✓	✓	✓	✓
		Technologists	✓	✓	✓	✓	✓	✓	✓	✓	✓
		Research Institutes	✓	✓	✓	✓	✓	✓	✓	✓	✓
Controller	H	Departmental Directors	✓	✓	✓	✓	✓	✓	✓	✓	✓
		Office Directors	✓	✓	✓	✓	✓	✓	✓	✓	✓
	O	Government	✗	✓	✗	✓	✓	✓	✓	✓	✓
		Health Authorities	✓	✓	✓	✓	✓	✓	✓	✓	✓

For instance, in the proposed taxonomy (Table 9.2), the actors 'Office Directors' and 'Departmental Directors' (in the category Controller) represents all directors in different offices and departments. However, this is not accurate in terms of analysis, as diverse categories of directors exist with different interests (e.g. IS Office Director, Director of Medical and Nursing, Director of Finance, Director of Management and Patient Records Office Director). In addition, it has been reported by Departmental Director A that:

'The Director of Finance is interested in EAI costs, when deciding towards the adoption of EAI, while I [the IS Office Director] am more interested in knowing about the IT Infrastructure, IT sophistication, Benefits, Barriers etc....'

Clearly, such a statement supports the authors' view that various directors do exist and there is therefore a need to identify all these types of directors. Therefore, the researchers requested to see business process models in an attempt to better explore the different types of directors. However, the IDEF0 models viewed were not of any help as they refer to a business sub-process that is not related to directors. Due to the limited number of the IDEF0 models that were examined by the authors, it is suggested that this issue should be investigated in more detail. Most of the interviewees mentioned that patients and citizens should have a principal role during the decision-making regarding the EAI adoption. This is in accordance with the normative literature, which indicates that there is a need for the development of an essential patient-centric healthcare IT infrastructure (DoH, 2004; Koutsouris et al., 2005). The Human Resource Director (Departmental Director B) mentioned the following:

> 'Patients and citizens should be organised in groups, so as to put pressure on the adoption of technologies, such EAI, that will improve the healthcare services provided to them....'

Factors and actors affecting the adoption of EAI

After testing the *actors' list*, the interviewees were asked to express their views regarding the mapping of actors against the factors that affect the EAI adoption process in healthcare organisations. The majority of interviewees mentioned that the factors influencing EAI adoption should be presented and explained to the multiple healthcare actors involved in the decision-making process. Thus, it *appears that the various influential factors should be examined in* relation to *the actors who affect and/or are affected by the EAI adoption.*

In addition, the empirical data indicated that the adoption of EAI technology in healthcare organisations is a process that is highly affected by multiple actors. It is worth reporting the views of the IS manager, who mentioned that:

> 'It is really important to explain to the multiple healthcare actors, the EAI adoption factors. The sooner they understand these factors, the easier the EAI adoption will be. Another issue that should be considered and indisputably affects the adoption from individuals is the power ... actually the decision of an office's director to adopt or not a technology can formulate the decision of his employee....'

Thus, the authors propose that the interrelationships between actors and issues, such as power, should be considered during the EAI adoption. This issue has been highlighted in the normative literature (Rogers, 1995) and thus, the authors propose that:

> 'the way that the different levels of actors' power can affect the decision towards the adoption of EAI is of high importance and should be investigated in depth'.

In Table 9.3, the authors present the results obtained by the combination of: (a) EAI influential factors and (b) the taxonomy of the healthcare actors (Table 9.2). Such a combination can provide a more detailed level of analysis. Horizontally, Table 9.3 illustrates the factors

Table 9.3 Mapping of actors and factors influencing the EAI adoption in HOSP

EAI adoption factors	Acceptor			Provider					Supporter						Controller			
	H			H		H	O			H		O			H		O	
	1	2	3	4	5	6	7	8	9	10	11	12	13	14	15	16	17	18
	P	NK	CI	C	NC	H	HD	HO	A	LP	R	S	T	RI	DD	OD	G	HA
1 Cost	○	○	●	●	●	●	●	●	○	○	○	●	●	●	●	●	●	●
2 Barriers	●	●	●	●	●	●	●	●	○	●	●	●	●	●	●	●	●	●
3 Benefits	●	●	●	●	●	●	●	●	●	●	●	●	●	●	●	●	●	●
4 IT support	○	○	○	●	●	●	●	●	●	○	○	●	●	●	●	●	●	●
5 Internal pressures	○	○	○	●	●	●	●	●	◐	○	○	◐	◐	●	●	●	●	●
6 External pressures	○	○	○	●	●	●	●	●	○	○	○	●	●	●	●	●	●	●
7 IT infrastructure	○	○	○	○	○	○	○	○	○	○	○	●	●	◐	●	●	○	○
8 IT sophistication	○	○	○	○	○	○	○	○	○	○	○	●	●	◐	●	●	○	○
9 Evaluation frameworks	○	○	○	○	○	○	○	○	○	○	○	●	●	◐	●	●	○	○
10 Organisational size	○	○	○	○	○	○	○	○	○	○	○	●	○	○	●	●	○	○
11 Telemedicine	●	●	●	●	●	●	●	●	●	●	●	●	●	●	●	●	●	●
12 Patient satisfaction	●	●	●	●	●	●	●	●	●	●	●	●	●	●	●	●	●	●
13 Security and confidentiality	●	●	●	●	●	●	●	●	●	○	●	●	●	●	●	●	●	◐
14 Compatibility	○	○	○	●	○	○	○	○	○	○	○	●	●	●	●	●	●	○
15 Physicians and administrators relationship	○	○	○	●	●	●	●	●	●	○	○	○	○	○	●	●	◐	○
16 Education	◐	◐	◐	●	●	●	●	●	●	○	○	○	○	○	●	●	●	●

influencing the EAI adoption process. Vertically, the healthcare actors are illustrated, grouped into Acceptors, Providers, Supporters and Controllers. Each of these categories is broken down into Human and Organisational lenses. Due to space limitations the authors refer to each of the actors using: (a) its initial letter and (b) the corresponding number given to them in Table 9.2. For instance actor number 3 refers to the Citizen (CI). To better understand the scope of these factors, the interviewees were asked to rank them appropriately. The ranking follows the scale of ranking used by Miles and Huberman (1994), which represents less important (○), medium important (◑) and most important (●).

Cost factor

The empirical data reveals that the Human and Organisational Providers, the Organisational Supporters (suppliers, technologists and research institutes) and the Human and Organisational Controllers (departmental directors, office directors, government and health authorities) are related to this factor (Cost). However, from the data retrieved, it appears that Clinicians and other actors are related to one or more parameters of Cost factor (e.g. training), whereas the actor Directors are interested in the cost savings that the EAI adoption will provide. In addition to this, the IS manager reported that:

'…Due to this interoperable IT Infrastructure, the hospital managed to increase productivity and reduce costs. A characteristic example is that in the laboratories of HOSP (due to the integration) we need 1/3 of the employees needed in a hospital that does not have an integrated system'.

This statement implies that with EAI there is a reduction of operational costs, an increment of productivity and efficiency. This is in accordance to the normative literature, which indicates that the adoption of EAI increases productivity and reduces costs (Khoumbati, 2005). However, the above-mentioned comment highlights an important barrier that relates to possible resistance to change. Therefore, the management of the organisation should be aware of all these issues, balance them and take appropriate decisions. For instance, the literature supports the fact that in similar cases organisations took the decision to either move employees from one department to another or expand their operations using the redundant staff. Clearly, these empirical and literature findings further support this research which seeks to better understand and analyze the actors and factors related to EAI in order to speed up its adoption and better manage EAI projects.

Barriers and benefits factors

The EAI adoption process in healthcare organisations is affected by multiple benefits and barriers. These factors appear to have a powerful effect all the actors interviewed, towards the adoption of EAI. Non-Clinician C mentioned that:

'The more informed we are [e.g. through workshops] during the adoption process, the more positive will be towards EAI adoption….'

As is extrapolated from the empirical data, the interviewees would like to be aware of the benefits, the barriers, the risks and the potentials associated with EAI. This is also a finding that has been reported in the normative literature (NHS, 1993; Siau, 2003).

From the description of the Cost factor reported above it appears that EAI may benefit specific actors or categories of actors but at the same time it may cause problems to others. Thus: It is important to investigate the interrelationships among a full range of benefits and barriers with actors involved in EAI adoption in healthcare to facilitate a deeper level of analysis and understanding of these factors.

IT support factor

The IT support is a factor that affects the Providers', Supporters' and Controllers' decision-making process towards EAI adoption, as the IS Office's provision knowledge, support and training to the multiple actors of HOSP. In support of this, Office Director A mentioned that:

> '…Since the beginning of the HOSP operation, HOSP realised the importance of the IS Office during the EAI life cycle. HOSP had employed specialised staff to support its IT Infrastructure. These employees provided knowledge, training and support to the multiple users'.

It appears that due to the complexity of EAI, the multiple actors seek specialised IT support. From the empirical evidence, it appears that the IT support is of great importance to the following HOSP actors:

- Human and Organisational Providers (clinicians, non-clinicians, hospital, hospital department and hospital office (sub-departments)).
- Administrators.
- Organisational Supporters (suppliers, technologists and research institutes).
- Human and Organisational Controllers (departmental directors, office directors, government and health authorities).

Internal and external pressures factors

The interviewees mentioned that the internal and external pressure factors are important and highly affect the following actors:

- Human and Organisational Providers (clinicians, non-clinicians, hospital, hospital department and hospital office (sub-departments)).
- Human and Organisational Controllers (departmental directors, office directors, government and health authorities).

Moreover, the suppliers' and technologists' decision towards the EAI adoption is influenced (medium importance) by these factors. *This highlights that the aforementioned actors cause or receive internal and external pressures during the EAI adoption process.*

IT infrastructure, IT sophistication, compatibility and evaluation framework of integration technologies factors

The empirical data indicates that the factors related to technological issues can be examined and analyzed as a group since they affect the same set of actors:

- Suppliers and research institutes (medium importance).
- Technologists, departmental directors and office directors (high importance).

To the rest of the actors, these factors have less effect on their decision towards the adoption of EAI. This finding suggests that *the technological factors should be studied in* relation to *the aforementioned actors to enhance the EAI adoption.*

Organisational size factor

Although HOSP has 35 offices, it provides specialised services to a large volume of the population geographically dispersed. The empirical data indicates that the organisational size affects the Human Controllers (departmental directors and office directors) decision towards the EAI adoption. Moreover, the Organisational Supporters consider that this factor affects them. It was reported by Office Director A, that:

> '...The larger the organisational size, the greater the need for integrating the heterogeneous systems and the propensity of EAI adoption and more difficult the EAI adoption process, as more actors (that should be managed) are involved....'

Telemedicine factor

Most of the HOSP actors (Acceptors, Providers, Controllers and Supporters) reported that they are highly affected by the telemedicine factor. Despite the fact that telemedicine applications have not yet been implemented in HOSP, the interviewees mentioned that it could affect the EAI adoption. This finding highlights the importance of implementing telemedicine applications, which can support the provision of healthcare services in emergencies or in cases where fast medical response and expert care is needed. Especially in Greece, due to its geographical landscape that includes tens of small islands and isolated areas, there is a high demand for telemedicine applications. Such HIS support communities and individuals in urban or rural areas and islands (Koutsouris et al., 2005).

Patient satisfaction factor

All the HOSP actors, identified through the IGOHcaps method, reported that the patient satisfaction factor affects the decision towards the EAI adoption. To this end the majority of actors reported that *the improvement of clinical processes and increase a patient satisfaction should be placed at the centre of the EAI solution.* Moreover, the director of patients record office (Office Director B) stated that:

> 'Always, in the beginning of the EAI adoption process, the patients and citizens are placed in the centre of attention and focus ... However, as the process (EAI adoption) continues, the focus shifts from patients/citizens to financial and technical issues ... thus, they (patients/citizens) are not anymore the protagonists of this process ... However, it should be highlighted that the EAI adoption and thus the integrated IT infrastructure will enhance the patients' satisfaction, who will get better services in HOSP ... patients should be treated as really demanding customers ... and their satisfaction should be the main priority of employees'.

Security and confidentiality factor

All the actors' decision towards the EAI adoption is affected by the security and confidentiality of patient data. This finding emphasises the need for patient data security and confidentiality. It appears that the success of the EAI adoption process depends to a large extent on the ability of EAI to protect the individual (patient, citizen and clinician, etc.) against unlawful use of personal information. This is along similar lines to the normative literature that suggests security and confidentiality is critical during the implementation and adoption of integrated solutions in a healthcare setting (Huston, 2001).

Physicians and administrators relationship factor

The physicians and administrators collaboration and close relationship is an important factor influencing the EAI adoption in healthcare organisations. Empirical evidence indicates how the Human Controllers (departmental directors and office directors) and Human Providers (clinicians and non-clinicians) are affected by this factor.

The physicians' role has been characterised as crucial during the adoption of integrated technologies (Chan et al., 2005; Stefanou and Revanoglou, 2006), as it can be a barrier during the EAI adoption process. Clinician D reported that:

> 'The communication and collaboration among physicians and administrators is important and can affect the EAI adoption, as both have a crucial role in the system's use and in the hospital's functions'.

Thus, the authors propose that: The interrelationships between the different actors might be studied, to enhance the understanding of the way that these interrelationships affect the EAI adoption process.

Education factor

HOSP has paid a lot of attention to the education of multiple users and the employment of specialised staff who can enhance knowledge and support the healthcare organisation. The increase in education can positively affect knowledge and understanding and thus, increase the EAI adoption (Khoumbati, 2005). In support of this, the IS manager reported that:

> 'The management of HOSP realised from the beginning the importance of the IT Office and has focused on the employment of specialised staff to support the IT Infrastructure … In Greece, only a few hospitals have paid attention to the development of a specialised IT Office'.

From the findings it appears that the following actors' decision towards EAI adoption is highly affected by the education factor:

- Human and Organisational Providers (clinicians, non-clinicians, hospital, hospital department and hospital office (sub-departments)).
- Human and Organisational Controllers (departmental directors, office directors, government and health authorities).
- Research Institutes.

Conclusions

The need to improve healthcare services through HIS integration has been highlighted and explained in this study. EAI is an emerging technology and although it is widely applied in many sectors, its adoption in healthcare is underutilised. For this reason, there is a necessity to investigate this area in more detail and contribute to the body of knowledge. This is of high importance as HIS are critical to human lives and thus information about their integration might be equally significant. In this chapter, the authors attempted to address this issue by reviewing the normative literature and building a conceptual model on the outcomes of this review. From the literature review it appears that previous published work on the adoption of EAI did not pay appropriate attention to human and social issues. Although EAI adoption in healthcare is a validated approach this explains why the uptake of EAI it has its limitations. Human and social aspects which are considerable and fundamental for the study of healthcare. To overcome this limitation, the authors propose a combination of the factor- (MAESTRO model) and actor-oriented (IGOHcaps method) approaches. This novel approach extends the normative literature and increases the level of analysis by providing a more detailed and systematic study of this phenomenon. The authors identified and categorised the actors related to the EAI adoption in healthcare since there was a void in the literature. In doing so, the authors produce a conceptual model that incorporates influential factors reported in previous studies (MAESTRO model) and combines them with the proposed method for healthcare actors' identification (IGOHcaps method). The model contributes towards a deeper understanding of EAI adoption in healthcare. The identification of the actors is based on theoretical works conducted by others. Hence, the justification and identification of actors is grounded in literature. The combination of actors- and factors-oriented approaches (a) supports managers and researchers in understanding which actors should be considered during the study of EAI adoption factors, (b) supports the multiple healthcare actors in the realisation of the factors related to the EAI adoption process and (c) might increase the adoption of EAI in healthcare. Consequently, it is suggested that this approach might reduce the resistance to change and speed up the adoption of EAI. Therefore, the services provided to patients and citizens will be improved. One of the limitations of this research is that the outcomes presented herein are based on a single-case-based strategy. Thus, the data and the observations derived from this case cannot be generalised. Nonetheless, it is not the intention of this chapter to offer prescriptive guidelines about which actors are affected and affect the EAI adoption process. Rather, it is to allow others to relate their experiences to those reported herein. Therefore, this chapter offers a broader understanding of the phenomenon of EAI adoption in the area of healthcare.

References

Carr, C. and Moore, S. (2003). 'IHE: A model for driving adoption of standards'. *Computerized Medical Imaging and Graphics*, 27(2–3), 137–146.

Chan, Y. E., Dekker, R. A. and Ramsden, J. D. (2005). 'Information systems and health care. III: Diffusing healthcare knowledge: A case study of the care delivery network'. *Communications of the Association for Information Systems*, 15(2005), 225–241.

Chau, P. Y. K. and Hu, P. H. (2002). 'Investigating healthcare professionals' decision to accept telemedicine technology: An empirical test of competing theories'. *Journal of Information and Management*, 39(4), 297–311.

Denzin, N. Y. K. (1978). *The Research Act: A theoretical introduction to Sociological methods*. McGraw Hill, New York, USA.

Doh (2004). 'The NHS Plan – A Plan for Investment, a Plan for Reform'. London: HMSO, Available at www.dh.gov.uk

Donlon, J. (2003). 'Health integration cost cutting'. *Journal of Health Information Management*, 17(4), 62–66.

Eisenhardt, K. M. (1989). *Academy of Management Review*, Vol. 14, pp. 532–550.

Fitzgerald, G. and Russo, N. L. (2005). 'The turnaround of the London Ambulance Service Computer-Aided Despatch system (LASCAD)'. *European Journal of Information Systems*, 14(3), 244–257.

Greenhalgh, T., Glenn, R., Macfarlane, F., Bate, P. and Kyriakidou, O. (2004). 'Diffusion of innovations in service organisations: Systematic review and recommendations'. *The Milbank Quarterly*, 82(4), 581–629.

Heeks, R., Mundy, D. and Salazar, A. (1999). *Why Health Care Information Systems Succeed or Fail*. Institute for Development Policy and Management. Available at: http://www.man.ac.uk/idpm/idpm_dp.htm#isps_wp (accessed 24th June 2004).

HIMSS (2004). *15th Annual HIMSS Leadership Survey Sponsored by Superior Consultant Company*, HIMSS.

Huston, T. (2001). 'Security issues for implementation of e-medical records'. *Communications of the ACM*, 44(9), 89–94.

Janesick, V. (2000). 'The choreography of qualitative research design'. In Lincoln, Y. S. (Ed.), *Handbook of Qualitative Research*. Sage Publications, Thousand Oaks, CA, pp. 379–399.

Khoumbati, K. (2005). *Investigating the EAI Adoption in Healthcare Organisations, School of Information Systems, Computing and Mathematics*. Brunel University, London.

Khoumbati, K., Themistocleous, M., Irani, Z. and Mantzana, V. (2006). 'Testing the Adoption of EAI in the Healthcare Sector'. *Submitted to Communications of the Association for Information Systems*

Koutsouris, D., Aggelidis, P., Berler, A. and Tagaris, A. (2005). *Integration of Healthcare Information Systems*, E-business-forum, Z3 research team, Athens.

Lafky, D. B., Tulu, B. and Horan, T. A. (2006). 'A User-driven approach to personal health records'. *Communications of the Association for Information Systems*, 17(46), 1028–1041.

Leape, L., Bates, W. and Cullen, J. (1995). 'Systems analysis of adverse drug events'. *Journal of American Medical Association*, 274(1), 35–43.

Lee, J., Siau, K. and Hong, S. (2003). 'Enterprise integration with ERP and EAI'. *Communications of the ACM*, 46(2), 54–60.

Lee, S. A. (1991). 'Integrating positivist and interpretative approaches to organisational research'. *Organisational Science*, 2, 342–365.

Lenz, R. and Kuhn, K. (2004). 'Towards a continuous evolution and adaptation of information systems in healthcare'. *International Journal of Medical Informatics*, 73(2004), 75–89.

Leonard, K. J. (2004). 'Critical success factors relating to the healthcare's adoption of new technology: A guide to increasing the likelihood of successful implementation'. *Electronic Healthcare*, 2(4), 72–81.

Mantzana, V., Themistocleous, M., Irani, Z. and Morabito, V. (2007). 'Identifying healthcare actors involved in the adoption of information systems'. *European Journal of Information Systems*, 16(01), 91–102.

Menachemi, N., Burke, D. E. and Ayers, D. (2004). 'Factors affecting the adoption of telemedicine – A multiple adopter perspective'. *Journal of Medical Systems*, 28(6), 617–632.

Mercer, K. (2001). 'Examining the impact of health information networks on health system integration in Canada'. *Leadership in Health Services*, 14(3), 1–29.

Miles, U. and Huberman, A. M. (1994). *Qualitative Data Analysis: An Expanded Sourcebook.* Sage Publications, Newbury Park, CA.

Mundy, D. and Chadwick, W. D. (2004). 'Electronic transmission of prescriptions: Towards realising the dream'. *International Journal of Electronic Healthcare*, 1(1), 112–125.

Neri, E., Thiran, J., Caramella, D., Petri, C., Bartolozzi, C., Piscaglia, B., Macq, B., Duprez, T., Cosnard, G., Maldague, B. and Pauw, J. (1998). 'Interactive DICOM image transmission and telediagnosis over the European ATM network'. *IEEE Transactions on Information Technology in Biomedicine*, 2(1), 35–38.

NHS (1993). *The Good European Health Record: Ethical and Legal requirements.* National Health Service (NHS) (accessed 23rd June 2004).

Pink, G. (1996). *Integrated Delivery Systems: Providing a Continuum of Healthcare.* University of Toronto, Toronto.

Puschman, T. and Alt, R. (2001). 'Enterprise Application Integration – The Case of the Robert Bosch Group'. *Proceedings of the 34th Hawaii Conference on System Sciences*, Big Island, Hawai, USA.

Ragupathi, W. (1997). 'Health care information systems'. *Communications of the ACM*, 40(8), 81–82.

Rodrigues, R. J., Gattini, G. and Aalmeida, G. (1999). *Setting up Healthcare Services Information Systems: A Guide for Requirement Analysis, Application Specification, and Procurement.* Washington, USA.

Rogers, E. M. (1995). *Diffusion of Innovations.* The Free Press, New York.

Siau, K. (2003). 'Health care informatics'. *IEEE Transactions on Information Technology in Biomedicine*, 7(1), 1–7.

Siau, K., Southbard, P. and Hong, S. (2002). 'E-healthcare strategies and implementation'. *International Journal of Healthcare Technology and Management*, 4(1–2), 118–131.

Spyrou, S., Bamidis, P., Chouvarda, I., Gogou, G., Tryfon, M. and Maglaveras, N. (2002). 'Healthcare information standards: Comparison of the approaches'. *Health Informatics Journal*, 8(1), 14–19.

Stefanou, C. and Revanoglou, A. (2006). 'ERP integration in a healthcare environment: A case study'. *Journal of Enterprise Information Management*, 19(1), 115–130.

Sutherland, J. and Willem, J. (2002). 'Enterprise application integration and complex adaptive systems'. *Communications of the ACM*, 45(10), 59–64.

Trimmer, K., Pumphrey, D. L. and Wiggins, C. (2002). 'ERP implementation in rural health care'. *Journal of Management in Medicine*, 16(2–3), 113–132.

Wanless, D., Charlesworth, A., Walker, I., Beck, M., Black, J., Blue, I., Brindle, S., Bucht, C., Dunn, S., Fairweater, M., Ghazi-Tabatabai, Y., Innes, D., Lewis, L., Patel, V. and York, N. (2002). *Securing our Future Health: Taking a Long-Term View.* HM Treasury, Available at: http://www.hm-treasury.gov.uk/wanless (accessed, May 2004).

Westrup, C. (1998). *What's in Information Technology.* Asian Institute of Technology, Bangkok.

Wilson, V. (2003). 'Asynchronous health care communication'. *Communications of the ACM*, 46(6), 79–84.

Yin, R. K. (1994). *Case Study Research: Design and Methods.* Sage Publications, Thousand Oaks, CA.

Chapter 10 ■■■

Evaluating the governance structure for public sector IT: The UK National Programme in the Health Service

W. L. Currie

■ Introduction

The UK National Health Service (NHS) was set up in 1948 to offer free healthcare at the point of delivery to all citizens. Since then, the NHS has rarely been out of the public eye as politicians, the media and citizens continue to debate how to allocate the £80 billion annual NHS public spend (Wanless Report, 2002). Tracking the political, economic and social history of the NHS suggests that professional dominance characterised the era between 1948 and 1979. During this period, clinicians acted as the dominant force in healthcare organisations, supported by administrative services to assist their tasks and activities (Currie and Suhomlinova, 2006). This changed from around 1980, as the Conservative administration launched the era of market mechanisms, where additional managers were hired to make the NHS more cost conscious and efficient (Burgoyne et al., 1997). Over the past three decades, the NHS has faced continuous restructuring with the introduction more recently of primary care trusts (PCTs), Foundation Hospitals and the more recent 'choice' for patients (Morrell, 2006). Yet despite relentless politically driven change, the NHS continues to suffer from serious shortfalls in its financial budgets and frontline services to patients (Pollock, 2005).

In 2002, the government decided to launch the largest civil IT programme worldwide in the name of the National Programme[1] for information technology (IT) (National Programme) (Wanless, 2002). Part of the rationale for pledging around £6.2 billion to this initiative was the belief that IT would play a central role in providing better healthcare services. The key objective promised: *To deliver a 21st century health service that is better for patients, citizens, clinicians and people working in the NHS through the efficient use of information and communication*

---

[1] There is a dedicated government website for the National Programme: www.connectingforhealth. nhs.uk.

technology (Granger, 2004). Planned over a 10-year period, the National Programme aims to deliver five systems across England:

1 NHS Care Records Service
2 Electronic Appointment Booking
3 Picture Archiving and Communications system (PACs)
4 Electronic Transmission of Prescriptions
5 IT Infrastructure and Network.

The National Programme is an ambitious attempt to complement the political agenda of 'New Labour' to transform healthcare. Government believes that information and communication technology (ICT) can play a central role in moving the NHS into the '21st century' by utilising the latest technologies to provide online medical records, giving patients the opportunity to 'Choose and Book' hospital appointments with their GP, to allow the speedy transfer of digital images (i.e. X-rays and scans) across the network, to enable patients to pick up their repeat prescriptions at the pharmacy without having to enter the GP surgery and to build a state-of-the-art, powerful broadband network to allow the capture, storage, manipulation and transfer of digital data and images.

Such a large-scale, multi-faceted and centrally planned IT-enabled initiative is a shift away from the traditional decentralised approach of introducing ICT into UK Healthcare. Starting in the early 1960s, the NHS had virtually no computers despite being an information intensive organisation. As the computer revolution got underway during the 1980s, the NHS procured tens of thousands of computers resulting in numerous disparate systems and applications (see Figure 10.1) (Brennan, 2005). One of the first computer systems was the patient administration system (PAS) introduced in the 1960s. This was followed by several different systems in the 1970s (laboratory), in the 1980s (management systems), in the 1990s (IT strategy like electronic patient records (EPR)), electronic record development and implementation programme (ERDIP) and electronic health records (EHR).

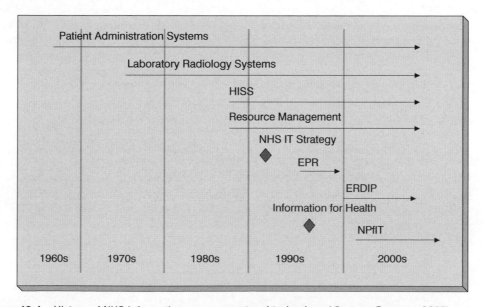

Figure 10.1   History of NHS information management and technology (*Source*: Brennan, 2005)

Notwithstanding a marked increase in the numbers of computers now used across the NHS, many clinical and administrative processes continue to use paper-based systems. Stories of lost or mislaid patient notes and images continue to circulate in the media and anecdotally. The National Programme is viewed by government as a way to resolve the inefficiencies that lead to inconvenience for staff and patients or potentially fatal mistakes that represent a complete failure in clinical governance.

Despite technical change being viewed as positive across the NHS, many question the monolithic National Programme in the context of past large-scale public IT programmes that have produced mixed results (NAO, 2004, 2006a). Successful IT projects are identified as, the Payment Modernisation Programme in the Department of Work and Pensions, which has transformed the payment of benefits and pensions by paying entitlements directly into recipients' bank accounts, the Transport for London 'Oyster' card, which is an electronic smartcard, and the Office of the Revenue Commissioners in Ireland, Revenue Online Service which enables customers to both pay their taxes and file their returns online (NAO, 2006b). Yet other projects have received high-profile media coverage and labelled as 'IT disasters'. These include: the Wessex Health Authority, the London Ambulance Service, the Child Support Agency and the Passport Office have led to serious questions about the leadership and management of public sector IT. Falling public confidence in government-run IT projects led to the creation of 'Gateway Reviews' (NAO, 2004) where IT projects are evaluated at various critical stages in their life cycle. Part of this initiative is to demonstrate that public money is not being wasted and that IT projects deliver on their promises. This has become more important as the annual IT spend has doubled since 1999 and is currently around £14 billion (NAO, 2004). With the launch of the National Programme, this figure will increase significantly, with some estimates that the total spend on the National Programme alone could reach as much as £20 billion.[2]

In this chapter, the author presents the findings from a longitudinal study on the National Programme covering the period between 2001 and 2006. This includes an analysis of data collected from 170 interviews with clinicians, hospital managers, IT suppliers and relevant healthcare agencies and groups. The focus of this study is to examine the relationship between the various stakeholders involved in developing and implementing the National Programme. An evaluation is made of the formal governance structure that comprise the development of an agency charged with running the National Programme – Connecting for Health. The author analyzes how this agency works with the various parties (i.e. politicians, NHS staff, IT vendors) in fulfilling the aims and objectives of the National Programme. Consideration is given to the importance attached to the procurement process where IT vendors are offered a 'carrot and stick' approach by Connecting for Health. Developing an effective IT procurement process is seen by Connecting for Health as a major step towards improving the evaluation of IT from selection to implementation. The relationship between public and private sector organisations is examined, in the context of euphemistic descriptions of 'strategic partnerships'. Building on an analysis of this relationship, consideration is given to the extent to which private IT vendors possess the necessary capabilities and skills to work with the NHS.

The chapter is structured as follows. First, an overview of the governance structure in UK healthcare is set out. Five key stakeholders are identified, each of whom plays an important

[2]www.E-health-insider.com. This site contains many articles and commentary on the National Programme.

role in the fulfilment of the National Programme. Second, a brief overview is given of research methods, data collection and analysis. Third, the findings from the case study on the National Programme are presented. The chapter concludes by highlighting a number of critical pressure points that are seriously damaging the progress of the National Programme and offer some insights for theory and practice.

■ The governance structure for IT in healthcare

The acronym NHS has become synonymous with the concept of reform in the past three decades (Morrell, 2006). Reforms have been wide ranging with the more recent ones in the form of PCTs, Foundation Hospitals, clinical governance, patient choice, in addition to other 'efficiency enhancing' initiatives, such as the private finance initiative (PFI) and out-sourcing. The focus here is IT-enabled reforms and initiatives where, since the early 1980s, the NHS has seen the introduction of total quality management, business process reengi-neering (BPR), the new public management, learning organisation and knowledge man-agement. The impetus behind these initiatives is politically driven to encourage the NHS to adopt the methods and practices of private sector firms (Pollock, 2005). One significant practice has been the contracting out of services, now commonly referred to as outsourcing. This extends beyond traditional 'blue collar' forms of work like catering and cleaning to include 'white collar' roles, such as management consultancy and the use of external firms to develop and implement information systems.

Notwithstanding ideological and practical concerns about the nature and extent of out-sourcing, the use of external firms to help the NHS become more 'market driven' has sig-nificant implications for the structure, culture and organisation of NHS work. The author's interest focuses upon the introduction of IT into the public sector in the form of the National Programme. Yet we are reminded that high-profile 'IT failures' offer many lessons on how to avoid the problems of introducing large-scale IT. These lessons often point to the failure to provide an effective governance structure for IT projects in addition to the common prob-lems of 'scope and scale creep' as new functionality and features are continuously added to the software design, which extends the project cost (over-budget) and delivery date (a late project).

Despite the introduction of Gateway Reviews (NAO, 2004) to oversee the progress of IT projects at various critical stages in their development, a more fundamental concern needs to be addressed in the form of governance structures for managing public sector IT con-tracts with external providers. This extends beyond the structural components of govern-ance structures (i.e. identifying roles and responsibilities of the various stakeholders) to the cultural dimension, which includes the values, attitudes and beliefs that individuals hold about their work. Clearly, within a highly institutionalised environment like healthcare (Scott, 2001) where clinicians undertake their work based upon many years of experience and training, extensive organisational change is unlikely to be accepted without some form of resistance. Yet Gateway Reviews and other formal-rationale approaches to project man-agement are unlikely to preclude further IT failures. This is almost certainly the case where the change management initiative fails to win the hearts and minds of the people for whom it is intended (NAO, 2006a).

One of the paradoxes about governance structures within healthcare is that, in spite of the institutionalised practices and procedures across the NHS, politicians continue to restructure the NHS (Harrison, 2004; Currie and Suhomlinova, 2006) by replacing previous initiatives with new ones. Part of this continuous restructuring is because healthcare is closely coupled with the political agenda of the current administration. As such, healthcare is bombarded with new initiatives and ideas such as 'patient choice'[3] as politicians seek to gain support from the electorate (Callaghan and Wistow, 2006). So, who are the key stakeholders in the National Programme? Based upon the literature review, six principal stakeholder groups are identified that play a central role in the governance structure:-

1 Government agencies and appointed representatives who use their regulatory, ministerial or influential powers to exercise decision-making and control over the healthcare system.
2 The influential medical bodies which represent clinical staff exert a high degree of power and influence over government policy and decision-making.
3 Clinicians (including consultants, hospital doctors, GPs).
4 Non-clinical healthcare management and staff who are charged with implementing change management initiatives.
5 External IT firms are increasingly securing large contracts to provide services to the NHS.
6 Patients through the initiative of 'patient choice' are increasingly being included in decision-making on healthcare.

The above stakeholders will exert their power and influence at various stages over the 10-year initiative. While government agencies and appointed representatives play a significant part in formulating the policy for the National Programme, other stakeholders will be charged with executing the policy. Since the procurement contracts have already been signed, much attention in the media now focuses upon the role of external IT vendors in meeting the various performance targets and deliverables. The views of clinicians and patients are also sought. This research study was therefore designed to encapsulate the views of all the relevant stakeholders, since it is thought that a deep understanding of public sector IT is only achieved by placing the 'IT artefact' within the broader context of the socio-political and interorganisational levels (Currie, 2004).

■ The research study

This study on the UK NHS began in 2001 at a time of heightened activity in this sector. As far back as 1998, the Department of Health (DoH) produced a strategy document which committed the NHS to lifelong EHR, *for everyone, with around the clock, on-line access to patient records and information about best clinical practice for all NHS clinicians* (Connecting for Health, 2004). This culminated in the NHS plan in 2000, which outlined a vision of healthcare service designed around the patient and a new delivery system.

By 2001, another report was produced which outlined the information systems needed to deliver the NHS plan and support patient-centred care and services. The following year,

---

[3] One of the more recent ideas is 'patient choice', which intends to put patients at the forefront of decision-making about the referral choices given to them by their GP and how they evaluate healthcare services they receive as 'consumers'.

the Wanless Report (2002) was published which offered several key recommendations for IT in the NHS. The report advocated an increase in IT investment, stringent, centrally managed national standards for data and IT, and better management of IT implementation in the NHS, including a National Programme. Later in 2002, another report was published – *Delivering 21st Century IT Support for the NHS – A National Strategic Programme* (DoH, 2002). Within it contained the plan for the governance structure to create a ministerial taskforce and recruitment of a director general for the National Programme for IT. In addition, it set up the Clinical Care Advisory Group, with representatives from many healthcare organisations. The main task for this group was the recommendation to create an NHS Care Record for each patient, with core information held in a national data repository. By October 2002, the National Programme was launched with the appointment of a Director General of NHS IT. The purpose was to *procure, develop and implement modern, integrated IT infrastructure and systems for all NHS organisations in England by 2010* (Connecting for Health, 2004).

As a longitudinal study on the UK healthcare system, it was imperative that a research method was compatible with the objective to identify and understand the governance structure in healthcare. More specifically, there was a desire to identify and explain the observed changes in the formal structure, the growing diversity of the supplier base, procurement of IT contracts and vendor management issues. The research agenda was designed to (a) identify the governance structure for overseeing the implementation of the National Programme, (b) understand and evaluate the contracts and relationships between the NHS and external suppliers, (c) gain a wider understanding of the effectiveness of the current governance structure in meeting the aims and objectives of the National Programme.

As an exploratory-descriptive study, a variety of individuals working across the NHS were interviewed. These included government representatives, professional groups within healthcare, NHS clinicians and administrators, and external IT suppliers involved in National Programme.

A literature review of the healthcare arena identified a number of studies on policy issues, yet few which systematically and rigorously examined how change management programmes are adopted and diffused throughout the healthcare sector. Whereas many studies considered the introduction of a change programme, usually involving an IT artefact (i.e. an enterprise resource management system or a PAS), or within a specific organisational setting (i.e. a hospital department) (Brown, 2001), there were virtually no studies that examined governance structures in terms of the different constituents in the adoption and diffusion of IT systems (i.e. government agencies, NHS executives, hospital trusts, IT suppliers and patients). Most of the studies were descriptive and lacked a historical dimension.

Data collection and analysis

Three methods of data collection were adopted. First, the researchers assembled a range of academic, government and industry studies on the healthcare sector. These studies were not restricted to the UK alone, but included articles and reports on healthcare services in many countries, regions and locations. This material proved invaluable for understanding some of the societal, economic, political, cultural and technical differences in healthcare nationally and internationally. Second, the researchers attended various trade fairs, conference, workshops and exhibitions on healthcare. Some of these events were focused on general topics (i.e. IT in healthcare, patient services, hospital management and professional best practice), with others more focused upon specific activities (i.e. the National Programme, presentation of the Wanless Report, IT strategy). These events generated many useful research contacts. Third, primary data collection commenced, where 170 interviews were conducted with a range of constituents.

A semi-structured interview schedule was used to enable interviewees to expand on their answers. This method of data collection was critical for allowing interviewees to raise additional themes, issues and concerns that they felt were important to the research study. Interviews with respondents took place over a 3-year period. Most of the interviews lasted around 2 hours. The interviews at the NHS hospitals were tape-recorded and the tapes were transcribed. Respondents were sent a transcript of the interview to verify it was a true account of what was discussed. Any errors were corrected. Since some of the interview content is politically contentious, the interviewees asked for themselves and their NHS hospitals to retain their anonymity.

The open-ended and semi-structured interviews were conducted during the first 4 years of National Programme project implementation, part of which was the negotiation of contracts to the service providers. Multiple informants were interviewed both within the NHS hospitals and with other constituents. During the first year of interviews, the scope of the study was extended as it was important to elicit data and information from a wider range of respondents engaged in the implementation of National Programme. These included IT service firms bidding for public sector IT contracts and doctors in general practice (external to the NHS hospitals). Respondents from IT service firms offered critical insights into the political and procurement processes within the NHS and public sector more generally. GPs offered useful insights about the communication channels underpinning the vendor responsibilities.

Following the first year of interviews, the researchers evaluated the data and refined the semi-structured interview schedule. It was recognised that given the range of constituents involved in the National Programme, the questionnaires needed to be more closely targeted to the professional and personal situation of the individual, as generic questions were less meaningful. The comments and insights from respondents were further compared with the policy documents and reports from government sources. While it is outside the scope of the present chapter to convey lengthy quotes from respondents, their comments were grouped together under specific themes from which it was possible to build up a rich picture of their observations, opinions and beliefs. The case study is focused almost entirely on the theme of the governance structure for the National Programme.

■ Case analysis: Evaluating the governance structure ■ for the National Programme for IT

Healthcare in the UK is a highly complex environment with the NHS providing patient services to around 60 million citizens, free at the point of delivery. The NHS was created in 1948 by a parliamentary act initiated by the Labour government following a national healthcare review after World War II. The current NHS organisation consists of parliament, a secretary of state for health, strategic health authorities (SHAs), under which NHS trusts, foundation trusts, PCTs, care trusts and non-NHS organisations reside. An independent regulator that monitors these organisations reports to parliament.

The past six decades have witnessed the NHS experiencing periods of both stability and change. As a highly institutionalised environment, the NHS has developed a 'public sector ethos' infused with the values of serving the public. Clinicians and healthcare workers have placed these values above issues of finance and cost effectiveness as treatment has been provided based upon medical need rather than ability to pay. Over the years, institutionalised mechanisms within the NHS have made changes difficult and highly controversial, as resistance is shown such by the powerful professional bodies that govern the conduct and performance of clinicians (McNulty and Ferlie, 2004). Successive governments have introduced policy documents to modernise the NHS with varying levels of success. One area has been in the use of ICT, as a means to enhance efficiency and performance. Healthcare is an information-rich business with 15% of hospital resources spent on gathering information. Doctors and nurses are estimated to spend up to 25% of their time collecting and using information (Audit Commission, 1995).

The proliferation of new entrants into the healthcare sector is a consequence of changing government policies over six decades. During the first three decades of the NHS, which can be characterised as the era of professional dominance (Klein, 2001; Harrison, 2004), healthcare workers, particularly clinicians, enjoyed a level of freedom to define and structure their working practices. This extended to choices about the types of technology adopted and diffused across the NHS. As a new era emerged in the 1970s, which embraced market mechanisms as a way to enhance efficiency and performance (Laing and Hogg, 2002; Harrison, 2004; Morrell, 2006), the healthcare system was increasingly inundated with various managerial fads and panaceas, like BPR and change management (Willcocks and Currie, 1997a, b; McNulty and Ferlie, 2002). An outcome of these interventions was that governance structures across the NHS were increasingly threatened, as NHS managers were keen to demonstrate 'best practice' examples through the adoption of the latest management ideas. Implicit in this view was that NHS organisations that had not embraced 'new ideas' ran the risk of being labelled as 'against modernisation' or, at worst, 'failing institutions'.

Up till the mid-1990s, the NHS governance structure for IT was decentralised or division based, although decisions about organisational-wide IT projects remained centralised at the level of the government and NHS executive. IT divisions were spread across several regional authorities, with medical functions centrally controlled. This precluded many small IT service firms from gaining a foothold in the NHS, as only their larger counterparts had the political, organisational and technical capacity to deliver large-scale IT work. In the late 1990s, the government increasingly recognised the opportunity to use IT to improve the delivery of service within the NHS. After a series of reviews of NHS IT service delivery, a more integrated and seamless IT organisation was recommended (DoH, 2000; Wanless, 2002).

The Wanless Report (2002) spearheaded the National Programme by providing cogent arguments to support increased IT investment in healthcare. One example was a comparison between IT spend in finance (which was £9000 per annum) and healthcare (£1000 per annum). Wanless concluded that healthcare IT spending was falling behind other industrial sectors and, therefore, it was failing to benefit from the latest technological advances. So against decades of under-investment in ICT, the National Programme was launched following the Wanless Report, with 'ministerial backing' (NAO, 2006a) and a large financial budget.

Formal governance structure

The formal governance structure for National Programme operates at three levels with defined reporting lines and links to other groups (see Figure 10.2). At the top level, governance is provided by the DoH – Departmental Management Board (DMB), chaired by the DoH permanent secretary. This is the senior decision-making body within the DoH and is the National Programme sponsor. The senior responsible owner (SRO) is the DoH Group Director for delivery who is a member of the DMB and who chairs the National Programme Board Executive which is an executive sub-group attended by all SROs for individual programmes and work streams. On a day-to-day basis, the management of the National Programme is the responsibility of the operational management team, chaired by the Chief Operating Officer, who reports to the National Programme Board and its Executive, and also chairs the National Supplier Board.

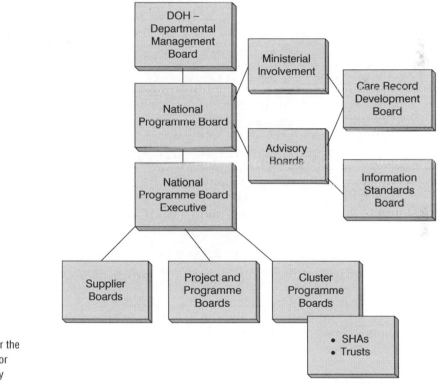

Figure 10.2
Governance system for the National Programme for information technology

Other agencies involved in auditing and reviewing the National Programme are part of the programme governance structure. These include HM Treasury, the National Audit Office and the Office of Government Commerce, all of which are represented on the National Programme Board. The Cabinet Office Committee, which reviews the ongoing progress of all large-scale IT projects, also plays a role.

The National Programme is structured around regional clusters following consultation with SHAs. After much discussion, England was split into five geographic regions (North West and West Midlands, North East, South and London) – each cluster comprising between five to seven SHAs – to work together on the procurement and implementation of National Programme services at local level. Five local service providers (LSPs) deliver applications at a local level. The LSPs work closely with local NHS IT professionals and are overseen by a Regional Implementation Director (RID) from the National Programme. The LSPs ensure that existing local systems are compliant with national standards and that data are able to flow between local and national systems. To do this, the National Programme plans to deliver upgrades or replacements to hardware and software as appropriate and implement core local training for NHS staff. All RIDs lead the implementation process across their individual areas. RIDs manage the National Programme support team and the relationship with the supplier, as well as coordinating deployment. A RID is part of the National Programme team and reports to the National Programme implementation director, but is also responsible to the cluster board for delivery.

The formal governance structure reflects the magnitude of the National Programme. Yet interviews with a range of respondents identified a paradox in that the effort to build a rigid governance structure with clear reporting lines and roles and responsibilities runs in parallel with almost constant restructuring and uncertainty within healthcare. One NHS Chief Executive commented:

'The formal structure is intended to clarify roles and responsibilities which is standard practice in any large-scale IT implementation. However, the current structure is not permanent as the government is planning to reduce strategic health authorities to only nine. This will have significant implications to decision-making structures as many chief executives will either be out of a job or moved to another role. At my hospital, the budgetary constraints have meant that we have had to postpone some of the work for the National Programme, but the constant restructuring also makes it difficult to implement IT change'.

The ongoing changes in the formal structure of the NHS produced two disruptive and negative outcomes. First, NHS restructuring was labelled by staff as producing 'change management fatigue' as they sought to interpret and implement revised government policies which could involve restructuring, targets and other performance initiatives. Many staff were concerned that structural changes did little to increase efficiency and performance, and instead contributed to low morale. Second, structural changes produced confusion, uncertainty and low morale. For example, a Director of ICT at one hospital said:

'In the past, the hospital was owned by the state. Now that we are part of the private finance initiative (PFI), the buildings are privately owned. If someone wants a new socket in their wall, I can no longer go and fit one in. I have to ask the leaseholders of the building to do this, and the cost is five times as much. This changes relationships within the organisation as everyone is either a provider or purchaser in this internal market'.

Comments of this nature were commonplace across the NHS as chief executives were more concerned about the uncertainties brought about by restructuring in conjunction with constant pressure to meet government targets with finite resources. Another common concern was the lack of communication between the senior echelons of the National Programme and the grass-roots level. A senior clinician commented:

> 'All throughout this programme, I feel there has been a lack of communication between the top and at local level. I don't think clinicians have been consulted about how the various components of the National Programme will change working practices. This needs to be made clear as people will just resist the changes otherwise.

> Despite the formal governance structure for the National Programme, the main concern of front-line NHS staff was that following decades of restructuring in healthcare, many NHS staff believed that the policy behind the National Programme could also change with a different political administration. This was in spite of the large-scale investment in this initiative and the 10-year trajectory for change'.

Procurement contracts

One aspect of the National Programme depicted as an example of good governance practice was the arrangements put in place for the procurement contracts for IT services. Much of the work of Connecting for Health is to provide 'effective and ongoing management of the National Programme contracts' (and to) 'provide a purchasing and procurement function to enable the provision of timely, effective and value for money goods and services, along with management of supplier relationships and commercial negotiations' (Connecting for Health, 2005, p. 39).

Since the five areas of the National Programme were planned across the NHS in England, the procurement contracts were sub-divided into the five regional clusters. Bids were invited from large IT vendors for specific projects in a cluster. Table 10.1 shows the major vendors who received contracts for the National Programme. Like other large-scale IT outsourcing contracts where there is high risk and reward for both parties, the nature of the contracts were shrouded in secrecy and defined as 'commercially sensitive' and 'confidential'. Connecting for Health (2005, p. 39) claimed to offer *advice and guidance on best practice, public procurement (which would) contribute to greater certainty of success.*

To avoid past problems in outsourcing contracts where IT vendors were likely to receive financial payment despite poor performance (NAO, 2004), Connecting for Health developed vigorous procurement contracts where the vendor would only be paid if they could demonstrate that work had been satisfactorily completed. While this suggests sound business practice, the reality of pursuing this course of action unveiled many serious problems in relation to the fulfilment of procurement contracts, coordinating work among key suppliers, development and integration costs and time schedules. The relationships and responsibilities among the contractor, NHS clinicians, managers and other staff, and IT vendors and their sub-contractors all conspired to produce a complex array of issues and problems as implementing the various IT projects was dependent upon the cooperation of these multiple stakeholders – all with different agendas.

In the area of the National Care Records Service, for example, a major contractor pulled out of contracts worth £2 billion in the autumn of 2006 with a promise to pay £63 million compensation to the NHS Connecting for Health. This contractor was the second largest supplier to the National Programme. The departing contractor then transferred its contracts

Table 10.1 Major vendors on the National Programme

Major Vendors – National Programme
- NASP purchasing and integrating nationally
- LSP delivering IT systems and services locally

Contracts (December 2004)	Service provision	Provider	Length (in years)
Care Records Service – NASP	National	British Telecom	10
Care Records Service – LSP	North East	Accenture*	10
Care Records Service – LSP	Eastern	Accenture*	10
Care Records Service – LSP	London	Capital Care Alliance (British Telecom)	10
Care Records Service – LSP	North West and West Midlands	CSC	10
Care Records Service – LSP	Southern	Fujitsu Alliance	10
National Network for the NHS (N3)	National	British Telecom	7
Choose and Book	National	Atos Origin	5
Contact (e-mail)	National	Cable and Wireless	10

to another contractor specifying a five-month handover period. Earlier in the year, the departing contractor made a £250 million loss provision against its National Programme contracts citing 'significant delays by one of the contractor's major subcontractors in delivering software' in addition to 'higher development costs, increased integration costs' and 'revised programme release schedules' (www.e-health-insider.com). Connecting for Health announced, 'The changes are presaged by NHS Connecting for Health and its suppliers' ongoing desire to ensure that delivery of new systems is rapid as is practicable within existing costs' (Computer Weekly, 28 September 2006). Another smaller supplier, experienced serious financial difficulties and was forced to negotiate a refinancing deal with the large contractor that had taken over from the previous one.

Many respondents commented that procurement contracts favoured the large firms over the smaller firms since the price of bidding was very high and only affordable to the well-resourced firms. Small firms were likely to be sub-contracted work by large firms, although risks increased in proportion to the numbers of firms involved in various contracts. One senior NHS manager said:

'The problem with the procurement contracts in the National Programme and elsewhere in the public sector is that IT contracts are treated like construction or railway contracts. A lot of effort is put in the area of purchasing capital equipment with less effort and money going towards the softer, change management issues. IT has to be seen as a service, not a product. By and large, the people that use IT are providing a service, whether internally or externally, and poor software development will lead to a poor service and users who do not want to use the IT'.

Where IT vendors are unable to fulfil a commercial contract, either through shareholder pressure (McNulty and Ferlie, 2004) or because of delays in developing and implementing software (Willcocks and Currie, 1997a, b), the termination of contracts does not bode well for the future success of the National Programme or the notion that private and public sector organisations enter into *strategic partnerships*.

Strategic partnerships

IT outsourcing contracts often euphemistically refer to strategic partnerships, more as an aspiration than a tangible outcome. One essential element of a strategic partnership is about sharing risks and rewards, and creating synergies from complementary competencies (Lacity and Willcocks, 2006). While the general public are encouraged to believe the National Programme may develop strategic partnerships between the NHS and IT vendors (Mohan, 2002), how this is expected to work in practice is the topic of much debate. One of the impediments to formulating a strategic partnership is the different working environment of these sectors, with private sector firms attempting to maximise their profits, and public sector NHS organisations focusing upon the needs of their patients.

These research findings suggest that closing the gap between the different aspirations of public and private sector organisations remains a challenge. Much of the criticism of the National Programme was that top-level negotiations between Connecting for Health and private firms had not embraced the concept of *user engagement*. One clinician said:

> 'I sat through three different bids from IT service firms. The firm I thought was the best failed to win the contract. I understand that this firm had already won other contracts so was perhaps not in a position to take on any more work. The firm that did win the contract did not impress NHS staff. It had very little idea of how we do things in the NHS and was just interested in introducing technology to fulfil its contractual obligations. When I asked questions about how the new software would work, I failed to get any detailed answers. I felt I was just expected to adapt to the new system'.

The concept of a strategic partnership between the NHS and private sector firms was largely dismissed as rhetoric. NHS staff expressed the most criticism about the distance between the key IT vendors and front-line NHS staff. Many staff felt that performance targets and punitive contractual arrangements were unlikely to encourage an atmosphere of trust and cooperation between the various stakeholders.

IT supplier diversity and capabilities

Despite the bureaucratic and politically charged atmosphere within the NHS, many IT vendors were keen to capitalise on the large-scale procurement contracts underpinning the

National Programme. Over the past two decades, the IT vendor marketplace has become more diverse. The large *generic* IT vendors pursue big clients, where they combine a range of IT and management capabilities and skills. More specialist IT vendors target specific industrial sectors (i.e. investment banking, hotel and catering) or applications (i.e. enterprise resource planning software, payroll systems). All three competencies are required in the National Programme as the various IT projects extend beyond simple process improvement to include process transformation. An IT Director commented:

'If you compare banking and the NHS, IT systems tend to be standardised in banking but non-standardised in the NHS. IT in the NHS has grown from the bottom up, and this is now creating problems for the National Programme, which is trying to create a uniform approach to IT across the NHS'.

One of the key challenges in the NHS was the sheer diversity of information requirements. Unlike banking, where an individual could have two or three bank accounts which transfer money from one to another, in addition to calculating interest and other routine banking services, no two patients in the NHS were alike. As such, the notion that NHS IT systems could be modelled or likened to banking or manufacturing systems was inappropriate. While payroll and billing IT systems were similar across industrial sectors, information such as patient medical records was a minefield of complexity, further complicated by issues about data security and protection, and even data ownership and availability. In regard to the National Care Record Service, where patient medical records were planned to be stored digitally and made available to specific NHS staff (i.e. GP, consultant, etc.), there was continuous debate on this area of the National Programme, even though the contracts to carry out the work had already been commissioned.

The low investment in IT services since the mid-1960s suggested that few IT vendors had developed the appropriate capabilities and skills to fully understand the political, organisational and financial complexities within the NHS. While the IT outsourcing market, which has expanded globally over the past 20 years, has witnessed heightened activity in financial services, manufacturing and retailing, contracts awarded in the healthcare sector were relatively low until recently.

The outsourcing that occurred during the 1980s and 1990s saw the loss of hundreds of potential IT jobs in healthcare. Graduates were unlikely to work in healthcare IT as the money was low compared with banking and even manufacturing. As IT work in healthcare was increasingly done by external firms, a wide knowledge gap started to appear between the NHS and IT industry. IT vendors were brought in to introduce new computer systems but had little idea about the complex business processes within healthcare. Equally, NHS staff understood the business and operations of healthcare but few knew how to translate this into a technical solution. As one long-standing IT Director commented:

'The IT outsourcing of past decades has meant that IT skills have been lost in healthcare. The focus has been to deliver packaged solutions, but computers and software alone rarely produce a seamless IT service. A lot of people with business knowledge of healthcare are now leaving. My concern is that we need to develop people within the NHS that have business and IT skills. External IT suppliers may be good at doing email, but they are not good at understanding how IT can help the day-to-day or minute-by-minute job of a doctor or nurse'.

Discussion and conclusion

The decision to launch a 10-year National Programme for IT was ambitious in the context of decades of low investment in IT across the NHS. With the introduction of the National Programme in 2002, the UK government set up a formal governance structure for overseeing the development and implementation of the various large-scale IT-enabled projects. However, these research findings suggest that, despite an attempt to apply 'best practice' methods and practices from standard project management approaches, the National Programme exhibits many of the shortcomings which have afflicted past 'IT failures'.

Comparing past and present approaches to IT investment in healthcare shows the traditional approach of localised implementation has shifted towards a centralised approach, where the agency – Connecting for Health – is involved in the procurement process for the various projects within the National Programme. While centralisation in an IT context means standardisation and uniformity of systems, this research shows that across the NHS, this policy was resisted by many clinicians who resented government attempts to 'impose' IT to change working practices without proper negotiation and consultation.

In terms of the National Care Records Service aimed to store patient medical records electronically to be made available to 'appropriate' clinicians as needed, this element of the National Programme had failed to win the widespread support of clinicians, particularly GPs who demonstrated a sense of 'ownership' and protectionism about their patients' data. Electronic medical records were also being discussed in the media as a potential security problem as data stored on external computer systems could be vulnerable to 'hacking' and other security lapses (i.e. unauthorised staff accessing patient data).

Similarly, the Choose and Book system, where a GP, together with his/her patient, can select a hospital, consultant, date and time for a referral appointment was also resisted by many clinicians. While this system within the National Programme was described as offering 'patient choice', GPs were frustrated by many functional and technical aspects of the system, and also stressed that patients often wanted an appointment at their local hospital, rather than taking up the option to travel far away. Recognising that GPs were not wholly embracing the Choose and Book system led government to consider incentive schemes to enable GPs to be paid a small fee for booking appointments. Patients were also surveyed to see if they had been offered appointment options by their GP as required by the new system.

Both these examples exemplify the shortcomings of designing monolithic IT systems at a centralised level. This was exacerbated by political involvement of ministers who wanted the systems to reflect current policy, specifically in the area of patient choice. While the formal governance structure for the National Programme clearly identified the various roles and responsibilities of the individuals under their specific domain, the serious problems arose in the design and implementation of the various systems. Like many software contracts, the IT solutions tended to be 'over-sold' to the NHS. This became increasingly apparent as the various IT vendors failed to meet the implementation timescales originally planned. This problem was further intensified by the lack of communication and coordination between NHS staff and IT vendors, in addition to budgetary constraints across the NHS.

While private sector clients also face the problem of 'over-selling' IT solutions, missed deadlines saw the high-profile National Programme attracting negative publicity with headlines describing the 'NHS's £20 billion computer catastrophe'.[4] Clearly, the rigid implementation deadlines imposed upon NHS managers and IT vendors served as a hostage to fortune, as the failure to meet performance targets offered the media a headline-grabbing story which rarely explored the finer points about the overall rationale for the IT system and potential benefits to the Health Service.

Despite the generally positive comments from respondents in the NHS about the benefits of IT in the abstract, the governance structure for the National Programme failed to address many of the softer issues of change management, particularly those around user engagement and managing the relationships between client and supplier. Connecting for Health tended to convey the National Programme as a national procurement strategy for IT, emphasising the corporate and contractual elements of dealing with suppliers. Yet the more serious concerns expressed by NHS staff were not simply confined to value for money matters and auditing, but how technology would change their working practices. While this was less contentious among hospital administrative staff, clinicians such as GPs were more resistant to IT-enabled change where they saw it as detrimental to their current activities, payment scales and rewards. Clinicians also enjoyed the support of their powerful representative bodies, such as the General Medical Council and Royal College of Surgeons.

Although the National Programme is ongoing where its fate is yet to be decided, this research study offers some useful insights on the design and implementation of governance structures for managing large-scale IT projects. Unlike many public sector IT initiatives, the National Programme is a colossal undertaking with five core projects planned across the whole of England. Notwithstanding best practice advice that suggests IT projects should be kept within a manageable scope and scale (Currie, 1994), the National Programme is a departure from this approach and carries a much higher risk of failure. Yet these findings show that addressing perceived and real risks by imposing a rigid governance structure in which tightly coupled procurement contracts act as a mechanism to control and reward IT vendors is only one side of the equation. For as the empirical data suggests, the extensive focus upon the procurement contracts and capital investment in hardware and software, has meant that fewer resources have been given to the softer issues in managing change. The negative consequences of this are witnessed by a major supplier terminating its contract, another smaller supplier facing financial difficulties and resistance from NHS staff who interpret the National Programme as a major IT solution imposed by government.

Faced with these challenges, this research suggests that greater efforts need to be placed on developing an IT policy for healthcare which is closely coupled with the business needs of

[4] Evening Standard (2006). 'Revealed: The man behind the NHS's £20bn computer catastrophe', pp. 22–23.

NHS staff and the capabilities and skills of IT firms. This policy needs to be closely related with a business delivery plan that incorporates the interests of all relevant stakeholders. While the last few decades have witnessed intensified IT outsourcing activity, academic literature suggests that outsourcing is not a panacea to reduce costs and improve services, but an alternative IT strategy that needs to be closely managed at all stages throughout the contract (Willcocks and Currie, 1997a, b). Similarly with the National Programme, the various IT outsourcing contracts which comprise the body of work are unlikely to produce successful results unless the governance structure incorporates a softer dimension where change is implemented at localised level by those engaged in change management activities alongside technical consultants.

The research findings suggest that developing a formal governance structure emphasising IT procurement as a key activity was no guarantee for successful project implementation. Evaluation of IT was largely a socially constructed activity (Currie, 1989) where clinicians and hospital managers balanced the advantages of investing in IT with other, often more important priorities, such as treating patients. The agency responsible for the National Programme was centralised and loosely coupled with the implementation of IT at the grassroots level. This meant that NHS staff acceptance of IT was left to chance, with many criticising both the vision and strategy of the programme.

In conclusion, it is suggested that as opposed to the National Programme being represented by politicians, NHS executives and the media as 'an IT project', it should be evaluated as a large-scale, IT-enabled change programme for healthcare which forms part of government policy. As this research shows, the National Programme is not simply an 'IT artefact' where success and failure factors can be measured by a narrow range of key performance indicators. Rather, the initiative is designed to transform healthcare services linked to government policy objectives on 'patient choice'. It would therefore be an oversimplification to evaluate the National Programme in isolation of how government policy both shapes and influences key stakeholders. This research points up serious shortcomings in the formal governance structure for the National Programme, not least because the informal workings in the NHS suggest that resistance to the programme has been underestimated by politicians and some NHS executives. This suggests that IT evaluation must therefore be placed in the broader context, where large-scale IT initiatives are embedded into the government policy agenda. The final outcome of the National Programme will therefore depend, not only on IT imperatives, but on whether politicians and NHS organisations continue to view IT as a means through which the policy agenda can be served to maximum advantage.

■ References

Audit Commission (1995). *For Your Information, a Study of Management and Systems in the Acute Hospital*. HMSO, London.

Brennan, S. (2005). *The NHS IT Project*. Radcliffe Publishing Ltd, London.

Brown, T. (2001). 'Modernization or failure? IT development projects in the UK public sector'. *Financial Accountability and Management*, 17(4), 363–381.

Burgoyne, J. G., Brown, D. H., Hindle, A. and Mumford, M. J. (1997). 'A multidisciplinary identification of issues associated with "contracting" in market-orientated health service reforms'. *British Journal of Management*, 3(39), 39–49.

Callaghan, G. D. and Wistow, G. (2006). 'Publics, patients, citizens, consumers? Power and decision making in primary health care'. *Public Administration*, 84(3), 583–601.

Computer Weekly (2006), 28th September, *www.computerweekly.com*

Connecting for Health (2005). *Business Plan*. Department of health, London. http://www.connectingforhealth.nhs.uk.

Currie, G. and Suhomlinova, O. (2006). 'The impact of institutional forces upon knowledge sharing in the UK NHS: The triumph of professional power and the inconsistency of policy'. *Public Administration*, 84(1), 1–30.

Currie, W. (1989). 'The art of justifying new technology to top management', in OMEGA – The International Journal of Management Science, October, 17(5), 409–418.

Currie, W. (1994). 'The strategic management of large scale IT projects in the financial services sector'. *New Technology, Work and Employment*, 9(1), 19–29.

Currie, W. (2004). 'The organizing vision for application service providers'. *Information and Organization*, 14(4), 237–267.

Department of Health (DoH) (2000). *NHS Plan: An Information Strategy for the Modern NHS*. Department of Health, London.

Department of Health (DoH) (2002). *Delivering 21st Century IT Support for the NHS*. Department of Health, London.

Granger, R. (2004). *The National Programme in the NHS in England*. www.connectingforhealth.nhs.uk.

Harrison, M. I. (2004). *Implementing Change in Health Systems: Market Reforms in Health Systems in the UK, Sweden and the Netherlands*. Sage Publications, London.

Klein, R. (2001). *The New Politics of the NHS*, 4th ed. Longman, Harlow.

Lacity, M. C. and Willcocks, L. P. (2006). 'Transforming back offices through outsourcing: Approaches and lessons'. In Willcocks, L. P. and Mary, C. (Eds.), *Lacity Global Sourcing of Business & IT Services*. Palgrave Macmillan, London, pp. 97–113.

Laing, A. and Hogg, G. (2002). 'Political exhortation, patient expectation and professional execution: Perspectives on the consumerization of health care'. *British Journal of Management*, 13, 173–188.

McNulty, T. and Ferlie, E. (2002). *Re-engineering Healthcare: The Complexities of Organisational Transformation*. Oxford University Press, Oxford.

McNulty, T. and Ferlie, E. (2004). 'Process transformation: Limitations to radical organisational change within public service'. *Organisation Studies*, 25(8), 1389–1412.

Mohan, J. (2002). *Planning, Markets and Hospitals*. Routledge, London.

Morrell, K. (2006). 'Policy as narrative: New labour's reform of the national health service'. *Public Administration*, 84(2), 367–385.

National Audit Office (NAO) (2004). *Improving IT Procurement. Report by the Comptroller and Auditor General, HC 877 Session 2003–4: 5 November*. The Stationary Office, London.

National Audit Office (NAO) (2006a). *The National Programme for IT in the NHS, 16 June*. The Stationary Office, London.

National Audit Office (NAO) (2006b). *Delivering Successful IT-Enabled Business Change, 15 November*. The Stationary Office, London.

Pollock, A. (2005). *NHS Plc: The Privatisation of our Healthcare*. Verso, London.

Scott, WW. (2001). *Institutions and Organisations*. Sage Publications, Thousand Oaks, CA.

Wanless, D. (2002). *Securing our Future Health: Taking a Long-Term View*. Final report of an independent review of the long-term resource requirement for the NHS. April. London.

Available at: www.hmtreasury.gov.uk/Consultations_and_Legislation/wanless/consult/wanless_final.cfm.

Willcocks, L. and Currie, W. L. (1997a). 'Pursuing the re-engineering agenda in public administration'. *Public Administration*, 75(4), 617–650.

Willcocks, L. and Currie, W. L. (1997b). 'Contracting out information technology in public sector contexts: Research and critique'. *Journal of the Australian and New Zealand Academy of Management*, 3(2), 34–49.

■ Strategic alignment and a culture innovation: Using the SPRINT methodology to meet two challenges of information age government

P. Kawalek and D. Wastell

■ Introduction

The need for alignment of information systems (IS) and organisational goals has been a consistent theme across management and IS literature (e.g. Beer, 1985; Checkland and Scholes 1991; Ciborra, 1997). Recent debates about the information age, e-business and e-Government have added to this by stressing the need for innovation and ongoing adaptability (e.g. Downes and Mui, 1998; Haeckel, 1999; Moss Kanter, 2001). It is argued that this fresh emphasis upon innovation and change is inconsistent with traditional approaches wherein the goals of an organisation are devised and passed outwards in a top-down fashion. Such traditional models generally depict goals as arising from senior management and being cemented into the rest of the organisation through rational planning and change management; a process through which the whole organisation is cast in the image of these goals. A contrasting view is that ongoing innovation percolates from different levels in the organisation. It may as readily be bottom-up as top-down. Thus, the organisation seeks to remake itself around new ideas from whatever their source. It is this intrinsic malleability of organisation and goals that gives vitality and viability. This kind of highly adaptive structure stands in stark contradistinction to the older model of a top-down bureaucracy whose credibility lies in the concreteness of its goals and the rigour of their implementation.

In essence then, the information age organisation must still seek alignment of IS and goals, but it should do this in a way that promotes adaptability through innovation. Alignment and innovation are thus key, and potentially competing, challenges of the information age. A descriptive analogy makes the point. An organisation is like a flotilla of boats, each one captained and crewed by sailors who navigate by the stars. The difficulty is, for our sailors, that they are blind. They cannot see the stars that they seek to follow. They can only imagine where they are. A process of debate ensues, different people having different instincts about the location of the stars and their relative importance to progress. The debate takes place within and between boats in the flotilla. Over a period of time a consensus begins to emerge, and the sailors find themselves able to steer the flotilla in a more or less common direction. 'Scientific' evidence is used to scrutinise the consensus, the sailors are able to judge their decisions by the ease, rapidity and comfort of progress. Now, imagine that our flotilla is made up of fishing boats, not only seeking a common direction but to maximise the number of fish that they catch. Traditionally, our sailors have found that the cohesion of the flotilla is positively related to the weight of the catch. In other words, they catch more fish if they sail more closely together. In order to facilitate this, leadership is assigned to the captain of one boat and this captain's opinions about the best direction of the flotilla are given more weight than the opinions of those with lesser status. Times change, and the flotilla finds itself hunting fish in choppier, fast-changing seas. Instead of cohesion, it becomes evident that the flexibility of the structure is most closely correlated to the weight of the catch. The flotilla is more successful if it allows different boats to pursue their own directions, responding rapidly to changes of instinct of their crews, to evidence about the rate and direction of progress, and to the most local conditions of the water surrounding their hull. Alignment has been sacrificed for innovation. Alignment is still important, the captain expends a lot of effort in just trying to keep the boats in the flotilla, but now it is understood that the different boats have a greater latitude of freedom to pursue their own vision, to respond to local variables.

The ideas underpinning all of this stem from that of the 'information age' itself. This notion that society has entered a post-industrial state has been proposed by a number of writers (e.g. Bell, 1973; Arthur, 1990) with the kernel of the argument being that the highly efficient transfer and management of information places a new premium on the value of that information, and enables new forms of organisation to exploit the information (e.g. Downes and Mui, 1998; Haeckel, 1999). At the same time, marketplaces themselves change and become increasingly irascible as the easy movement of information catalyses both local entrepreneurship and globalisation. This thesis is subject to ongoing scrutiny. The boom and bust of the dot.com provides ammunition for convert and sceptic alike. A sober post-boom assessment suggests that the significance of the information age will vary from sector to sector (*BusinessWeek*, 2001, 2003). Manufacturers may use the Internet to smooth their supply chains, but will still have to make high-quality products. Travel companies may utilise the Internet to enhance their yield management, but will still have to provide the right destinations and hassle-free journeys. On the other hand, the entertainment industry will be more deeply transformed as it increasingly sells its products in digitised format. Financial transactions will also be digitised. Banks will do still more business over the Internet and still less over the counter. Government departments also trade primarily in information. They will become leaner and better integrated.

This argument is further extended by the emergence of Web 2.0, synonymously known as 'social computing' and 'social media'. Essentially, the Web now permits strands to be woven between knowledge management, media studies, corporate communications and social networking. The implications for business and government organisations may be many. McAfee has coined the term 'Enterprise 2.0' to explore how 'freeform' software tools will challenge how businesses operate in the future (McAfee, 2006). Elsewhere, Kawalek (2006) has presented an 'Anna Eagin Hypothesis'; the idea that the bureaucratic norms of organisations will be challenged simply through the recruitment of a younger, Web 2.0-savvy workforce.

The task of encouraging innovation while ensuring the alignment of IS and organisational goals is therefore central to all organisations in this ongoing 'information age'. In this paper, this problem is placed in the context of organisational change through Business Process Reengineering (BPR). The domain is government. A BPR methodology is described which attempts to address the key issues of alignment and innovation. The methodology is known as SPRINT (Salford Process Reengineering method Involving New Technology) and was developed collaboratively with the information technology (IT) department of a local public administration, the city of Salford (a novel feature itself, which was seen as key to its adoption in practice). SPRINT has been strongly influenced by the original philosophy of Business Process Reengineering (Davenport, 1992; Hammer, 1990) as BPR was felt to embody a set of precepts that are critical to achieving real benefits from information and communications technology (ICT) investment, principally a concern to exploit the transformatory power of ICT disciplined by the necessity to pay constant attention to the needs of the business. SPRINT represents the accumulation of many years of experience of the authors in the BPR field (e.g. Wastell et al., 1994; Warboys et al., 1999). This work recognises the contested, problematic nature of the term 'BPR' itself. It has also been influenced by recent thinking in the area of change management and strategic alignment, principally the need to adopt a participative, improvisational approach to change (Orlikowski and Hoffman, 1997), a bottom-up 'design approach' to strategic alignment (Ciborra, 1997; Simonsen, 1999) and the need to embed a culture of innovation across organisational strata (Haeckel, 1999; Moss Kanter, 2001).

It follows that key challenges for SPRINT in practice, in the domain of information age government, are as follows:

- To facilitate process innovation while promoting the alignment of IS and business goals.
- To inculcate an ongoing culture of innovation.

SPRINT forms a key element in the City of Salford's recently elaborated Information Society Strategy (Salford City Council, 1999). The Strategy's visionary aim is to harness the potential of ICT in order to enhance local democratic processes and to improve the social and economic well-being of the people of Salford (through improved service delivery, greater social inclusion, and development of the local economy). The Strategy sets out 10 key work programmes involving specific initiatives such as 'One-stop shops' and a move towards more flexible work patterns (e.g. home-working). ICT is integral to all these programmes, and all are predicated on a philosophy of fundamental change in the way that the city operates. To underpin the initiatives, a strategic methodology was required focusing on the innovative use of ICT to realise radical transformation; one of the work programmes was explicitly targeted at the development of such a methodology, which has come to be known as SPRINT.

SPRINT: general precepts

Before discussing the practical aspects of the methodology, the main philosophical principles underpinning SPRINT will be described. SPRINT has the following key characteristics:

Breadth of vision and depth of understanding: BPR projects are inherently complex in that many groups and individuals within the organisation will be directly or tangentially impacted. Recognising this, SPRINT stresses the importance of seeking out and examining all stakeholder perspectives in order to appreciate the complexity of the problem and the different views that people hold. SPRINT also advocates the development of a rigorous *evidence-based* understanding of processes. It is important to know what goes on now, why things are the way they are and what the important contextual factors are. Ethnographic methods (i.e. detailed, immersive investigation) are recommended to achieve this depth of understanding (Martin et al., 1998).

Learning and Knowledge Management: BPR projects are regarded as opportunities for organisational innovation. Learning and knowledge management are thus seen as key to successful BPR and the methodology actively aims to stimulate innovative thinking and to nurture radical ideas. Following Wastell (1999), BPR projects are regarded as Transitional Spaces, that is as 'supportive learning environments' in which users are encouraged to reflect critically on current processes and experiment with new process designs (using various modelling techniques). To support the management of knowledge within and across BPR projects, extensive use is made in SPRINT of intranet technology. A Web site is created for each SPRINT project which acts as a shared repository for the project's working documentation and allows access to the experience and knowledge gained in other projects.

An emphasis upon innovation through participation: Localised innovation and learning become more important as certainty decreases (Haeckel, 1999; Moss Kanter, 2001). The design of SPRINT recognises that a key part of any transformation project may be to overturn a traditional ethos of top-down management and to implant a new culture of innovation, based upon the insights of staff at all levels in the organisation. The SPRINT 'expert' practitioners from the IT team might themselves be part of the transitional space as the organisation makes this change. As end-users become skilled with SPRINT, they will become more able to develop ideas independently, and more eager to implant them in their organisation. A participative approach is therefore indispensable to the effectiveness of SPRINT as a means of generating innovation. This thinking draws upon a well established lineage of ideas in IS. Blackler and Brown (1986) distinguish two paradigms that drive IT-based organisational change: The *Task and Technology* approach, in which technology is used Tayloristically to increase efficiency by deskilling and automating the role of the human agent, and *the Organisation and End User* paradigm, in which the emphasis is on the potential of technology to create new organisational possibilities and to augment the human role. SPRINT embraces the latter, which, in essence, reflects a socio-technical approach to IS design (Mumford, 1986; Wastell and Newman, 1996; Warboys et al., 1999). This importance of *user participation* in innovation and design may seem to be at odds with the popular perception of BPR. Although BPR has come to be seen as a sinister Tayloristic force, it is worth remarking that much of its founding philosophy is decidedly socio-technical in spirit (see Davenport, 1992).

Designed-in strategic alignment: It follows that while SPRINT places considerable emphasis on the achievement of recognisable business benefits, it eschews a classical top-down approach to achieving business alignment. The authors concur with recent critiques of the rational paradigm (e.g. Hackney and Little, 1999; Ciborra, 1997) which stress the emergent, practice-based nature of the 'strategy process'. Alignment is seen as an integral part of the ongoing process of BPR, not as something in advance of and separate from the design work itself. In Ciborra's terminology, alignment is something that should be *taken care of* throughout the design process. Haeckel (1999) makes a similar argument, proposing that strategy should be seen as a 'Design for Adaptation', which is fulfilled by the ensuing process of organisational development. SPRINT contributes to this by exhorting BPR participants to address themselves to business goals at all stages in a BPR project, from goal identification in the analysis phase through to, goal development and the establishment of rigorous mechanisms to track and manage the achievement of business benefits (Serafeimidis and Smithson, 2000) in the implementation phase.

An incremental, improvisational change model: BPR is often associated with the idea of large-scale, rapid change. However, the idea that organisational change can proceed on a one-shot Lewinian basis (unfreeze-change-freeze) has been called into serious question in an IS context (Macreadie and Sandon, 1999). The demands on the organisation are potentially huge, in terms of human and technical resources (Benjamin, 1993) and the risk of resistance is high (especially in a public sector organisation with strong collective traditions). SPRINT rejects the idea of change as a discrete, convulsive event, imposed on the organisation. The authors' approach draws its inspiration from the improvisational change model of Orlikowski and Hofman (1997). Change should not be determined by a top-down plan, but rather guided by a set of business objectives, and enacted through a series of incremental steps emphasising continuous reflection and adaptation to changing circumstances. Each step should be seen as a learning experiment, in which a new ICT-enabled process is implemented, evaluated and refined. The ethos should be one of excitement, fun even, not of fear. It goes without saying that a participative approach is key, with users leading the prototyping process and colleagues involved in giving feedback. Of course, a plan is required but only as a coordinating device and as means for managing progress; the plan does not drive the change.

Flexibility and extensibility: A danger with methodologies is that they can become an end in themselves, with users following the method's prescriptions in a slavish fashion rather than thinking for themselves (Wastell, 1997). To guard against this, SPRINT has been deliberately designed with a minimum of procedural structure; in essence, it comprises a tool-box of recommended techniques within a loose, general framework of tasks and phases. Users should be familiar with SPRINT's structure, tasks and tools but they are encouraged interpret and adapt the methodology according to the particular circumstances of the project they are undertaking. For instance, if they think that some new tool or method is ideally suited to solving a particular problem, they are encouraged to adopt it and bring it into the framework.

■ An overview of SPRINT

This section provides practical information regarding SPRINT. First, project organisation and management are considered, including the roles that participants are expected to play. Details of the method itself (phases and tasks) are then given.

People and project management

SPRINT recommends that two groups be established to manage a BPR project: a **Steering Group** and the **BPR team**. The former should include: the departmental director for all operational areas impacted by the project; the BPR project manager and Lead BPR consultant; together with senior representatives from Human Resources (HR) and ICT services. Leadership at such a senior level is critical; given the radical nature of BPR, it is vital that such commitment is made from all those departments that will be directly impacted.

Membership of the BPR team comprises: a Senior User at deputy director level, who plays the role of Project Manager; a Lead BPR consultant and supporting consultants; HR and ICT experts. Early projects required that operational groups whose work will be directly affected by the initiative should be represented on the Team by one or more 'Practice Representatives'. More recently, the idea of the 'e-envoy' has been developed. These are individuals who are recognised for their innovative thinking, and are able to work with organisational and ICT-related issues. Staff members of any level of seniority can participate as an e-envoy.

The rationale of the BPR team is to undertake the detailed investigative work of Phases 1 and 2 of SPRINT and to oversee the implementation activity in Phase 3. It is strongly recommended that the core team stay together throughout the entire project thereby ensuring continuity and ownership.

Members of the BPR team are required to play two roles: an **operational role** (i.e. carrying out the technical work that is required) and a **review role**. The role of reviewer is to examine BPR ideas that are made by the team, actively challenging conservatism in the project; reviewers should try to prevent the project from too readily taking an incremental, stepwise approach.

Phase 1: Understanding process context

SPRINT comprises 3 main phases (see Figure 11.1). Each phase is defined in terms of a set of aims, and there are a set of tasks within each phase intended to help the realisation of these aims. Although the impression may be gained of a tightly defined structure, this is emphatically not the case. The division into phases and tasks is merely to provide a loose organisational framework to allow the work to be structured and divided up amongst the BPR team. There is no requirement, for instance, for tasks to be performed in strict sequence and there are no dogmatic injunctions on the use of particular techniques.

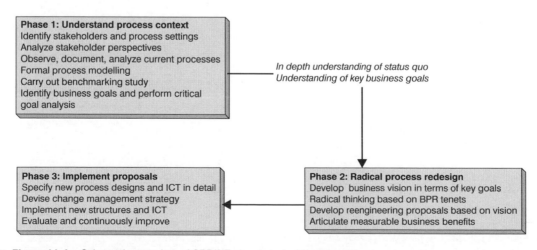

Figure 11.1   Schematic overview of SPRINT showing phases and tasks

Phase 1 is essentially one of analysis. The aims are:

- To understand the business context of the BPR project by considering all relevant perspectives, and to analyze the effectiveness and efficiency of current processes in this broader context.
- To generate preliminary ideas for process improvements (technical and organisational).
- To help develop the business vision on which the detailed BPR proposals in Phase 2 will be founded.

The emphasis on understanding the business context is crucial. This forces the BPR team to stand back from the original remit which may focus too narrowly on a particular process or processes. 'Zooming out' in this way will assist in identifying and understanding the real business goals that should be addressed and will lead towards the identification of more radical reengineering opportunities.

Of the various tasks carried out in Phase 1, two require further comment. The construction of formal process models is a key feature of SPRINT. To this end, a modelling method known as *Role Activity Diagramming* (RAD) is proposed as the technique of choice. The authors' previous BPR experience has demonstrated the accessibility and the efficacy of this simple method which makes use of a small number of relatively straightforward constructs (primarily Roles, Activities and Interactions). For a detailed description see Warboys et al. (1999).

Critical goal analysis (CGA) is another important technique. This task constitutes the crux of Phase 1 as it is the primary means for addressing the alignment issue. CGA focuses all strands of enquiry on two pivotal questions: What are the business goals relevant to the process context? How well are they supported by the current processes and support systems? For each business goal, a number of key issues must be addressed, including: What is the goal? Who are the primary stakeholders? How does it relate or divert from the strategic aims of the Council, especially to the themes of the Information Society Strategy? How well is the goal currently achieved and how should it be measured (i.e. what metrics could be used)? SPRINT recommends the use of a Goal Network Diagram to depict the set of goals and their interrelationships. An example is shown in Figure 11.2.

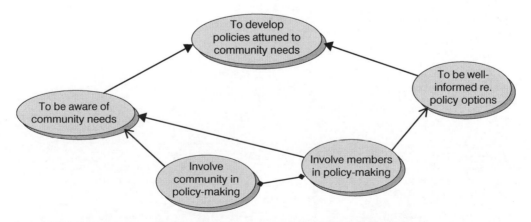

Figure 11.2　Part of the Goal Network Diagram for the Decision-Making (DM) Case Study. Links between goals are either positive (arrows) or inhibitory (diamonds)

Phase 2: Radical process redesign

The analytical work of Phase 1 constitutes essential preparation for the second phase of SPRINT, the aim of which is to devise a set of process reengineering proposals. These will embrace the use of ICT to underpin new processes aimed at dramatic improvements in the City Council's performance, in relation to its general strategic objectives and the specific aims of the Information Society Initiative. The first 'task' in Phase 2 is to develop a business vision in terms of key goals and critical success factors for achieving the goals. It is vital to assess the importance of each goal and the effectiveness of current process support. Although the articulation of a clear business vision might suggest a conventional top-down IS design and planning process, this is not how the business vision is intended to function. Its role is simply to provide a panoramic view of the organisation's key goals as currently understood and to enable a set of priorities to be established to guide subsequent design work. Initially, the BPR team lead the work, although key stakeholders also participate and increasingly take over this important alignment activity. A high-priority goal is one which is judged to be important to the organisation but not well-supported in terms of current processes. Table 11.1, from the first of the featured case studies, furnishes an example.

Having established a clear business context, the next task requires the BPR team to reflect, in a radical way, on reengineering opportunities. The aim of BPR is to change the way the organisation operates by taking full advantage of the potentialities of ICT to enable new ways of working. Innovative thinking can stimulated in a number of ways: via literature research, the results of best practice investigations, existential reflection. Although it cannot be reduced to technique, SPRINT provides a set of 'revisioning heuristics' based on Hammer's early work (Hammer, 1990) to aid in the search for new ideas.

The end point of Phase 2 is a set of reengineering proposals which embody new process designs (again using the RAD notation wherever appropriate) enabled by the innovative application of ICT. Crucially, each proposal must be supported by a detailed business case, including the specification of a set of metrics (ideally quantitative) to aid in the delivery of real business benefits and to establish an ongoing feedback loop to facilitate continuous process improvement.

Phase 3: Implementation and continuous improvement

The aim of the third phase of SPRINT is to implement the reengineering proposals developed in Phase 2. As noted above, the original BPR team remain in place in order to supervise this stage, although the overall team will typically become much larger via the co-option of additional individuals (e.g. training specialists, ICT specialists, relevant line managers, user representatives) in order to carry out the detailed changes that are required to implement the proposals. Implementation can be a long, arduous process and strong user leadership is absolutely essential at this stage to carry through the desired changes into working practice. Many tasks are entailed:

■ An incremental implementation plan is required to provide an overall organisational framework. It must be determined whether the proposals are to be implemented serially, or concurrently if there are important areas of synergy and there is sufficient resource available;

- The process designs must be re-examined and translated into new working structures and procedures;
- Training must be addressed, courses and documentation devised, and staff trained;
- Requirements for new ICT must be elaborated in appropriate detail to allow the development of the necessary ICT systems (by whatever method is deemed appropriate, in-house development, packages etc.);
- Crucially, a positive attitude towards evaluation must be established and appropriate mechanisms put in place to gather whatever data is required to provide feedback on the new systems and processes, whether this be soft data (e.g. interview feedback) or quantitative metrics. It is vital that the ethos of learning, experimentation and further innovation be maintained throughout.

In principle, this final phase continues indefinitely: the new process designs should be the subject of continuous monitoring and critical evaluation (assisted by the metrics framework). SPRINT thus recommends that the BPR team remain in place on an ongoing basis, considering incremental improvements or indeed radical process changes (akin to the original BPR effort).

SPRINT in action

SPRINT has been deployed on many major projects within Salford, Leeds and across the sector. Three of the Salford cases are described briefly in order to give details of the difficult pressures that develop around the building of alignment and the cultivation of innovation. The descriptions follow in chronological order of project start.

The decision-making project

Profound changes to the nature of local government in the UK form the background to the decision-making (DM) project. At the behest of national imperatives, local government engaged in a process of democratic renewal, wherein decision-making processes were the subject of fundamental change (Wilson and Game, 1998). The traditional method of decision-making involved a set of committees, chaired and staffed by elected representatives, with a committee devoted to each area of the Council's work (Housing, Social Services and so forth). The most common model that replaced this method was that of cabinet-style government, although further reforms are ongoing. The cabinet model involves the constitution of a small, centralised decision-making body of 'Lead Members' (the Cabinet) and a considerably extended system of delegation of power through the executive. Each Lead Member has decision-making power for a given operational area; in effect, they resemble ministers in the Westminster system.

In early 1999, a conventional ICT project had been instigated to address issues of IS support for the administrators who would service the new structure. This came to focus upon the issue of 'text retrieval' – the ICT search facilities used by administrators when responding to requests for information made by elected members. Over a period of time, concerns developed that this project was too narrow, that it had failed to address the broader issues regarding the enhancement of local democracy embodied in the Information Society vision. At best, text retrieval could only achieve marginal improvements to the existing administrative process. What was needed was a wider and deeper study that would coalesce a more radical vision of change as a precursor to defining a more fitting ICT solution. The decision was thus made for members of the then nascent BPR team to deploy SPRINT on the project. It was used to facilitate a broad enquiry among all concerned stakeholders about how the decision-making structure should work, and how it could be supported through ICT.

Interviews with key stakeholders were carried out (elected members, council officers, community representatives) supplemented by detailed ethnographic observation of the administrative process supporting the committee decision-making system (still operating at that time). Essentially, the support process was a paper-based one involving the circulation of agenda packages in advance of committee meetings. These packages included an agenda, the minutes of the previous meeting, and a set of detailed reports relevant to the agenda items.

A Role Activity Diagram for the support processes was constructed and a CGA carried out. This promoted a highly productive discourse amongst stakeholders about how the existing process operated and its relationship with the goals of the organisation. This was important as it forced stakeholders to confront the fact that the existing support mechanisms were not effective (e.g. see Table 11.1). Very few of the Council's goals regarding effective and responsive decision-making were effectively supported by the existing process; few indeed were even tangentially addressed. For instance, effective decision-making was impeded by the fact that large volumes of documentation would be delivered to councillors just a few days before a committee meeting. How were they expected to read it all in such a short time? How were they expected to identify the parts relevant to their constituents? Equally, the need to involve the community in the decision-making process was severely inhibited by a lack of ready access to documentation. It was clear that here was a process that was severely out of alignment with its goals.

Table 11.1 Summary of the Business Vision for the case study. The gap column indicates the degree to which the goals were supported by the original process

Business goal	CSF/sub goal	Gap	Priority
Effective representation of community interests	Support representative role of members	Mod	High
	Support direct involvement of community in decision-making	Low	High
Policy development attuned to needs of city	Support policy development role of elected members	High	Mod
	Better community consultation	High	Mod
	More effective policy coordination	High	Mod
	Effective policy monitoring by elected representatives	Low	High
	More rapid decision-making	Mod	High

Phase 2 led to the rapid formulation of a design proposal centred around the creation of a comprehensive information repository (CIR) for the Council and the transformation of the role of the committee support staff to that of information managers. All documents (reports, agendas, minutes) would in future be stored in the CIR directly by their authors. They would be indexed rigorously in terms of the policy issues they addressed and the areas of Salford that they related to. The committee support staff would no longer simply act as 'paper pushers' but would take responsibility for ensuring that documentation was correctly classified; they would also monitor the quality of reports and actively seek out additional material. In short, the BPR proposal envisaged the creation of an information management (IM) function within the Council. This would underpin major changes to the processes of information dissemination and retrieval. Additionally, it would promote better alignment with the goals of the process by providing a speedier and customisable service. Documents would be circulated to elected members electronically, thus reaching them more quickly. Members would also be able to register their interests (e.g. policy issues, their ward) and information would be proactively supplied to them based upon this profile. Retrieval also would no longer depend on the committee support staff, elected members could search for electronically held documents using the indexes provided for them. Thus, from its original concerns with 'text retrieval', the use of SPRINT had enlarged the scope of the project to consider the whole process of decision-making more broadly, and the related HR, business process and ICT issues. In time, it was proposed, the benefits would become still greater with community stakeholders able to utilise the CIR in a similar way to the elected members.

Births, deaths, marriages (BDM)

A later engagement for SPRINT followed in the area of the registration of births, deaths and marriages (BDM). One BPR consultant took primary responsibility for the engagement, working closely with two managers of the service (one is a senior manager). The BDM service in Salford is located in a large, converted Victorian house about one mile away from the City Council's main offices. It houses a reception desk where members of the public come in to report for appointments (e.g. to register a death) and to make ad-hoc queries. The majority of transactions, however, feature a telephone call. The office receives close to 34 500 telephone calls per annum. Many of these relate to appointments, with copy certificates and family history being other prominent service requests.

It became clear that the short walk between the City Council's main offices and the BDM office was associated with a marked contrast in available technology. The BDM office had no e-mail facilities and fee payments could only be accepted by cash or cheque. PC-based records for BDM existed only for the years following 1994.

Staff reported problems with overstretch at peak times. Queues would build at the service counters and on the telephone lines. An interesting problem would be posed by individuals researching family history; a fast-growing area of activity. They might come into an office or make a telephone enquiry with a friendly, long-winded and time-consuming set of questions about their ancestors. Behind them in the queue might be the traumatised relatives of a recently deceased person.

The enquiry into service goals and alignment identified a number of important service metrics, relating to times taken to answer queries from the public. All targets were being met, although the targets themselves were not always ambitious (e.g. customers coming in to the office should be seen by reception staff within 30 minutes). Looking forward, the discussion highlighted a set of proposals made at national level by the National Audit Office (NAO, 2002). This focused on service developments around the needs of families and individuals. It highlighted the need to be open to the prospect of partnerships within the public sector (e.g. hospitals) and beyond to the private sector (e.g. local wedding or funeral services, family history services). Another set of ideas from central government for modernisation was also influential. This was the idea that government services in general could be increasingly organised around 'life events'. This proposal suggests that much of the public's engagement with government is predictable, taking place in response to defined life episodes. Births, deaths and marriages are three such life events. It was likely that in the future the act of registering one of these events would initiate a network of information exchanges with the benefit being that the customer needs to engage only once with government over a particular episode.

Beyond a general discussion of these central government initiatives, the discussion of service goals faltered. There were pressing objectives and a number of popular proposals. These focused on the use of the corporate call centre to provide basic information to the public (thereby freeing the specialist resources in the BDM centre), and the provision of e-mail for communications within the council. However, these were clearly incremental in nature, designed to fix existing service deficiencies. The existing goals of the service were not called into question and there was no obvious realignment of the service around the modernising agenda of central government. The agenda, and all of its radical potential, remained some way distant. Instead, it was acknowledged that the BPR project 'set the groundwork' for more extensive service reorganisation, but the time scale and means for achieving these more fundamental changes were not established.

Social Services

The third of the case studies is the most recent. It reflected a growing awareness that while SPRINT was being used to successfully deliver change to the organisation, it was falling some way short as a means of inculcating an ongoing ethos of innovation. As a result, the BPR project in social services introduced a new concept, that of the 'e-envoy'. This new concept conferred a new authority upon selected primary users from the operational division engaged in the study. The mission of the e-envoy was to think creatively about change possibilities and to represent these ideas to the operational division. Staff were asked to apply for the post of e-envoy prior to the commencement of the BPR study. They were asked to include a statement describing their feelings and ideas about e-Government and service innovation. Consistent with the need to infuse a culture of innovation, the designation as e-envoy was an indefinite one but most activity was to be concentrated in a period of about three months. During this time, the e-envoy worked exclusively on SPRINT projects, while temporary staff were bought in to fulfil the postholder's normal day-to-day job.

The advertisement of an e-envoy position in Social Services bought forward two applicants, both qualified social workers. One had substantial Internet experience. Neither had taken an active part in major organisational change programmes. After consultation it was decided that both should be appointed to the post, with two temporary staff being bought in to provide cover. Following an initial period working on the SPRINT analyses, it was also decided to extend the period of the e-envoys' BPR activity to five months. By this stage, it was also clear that the BPR team would play only a supervisory role in the Social Services project, a position that was a significant retrenchment from that taken in the DM and BDM projects. The social workers quickly became adept at using SPRINT and soon found their way to generating some noteworthy innovations.

The social services case is an interesting one for in some ways it became the most potentially radical of all SPRINT projects. Among the many ideas developed by the e-envoys was the restructuring of the service around self-contained practices (analogous to GP practices) and the development of a new, independent, Internet-based information service. This would be responsible for the sourcing and maintenance of care information (e.g. care home vacancies). These ideas align with the overriding goals of the social care function, to provide high-quality care to members of society. However they deviate sharply from some deeply entrenched goals of the organisation itself: to maintain itself as an entity and to retain control over the information it uses. This radicalism was sometimes the source of tension. The BPR team insisted on promoting alignment, using SPRINT to ensure that the social workers thought about the existing goals of the service and whether any particular innovation conforms to or diverts from them. The social workers had been working differently, instinctively seeing the virtue of an innovation and then giving a post-hoc view of how the innovation does or does not fit in with the goals of the organisation. They tended to view SPRINT's requirement that they pre-think alignment issues in Phase 1 as a restriction on their creative operation. 'I don't know who owns this process', complained one social worker, 'but it's not us'. At one stage, colleagues of the social workers in the Social Services directorate also raised concerns about the innovative nature of the ideas. They sought to remind the e-envoys about legacy issues arising from a recently sourced software package. It was argued that they should not propose any initiative that was inconsistent with the functionality of this software.

As controversy peaked, the Social Services project entered a crucial period. The redesign ideas of the e-envoys became increasingly well-focused and well-described. The ideas lost none of their radicalism but were accompanied by a number of less profound, more incremental changes. It was these less radical changes that became the agreed outputs of the study. The radical ideas were lost in some uncertain responses and, eventually, the greater wave of reform emanating largely from central government. From the point of view of the e-envoys themselves, the project was unsuccessful. They faced the problem of selling their radicalism to their colleagues, but this proved difficult. The adoption of small-scale, incremental changes did not compensate for the setting aside of the boldest ideas. This dynamic was interesting given that the appointment of e-envoys was originally motivated by the wish to source ideas directly from operational staff and to build a focus for ongoing innovation in the operational division. It seems that radicalism is still radicalism and will be difficult to sell, whatever its source.

Discussion

It would be easy to fashion these experiences into a typical tale of top-down managerial philosophy vs. bottom-up, innovative thinking. In one corner one could see the conservatism of managers and in the other the free-thinking, and potential unruliness, of more junior staff. This tale of two perspectives would be a highly misleading depiction. Neither alignment nor innovation wholly resides within the remit of management or junior staff.

Each has the potential to promote alignment and to promote innovation, as each is able to disrupt alignment and dampen innovation.

It is more useful to think about alignment and innovation as both being desirable properties of the government system, in this case the Salford government system. Then one can see how one systemic property, innovation, has the potential to either undermine the other (alignment) or to enhance it. This, then, is a dialectic between meta-system and operational system (e.g. Beer, 1985). The meta-system seeks sufficient alignment to give coherence to the whole operation of the system. The operational system will sometimes seek freedom from this alignment in order to pursue a new goal that arises from its engagement with the business environment.

The net effect is that while a reduced emphasis on alignment is consistent with an increased emphasis on innovation, alignment is still important. This leaves managers in government institutions like Salford with the problem of trying to loosen and then refasten the stays of alignment, before organisational coherence unravels and the synergies and connections of organisational life are lost. The three SPRINT case examples reveal the difficulty of controlling this relationship. They reveal also how ownership of the change initiative by the operational division does not necessarily imply either a more or less radical approach.

The projects can all be described as being successful up to a point. The DM and BDM projects have both been associated with needed changes in the departments concerned. The Social Services project left a less certain imprint but was still generally well-regarded. However, if Salford is to develop its capabilities as a developing, information age organisation, then another order of challenges must be met. These were set out above:

■ To facilitate process innovation whilst promoting the alignment of IS and business goals.
■ To inculcate an ongoing culture of innovation.

In the DM project, the BPR consultants took a hands-on approach to the development of the new design. They worked closely and shared responsibility with end-users and managers. They clearly demarcated ownership of the project: it resided with the manager of the committee staff. The result was a successful implementation. The CIR was born with the name SOLAR (Salford Online Archive), and gave rise to a number of business benefits (e.g. more rapid dissemination of reports). However, the most radically innovative ideas were left on the shelf. The idea of reconstituting the committee support function as an IM function has not been implemented. Neither has the proposal that authors of documents should input them directly to SOLAR. Both of these innovations would enhance the alignment of the service with its declared goal of supporting policy development. This would be achieved by further speeding up the process and by ensuring the development of a rigorously catalogued library of reports for further policy development. Retracing the steps of the project reveals that BPR team members proposed both of these fundamental ideas. They were supported by the Senior Manager and his staff. Nonetheless, the failure to implement them speaks eloquently. Judged against this challenge then, that of promoting alignment, the DM project was only partially successful. Perhaps what is being described exemplifies the difference between formal service goals and the tacit goals of those carrying out the service. Yes, all sides agreed that the radical innovations would improve the contribution of the service to its formal goals. But how well-accepted are these goals? Do they conflict with another set of goals, the internalised goals of the service providers themselves? These internalised goals might dictate that service innovations are kept within a 'comfort-zone' of current process and technology know-how. Hence, in this case, the very idea of under-stood and accepted business goals has proved to be an oversimplification. This has impor-tant ramifications for the challenge of developing an ongoing culture of innovation. The DM project remains stuck fast on these issues. The SPRINT ethos of stepwise, incremental organisational development will not necessarily dislodge the caution of the project owners.

In the case of BDM, we again see a BPR expert taking a hands-on approach to the develop-ment of design ideas. However, again, following the SPRINT prescription, ownership resides with the manager of the BDM function. The BPR expert worked closely with this manager and her subordinate staff. The radical agenda is identified, to some extent it is pre-packaged, as it resides in a governmental vision for service development incorporating partnership and utilising the concept of life events as a new portal for government services. However, the BPR project did no more than prepare the 'groundwork' for this new vision. This radical vision remains remote, with only the most pressing needs being met by the BPR. If this is a sen-sible outcome, it is also conservative: the idea of introducing e-mail and call centre support facilities was not bold! Perhaps the most glaring shortcoming is the fact that the study has not brought forth a plan for building on this groundwork. Yet, an interesting footnote is that in this case the BPR consultant admitted to a sense of frustration. She saw the opportunity to develop a new model around integrated services. Taking bereavement as an example, the function of registering a death could have cross-departmental implications, embracing social services, housing and other relevant areas. By providing a range of services, staff would be able to sort out a number of difficulties for bereaved friends and relatives in one single coun-selling session. When asked why this idea did not figure in the SPRINT design activity, she replied that she felt constrained to work with the needs and preferences of the client. From their technologically disadvantaged position, even the introduction of e-mail felt radical.

Later, however, in the context of other projects in Salford, these more radical ideas were reintroduced. Many of the measures were taken forward by aligning them with other cor-porate goals, for example those of good customer service and cross-departmental informa-tion sharing. Although the full vision of the BPR analyst has not been realised, the project seemed to enter its most radical phase after its formal completion!

The third case adds a further twist. Here, some operational staff were selected for their inno-vative thinking and were given a special status, that of 'e-envoy'. We see a role reversal take place. In the BDM case, the BPR consultant had been unable to develop some radical ideas because the study was owned by the operational managers. These operational managers were content with more mundane initiatives. This time, it was the e-envoys who felt frustrated as the BPR team and SPRINT itself appeared, at least for a time, to act as a brake on their ambition. One e-envoy complained about the ownership of the study. Nonetheless, progress was made and the e-envoys developed their proposals. However, the selling of the proposals remained a daunting task. That the e-envoys belonged to the affected department mattered lit-tle, it seems, when the proposals involved a significant realignment of organisation and goals.

Nonetheless, the case showed how operational experts, freed from their day-to-day activi-ties, can quickly cut inwards to the heart of an issue. In this light, the impatience of the social workers with the BPR team and the SPRINT methodology might actually be a positive sign. It signifies a creative tension as the expert practitioners require the BPR consultants to operate more quickly and to engage with constructive design ideas. A hallmark of the case has been the readiness of the e-envoys to roll back the alignment issue: to focus upon the goals that are really important to the work and to dismiss other goals and constraints that might be seen to hinder this. Hence, there has been a detailed debate about ways and means of providing more effective client care. Little else has mattered. Moreover, as they return to their operational role the e-envoys will provide a focus for ongoing innovation and change.

Conclusions

The cases exemplify just how difficult it is to meet the challenge of remaking government for this, so-called information age. The rhetoric suggests that radical solutions should be the norm, that new technology should be a catalyst amid a range of organisational and cultural changes. In fact we tend to find a different outcome: we have reported projects that start with high ambition but then slip backwards to a positive but appreciably more modest result.

Looking forward, the development of e-envoys, innovative thinkers who are given time to develop their ideas, does seem to be a key development. It injected a more radical spirit into the design process and, critically, sources this radicalism from the operational department itself. The reader will recall that in the DM and BDM cases it was the BPR consultants who were the frustrated radicals. In Social Services case, this distinction belongs to the e-envoys. The rebranding and further development of the concept of the e-envoy is likely to be an important topic in the further development of SPRINT. However, it will not be enough. The Social Services case describes how radicalism is difficult to sell whatever its source. Our social work e-envoys admitted it was revealed that the vaulting ambition of the BPR project in Social Services was thwarted and that it too resulted in a positive but modest outcome for the department.

So what lies beyond these projects, and what, if anything, can engender a spirit of change that matches the ambition of the e-Government literature? The general management literature provides many clues. Moss-Kanter's approach to systemic change through 'the change wheel' prescribes a set of ten different elements that must be adjusted in order to ignite organisational change (Moss-Kanter, 2001). Using her model to provide a quick diagnostic of the SPRINT projects described above, it might be argued that too little attention has been given to quick wins, to new reward structures and to communication with the operational staff likely to be most affected by the changes. This latter point has a particular relevance to the Social Services case and the difficulty of the e-envoys in 'selling' their ideas to their colleagues. Other literature such as Livingston's delineation of the Primary Working Group and the potential of 'skunk works', or Christensen's depiction of product innovation, suggest an alternate strategy in the change process. This is to build new satellite service operations and allowing them to run alongside, and potentially take over, from the older structures (Christensen, 1997; Livingston, 1990). In these ideas might reside the vital combination of elements that will make up the vital elixir, the fuel for ongoing innovation. A case that deployed these more radical ideas is described in Kawalek (2007). However, none of the SPRINT cases described above has yet on an individual basis been able to successfully seed a process of ongoing innovation although, more widely, the actions of the SPRINT team are still associated with the organisation's ongoing quest for development.

Beyond all of this, a resounding note of caution is necessary. Organisational transformation is a fundamentally challenging prospect. The literature across the public and private sectors is replete with cases of failure (e.g. Davenport, 1992; Cabinet Office, 2000) Then when change does take root, the financial and organisational costs can be high (*BusinessWeek*, 2001). In this light then, perhaps we should be prepared to accept that the birth of the so-called information age government will be made of a huge number of change projects as people try to apply new technologies and ideas to their organisations. A few of these projects will be heralded as great successes. Some will be seen as dramatic failures. Many will be some way in between these poles; modest successes or modest failures.

References

Arthur, B. (1990). 'Positive feedbacks in the economy'. *Scientific American*, February 1990.

Beer, S. (1985). *Diagnosing the System for Organizations*. John Wiley & Sons, Chichester.

Bell, D. (1973). *The Coming of Post-Industrial Society*. Basic Books, New York.

Benjamin, R. et al (1993). 'Managing information technology enabled change'. In Avison, *Human, Organisational and Social Dimensions of Information Systems Development*. IFIP, North Holland, pp. 381–398.

Blackler, F. and Brown, C. A. (1986). 'Alternative models to guide the design and introduction of new technologies into work organizations'. *Journal of Occupational Psychology*, 59, 287–313.

BusinessWeek (2001). *Rethinking the Internet*, March 21, 2001.

BusinessWeek (2003). *The E-Biz Surprise*, May 12, 2003.

Cabinet Office (2000). *e.gov Electronic services for the 21st Century*, Performance and Innovation Unit, September 2000.

Checkland, P. and Scholes, J. (1991). *Soft Systems Methodology in Action*. Wiley, Chichester.

Christensen, C. M. (1997). *The Innovators Dilemma: When New Technologies Cause Great Firms to Fail*. Harvard Business School Press, Boston.

Ciborra, C. (1997). 'De Profundis? Deconstructing the concept of strategic alignment'. *Scandanavian Journal of Information Systems*, 9, 67–82.

Davenport, T. (1992). *Process Innovation: Reengineering Work through Information Technology*. Harvard Business School Press, Boston, 1992.

Downes, L. and Mui, C. (1998). *Unleashing the Killer App*. Harvard Business School Press, Boston.

Hackney, R. and Little, S. (1999). 'Opportunistic strategy formulation for IS/IT planning'. *European Journal of Information Systems*, 8, 119–126.

Haeckel, S. H. (1999). *Adaptive Enterprise: Creating and Leading Sense and Respond Organizations*. Harvard Business School Press, Boston, Massachusetts.

Hammer, M. (1990). 'Reengineering work: Don't automate, obliterate'. *Harvard Business Review*, July–August, pp. 104–112.

Kawalek, P. (2006). The very ordinary case of Anna Eagin, http://mbsmis2006.blogspot.com/2006/10/very-ordinary-case-of-anna-eagin.html (accessed April 15th 2007).

Kawalek, P. (2007). The bubble strategy: A case study of dynamic, defensible processes of change in Salford. *International Journal of Public Sector Management*, (20)3, pp. 178–191.

Livingston, W. L. (1990). *Friends in High Places*. FES Publishing Ltd, New York.

Macreadie, R. D. and Sandon, C. (1999). 'IT-enabled change: Evaluating an improvisational perspective'. *European Journal of Information Systems*, 8, 247–259.

Martin, D., Wastell, D. and Bowers, J. (1998). 'An Ethnographic Systems Design Method: The Development and Evaluation of an Internet-based Electronic Banking Application'. *Proceedings of the 8th European Conference on Information Systems, Aix-en-Provence.*

McAfee, A. P. (2006). *Enterprise 2.0: The Dawn of Emergent Collaboration, Sloan Management Review,* (47)3.

Moss Kanter, R. (2001). *Evolve, Succeeding in the Digital Culture of Tomorrow.* Harvard Business School Press, Boston.

Mumford, E. (1986). *Using Computers for Business Success: The ETHICS Method.* MBS Press, Manchester.

National Audit Office (2002). *Better Public Services Through e-Government,* HC 704 I-III, Parliamentary Session 2001–2002, National Audit Office, London.

Orlikowski, W. and Hoffman, J. D. (1997). 'An improvisational model for change management: the case of groupware technologies'. *Sloan Management Review,* 38, 11–21.

Salford City Council (1999). *People Not Technology Internal report.*

Serafeimidis, V. and Smithson, S. (2000). 'Information systems evaluation in practice: A case study of organisational change'. *Journal of Information Technology,* 15, 93–105.

Simonsen, J. (1999). 'How do we take care of strategic alignment: constructing a design approach'. *Scandanavian Journal of Information Systems,* 11, 51–72.

Warboys, B. C., Kawalek, P., Robertson, I. and Greenwood, R. M. (1999). *Business Information Systems: A Process Approach.* McGraw-Hill, London.

Wastell, D. G. (1996). 'The fetish of technique: methodology as a social defence'. *Information Systems Journal,* 6(1), 25–40.

Wastell, D. (1999). 'Learning dysfunctions and information systems development: Overcoming the social defences with transitional objects'. *MIS Quarterly,* 23, 581–600.

Wastell, D., White, P. and Kawalek, P. (1994). 'A methodology for business process redesign: Experiences and issues'. *Journal of Strategic Information Systems,* 3(1), 23–40.

Wastell, D. and Newman, M. (1996). 'Information systems design and organisational change in the ambulance services: A tale of two cities'. *Accounting, Management and Information Technologies,* 6, 283–300.

Wilson, D. and Game, C. (1998). *Local Government in the United Kingdom.* Macmillan, London.

Chapter 12 ■■■

Social dimension of IT/IS evaluation: Views from the public sector

S. Jones

■ Introduction

This chapter discusses Information Systems (IS) evaluation methods and IS evaluation practice in the UK public sector. The chapter may inform academics and researchers with interests in the area of IS evaluation, especially in the public sector domain. The chapter may also inform IS practitioners, functional managers, senior executives and external assessors in the UK public sector faced with IS evaluation issues.

The chapter contends that IS evaluation is an under-developed and under-managed area, which has been traditionally neglected in the UK public sector. This is an important omission that has now become critical. This is due to a continuing increase in IS expenditure in general, together with several major central government modernisation and improvement initiatives, which require the UK public sector to deploy and evaluate IS.

The UK central government has in recent years concentrated on reforming the UK public sector, with the aim of making these organisations more efficient, effective, responsive and citizen orientated. Consequently, several important central government sponsored initiatives have emerged and been given priority status. These include the e-Government (e-Gov) programme, public sector collaboration, the transformation agenda, the national IS strategy and independent external performance assessment. The public sector is experiencing increasing levels of IS expenditure and complexity, and IS deployment is now prevalent in all aspects of public sector service delivery. Furthermore, traditionally there has been uncertainty and unpredictability associated with IS costs and benefit assessments in the public sector. Indeed, government IS projects have had a mixture of both success and failure, with many costly failures and value for money issues being evident.

The prevailing situation highlights the need for IS evaluation to be undertaken in public sector organisations. Indeed, for the first time, there is a requirement for an annual review of public sector IS expenditure to be undertaken, which will be presented to Parliament (Cabinet Office, 2005). IS evaluation therefore, is an important high-level issue. Furthermore, there is now a requirement for the public sector to undertake IS evaluation.

The current and dominant IS evaluation methods are primarily based on economic and technical factors. However, these are problematic and largely inappropriate for use in the public sector. This is due to difficulties with defining and measuring productivity, cost savings and value in a non-profit-making sector with a remit to serve the public. The chapter argues that emerging interpretive IS evaluation approaches, which consider human and organisational aspects of IS deployment and impact, may be more suitable in this domain. These approaches may help satisfy central government IS evaluation requirements and improve future IS evaluation processes. At a local level, these approaches may assist with organisational learning and IS knowledge sharing.

There is a paucity of interpretive evaluation approaches in the literature and a general absence of usage of these approaches in public sector practice. The chapter therefore, elicits and suggests tentative guidelines for interpretive IS evaluation. These guidelines are presented with the aim of generating further discourse and to assist with the development and implementation of interpretive IS evaluation approaches.

This chapter is structured as follows. The chapter begins with an introduction above, which outlines the area under review. This is followed by background and context to the subject, which includes a short history with regard to public sector performance and IS evaluation. The chapter continues with a review of government initiatives and IS deployment in the public sector. This includes a discussion of the modernisation and improvement agenda of central government, together with past, present and future aspects of IS investment. This is followed by a discussion of IS evaluation, which includes brief academic and practitioner perspectives. The chapter continues with a review of the two main IS evaluation approaches, including a table, which summarises the characteristics of the two approaches. This is followed by a discussion of the emerging and salient issues in relation to IS evaluation in the public sector. Arising from this discussion, proposed tentative guidelines for interpretive IS evaluation are extrapolated and presented. These guidelines aim to generate discourse and assist both practitioners and researchers when considering IS evaluation approaches. The chapter ends with a summary and conclusion, which suggests that interpretive IS evaluation may be more helpful, useful and appropriate for understanding IS impact in public sector organisations. The summary and conclusion also calls for further work to be undertaken by both researchers and practitioners.

The chapter now continues with a background and context to the subject area. This is presented in the next section.

Background and context

According to Weber (1919), a bureaucracy is characterised by several factors. These include a labour force based on functional specialisation, a hierarchy of authority, a system of rules which limit discretion, written records of activities, impersonality and a career structure based on technical rather than managerial competence. Bannister (2001) maintains that the characteristics of bureaucracy are most evident in the public sector.

Historically, from a performance perspective, the UK public sector has been primarily concerned with aspects such as cost savings and productivity. However, in recent years, the UK central government has required UK local government to redefine functional processes to improve public sector service delivery (Cabinet Office, 1999). Consequently, in the last decade, there has been a major shift of emphasis towards public service modernisation and improvement. Six main concepts have emerged as key public sector evaluation measures, namely efficiency, effectiveness, economy, performance, quality and assessment. These evaluation concepts apply to all areas of public sector service delivery, as the UK central government focuses on public sector modernisation and improvement.

The modernisation and improvement agenda has acknowledged that IS investment is one important area (Wilson and Game, 2006). Consequently, public sector organisations have increasingly introduced IS to assist with this initiative. The UK central government initiatives and IS deployment are discussed in the next section.

Government initiatives and IS deployment: past, present and future

UK public sector IS investment continues to increase annually. The UK central government Cabinet Office (2005) estimated that this expenditure would be in excess of £14 billion in 2006. Kable (2007) estimates that IS expenditure was £15.9 billion in 2007. Furthermore, Kable (2007) anticipates that IS expenditure will increase annually from 3% in 2008 to 6% in 2012. This will result in an anticipated public sector IS expenditure of over £20 billion in 2012. Significantly, the estimated percentage increase in IS expenditure is greater than the estimated percentage increase in overall public sector expenditure. This is clearly because IS investment is regarded as essential to deliver the modernisation and improvement programme of central government.

IS in the public sector now forms an integral part of service delivery and is a key and vital resource (Irani et al., 2005). IS pervades almost all functional aspects within public sector organisations and is intrinsic to the working life of most professionals and administrators.

IS deployment can reduce costs and improve organisational efficiency and effectiveness (Heeks, 2001). However, against this perspective, there is concern that IS investment does not always deliver value or sufficiently meet original objectives (Irani and Love, 2002). The term the 'IT productivity paradox' emerged to describe this phenomenon in the early 1990s (Brynjölfsson, 1993). Initially, this term was associated with the private sector. However, it is now widely acknowledged that the term is also very relevant to the public sector. Bannister (2001) for example, argues that the public sector has had some successful IS projects, but most senior civil servants responsible for IS are concerned with returns on IS investments. This is because the overall costs of IS implementations often outweigh any efficiencies and cost savings. A recent review of UK public sector IS challenges concluded that many chief executives are concerned with value for money from IS investments and the role of IS in organisations (SOCITM, 2007). These concerns have emerged primarily due to the increasing level of IS investment in the public sector. Irani and Love (2001) conclude that many public sector organisations continue to express discontentment with returns from IS expenditure, despite substantial and increasing IS investment. Jones and Hughes (2001) highlight that IS deployment also often delivers unforeseen outcomes, disadvantages and disbenefits, which can have a detrimental impact upon the overall success of any IS investment.

In 2000, the UK central government published ambitious targets, in the public sector modernisation and improvement agenda, to deliver all government services electronically to the general public by December 2005 (Cabinet Office, 2000). Central government announced that this would be achieved by implementing transactional online Web-based services via the Internet. These services are available 24 hours a day and seven days a week. This has required significant additional public sector IS investment in e-Gov systems. Indeed, all local authorities in England were provided with funding of £0.9 m to help achieve e-Gov targets. Some councils led on national e-Gov projects and innovations. Furthermore, the public sector engaged in partnerships, collaboration and mutual assistance to improve and hasten e-Gov advances. An interim review of e-Gov targets reported that a great deal of work had been undertaken and that sufficient progress had been made (Office of the Deputy Prime Minister, 2004).

The UK e-Gov programme officially ended in 2006, although enhancements and future developments will be ongoing. It has been claimed that the 2000 vision of all local councils providing all local services online by December 2005 has been achieved (Office of the Deputy Prime Minister, 2006). However, while this may be the official view, it is unclear to what extent this major e-Gov investment has been successful in practice, in terms of added value or benefit to service delivery. Indeed, SOCITM (2007) notes that most public sector Web sites are not sufficiently transactional and that there has been no significant improvement in tangible benefits or service delivery to the citizen. This has been due to several inhibiting organisational factors in relation to e-Gov, including indifferent senior management, inadequate staff resources, lack of direction, lack of political will and departmental autonomy. SOCITM (2007) argues for a radical transformation of public sector customer services through future e-Gov deployment. This transformation should focus on the customer and profoundly alter the culture, behaviour and processes within organisations. This, in turn, should lead to real differences in the way that public sector customers receive services over the Internet.

Gershon (2004) undertook an independent review of public sector efficiency. This review concluded that public sector collaboration and cooperation would help maximise efficiency. The philosophy underpinning the review is that collaboration will improve and increase any value or benefit. For example, public sector collaboration with IS procurement may yield improved benefits to organisations, such as lower costs, shared risk, improved contract negotiations and greater product demand aggregation. Moreover, Gershon (2004) suggested that shared services between public sector organisations may deliver benefits and improvements. Indeed, some IS service delivery collaboration projects are already planned or operational. This scenario will place the public sector under scrutiny in relation to IS value and benefit evaluation. Clearly, it will be important to assess and understand whether IS collaboration reduces costs and delivers value and benefits to public sector organisations and citizens.

Sir David Varney's report (2006) with regard to public sector service transformation is another critical narrative that calls for improved public sector services for citizens and businesses. The report argues that improved public sector productivity, efficiency and communication will lead to improved public sector service delivery. This will result in improved value for money for the taxpayer. Varney (2006) also highlights the need for the culture of the public sector to be more business oriented and customer focused.

Currently, the UK central government continues to be concerned with local government modernisation and improvement. Consequently, central government has increasingly made available considerable and specific ring-fenced funding to local government to drive this improvement agenda forward. However, unlike the e-Gov programme, in which every local authority received funding, this ring-fenced funding is awarded to local authorities through a bidding process. This process is based on local authorities submitting organisational service improvement plans, which are subsequently reviewed. These plans aim to improve local government performance or service delivery, such as the introduction of a staff performance management framework, the implementation of a citizen contact centre or the development of a new IS or e-Gov system. A significant number of these improvement initiatives rely heavily on IS implementations to help achieve objectives. However, despite the introduction of many improvement initiatives and associated IS throughout the UK public sector, it is unclear to what extent this improvement programme has been successful in practice. This is because there has been insufficient evaluation of both the improvement programme and any associated IS investment.

Looking to the future, the UK central government has announced an ambitious national public sector IS strategy that calls for further service improvements to be made via IS deployment (Cabinet Office, 2005). This will be achieved, at least in theory, by further implementing major IS to radically improve public sector performance. The central government IS strategy, *Transformational Government: Enabled by Technology*, identifies key issues, concepts and practical implications. The main areas are leadership, governance, portfolio management, IS professionalism, reliable project delivery, supplier management and innovation. The strategy is high level and not sufficiently specific to individual local authorities. It acknowledges that further work needs to be undertaken, in consultation with local government, to ensure that the IS strategy is developed for individual local authorities and communities, to achieve local aims and objectives. That is to say that any individual local authority IS strategy, should follow the overall direction of the national strategy, but with regard to specific, local and regional priorities of local councils and citizens. Notwithstanding the fact that political priorities often change in the public sector (SOCITM, 2007).

The transformational government strategy contends that there are improvement opportunities in transactional services, such as tax and benefits, which will help enable front-line public sector staff to be more efficient. The strategy also maintains that these opportunities will support effective policy development and outcomes. Moreover, the corporate services reform and infrastructure investment will enable front line public sector staff to take advantage of the latest IS technologies. The strategy notes that although the annual UK public sector IS expenditure is approximately £14 billion there is no comprehensive overview, assessment or evaluation of this expenditure. The strategy also states that, in future, IS project milestones and operational costs will be measured and monitored. Indeed, for the first time, the Cabinet Office and HM Treasury will review annual IS expenditure, project progress and achievement against plans. An annual report will also be published to Parliament and audited by the National Audit Office. This is an extremely important development, which has radically raised the profile of IS evaluation in the public sector.

The UK central government has further raised the profile of public sector scrutiny and evaluation, by introducing the Comprehensive Performance Assessment (CPA) (Office of the Deputy Prime Minister, 2002). CPA is an important, current and evolving issue within the UK public sector. The philosophy underpinning CPA is that all local authorities must ensure that business processes and services are operating successfully and performing well. The critical aspect of CPA is an external performance assessment. This assessment is undertaken by independent external audit bodies, such as the Audit Commission and the National Audit Office. Key components of this assessment include the evaluation, benchmarking and comparison of local government organisational and service delivery performance. CPA includes the strategic planning, corporate governance, function and operation of all aspects of a public sector organisations, including the IS service. The CPA process itself continues to evolve. Increasingly, the approach taken by external audit bodies is to require public sector organisations to undertake an internal evidence-based self-assessment. This self-assessment is then reviewed and validated, or otherwise, during the external assessment process. Self-evaluation and associated self-evaluation approaches are now key issues in the UK public sector. Senior executives are therefore becoming increasingly engaged with CPA and seek appropriate evaluation approaches that can assist with the assessment process.

To summarise this section, there are several important issues that are raising the profile of IS evaluation in the UK public sector. These include the significant and growing level of IS expenditure, increasing IS complexity, uncertainty and unpredictability associated with IS costs and value assessments, IS disbenefits, e-Gov initiatives, IS interorganisational collaboration, the service transformation report, the modernisation and improvement agenda, the national IS strategy and CPA. This current and complex situation highlights the need for IS evaluation to be undertaken in public sector organisations. IS evaluation is discussed in the next section.

■ IS evaluation

According to Willcocks and Lester (1999), IS investment is both costly and risky. Any IS investment therefore, should be evaluated to assess the value and benefit to the organisation. IS evaluation is an important process that provides feedback to managers and assists with organisational learning processes (Irani and Love, 2002).

Willcocks and Lester (1999) maintain that it is difficult to evaluate IS in organisations unless there is a clear, documented, systematic, analytical and formal approach. Outwardly, this method appears to be both necessary and appropriate. Furthermore, it is difficult to argue against this approach conceptually, especially when large costs and risks are involved. However, Remenyi and Sherwood-Smith (1999) note that many public sector IS investments are not evaluated and furthermore, when IS evaluation is undertaken, it is rarely rigorous. Various reasons are cited, including that it is too costly and too resource intensive. Therefore, IS evaluation that demonstrates clear value and benefit from IS deployment is rarely achieved in public sector practice. Indeed, despite the apparently obvious requirement for IS to be formally evaluated, many authors (Hirschheim and Smithson, 1999; Walsham, 1999; Land, 2001; Remenyi et al., 2004; Irani et al., 2005) contend that it is extremely difficult to formally assess IS investments. This is due to the complex nature and unpredictability of IS deployment in organisations, which usually leads to a portfolio of tangible and intangible benefits and disbenefits.

Bannister (2001) highlights the issue that there are many important organisational differences between the public sector and the private sector, which influence IS evaluation attitudes, options and approaches in the public sector. These include cultural, structural, technical and resource differences. Bannister (2001) also maintains that there are many important IS factors that distinguish public sector IS from private sector IS. These IS factors also influence IS evaluation in the public sector. For example, public sector IS projects are often undertaken on a large scale and often endeavour to deal with a national, regional or local issue. Public sector IS projects tend to implement unproven technologies and newly developed systems, because these systems are often sponsored by central government. There is usually non-interactive, hierarchical and bureaucratic decision-making in relation to any IS acquisition. There is rarely any user or citizen consultation regarding IS deployment, even regarding systems such as e-Gov that interact with the citizen. Any IS problems can usually be resolved by allocating additional resources or increasing project timescales. IS mistakes, project overruns and project overspends are rarely admitted. Public sector organisations are not subject to risks, such as bankruptcy or management take-over. IS projects are also often implemented as a result of statutory, parliamentary or European Union (EU) regulations, in response to politicians and political objectives. An excellent example is the National Programme for Information Technology (NPfIT) in the UK National Health Service. This is the largest public sector IS project in Europe, with estimated costs of £20 billion. The project has exhibited all of the above characteristics (House of Commons Public Accounts Committee, 2007).

Heeks (2001) highlights one fact that the public sector delivers a large number of diverse and important services to the general public and that this diversity impacts upon IS evaluation. The services provided include education, social services, highways, housing, planning and environmental services. These services are of a significant range, size, breadth and depth. The services are not always strongly connected or interrelated. Therefore, the diversity, complexity, number and large scale of public sector services also influences any IS deployment and IS evaluation approach.

Introna (1997) argues that there are strong political factors in the public sector that have major implications for IS investment and evaluation. These political aspects, while sometimes present in the private sector, are always more prevalent and far stronger in the public sector. These factors include political and hierarchical pressure for short-term IS solutions, perhaps to meet an immediate political crisis or to gain political ground, at the expense of planning and longer-term strategy. For example, the implementation of IS to pay urgent foot-and-mouth disease compensation payments to local farmers will usually override any IS strategic planning. Introna (1997) also argues that politics, power and influence between internal departments are far more dominant in public sector organisations. In this political climate, internal departments within the same organisation compete with each other for recognition, status and resources, sometimes to the detriment of the aims of other departments and corporate objectives. Often, internal departments do not have common goals. Indeed, these goals can sometimes be conflicting. For example, the finance department may wish to reduce revenue costs but a front-line service may wish to invest in IS, which will increase revenue costs. The strong political, power and competitive culture in public sector organisations therefore has implications for all organisational issues, including IS evaluation.

Bannister (2001) contends that there are inherent difficulties with IS evaluation in the public sector. This is because the objectives of the public sector are to serve the public and it is thus difficult to define appropriate evaluation measures for an organisation with these particular objectives. There are also clear categories of IS projects that do not aim to improve the efficiency or cost effectiveness of a public sector organisation. Bannister (2001) notes that these projects require an approach to IS evaluation that does not measure efficiency or effectiveness. For example, mandatory work that the organisation is compelled to undertake, such as new legal requirements to monitor environmental factors, which necessitate the introduction of IS. In these cases, many organisations argue that there is no need to undertake any justification, because the IS investment must proceed (Jones and Hughes, 2001). Walsham (1999) also maintains that many public sector IS projects do not aim to reduce costs or improve productivity and therefore IS evaluation is extremely complex and difficult in public sector practice. Indeed, with the modernisation and improvement agenda of the UK central government, it is clear that it is the improvements that are required, not necessarily cost reductions. Bannister (2001) further maintains that senior management in the public sector often ignores the IS investment appraisal process. The reason given is that any appraisal process would unnecessarily delay the acquisition and deployment of IS.

Bannister (2001) argues that many of the current formal IS evaluation approaches are not relevant in the public sector. This is because the concepts of value, cost–benefit and productivity, whilst relatively straightforward to define in a manufacturing, business and private sector environment, are very complex to define in a public service environment. Bannister (2001) maintains that measures of productivity, such as financial payback and return on investment, usually have little meaning in public sector service delivery. These measures therefore, are largely inappropriate in the public sector. The concept of Value for Money (VFM) is often regarded as the most appropriate evaluation model for use in the public sector. However, this has met with limited success in practice, especially in relation to IS projects. This is mainly due to the complexity of VFM and the difficulty in defining IS value.

Hirschheim and Smithson (1999) note that in practice, IS investment decisions and any subsequent post-implementation evaluation are usually left to IS management and functional service management. However, these managers do not normally utilise the operational system. The IS user community therefore, has little or no involvement in the IS procurement decision and any subsequent post-implementation evaluation. Remenyi et al. (2004) concur with this view and contend that traditionally, in the IS field, attention has been given to technological components, project management and systems development methods but not IS evaluation. Sauer (1993) concludes that this is an important omission that can lead to ineffective or failed IS investments, which in turn, can result in serious consequences.

Hirschheim and Smithson (1999) argue that any IS evaluation undertaken by IS professionals usually concentrates on the technical aspects, such as technical compatibility, system availability and functional response times. Similarly, Kumar (1990) concludes that the main reason for undertaking any post-implementation IS evaluation was to formally end the project and to disengage the IS department from the work programme. This suggests that IS evaluation can be ritualistic. It is clear, therefore, that in public sector organisational practice, insufficient attention has been given to evaluating the appropriateness of the IS for successfully supporting the service function.

The prevailing IS evaluation situation in the public sector is deficient because an assessment of the impact of the IS on the service delivery function is not undertaken. It is difficult, therefore, to assess the impact and contribution of IS. This is now a key issue, due to the drive from central government for public sector organisations to modernise, improve and assess service delivery. Clearly, from an IS evaluation perspective, what is of paramount importance to an IS user is not whether the IS is efficient and effective in its technical operation, but rather the extent to which it is useful and successful in practice (Jones and Hughes, 2001). Indeed, there are many examples of good technical IS solutions being introduced, in which the anticipated benefits were not realised. Moreover, there have been some unsuccessful IS solutions implemented that have resulted in seriously detrimental consequences. These consequences are often as a result of the social and organisational aspects not being appropriately considered (Irani and Love, 2002).

The historical and current situation has led many authors (Earl, 1992; Farbey et al., 1999; Walsham, 1999; Wilson and Howcroft, 2000; Serafeimidis and Smithson, 2000; Irani et al., 2005; Jones et al., 2007) to argue that IS evaluation is a key senior executive issue in the public sector. These authors highlight that IS evaluation has traditionally been neglected and called for improved evaluation practice. Furthermore, the UK central government has also consistently highlighted the need for improved public sector evaluation, including IS evaluation (Office of the Deputy Prime Minister, 2002; Gershon, 2004; Cabinet Office, 2005; Varney, 2006; House of Commons Public Accounts Committee, 2007). There is, in short, an abundance of academic study and government literature in relation to IS evaluation. Furthermore, there is increasing awareness, interest and concern in public sector organisations with regard to IS evaluation practice. However, academics, government officials and practitioners still acknowledge that there are difficulties and complexities with IS evaluation in the public sector.

This section has discussed IS evaluation, especially in the public sector. The next section reviews current IS evaluation approaches.

■ IS evaluation approaches

Many models have been devised and developed in an attempt to evaluate and measure IS efficiency and effectiveness in both public and private sector organisations. Irani (1998) has classified over 50 IS evaluation methods that aim to assist with this process. Land (2001) contends that there are over 60 methods available, which are categorised into five main groups.

Strassman (1997) maintains that there is widespread disagreement, in practice, over the usefulness of IS evaluation approaches and over which model to adopt. Walsham (1999) contends that there is disagreement as to the measures and subsequent method of analysis to include in any IS evaluation approach. Land (2001) argues that IS evaluation is difficult and that senior decision-makers regard IS evaluation as problematic. This is because it is difficult to predict IS costs, risks, benefits, impact and lifetime. At present, there is little consensus amongst researchers and practitioners as to which approach, instrument or methodology is appropriate for IS evaluation. This is especially the case with IS evaluation in the public sector.

Serafeimidis and Smithson (2000) maintain that in common with much of the IS field, IS evaluation has been dominated by the scientific, positivist and mechanistic paradigm.

Walsham (1999) concurs with this view and contends that where public sector organisations have undertaken IS evaluation, attention has been given to formal, quantitative and prescriptive methods. These methods attempt to define and measure IS costs and benefits. Hirschheim and Smithson (1999) also note that where public sector organisations have evaluated IS, mechanistic methods have been adopted. There are many of these formal and prescriptive IS appraisal models that have been developed from the modernist, positivist and philosophical perspective. These mechanistic methods are discussed in the next sub-section.

Mechanistic IS evaluation approach

Mechanistic approaches to IS evaluation are formal methods that are primarily concerned with monetary costs and benefits. The philosophical perspective of this approach is that of rational and objective analysis and decision-making. These mechanistic approaches are primarily based on economics. There are several commonly used financial indices that are calculated and used, which are based on economic performance. These include return on investment (ROI), return on shareholders equity (ROE), return on assets (ROA), discounted cash flow (DCF), net present value (NPV), cost–benefit analysis (CBA) and Payback. These formal and prescriptive mechanistic methods are used to plan, calculate, manage and monitor IS costs and financial benefits. The aim of these methods is to demonstrate or prove that financial value and benefit is being obtained from any IS investment. These techniques are usually employed by company accountants, IS management, functional management, IS consultants and IS suppliers.

Formal evaluation approaches based on quantification, financial and technical criteria have considerable legitimacy (Irani et al., 2005). However, these prescriptive methods have had limited success in public sector practice (Walsham, 1999). Furthermore, the usefulness of these methods has been cause for much discourse, especially in the public sector domain (Farbey et al., 1999; Walsham, 1999; Serafeimidis and Smithson, 2000; Irani and Love, 2001). Remenyi et al. (2004) argue that these formal and mechanistic IS evaluation tools are not well understood by IS stakeholders or IS staff and line managers, which is problematic. Furthermore, Powell (1999) concludes that none of these methods has found universal favour.

Introna (1997) contends that formal mechanistic IS evaluation, when undertaken, is more likely to be a symbolic expression of accountable and objective management, to perpetuate an image of the rational manager, rather than an accurate method to aid decision-makers. Wilson and Howcroft (2000) support this view and argue that politics and power play an important role in the IS evaluation, especially in the public sector. Senior decision-makers and the political environment will, strongly influence discourse and outcome, when applying IS mechanistic methods.

Mechanistic approaches to IS evaluation based on static accounting techniques and technical aspects are increasingly coming under scrutiny (Irani et al., 2005). In the public sector, these approaches have had limited success, do not command a high level of confidence and are increasingly being recognised as inadequate (Hirschheim and Smithson, 1999; Walsham, 1999; Serafeimidis and Smithson, 2000; Irani et al., 2005). Irani and Love (2002) contend that traditional appraisal techniques can work well for decisions concerning the replacement of private sector business items, such as manufacturing capital equipment. However, these techniques are very myopic and deficient for the appraisal of complex public sector IS that aim to improve service delivery.

Progressive methods, such as the Benefits Management approach (Ward, 1990) and the Active Benefits Realisation (ABR) approach (Remenyi et al., 1998), which outline a comprehensive benefit management framework for IS development and include both quantitative and qualitative evaluation factors, have also had limited adoption in practice (Walsham, 1999). This has mainly been due to their large scope, complexity and laboriousness. For example, there are many evaluation factors to consider and a continuous and iterative approach is adopted, which is applied to each stage of the life cycle of the IS development or procurement.

The growing number of well-developed, predominately mechanistic, methods for assessing returns, even those that have emerged from practice such as the Information Technology (IT) balanced scorecard, are viewed with much scepticism by IS practitioners and key IS stakeholders (Hirschheim and Smithson, 1999). Willcocks and Lester (1999) also illustrate that even when these prescriptive IS evaluation procedures exist, perhaps as part of an overall IS project plan, the process is usually not undertaken rigorously or not undertaken at all. Jones and Hughes (2001) highlight that the stakeholders cite various reasons, including it is too difficult, too time consuming, too costly and not necessary. Walsham (1999) concludes that IS evaluation is extremely complex and that formal, prescriptive evaluation is of little value, especially in public sector practice.

In the last decade, growing consideration has been given to the wider organisational and social aspects in relation to IS evaluation. Hirschheim and Smithson (1999) note that traditionally, the social and organisational dimensions of IS evaluation have largely been ignored. Irani et al. (2005) concur with this view and contend that this has led to a simplistic notion of IS evaluation based on metrics, which is dysfunctional. Many authors (Hirschheim and Smithson, 1999; Walsham, 1999; Serafeimidis and Smithson, 2000; Wilson and Howcroft, 2000; Jones and Hughes, 2004; Irani et al., 2005) have called for the development and deployment of interpretive IS evaluation approaches. These approaches are concerned with gathering, evaluating and understanding social and organisational perspectives of IS deployment. Interpretive approaches may be more suitable for many aspects of IS evaluation, especially in the public sector domain, where government initiatives now require internal self-assessment and evaluation. This interpretive approach is discussed in the next sub-section.

Interpretive IS evaluation approach

Historically, many IS observers (Mumford and Weir, 1979; Checkland, 1981; Walsham, 1993; Introna, 1997; Hirschheim and Smithson, 1999; Avison and Elliot, 2006) have argued that IS are predominantly social systems and therefore, the social aspects of IS are significant. Some authors (Hirschheim and Smithson, 1999; Walsham, 1999; Serafeimidis and Smithson, 2000; Irani et al., 2005) have also argued that adopting an IS evaluation approach based on interpreting and understanding social and organisational aspects of IS would improve IS evaluation. The perspective of this interpretive approach is that IS evaluation is a socially embedded process and therefore, the views of the social actors using any IS are important. These social actors are in a particular, unique, individual, contextual and organisational IS situation. Consequently, these IS users are in a good position to assess IS, offer opinion and advise senior executives of the usefulness and success, or otherwise, of the IS. Remenyi et al. (2004) contend that IS evaluation would be improved if the evaluation included an assessment of human views and values. An interpretive IS evaluation approach, therefore, is concerned with understanding the views of the social actors in an IS organisational setting, and appreciates the value of contextual, qualitative and subjective data for IS evaluation purposes.

Mechanistic IS evaluation methods based on economic measures ignore human, organisational and contextual dimensions. This appears to be a major omission. Wilson and Howcroft (2000) argue that these aspects are very important to IS evaluation, especially in public sector organisations, where the objective is to serve the public. Wilson and Howcroft (2000) further contend that the significant social, political, contextual and organisational perspectives that are inherent in any IS evaluation process, are usually neglected. Remenyi et al. (2004) also argue that IS stakeholders and users are important in any IS evaluation process, but note that this potential is not utilised. Remenyi et al. (2004) further highlight that although IS users are usually an important source of information during the analysis and design stages of any IS development life cycle, they are rarely involved in IS evaluation processes. Walsham (1999) maintains that it is important that IS users evaluate the success of IS after implementation and evaluate any potential future IS enhancement before committing further resources.

Heeks (2001) provides an interesting insight into the difficulties associated with formal IS evaluation methods in the public sector and contends that it is better to understand the 'wetware between the ears' rather than evaluating IS costs and benefits, again illustrating the importance of contextual user opinion, rather than metrics, in any IS evaluation in public sector organisations. Irani et al. (2005) highlight the potential importance of interpretive IS evaluation approaches and conclude that user assessments, which include human and organisational factors, should be included within any IS evaluation. Interpretive IS evaluation, therefore, can help organisations understand IS in social and organisational contexts and has the potential to produce deep and critical insights into IS phenomena.

Minzberg (1994) argues that, in practice, some of the most effective managers rely on the softest forms of information and that hard quantitative data seems to be of relatively little importance. Rockart (1979), in his seminal paper on critical success factors, although not appearing to explicitly recognise the interpretive perspective, gave an important insight into the differing interpretive world views of individuals when he noted that top executives usually undertake subjective assessment and evaluation when taking decisions, rather than accept quantifiable measures. Introna (1997) maintains that people tend to manage without formal management information and that decision-making is an immensely complex process, which involves sophisticated, subtle and sub-conscious cognitive elements. With regard to IS evaluation, Introna (1997) maintains that social interaction and user perception in organisational contexts play an important interpretive role. For example, just because an IS implementation is successful, or indeed unsuccessful, in one organisation, it does not necessarily follow that it will be successful, or indeed unsuccessful, in another organisation.

Generic evaluation is an important process that is undertaken by individuals in everyday life, in an attempt to gauge how well something meets a particular expectation, objective or need. These are not formal, overt, evaluation processes but informal, covert processes, in which context and perception play a key role. Nonetheless, they have significant importance to the individuals and peer groups concerned. With regard to IS evaluation, these opinions may also be of importance to an organisation and external audit bodies. Yet they are rarely, if at all, requested or valued.

Interpretive IS evaluation aims to understand IS from the point of view of the participants who are directly involved with the IS. The objective of this approach is to gauge and understand the success, or otherwise, of the IS in an organisational context, not to measure economic factors. This approach may be more appropriate for public sector IS evaluation, where the objective is to serve the public and improve service delivery. This concludes the discussion of interpretive IS evaluation approaches. A summary of IS evaluation approaches is presented in the next sub-section.

Summary of IS evaluation approaches

A summary of the characteristics of the mechanistic and interpretive approaches to IS evaluation is adapted and enhanced from Jones and Hughes (2001) and presented in Table 12.1. The table is for illustrative purposes, to draw attention to the contrasts, and does not suggest polarised positions.

Table 12.1 Characteristics of approaches to IS evaluation (adapted from Jones and Hughes, 2001)

Mechanistic IS evaluation approach	Interpretive IS evaluation approach
Concerned with IS evaluation methods objectively, irrespective of context	Concerned with IS evaluation interpretively, in organisational contexts
Traditional formal mechanistic methods dominate	New informal interpretive methods emerging
Overt and formally documented process	Covert and non-documented process
Financial, economic and technical factors dominate	Social, human and organisational factors considered
Attempt to define, measure and score	Attempt to gauge, understand and learn
Undertaken in isolation by accountants, functional management, IS suppliers and IS practitioners	Undertaken individually and in collaboration by IS users and stakeholders
Considers positive aspects and benefits	Considers positive and negative aspects, and both benefits and disbenefits
Legitimises IS investment decisions	Engages with stakeholders to understand IS impact
Espouses single objective view	Seeks multiple-stakeholder subjective views
Claims to be apolitical	Recognises IS evaluation as a political process
Official, rational management view of IS implementation and cost-effectiveness	Unofficial, subjective stakeholder views of IS implementation and impact
Concerned with justification and decision-making	Concerned with knowledge sharing and organisational learning to improve future IS evaluation processes
Static view	View may change over time

This concludes the section on IS evaluation approaches. A discussion of the emergent salient IS issues, with regard to IS evaluation in the public sector, is presented in the next section.

Discussion of emergent salient issues

IS evaluation is now a key and current issue in the UK public sector. However, many public sector organisations do not give IS evaluation sufficient attention. IS evaluation, when undertaken, is conducted via formally documented mechanistic processes, based on economics. These mechanistic methods measure broad costs and perceived accrued financial benefits. In addition, the operation of IS may be monitored and measured in terms of the technical aspects, such as response times and IS availability. Post-implementation IS project reviews are sometimes undertaken. However, these reviews usually have the objective of formally completing or signing-off the task and disengaging the IS department from the IS project. These prescriptive approaches to IS evaluation have inherent credibility issues and are often ritualistic rather than substantive. Therefore, senior and functional managers are currently unable to sufficiently evaluate IS impact with these methods, either prior to IS acquisition or subsequent to any IS implementation.

IS deployment is often unfavourably perceived by senior management and IS stakeholders. This is primarily due to the perception that IS is not achieving expectations. This prevailing scenario is of concern to IS managers and IS practitioners in the public sector. IS managers are aware that there is an increasing focus on the difficulty in demonstrating IS returns, via current IS evaluation practice. They are also concerned that poor IS implementations are often cited as the reason why public sector organisations underperform or fail to reach their strategic objectives. However, against this background they are under constant pressure to develop and implement IS solutions to organisational and service delivery problems.

Clearly, there is a need to evaluate IS that supports the modernisation and improvement agenda of UK central government and also to evaluate IS collaboration projects, to establish to what extent these initiatives are successful in practice. However, many public sector organisations currently do not undertake IS evaluation sufficiently. Therefore, senior IS stakeholders and senior executives should perhaps more fully recognise that IS evaluation is an important activity which should be undertaken. This may be more problematic with inter-organisational IS collaboration, due to the potential for increased complexity of any proposed IS solution across multiorganisations.

The difficulties associated with traditional, formal and mechanistic IS evaluation in the public sector suggests that the world views of social actors using IS in organisational contexts could be useful. Therefore, these views should be captured and interpreted to help gauge and understand the impact of IS implementations in organisational settings. Individuals have important opinions based on their knowledge, experience, background, understanding, intuition and subjective judgement. It may be helpful to complement the traditional, formal mechanistic approaches to IS evaluation with an interpretive approach based on subjective and soft data, which is grounded in opinion and world views. Within organisations, informal, interpretive IS evaluation is taking place in the IS user community, but it is not being articulated, requested or interpreted. User opinion is therefore largely ignored.

In public sector organisations, IS are deployed primarily to improve service delivery, assist with strategic direction and achieve corporate objectives. IS are not necessarily implemented to deliver financial benefits or cost savings. These systems should be owned and evaluated by the IS stakeholders that use the IS to achieve organisational objectives. In practice, IS users tend not to be concerned with IS metrics, they tend to be concerned with the successful introduction and operation of IS to support and improve service delivery and job functions. The public sector environment, rather than the private sector environment, would appear to be more suited to an interpretive approach to IS evaluation. This is because the public sector is non-profit making and service orientated, unlike the private sector, which is profit and business orientated.

An appropriate organisational culture may have to be in place to facilitate interpretive IS evaluation. This culture may present a challenge to some public sector organisations, especially those that have a traditional and bureaucratic environment. The objective of IS evaluation is to understand and improve the outcome of IS implementations. IS ownership and collaborative IS evaluation is therefore required from IS users. Furthermore, senior management and external audit bodies should value interpretive IS evaluation findings and be prepared to be informed. Interpretive IS evaluation recognises that IS stakeholders will articulate both rational and irrational views. These views are explicitly sought, exposed, recognised and considered in any IS evaluation approach. There may be differences in stakeholder opinion and stakeholders would need to articulate concerns and views to share information, understanding, knowledge and learning about IS. These individual and subjective views may also change over time as the context and circumstances change. Clearly, it is not possible to measure user assessments exactly. It is only possible to gauge and understand user opinion.

Organisations may need to direct resources into IS evaluation to improve evaluation practice. A role could be developed for an interpretive IS evaluation facilitator to assist with the process. With the significant expenditure on IS in the public sector, this resource would be sufficiently employed and may improve IS evaluation practice. Furthermore, the information provided by this role may highlight other value, benefit and service improvement aspects, which may be considered by senior executives. In cases where the IS has been unsuccessful, the information provided could also include recommendations as to whether or not the particular IS should continue to be utilised by the organisation.

Interpretive IS evaluation could be undertaken at three main stages of any IS project. Firstly, initial IS evaluation at the feasibility stage prior to acquisition to assess the suitability of the IS for the specific service or corporate function. Secondly, ongoing IS evaluation during the implementation stage to provide important feedback with regard to progress and the continuing suitability, or otherwise, of the IS. Thirdly, IS evaluation at the post-implementation stage to gauge the usefulness and impact of the IS in organisational context. Interpretive IS evaluation should not be complex. Evaluation aspects to consider should be straightforward and easily understood, which the organisation wishes to gauge to establish to what extent IS deployment has been successful. For example, faster processing of transactions, such as housing benefit applications, improved strategic information for policy making, easier access to information, user or citizen feedback that confirms that the IS is useful in practice and improves service delivery.

One of the issues associated with interpretive IS evaluation is the articulation, documentation and interpretation of tacit stakeholder knowledge and opinion (Serafeimidis and Smithson, 2000). However, there are current software products that facilitate the storage, management, access and reusability of information. This information is held in a knowledge base and can be utilised in a collaborative and reusable way. The adoption of agent-based collaborative knowledge base, web 2.0 and sharepoint software may assist with obtaining, storing, disseminating and understanding tacit knowledge and experience that is intrinsic to interpretive IS evaluation.

IS evaluation is an under-developed, under-managed and under-utilised area in UK public sector practice. However, public sector organisations can increasingly ill afford to neglect and ignore IS evaluation. This is primarily due to the demands of major central government initiatives, such as the modernisation and improvement agenda, Gershon report, collaborative IS operations, transformation report, national IS strategy and CPA. All these initiatives require the public sector to undertake IS evaluation. IS managers, IS practitioners and functional managers will need to articulate the importance of IS evaluation to senior executives and external performance assessors, rather than defend current practice. The future outlook may improve if public sector organisations give sufficient attention to IS evaluation and seek interpretive IS evaluation approaches to complement mechanistic IS evaluation methods. These interpretive approaches may be more suitable for public sector internal IS evaluation and more aligned to external assessment processes.

If IS evaluation is improved, in terms of methods, acceptance and practice, then more informed decisions can be made with regard to IS. There is an emerging view that interpretive approaches can offer insight into IS impact, which is more appropriate in public sector organisations, where business concepts, such as competitive advantage and economic measurement, are largely irrelevant. However, there is a general absence of interpretive evaluation methods, in both theory and practice.

This concludes the discussion section. Arising from the literature and discussion, interpretive evaluation guidelines have been elicited. These are presented in the next section.

Tentative interpretive IS evaluation guidelines

As highlighted in the discussion above, subjective IS evaluation is an inherent, contextual and continuous process by individuals in organisations. IS use is governed by attitudes to IS. Improving IS evaluation practice therefore, may lie in the experiences of multiple IS stakeholders rather than in the development of other formal quantitative methods. IS evaluation is predominantly grounded in tacit knowledge and user opinion. This evaluation is a local, embodied, emergent and contingent process, in which the views may change over time and in light of future events.

There is a paucity of interpretive IS evaluation approaches in the literature. Where they are covered, they are not covered extensively. There is also an absence in the literature of studies that research interpretive IS evaluation in practice. Therefore, interpretive evaluation guidelines have been drawn from the literature and discourse in this chapter. The guidelines have been developed intuitively to act as an aide-memoire to public sector organisations and researchers. The aim is to help, inform and improve IS evaluation practice and research. These guidelines are tentatively suggested and presented below:

1 Senior executives should engage more with major IS investment decisions to improve the IS investment decision-making process.
2 Organisations should adequately resource IS evaluation to ensure that IS evaluation is sufficiently undertaken.
3 Organisations should ensure that a senior executive sponsors IS evaluation to demonstrate the high importance of the process.
4 Organisations should specify who is responsible for IS evaluation to clarify responsibility.
5 Organisations should consider the appropriateness and validity of formal mechanistic and technical IS evaluation techniques to alleviate the perception that IS evaluation is ritualistic.
6 Organisations should consider employing an interpretive IS evaluation approach that complements mechanistic methods to improve IS evaluation practice.
7 Organisations should overcome political barriers and adopt a suitable culture for facilitating an interpretive IS evaluation approach to improve the process.
8 Organisations should ensure that any interpretive IS evaluation approach specifies the IS perspective sought, such as stakeholder, client, IS practitioner, IS user and wider community to ensure the appropriate stakeholders are included.
9 Organisations should consider evaluating aspects other than productivity and costs, such as user satisfaction and service delivery enhancement to improve the understanding of IS success and impact.
10 Organisations should consider the use of knowledge-based collaborative software to improve the interpretive IS evaluation process.
11 Organisations should identify and share IS evaluation best practice to improve IS evaluation in the public sector.

Table 12.2 contains suggested practical guidelines for public sector organisations and researchers that wish to consider interpretive IS evaluation.

■ **Table 12.2** Practical guidelines for interpretive IS evaluation

Characteristics of interpretive IS evaluation	Suggested actions for public sector organisations and researchers
Concerned with IS evaluation interpretively, in organisational contexts	Acknowledge that mechanistic IS evaluation methods are insufficient and that interpretive IS evaluation may complement mechanistic methods
New informal interpretive methods emerging	Investigate and explore these new interpretive evaluation approaches
Covert and non-documented process	Expose and document stakeholder views

(*Continued*)

■ **Table 12.2** (Continued)

Characteristics of interpretive IS evaluation	Suggested actions for public sector organisations and researchers
Social and organisational factors considered	Acknowledge the importance of social and organisational perspectives
Attempt to gauge, understand and learn	Develop appropriate collaborative enquiry approaches
Undertaken informally by IS users and stakeholders	Recognise informal process and acknowledge importance
Consider positive and negative aspects, and both benefits and disbenefits	Consider both positive and negative IS impact
Engage with stakeholders to understand IS impact	Appoint IS evaluation facilitator to engage and elicit stakeholder views so that they can be understood and disseminated
Seek multiple-stakeholder subjective views	Obtain multiple-stakeholder subjective views
Recognise IS evaluation as a political process	Acknowledge and address the political situation
Unofficial, subjective stakeholder views of IS implementation and impact	Obtain unofficial subjective stakeholder real-world interpretive view to understand IS impact
Concerned with knowledge sharing and organisational learning to improve future IS evaluation processes	Develop knowledge-sharing networks and threaded discussion boards
View may change over time	Undertake Interpretive IS evaluation periodically

The above suggested practical guidelines for public sector organisations and researchers map on to the characteristics of interpretive IS evaluation and have been elicited from the discourse in this chapter. These actions are presented with the aim of informing and assisting public sector organisations and researchers when considering interpretive IS evaluation.

■ Conclusions

This chapter was motivated by a concern for IS evaluation methods and their use in the public sector. This is a current, relevant and important issue, primarily due to the modernisation and improvement agenda of UK central government. This agenda has resulted in several major government initiatives that require significant public sector IS expenditure and corresponding IS evaluation.

The chapter highlights that there are a significant number of IS evaluation methods available. However, it is prescriptive and mechanistic methods based on economic and technical factors that dominate. These methods may be suitable for private sector organisations, because economic, financial and productivity factors are highly relevant in the private sector. However, they are mainly inappropriate for public sector organisations. This is because economic factors are largely irrelevant in the public sector domain, where the objective is to implement policy and serve the public.

Mechanistic methods contain very few or no user and organisational perspectives with regard to IS evaluation. However, this chapter has argued that IS evaluation is a human activity and an important social process. Thus interpretive IS evaluation is undertaken in a knowledgeable, reflexive, continuous and tacit way by IS users, including citizens, in public sector service delivery contexts. These opinions, which may change over time, consider both benefits and disbenefits. Therefore, to understand and gauge the success, impact and usefulness of IS from an organisational and human perspective, user opinion should be obtained.

Interpretive IS evaluation aims to inform and provide an improved understanding of IS implementations and also aims to improve organisational learning and future IS evaluation processes. This approach provides a richer and more practically oriented approach and therefore, may be more suitable to the culture, structure, corporate and service delivery aims of the public sector.

Tentative interpretive IS evaluation guidelines have been elicited from the discussion to inform and aid researchers and organisations. Through the discourse presented in this chapter, further research and practical work could be undertaken. The conceptual ideas and the tentative guidelines for interpretive evaluation could be formally explored by IS researchers using a research approach, such as action research. Moreover, the ideas and guidelines could be explored in practice by public sector organisations to understand to what extent they are successful in practice.

References

Avison, D. and Elliot, S. (2006). 'Scoping the discipline of information systems'. In King, J. L. and Lyytinen, K. (Eds.), *Information Systems: The State of the Field*. Wiley, Chichester, UK.

Bannister, F. (2001). 'Dismantling the silos: Extracting new value from IT investments in public administration'. *Information Systems Journal*, 11(1), 65–84.

Brynjölfsson, E. (1993). 'The productivity paradox of information technology'. *Communications of the ACM*, 35(1), 9–43.

Cabinet Office (1999). *Modernising Government*. HMSO, London, UK.

Cabinet Office (2000). e.*Gov – Electronic Government Services for the 21st Century*. Performance and Innovation Unit, HMSO, London, UK.

Cabinet Office (2005). *Transformational Government: Enabled by Technology*. HMSO, London, UK.

Checkland, P. (1981). *Systems Thinking, Systems Practice*. Wiley, Chichester, UK.

Earl, M. J. (1992). 'Putting information technology in its place: A polemic for the nineties'. *Journal of Information Technology*, 7, 100–108.

Farbey, B., Land, F. F. and Targett, D. (1999). 'Moving IS evaluation forward: Learning themes and best practice'. *Journal of Strategic Information Systems*, 8(2), 189–207.

Gershon, P. (2004). *Releasing Resources to the Front Line: Independent Review of Public Sector Efficiency*. HMSO, London, UK.

Heeks, R. (2001). *Reinventing Government in the Information Age*. Routledge, London.

Hirschheim, R. A. and Smithson, S. (1999). 'Evaluation of information systems: A critical assessment'. In Willcocks, L. and Lester, S. (Eds.), *Beyond the IT Productivity Paradox.* Wiley, Chichester.

House of Commons Public Accounts Committee (2007). *Department of Health: The National Programme for IT in the NHS.* TSO, London. http://www.publications.parliament.uk/pa/cm200607/cmselect/cmpubacc/390/390.pdf

Introna, L. (1997). *Management, Information and Power.* Macmillan, London.

Irani, Z. (1998). *Investment Justification of Information Systems: A Focus on the Evaluation of MRPII.* PhD Thesis, Department of Engineering Systems, Brunel University, UK.

Irani, Z. and Love, P. D. E. (2001). 'The propagation of technology management taxonomies for evaluating investments in information systems'. *Journal of Management Information Systems,* 17(3), 161–177.

Irani, Z. and Love, P. E. D. (2002). 'Developing a frame of reference for *Ex-ante* IT/IS investment evaluation'. *European Journal of Information Systems,* 11(1), 74–82.

Irani, Z., Love, P. E. D., Elliman, T., Jones, S. and Themistocleous, M. (2005). 'Evaluating e-government: Learning from the experiences of two UK local authorities', *Information Systems Journal, Special Issue on e-Government,* 15, 61–82, Blackwell Publishing Ltd.

Jones, S. and Hughes, J. (2001). 'Understanding IS evaluation as a complex social process: A case study of a UK local authority'. *European Journal of Information Systems,* 10, 189–203.

Jones, S. and Hughes, J. (2004). 'Information systems evaluation: Getting closer to the organisation'. *Journal Enterprise Information Management,* 17(4), 245–248.

Jones, S., Hackney, R. and Irani, Z. (2007). 'Towards e-government transformation: Conceptualising customer engagement – a research note'. *Transforming Government: People, Process and Policy,* 1(2), Emerald Group.

Kable (2007). *UK Public Sector Overview to 2012,* http://www.kable.co.uk/kabledirect/index.php?option=com_content&mCCountryOrgID=410&task=view&id=1172982

Kumar, K. (1990). 'Post implementation evaluation of computer based IS: Current practices'. *Communications of the ACM,* 33(2), 202–212.

Land, F. F. (2001). IS evaluation: Recent trends, Keynote Speech, *NUKAIS Information Systems Evaluation Seminar,* Priestley Hall, Leeds Metropolitan University, 27th February, 2001.

Minzberg, H. (1994). The fall and rise of strategic planning. *Harvard Business Review.* January–February, 107–114.

Mumford, E. and Weir, P. (1979). *Computer Systems in Work Design: The ETHICS Method.* Wiley, New York.

Office of the Deputy Prime Minister (2002). *Comprehensive Performance Assessment: An Introduction.* ODPM, London. https://www.odpm.gov.uk/index.asp?id=1123805

Office of the Deputy Prime Minister (OPDM) (2004). *One Year On: The National Strategy for e-Government.* ODPM, London. http://www.localegov.gov.uk/Nimoi/sites/ODMP/resources/local%20e-gov%201Year%20On%20Doc_21.pdf

Office of the Deputy Prime Minister (2006). *New Localism: Citizen Engagement, Neighbourhoods and Public Services: Evidence from Local Government.* ODPM, London. http://www.communities.gov.uk/index.asp?id=1505673

Remenyi, D., Sherwood-Smith, M. and White, T. (1998). *Achieving Maximum Value from Information Systems: A Process Approach.* Wiley, Chichester.

Remenyi, D. and Sherwood-Smith, M. (1999). 'Maximise information systems value by continuous participative evaluation'. *Logistics Information Management,* 12(1–2), 12–21.

Remenyi, D., Money, A., Sherwood-Smith, M. and Irani, Z. (2004). *Effective Measurement and Management of IT Costs and Benefits.* Butterworth-Heinemann, Oxford.

Rockart, J. F. (1979). 'Chief executives define their own data needs'. *Harvard Business Review*, 57(2), 81–93.

Powell, P. L. (1999). 'Evaluation of information technology investments: Business as usual'. In Willcocks, L. and Lester, S. (Eds.), *Beyond the IT Productivity Paradox*. Wiley, Chichester.

Sauer, C. (1993). *Why Information Systems Fail: A Case Study Approach*. Alfred Walter, Oxford.

Serafeimidis, V. and Smithson, S. (2000). 'Information systems evaluation in practice: A case study of organisational change'. *Journal of Information Technology*, 15(2), 93–105.

SOCITM (2007). *The Technology Challenge in 2007*. Society of Information Technology Management, Northampton, UK.

Strassman, P. (1997). *The Squandered Computer*. Information Economic Press, New Caanan, CN.

Varney, D. (2006). *Service Transformation: A Better Service for Citizens and Businesses, a Better Deal for the Taxpayer*. HM Treasury, London.

Walsham, G. (1993). *Interpreting Information Systems in Organisations*. Wiley, Chichester.

Walsham, G. (1999). 'Interpretive evaluation design for information systems'. In Willcocks, L. and Lester, S. (Eds.), *Beyond the IT Productivity Paradox*. Wiley, Chichester, pp. 363–380.

Ward, J. M. (1990). 'A portfolio approach into evaluating information systems investment and setting priorities'. *Journal of Information Technology*, 5(4), 222–231.

Weber, M. (1919). Bureaucracy. In Gerth, H., Wright, C. and Mills, T. (Eds.), *From Max Weber: Essays in Sociology*. Routledge, London, pp. 196–244.

Willcocks, L. and Lester, S. (1999). 'IT: Transformer or sink hole'. In Willcocks, L. and Lester, S. (Eds.), *Beyond the IT Productivity Paradox*. Wiley, Chichester.

Wilson, D. and Game, C. (2006). *Local Government in the United Kingdom*. Macmillan, London, UK.

Wilson, M. and Howcroft, D. (2000). Politics of IS Evaluation: A Social Shaping Perspective. *Proceedings of the International Conference on Information Systems*, December, Brisbane, Australia.

Chapter 13

▪ Benchmarking e-Government: Improving the national and international measurement, evaluation and comparison of e-Government

R. Heeks

▦ Introduction: Why benchmark?

e-Government benchmarking means undertaking a review of comparative performance of e-Government between nations or agencies. e-Government benchmarking studies have two purposes: internal and external. The internal purpose is the benefit achieved for the individual or organisation undertaking the benchmarking study. The external purpose is the benefit achieved for users of the study.

Little or nothing is made explicit about internal purpose in benchmarking studies. It could be synonymous with the external purpose but equally it could relate to a desire to raise the profile or perceived expertise and legitimacy of the individual or organisation in e-Government, or it could relate to a desire to attract funds or win additional e-Government business. Where a benchmarking report has a sales and marketing function, this could be in tension with public sector reform goals. At the very least, it makes sense to ensure that study implementers are themselves clear about their internal purpose even if this is not publicised.

Recommendation 1: Clarify the internal purpose of benchmarking

External purpose is a more complex issue to deal with and will involve an iterative identification of demand (or need) for e-Government benchmarking information, identification of the audience for the study and evidence about the use to which study findings will be or are being put (see Figure 13.1, developed from Janssen et al., 2004).

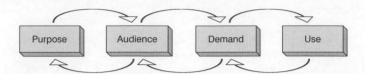

Figure 13.1   Determining the external purpose of e-Government benchmarking

The main audience for e-Government benchmarking is e-Government policy-makers: this is sometimes explicit (e.g. UN, 2005), sometimes only implicit (e.g. Accenture, 2006) and sometimes absent (e.g. West, 2006). Typical sub-audiences may include other e-Government practitioners such as consultants, private information technology (IT) firms and lower-level public officials, and academics (UN, 2005).

Deriving from the main audience, the main purpose of benchmarking is typically either:

- *Retrospective achievement*: Letting policy-makers know in comparative terms how their country or agency has performed in some e-Government ranking (e.g. 'It is a useful tool … to gain a deeper understanding of the relative position of a country vis-à-vis the rest of the world economies' (UN, 2005, p. 13)) and/or
- *Prospective direction/priorities*: Assisting policy-makers with strategic decision-making about e-Government (e.g. 'we aim to help governments identify the course of action that will most likely deliver high performance in e-Government' (Accenture, 2004, p. 2)). For some studies, prospective guidance may be more at the tactical level of individual e-Government projects; for example, offering lessons learned or best practice for such projects (e.g. OeE, 2001).

There is also an audience hardly ever mentioned – citizens, civil society organisations (CSOs) and opposition politicians – for whom benchmarking may provide a purpose of:

- *Accountability*: Enabling governments and agencies to be held to account for the resources they have invested in e-Government. Ministries of Finance/Treasuries may share an interest in this purpose. In relation to all these groups, e-Government officials may have their own purpose of using benchmarking in order to justify politically their past and future investments in e-Government.

There is little explicit evidence about the demand for benchmarking studies, though in some cases they arise out of e-Government practitioner forums (e.g. Capgemini, 2004) or are conducted by e-Government agencies (e.g. OeE, 2001). One can make an assumption in such cases that benchmarking has been demand-driven. However, in general, there is a knowledge gap around the demand for benchmarking data.

This issue is of particular relevance to benchmarking *readiness* for e-Government because a Eurocentric perspective might suggest that the time for such studies is past. As e-Government activity grows over time, the key issues – and, hence, the demand for benchmarking data – are felt to change over time, as illustrated in Figure 13.2 (adapted from OECD, 1999; ESCWA, 2005).

In part these changes could be ascribed to the policy life cycle, illustrated in Figure 13.3 (adapted from Stone, 2001; Janssen et al., 2004).

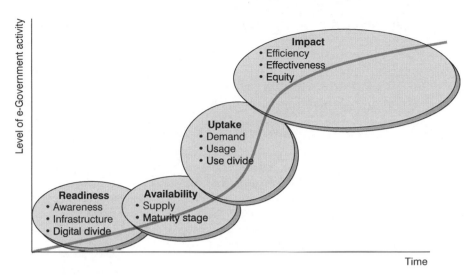

Figure 13.2   Changing e-Government issues over time

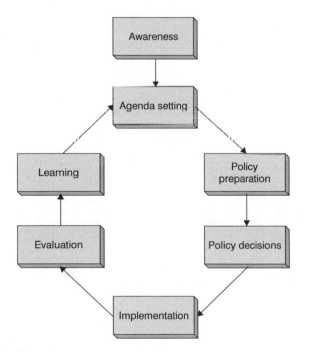

Figure 13.3   The policy life cycle

The demand (and thus external purpose) for e-Government benchmarking is likely to change as policy-makers move through the cycle:

- For policy-makers entering the *awareness stage*, the demand might simply be for help in understanding what e-Government is.
- For policy-makers at the *agenda-setting stage*, demand might come more from those seeking to encourage adoption of e-Government onto the policy agenda, focusing on

the carrot of good news/benefits stories and the stick of poor comparative benchmark performance.

■ At the *policy preparation stage*, policy-makers will likely demand an understanding of alternatives and priorities, comparisons with other countries and best/worst practices.

■ Finally, at the *evaluation stage*, they may demand both comparative performance data and the reasons behind that comparative performance in order to move to *learning*.

At a broader level, however, one may see that, once a policy cycle is completed, policy-makers move on to a new cycle, with a new issue. One can therefore hypothesise a set of e-Government policy cycles that move through the Figure 13.2 issues: a readiness cycle giving way to an availability cycle, then an uptake cycle and so forth. In the industrialised countries, there might be a sense of this from the changing nature of studies (see also EAG, 2005). Table 13.1 shows the main focus of 64 e-Government benchmarking reports (developed from eGEP, 2006a), where there has been a change of modal interest from readiness to availability to uptake to impact over time.

Table 13.1 Main focus of e-Government benchmarking studies over time

Year	Readiness	Availability	Uptake	Impact
2000	**XXXXX**	XXX	XXXX	
2001	XX	**XXXXXX**		
2002	XXX	**XXXX**	X	XX
2003	XXXXX	XXXXXX	**XXXXXXXX**	XXXXXX
2004	X	**XXXXXXXX**	XXXX	XXXXX
2005			X	**XXXXXXX**
2006				**X**

So, is the era of concern about readiness already gone? Arguably not in all countries. Industrialised country governments and some benchmarking reports written for those governments may be moving to a level of e-Government activity and a policy cycle beyond issues of readiness. But that is not necessarily true of the majority of the world's nations, in which the seven core elements of readiness for e-Government still appear to be part of current agenda and policy discussions (Heeks, 2002; UNESCO, 2005): data systems infrastructure, legal infrastructure, institutional infrastructure, human infrastructure, technological infrastructure, leadership and strategic thinking and e-Government drivers.

Recommendation 2: Clarify the external purpose and audience for benchmarking

Recommendation 3: Commission a quick study on demand for benchmarking data

Evidence on *demand* for e-Government benchmarking data can help guide the purpose and content of a study. Evidence on *use* of e-Government benchmarking data can help guide evaluation of a study, and the purpose and content of any subsequent studies. Governments performing well in e-Government rankings certainly do make use of that fact in press releases and other publicity (see e.g. TBCS, 2004; USA.gov, 2007). There is an assumed use of data to guide e-Government strategy (e.g. Janssen et al., 2004). And there is informal evidence that rankings are used to justify continuing investment in e-Government (Anonymous, 2006). Hence, there is also informal evidence that policy-makers – especially politicians – will complain to benchmarkers about poor/falling rankings, and will prioritise activities that sensitivity analysis has shown will help maintain or improve rankings (ibid.). As per demand, though, there seems to be very little formal evidence about key usage issues: Do policy-makers and others make use of the data provided by benchmarking studies? If so, what data do they use? And how exactly do they use it? Without such evidence we are limited in our ability to evaluate the impact and value of e-Government benchmarking studies, and in our ability to guide future studies.

Recommendation 4: Commission a quick study on usage of benchmarking data

Recommendation 5: For regular benchmarking series, create a user panel to provide feedback

What to benchmark?

Scope of e-Government

Components of e-Government

We can readily categorise the nature of e-Government, as per Figure 13.4 (adapted from Heeks, 2002).

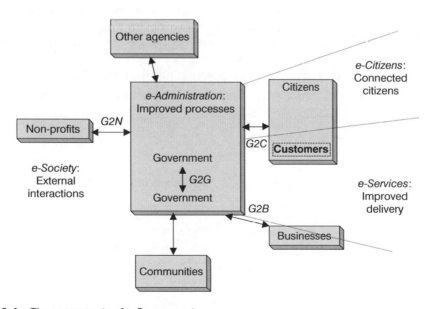

Figure 13.4   The components of e-Government

Within this potentially broad scope of e-Government, the majority of benchmarking studies have focused on citizen-related e-services (Janssen, 2003; Kunstelj and Vintar, 2004). One may see acknowledgement of the constraints this places on benchmarking (e.g. see UN, 2005,

p. 14). Nonetheless, these are constraints that – within the time and cost boundaries that all benchmarking studies must work to – one might try to break free from.

Why? In an overall sense, because there are question marks over citizen-related e-Government:

- Citizen contact with government is relatively rare. In the USA, for example, only half of survey respondents had contacted any level of government in the previous year and, of those, two-thirds rated their contact rate as less than every few months (Horrigan, 2005). Citizen contact levels with government in Europe average 1.6 times per year (Millard, 2006). Likewise, use of e-Government by citizens is relatively rare – the number of citizens accessing e-Government in the past one year is about one-half to one-third the number who have ever accessed e-Government, suggesting up to two-thirds of those using government Web sites do so less than once a year (Accenture, 2005).
- The total number of citizens ever making use of e-Government worldwide is relatively small. Figures for the majority of developing countries are lacking but we can estimate these, given we have an estimate of the number of Internet users in developing countries (e.g. ITU, 2007 for 2005 estimates). We then need an estimate of the proportion of Internet users who have ever accessed e-Government. In industrialised countries, this figure is approximately two-thirds (TNS, 2003; Accenture, 2004; Horrigan, 2005). It is likely to be much less in developing countries given the far more limited availability of e-Government services. Data from TNS (2001, 2002, 2003) gives figures ranging from 10% of Internet users ever using e-Government at the lowest end of developing/transitional economies to around 40% (for Malaysia) at the highest end. This is a significant range so, in taking 25% of Internet users as an average figure it must be recognised that this is a very rough average. We can use it, though, to provide estimates for the apparently very small fraction of citizens in developing countries that has ever accessed e-Government (see Table 13.2). Figures for other countries (Europe including Russia and other transitional economies, Japan, Israel, Canada, USA, Australia, New Zealand) use an average 60% of Internet users ever accessing e-Government. Put together, these imply that not much over one-in-fifteen of the world's population has ever accessed e-Government.

Table 13.2 Very rough estimate of citizen use of e-Government in developing and other countries

Region	Ever accessed e-Government	
	Absolute (in million)	Population (%)
Africa	8.3	0.9
America	21.3	3.9
Asia	75.2	2.0
Oceania	0.11	1.3
DCs Total	105	2.0
Middle- and high-income countries	336	26
World Total	441	6.9

■ There appears to be a negative relationship between citizen attitudes to e-Government and usage rates/sophistication of e-Government for citizens: attitudes are most positive in those countries with the lowest rates of e-Government use/sophistication, and vice versa (Graafland-Essers and Ettedgui, 2003; Accenture, 2005). One (small) study of disadvantaged users in the USA found that, following training, two-thirds had visited a government Web site but that not a single one intended to do so again (Sipior and Ward, 2005).

■ By far the main use of e-services by citizens is to access information from government Web sites rather than actual services (only 10–25% of e-Government users undertake transactions (TNS, 2003; Accenture, 2004), and even for e-Government 'front-runner' services only 5–10% of transactions are undertaken online: the remainder still occur offline (Ramboll Management, 2004)). But this acquisition of data is just the first step in an information chain (see Figure 13.5) that requires the presence of many other resources if it is to lead to a developmental impact on citizens' lives. To turn that e-Government-based data into an impact requires that the data be assessed, applied and then acted upon. This requires money, skills, knowledge, motivation, confidence, empowerment and trust among other resources. Yet e-Government itself does nothing to impact these other resources. It is therefore only one small part of a much bigger picture required to make an impact on citizens' lives.

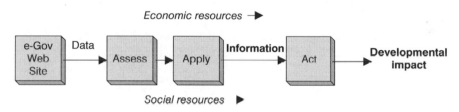

■ **Figure 13.5**   Citizen use of e-Government data – The information chain

We can also frame an argument for the necessity of benchmarking beyond just citizen e-services in terms of the other e-Government components. First, *G2B* – with the goal of improving public service to business – should not be ignored. Of those benchmarking reports that do encompass e-services, most focus only on citizens and ignore businesses as users; yet there is evidence of a need to reverse this emphasis:

■ In 2002, in the EU, the most popular e-Government service for citizens (library book search) was used by less than 10% of citizens; the most popular e-Government service for businesses (online submission of statistical data) was used by 23% of businesses (Graafland-Essers and Ettedgui, 2003).

■ In 2003, in the UK, 18% of citizens had some online interaction with government (TNS, 2003) but 35% of UK businesses did so (DTI, 2004).

■ Economic return on investment in e-Government can be calculated via its impact on three cost stages of interacting with government: finding relevant government procedures, understanding government procedures and complying with government procedures (Deloitte, 2004). From this approach, it is government interaction with businesses much more than citizens which delivers e-Government ROI.

■ Perhaps reflecting this notion of higher demand and higher returns plus higher IT readiness among businesses, G2B services are more developed. In 2004, in the EU, 68% of sampled e-Government-for-business sites offered full electronic case handling compared to just 31% of e-Government-for-citizens sites (Capgemini, 2005).

Second, because *G2G* – with goals such as cutting costs, decentralising power, managing performance and improving strategic decision-making – should not be ignored. e-Administration has not been addressed by global benchmarking but it has a key role to play:

- In terms of most e-Government stage models, the final stage (be it called integration, transformation, sharing, etc.) requires back-office changes; in other words significant G2G developments (Goldkuhl and Persson, 2006).
- In practice, the most successful approaches to e-Government are characterised by a 'dual focus on back office integration and front office service delivery' (BAH, 2002, p. 18) so that 'back office changes are required to achieve results' (Capgemini, 2004, p. 3; see also Kunstelj and Vintar, 2004).
- Benefits of e-Government are perceived mainly to relate to change in internal government agency processes (NOIE, 2003; Capgemini, 2004).

Third, because *e-citizens* applications – with goals of talking to citizens and listening to citizens – should not be ignored:

- e-Citizens applications cover issues of e-accountability, e-participation and e-democracy, the goals of which are fundamental to good governance (Kaufmann et al., 2005). Concern about delivery of good governance therefore requires concern about e-citizens.
- Without a focus on e-citizens applications, there is a danger of digital exclusion; in other words of the inequalities between the 'haves' and 'have nots' being exacerbated by e-Government (EAG, 2005).

Fourth, because *e-society* applications – with goals such as working better with business, developing communities and building partnerships – should not be ignored.

- Reform based on new public management attempts to shrink the role of the state to 'steering not rowing', thus requiring a stronger partnership role with private and CSOs that will join the state as service providers (Heeks, 2001).
- For many countries the state's capacity is much less than necessary to deliver on its roles. It is therefore obliged to rely on other organisations – largely those of civil society – particularly for service provision (Edwards, 2003).

Recommendation 6: Seek ways to incorporate the breadth of e-Government components within benchmarking

Levels of e-Government

We can categorise at least five potential levels of e-Government, as per Figure 13.6.

The majority of benchmarking studies have focused on national e-Government. National e-Government provides, of course, an appropriate basis for cross-national benchmarking. For some countries, it represents the only location for e-Government. However, this does bring with it some limitations:

- In industrialised countries between one-half and fourth-fifths of government contacts are at sub-national level (Carbo and Williams, 2004; AGIMO, 2005; Horrigan, 2005). In developing countries, it is local governments particularly that are the main point of contact for delivery of services and for delivery of National Programmes (Amis, 2001; Page, 2006).

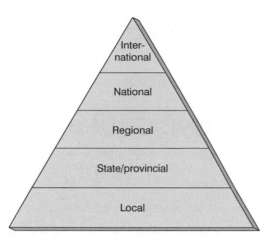

Figure 13.6   Levels of e-Government

Hence they are a critical location for applying Information Communication Technologies (ICTs) in pursuit of national development goals (Jensen, 2002).

■ Lower tiers of government may be more innovative in e-Government than the national level due to lower barriers to change (e.g. Paquet and Roy, 2000). In many countries, this may be more than counter-balanced by the severe resource constraints, leading to diffusion graphs similar to that portrayed in Figure 13.7. Even in this situation, though, e-Government at lower tiers is of increasing importance over time: one straw in the wind is the e-Government case studies listed at the World Bank e-Government Web site (World Bank, 2007a) of which more than half are at state and local level.

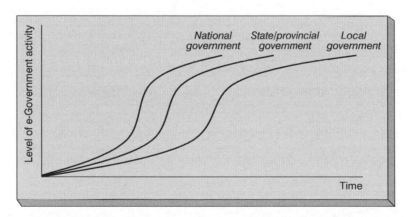

Figure 13.7   Hypothesised diffusion of e-Government at different levels of government in poorer countries

Recommendation 7: Seek ways to incorporate appropriate levels of e-Government within benchmarking

Channels of e-Government

e-Government can be defined as the use of information and communication technologies by public sector organisations. As such it encompasses a variety of potential delivery channels (see Figure 13.8, adapted from Cabinet Office, 2000).

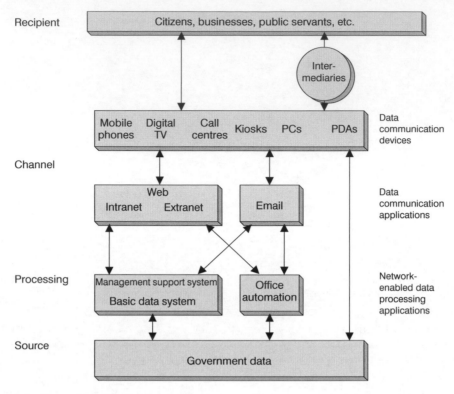

Recipient

Channel

Processing

Source

Figure 13.8   The architecture of e-Government

By and large, the focus of benchmarking studies has been Web-based communication deliv-ered via a PC. The assumption – explicit within industrialised country-focused studies; implicit otherwise – is that the PC will be directly accessed by the recipient. However, even in industrialised economies this reflects neither practice nor preference in interaction with government:

- *Telephony dominates channel usage in some situations*: Accenture (2005) reports 63% of indus-trialised country respondents contacting government by telephone; compared to 31% using the Internet over a 12-month period.
- *In-person visits dominate in other situations*: An Australian survey reports half of gov-ernment contacts to be face-to-face compared to one-fifth undertaken via the Internet (AGIMO, 2005).
- Survey data also reflects an ongoing preference for telephone or in-person channels espe-cially for transactional, problem-solving, urgent and complex interactions (AGIMO, 2005; Horrigan, 2005; Streib and Navarro, 2006).

These figures are changing over time – visits to government Web sites are growing; the profile among Internet users (a grouping which has only plateaued in size in a few of the industrialised economies) is more pro-Internet; and there seems to be a fairly ready incor-poration of government Web sites into citizens' information searches (Graafland-Essers and Ettedgui, 2003; Accenture, 2004). However, we should not seek to deny the reality of current usage and preference patterns.

Recommendation 8: Encompass the multi-channel realities of government interactions, for example, by investigating channel integration

Data from developing countries is very limited but suggests a 'same but more so' picture. For example, Accenture (2005) reports that in emerging economies 67% of those with a home phone (a sample significantly skewed towards higher-income groups) had used in-person interactions with government compared to 11% using online channels in the past year. To this, we can add two further issues:

- Given Internet usage rates of, for example, less than 3 per 100 population in Africa (and with that usage heavily skewed towards a small high-income fraction of the population), models of e-Government anticipating direct use of the Web by citizens are inappropriate for the majority of the world's population for the foreseeable future (Heeks, 1999; ITU, 2007). If e-Government services are to impact this group, it will be through intermediated models: for example, assisted use at a village kiosk or town telecentre. Even in industrialised countries, intermediation is significant: 42% of European e-Government users reported accessing information or services on behalf of others (Millard, 2006).
- Developing country governments and related international actors during the final years of the 20th century and first years of the 21st have been telecentre-focused. As a result they have, to some extent, been blindsided by the growth of mobile telephony in developing countries. Yet, for example, there are now over five times more mobile phones than PCs in Africa, with growth rates for the former being over 50% per annum, while the latter grows at just over 10% per annum (ITU, 2007). Even in Europe, cell phone usage outstrips that of PCs and there is intense interest in m-Government: delivery of government information and services to phones (e.g. Cross and MacGregor, 2006).

Recommendation 9: Take account of intermediated access to e-Government

Recommendation 10: Investigate ways to incorporate m-Government into benchmarking

e-Government value chain

Figure 13.9 illustrates the 'e-Government value chain' – a summary of the way in which e-Government turns inputs into outcomes (developed from Flynn, 2002; Janssen et al., 2004; Capgemini, 2005). Benchmarking studies can choose to measure simple indicators from this chain, as described in Table 13.3, or calculated indicators, as discussed later.

Table 13.3 is not intended to be statistically representative. However, its profile does reflect other evidence (e.g. Janssen, 2003; Kunstelj and Vintar, 2004; eGEP, 2006a) that benchmarking tends to focus on the core of the value chain – intermediates, adoption and use – rather than the main upstream (precursors, inputs) or downstream (impacts, outcomes, to some degree outputs) elements. As summarised in Figure 13.10, this probably occurs because the core measures are a compromise between ease/cost of measurement and developmental/comparison value. However, this does create limitations in that most critical of benchmarking activities: understanding the value of e-Government. The particular emphasis on intermediates is also problematic because it is not a proxy for the further-downstream measures of adoption and use: in other words, countries/agencies with very sophisticated Web sites can have low levels of use and vice versa (BAH, 2002; Wattegama, 2005).

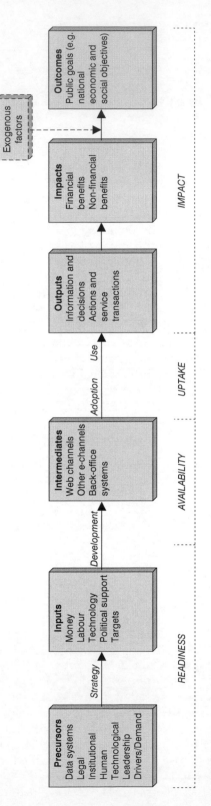

Figure 13.9 The e-Government value chain

■ **Table 13.3** e-Government measures, indicators and methods used in benchmarking studies

Value chain stage	Sample measure	Sample indicator	Sample data-gathering method
Precursors	Telecommunications infrastructure	Mainline phones per 1000 population (UN, 2005) Internet users per 1000 population (UN, 2005)	Official statistics: International agency (UN, 2005)
	Human resource infrastructure	UNDP education index (UN, 2005)	
Strategy	Presence of e-Government strategy		
Inputs	Money	Annual government expenditure on IT (Heath, 2000)	Official statistics: Government (Heath, 2000)
Development	Development best practices	Extent of use of public-private partnerships (OECD, 2004) Lessons learned (OeE, 2001)	Internal self-assessment (OeE, 2001, OECD, 2004)
Intermediates	Quality of government Web sites	Navigability rating for Web site (Moore et al., 2005; Petricek et al., 2006) Nodality of Web site (Petricek et al., 2006) Bobby/W3C accessibility of Web site (Choudrie et al., 2004; Cabinet Office, 2005; UN, 2005) Privacy rating for Web site (Choudrie et al., 2004) Connectivity of e-government sites to NGO sector (Kuk, 2004)	Third-party Web assessment (BAH, 2002; Accenture, 2005; Cabinet Office, 2005; Capgemini, 2005; Moore et al., 2005; UN, 2005; West, 2006) Web metrics and crawlers (Choudrie et al., 2004; Kuk, 2004; Cabinet Office, 2005; UN, 2005; Petricek et al., 2006)
	General features of government Web sites	Presence/absence of e-mail address (West, 2006) Presence/absence of credit card payment system (West, 2006)	Internal self-assessment (BAH, 2002)
	Participation-specific features of government Web sites	Percentage of countries explaining e-consultation, and informing citizens of ways to provide input (UN, 2005)	
	Government Web site maturity	Level of Web site on three-stage model (Accenture, 2005) Level of Web site on four-stage model (Capgemini, 2005) Level of Web site on five-stage model (UN, 2005)	
	Government-specific infrastructure	Percentage of government staff with a PC (BAH, 2002) Percentage of government services available online (BAH, 2002)	

(Continued)

■ Table 13.3 (Continued)

Value chain stage	Sample measure	Sample indicator	Sample data-gathering method
Adoption	Prospective attitude towards use of e-government by citizens	Awareness of specific e-government services (Graafland-Essers and Ettedgui, 2003)	Mass citizen survey (Graafland-Essers and Ettedgui, 2003; TNS, 2003; Accenture, 2004, 2005; Horrigan, 2005)
		Percentage of adults feeling safe to transmit personal data to government via Internet (TNS, 2003)	Focus group (NOIE, 2003)
		Channel preferences of citizens – phone, online, mail, in person (Graafland-Essers and Ettedgui, 2003;Accenture, 2005;Horrigan, 2005)	Internal self-assessment (OECD, 2004)
		Likely benefits of e-government perceived by citizens (Graafland-Essers and Ettedgui, 2003)	Pop-up survey (Freed, 2006)
		Barriers to e-government use perceived by citizens (NOIE, 2003; Accenture, 2004)	
		Expectations of e-government perceived by citizens (Freed, 2006)	
	Adoption of best practices	Presence/absence of incentives for e-government uptake (OECD, 2004)	
Use	Use of e-government by citizens	Percentage of adults using online services in past year (Graafland-Essers and Ettedgui, 2003; TNS, 2003)	Mass citizen survey (Graafland-Essers and Ettedgui, 2003;TNS, 2003; Accenture, 2005; Horrigan, 2005)
		Percentage of e-government users getting information about welfare benefits (Horrigan, 2005)	Mass business survey (DTI, 2004)
	Use of e-government by businesses	Percentage of businesses making online payments to government (DTI, 2004)	
	Experience of e-government use by citizens	Percentage of contacts in which previous contact was recalled (Accenture, 2005)	

Outputs	Retrospective attitude towards use of e-government by citizens	Satisfaction rating with particular e-government services (Accenture, 2004; Ramboll Management, 2004; Horrigan, 2005; Freed, 2006)
		Level of citizen complaints about e-government service (Freed, 2006)
		Mass citizen survey (Accenture, 2004; Horrigan, 2005)
		Pop-up survey (NOIE, 2003; Ramboll Management, 2004; Freed, 2006)
		Perceived improvement to information access (NOIE, 2003)
Impacts	Citizen benefits	Time saved (Capgemini, 2004; Ramboll Management, 2004)
		Interview: Internal self-assessment/internal administrative records (NOIE, 2003)
	Financial benefit	Financial savings perceived by officials (NOIE, 2003)
		Interview: Internal self-assessment (BAH, 2002)
		Nature of changes to government processes (BAH, 2002)
		Questionnaire: Internal self-assessment (Capgemini, 2004)
	Back office changes	Changes in process time (Capgemini, 2004)
		Pop-up survey (Ramboll Management, 2004)
Outcomes	Employment levels	

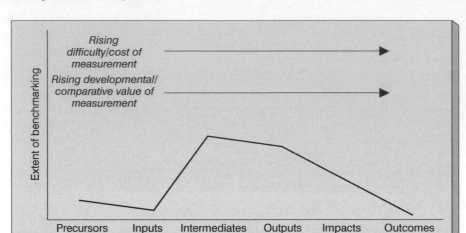

Figure 13.10   Usage of different indicators in e-Government benchmarking

Recommendation 11: Where feasible incorporate more downstream (outputs, impacts) measures into e-Government benchmarking

There are related indicator sets for at least three of the underemphasised measures – demand precursors, impacts and outcomes – that are relatively easily available for a large spread of countries (see Table 13.4). Unfortunately, there are many additional factors involved in the relation between these general indicators (of attitudes, governance and development) and core e-Government indicators. Certainly, any correlation exercise involving outcomes would be fairly pointless: the causal path from e-Government to outcomes is too indistinct. For the other indicator sets – demand and impacts – correlation is also of questionable value given the likely limited impact of these more general demand indicators on e-Government, and of e-Government on general governance indicators of corruption, trust, perceptions of accountability and bureaucracy, etc. Nonetheless it may be worth undertaking some exploratory correlations to see if any patterns emerge.

Table 13.4   Demand, impact and outcome data from non-e-Government sources

Value chain element	Sample indicators
Precursors: Demand	Relative importance of security, democracy and economy (WVS, 2005)
	Level of political activity (WVS, 2005)
	Contribution of technology (WVS, 2005)
Impacts	Trust/confidence in government (GI, 2005; WVS, 2005)
	Level of corruption (Kaufmann et al., 2005; TI, 2006)
	Perceptions of democracy (GI, 2005)
	Governmental effectiveness (Kaufmann et al., 2005; IMD, 2006)
Outcomes	National development indicators (World Bank, 2007b)
	Millennium development goals (UNSD, 2007)

Recommendation 12: Conduct exploratory correlations between demand, impact and core e-Government indicators

Using calculated indicators

The discussion above relates to simple indicators, which form by far the majority of those reported. A number of benchmarking studies use composite indicators (e.g. for the purposes of national rankings). Composites have been criticised (e.g. UIS, 2003) for their subjectivity and inaccuracy; some also lack transparency – it is unclear how they are researched or calculated. A guide to good practice in use of composites would include (eGEP, 2006a, p. 45):

- Developing a theoretical framework for the composite.
- Identifying and developing relevant variables.
- Standardising variables to allow comparisons.
- Weighting variables and groups of variables.
- Conducting sensitivity tests on the robustness of aggregated variables.

Recommendation 13: Follow good practice procedures when using composite indicators

Other than the composite calculation of national rankings, there appears to be relatively little use of calculated indicators in the benchmarking of e-Government (see Table 13.5). Some of these existing indicators could usefully be extended.

Table 13.5 Calculated indicators used in e-Government benchmarking

Calculated indicator	Example	Method
Benefit/Cost ratio	Expected financial benefit (impact)/financial cost (input) (NOIE, 2003)	Interview (internal self-assessment/internal administrative records)
Demand/ supply match	Preference for online channel in particular services vs. online sophistication of that service (Graafland-Essers and Ettedgui, 2003)	Mass citizen survey
Comparative service development	Stage model level of citizen services vs. business services (Capgemini, 2005)	Third-party Web assessment
	Stage model level of different service cluster areas (Capgemini, 2005)	
National ranking	Composite of features and stage model level for national Web sites (West, 2006)	Third-party Web assessment
	Composite of ICT and human infrastructure with stage model level for national/other Web sites (UN, 2005)	
	Composite of stage model level, integration and personalisation of national Web sites (Accenture, 2005)	

Benefit/cost ratio: Ways of measuring benefits are discussed later. However, there is a notable black hole in e-Government benchmarking of relevance to benefits: e-Government failure. Partial failures – e-Government projects in which major goals are unattained and/or in which there are significant undesirable impacts – do produce a workable system which typically would be included within benchmarking. However, total failures – e-Government projects that are never implemented or are implemented but immediately abandoned – will, by definition, not be included in normal benchmarking. Yet one can estimate that between one-fifth and one-third of all e-Government projects fall into the total failure category (Heeks, 2000; Heeks, 2003). Such all-cost, no-benefit projects need to be included in overall benefit/cost calculations for e-Government.

Demand/supply match: There is a significant bank of data on e-services supply measures such as Web site maturity and quality. This can be compared to demand data: either country-specific ratings of demand from a commissioned survey, or more generic data gathered from other sources. This has sometimes been found to indicate a mismatch between what users want and what e-Government provides (Graafland-Essers and Ettedgui, 2003).

Comparative service development: Comparison of the maturity of different service clusters gives an insight into government priorities. For example, in Europe, government-centred applications (tax gathering, registration by citizens/businesses) have a greater maturity than more citizen-centred applications (service delivery, provision of permits/licences) (Capgemini, 2005). One could see this as evidence of a lack of citizen-centricity in government. This idea – of comparing government-centred and citizen-/user-centred application maturity – can be utilised in other benchmarking studies. One could combine this basic demand understanding to compare maturity of, for instance, applications aimed more at traditionally male interests/roles vs. traditionally female interests/roles; or to compare applications prioritised more by poor citizens vs. those prioritised more by wealthy citizens.

National ranking – Stage models. All the national ranking models listed here rely centrally on a stage model of e-Government. Stage models vary somewhat but a typical formulation runs from Information (static information) to Interaction (information searches and form downloads) to Transaction (completing transactions online) to Integration (joining-up of online services between agencies) (Goldkuhl and Persson, 2006). There are at least two problems with this approach, caused partly by the fact that stage models have their origins in private sector e-commerce models. First, they assume online transaction to be the 'nirvana' of e-Government, yet nirvana might actually be the proactive completion of the transaction within government or even its elimination (Janssen, 2003). Second, having a single-stage model conflates two separate dimensions: the sophistication of a service (a front-office measure of how much can be accomplished online) and the integration of a service (a back-office measure of the degree to which elements of a user-focused process are dispersed or integrated) (Kunstelj and Vintar, 2004). The latter authors therefore propose a revised conceptualisation of stage models, as illustrated in Figure 13.11. Accenture's move in 2005 to build a two-dimensional ranking system based on service maturity (a basic sophistication model) and customer service maturity (incorporating aspects of integration but also further customer-centric ideas) can be seen as innovative in this regard.

Basing rankings on stage models also means that, despite caveats (e.g. UN, 2005, p. 18), higher positions in ranking tables are seen as better. Rankings thus have a significant power to both (mis)guide political decision-making and to attract criticism and lobbying of

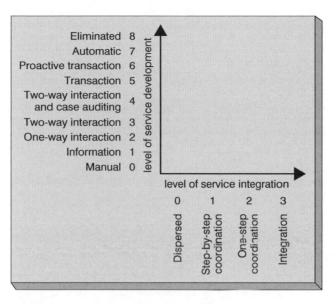

■ **Figure 13.11**   Two-dimensional e-Government Web stage model

benchmarkers (Anonymous, 2006). Some are therefore questioning rankings and Accenture (2006) abandoned its country rankings to focus more on ideas, good practice and lessons.

National ranking – Precursors: National e-Government rankings undertaken by the UN are virtually unique in including some precursors (telecommunications infrastructure indicator and human development indicator). This could be extended to correlate e-Government maturity levels or usage levels with a full set of the precursor indicators identified above (data systems, legal, institutional, human, technological, leadership, drivers/demand) via analysis of variance to see which precursors appear more or less important (see also the idea of 'pathway diagrams' in the 'How to report' section).

Recommendation 14: Investigate extended use of calculated benchmarking indicators

Using standard public sector indicators

It is also possible to compare Table 13.5 with a standard indicator set for public sector performance (see Table 13.6, adapted from Flynn (2002): the examples chosen here are G2C e-services given its domination of benchmarking, but they could equally be applied to other components of e-Government).

The comparison shows that only one calculated standard indicator was found in the review of benchmarking; benefit/cost ratio which is one external efficiency measure, but undermined at least in the cited case because it is (a) self-reported only, and (b) refers only to expectations, not reality. The only other typical indicator used is quality, as reflected in relation to both intermediates (e.g. stage maturity or navigability of e-Government Web sites) and outputs (e.g. citizen satisfaction with e-Government services).

■ Table 13.6 Standard indicators for government and e-Government performance

Indicator	Explanation	e-Government example	Benchmark
Economy	The amount of inputs used	Expenditure per capita on IT in government	None
Internal efficiency	The ratio of inputs:intermediates	Cost per Web site produced per year	Minimisation
External efficiency	The ratio of inputs:outputs (use)	Cost per citizen user of government Web sites per year	Minimisation
Internal effectiveness	The fit between actual outputs (use) and organisational objectives or other set targets	The extent to which underserved communities are users of e-government services	Maximisation
External effectiveness	The fit between actual impacts and organisational objectives or other set targets	The extent to which citizens are gaining employment due to use of an e-government job search service	Maximisation
Quality	The quality of intermediates or, more typically, outputs (use)	The quality of e-government services as perceived by citizen users	Maximisation
Equity	The equitability of distribution of outputs or impacts	The equality of time/money saved by e-government service use between rich and poor citizens	Maximisation

The first three standard indicators listed in Table 13.6 would be potentially usable only if figures on government IT spending are available. Per-application figures would be most useful but they appear very rarely (Nicoll et al., 2004 is an exception, providing an estimate of US$12 000 to US$750 000 redesign costs per e-Government Web site; and US$150 000 to US$800 000 annual recurrent costs per e-Government Web site). More general figures on ICT spending in government are available for some countries (see World Bank, 2007c) but one must then grapple with the limitation of relation between this figure and available intermediate or output measures: How appropriate is it, for example, to relate total ICT spending solely to Web sites, when that spending likely covers many other areas of computerisation?

Effectiveness measures can be and are used for benchmarking e-Government, though hampered by the relatively limited attention they have received to date. Finally, equity measures are relatively easy to adopt, at least for those benchmarking activities relying on surveys since equity-related questions – about the income, education, age, location, etc. of respondents – are often included in the survey. As discussed later, one may also proxy these with general Internet use demographics.

Recommendation 15: Investigate greater use of standard indicators, but recognise barriers to their use

Benchmarking change

Many benchmarking studies of e-Government are one-offs and rely on one-time, cross-sectional measures. Even regular benchmarking studies tend to focus mainly on their static data with somewhat perfunctory consideration of change in indicators over time. Yet it is the ability to bring about change that, presumably, policy-makers and other audience members are particularly interested in. National or agency rankings, for example, might look very different if based on degree of change over one-, two- or three-year time scales rather than based on static measures. eGEP (2006b) proposes relying solely on the annual change in an indicator as the benchmarking measure for e-Government because this circumvents the problem of standardising indicators across countries. One could then investigate top performers further via quantitative correlational and qualitative causational analysis to try to understand what explains their performance; providing important lessons. From this perspective, one likely causal component – missing from almost all e-Government benchmarking – is the capacity of government agencies to enact a learning cycle of evaluation, reflection, planning and action (IAB, 2003).

Recommendation 16: Give equal emphasis where possible to measures of change over time

Matching e-Government supply to demand is one of the main likely priorities for change. Given this, adoption data is of especial interest. It is not particularly appropriate for benchmarking: comparing perceived pros and cons of e-Government or channel preferences across countries is of limited value. But for individual countries or agencies a sense of why their target users do and do not use e-Government provides valuable guidance for change (e.g. see Graafland-Essers and Ettedgui, 2003; Accenture, 2004). This is part of a slightly broader point that it is the processes within the e-Government value chain – adoption to some extent but strategy and development much more – that are the activities of change which most benchmarking study users are actually engaged in. Yet these activities are rarely the subject of benchmarking, tending more to form a patchy qualitative background from which readers must draw their own conclusions and only occasionally (e.g. OeE, 2001) being placed centre-stage. (Another exception is the Balanced e-Government Index (Begix), which incorporates a well-balanced set of indicators around benefits, efficiency, participation, transparency and change management (Bertelsmann Foundation, 2002); unfortunately its actual content and implementation methods are unclear – see http://www.begix.net). One proposed approach to address this – given the complexities of measuring qualitative processes such as change – is 'bench-learning': a peer-to-peer exchange of change-related lessons and practices requiring less standardisation and fewer 'public relations biases' than the typical top-down/external form of benchmarking (eGEP, 2006b).

Recommendation 17: Recognise the importance of change practices in benchmarking

Recommendation 18: Consider the relevance of a benchlearning approach

Benchmarking public value

'Public value' has become something of a buzz term invoked in relation to e-Government benchmarking, though sometimes without a clear connection to what is actually measured (e.g. Accenture, 2004). Public value is intended to be the equivalent for the public sector of private value: the returns that businesses deliver for their shareholders. In general, public value can be defined as 'the value created by government through services, laws, regulation and other actions' (Kelly et al., 2001, p. 4). It is therefore in tune with the 'integrate' approach described in Box 13.1 and a reminder that we should not really be interested in measuring e-Government *per se*, but in measuring what e-Government achieves: a message not understood by many governments in setting their technocentric initial targets for e-Government.

■ Box 13.1   Beyond e-Government?

Aside from the particular benchmarking issues, is it time to stop focusing on e-Government? Strategy in government moves through four stages of relations between information and communication technologies (ICTs) and public sector reform (Heeks and Davies, 2001):

- *Ignore*: ICTs are entirely disregarded in considering reform.
- *Isolate*: ICTs are included but disconnected from the reform process.
- *Idolise*: ICTs become a centrepiece of reform, seen as the transformative lever.
- *Integrate*: Reform goals are the ends, and ICTs are an integral means to achieve those ends.

The peak of interest in e-Government occurs when groups of officials enter the 'idolise' phase, creating a demand spike for data from studies and reports. But what happens after this? In some cases, there is a post-hype bursting of the dot.gov bubble, with officials simply falling out of love with e-Government and moving on to seek the next silver bullet. In other cases, there is a move to the 'integrate' approach, with ICTs sub-sumed within a broader vision of and interest in transformation. In either situation, there will be a fall-off in demand for e-Government data.

Evidence for this analysis is scanty but a few straws in the wind can be claimed:

- The US National Academy of Public Administration's ending of its e-Government programme and the absence of e-Government from its 2006 'big ideas' list.
- 2003 being the peak year for number of e-Government benchmarking studies reported by eGEP (2006a).
- The virtual 'without a trace' disappearance of the once much publicised e-Government targets in the UK.
- Accenture's 2005 and 2006 refocusing and rebranding of its annual e-Government survey to centre on customer service.

But how can this rather vague concept be translated for measurement of e-Government? Here, two ideas are offered. First, the public value of e-Government can be broken down into three main areas, as described in Figure 13.12 (adapted from Kearns, 2004).

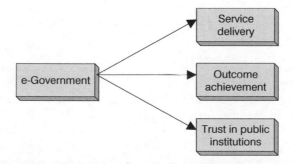

■ **Figure 13.12**   The public value of e-Government (Kearns approach)

These can be developed into a set of indicators, as shown in Table 13.7 (developed from Kearns, 2004).

Table 13.7   Indicators for e-Government's public value (Kearns approach)

Value domain	Indicator	Description
Service delivery	Take-up	The extent to which e-government is used
	Satisfaction	The level of user satisfaction with e-government
	Information	The level of information provided to users by e-government
	Choice	The level of choice provided to users by e-government
	Importance	The extent to which e-government is focused on user priorities
	Fairness	The extent to which e-government is focused on those most in need
	Cost	The cost of e-government information/service provision
Outcome achievement	Outcome	e-Government's contribution to delivery of outcomes
Trust in public institutions	Trust	e-Government's contribution to public trust

Public value can thus be seen as a new perspective since none of these indicators is covered by standard e-services G2C benchmarking (even though this interpretation of public value is largely focused on e-services rather than, say, e-administration or e-citizens). Take-up, satisfaction and cost have all been part of some benchmarking studies, and the importance measure is very similar to demand/supply match. As noted, the causal distance between e-Government and outcomes is too great, so outcomes must be measured by proxies such as outputs or impacts which some benchmarking does cover. The indicators of information, choice, fairness and trust do not appear to have been covered by any mainstream e-Government benchmark studies. There is therefore significant potential for an original approach to e-Government measurement.

A second approach takes a rather broader perspective that could potentially encompass all components of e-Government, again with three main areas as described in Figure 13.13 (developed from eGEP, 2006b).

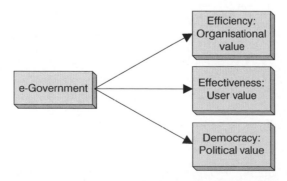

Figure 13.13   The public value of e-Government (eGEP approach)

Again, these can be developed into a set of indicators, as shown in Table 13.8 (developed from eGEP, 2006b). There is still some bias here against e-administration/G2G, with no inclusion of user impact related to improvements in decision- and policy-making, and against e-society/G2N, with no inclusion of government's e-enabling of civil society and communities. This is because the framework is based on an understanding of e-Government users only as taxpayers (efficiency), consumers (effectiveness) and citizens/voters (democracy). However, eGEP's work combines a significant depth of analysis with an understanding of real-world limitations to produce a valuable set of ideas on benchmarking indicators.

Table 13.8 Indicators for e-Government's public value (eGEP approach)

Value domain	Indicator	Sample measures
Efficiency: Organisational value	Financial flows	Reduction in overhead costs Staff time saving per case handled
	Staff empowerment	Percentage of staff with ICT skills Staff satisfaction rating
	Organisation/IT architecture	Number of redesigned business processes Volume of authenticated digital documents exchanged
Effectiveness: User value	Administrative burden	Time saved per transaction for citizens Overhead cost-saving for businesses (travel, postage, fees)
	User value/satisfaction	Number of out-of-hours usages of e-government User satisfaction rating
	Inclusivity of service	e-Government usage by disadvantaged groups Number of SMEs bidding for public tenders online
Democracy: Political value	Openness	Number of policy drafts available online Response time to online queries
	Transparency and accountability	Number of processes traceable online Number of agencies reporting budgets online
	Participation	Accessibility rating of e-government sites Number of contributions to online discussion forums

Recommendation 19: Consider new indicators of e-Government public value which may be of use in benchmarking

How to benchmark?

Selecting data-gathering methods

We can identify from the review and Table 13.3 given above a series of different data-gathering methods for e-Government benchmarking and can summarise three features of each method as shown in Table 13.9 (adapted from eGEP, 2006b, p. 20):

- *Cost*: The time and financial cost of the method.
- *Value*: The value of the method in producing data capable of assessing the downstream value of e-Government.
- *Comparability*: The ease with which data produced can be compared across nations or agencies.

Table 13.9 Comparing e-Government benchmarking data sources

Method	Cost	Value	Comparability
Official statistics	Low	Low	High
Internal self-assessment	Low–Medium	Medium	Low
Third-party Web assessment	Medium	Medium	High
Web metrics and crawlers	Medium	Medium	Medium–High
Pop-up survey	Medium	Medium–High	Medium–High
Focus group	Medium	High	Low–Medium
Internal administrative records	Medium–High	Medium–High	Low–Medium
Mass user survey	Medium–High	High	Medium–High

There is a fourth issue that should also be included when considering data-gathering methods: data quality. This is an issue hardly addressed by most benchmarking studies, and there seems to be an implicit assumption that the quality of benchmarking data is high. However, this is not always the case with apparently 'solid' indicators, in fact, being based on subjective and partial original data (see Janssen, 2003; UIS, 2003; Minges, 2005). If the data quality of methods does need to be assessed or compared, the CARTA checklist can be used (Heeks, 2006):

- How *complete* is the benchmarking data provided by this method?
- How *accurate* is the benchmarking data provided?
- How *relevant* is the benchmarking data provided?
- How *timely* is the benchmarking data provided?
- How *appropriately presented* is the benchmarking data provided?

Recommendation 20: Select data-gathering methods on the basis of their cost, value, comparability and quality

Other general methods issues

Measurement transparency: In some benchmarking studies (e.g. Bertelsmann Foundation, 2002) it is not possible to understand either how the benchmarking data was gathered, nor how it was analyzed, nor how it was used to calculate any indices or rankings. Other studies (e.g. UN, 2005) are very clear about all these elements. The problem with the former approach is that it raises suspicions that researchers either do not wish their methods to be understood (and, hence, criticised) or that they seek to extract rents from proprietary methods that others cannot reuse. In either case this devalues the benchmarking findings. A combination of data-gathering transparency and perceived objectivity is also seen by some benchmarkers as a necessary defence against complaints from policy-makers about poor or falling rankings (Anonymous, 2006).

Recommendation 21: Be transparent about benchmarking methods

Output/impact measurement: Measures beyond adoption in the e-Government value chain are needed to judge the value of e-Government. Most of the impact examples given in Table 13.3 were measured by self-assessment; a method with distinct drawbacks, as noted below. As also discussed later, there may be emerging opportunities to use Web metrics/crawlers to assess some outputs/impacts but only in certain situations. In general, then, output and impact measurements require some form of survey. Surveys have been used for this but survey data to date seems to have concentrated mainly on adoption and use, so there is obvious potential for change.

Recommendation 22: Make greater use of survey methods to assess e-Government outputs and impacts

Partnerships in data gathering: As can be seen from Table 13.3 and from the reference list, there are many e-Government benchmarking studies at global, regional and national level. This inevitably means there is duplication of data-gathering activity. For example, annual global third-party Web assessment is undertaken by West (2006) and the UN (2005). Consulting firms Accenture, Capgemini and Deloitte have all undertaken similar regular third-party Web assessments for e-Government sites in Europe and beyond. There are also studies repeating this activity for individual nations (e.g. Abanumy et al., 2005). Likewise there are a number of apparently similar, apparently simultaneous mass surveys in various countries encompassing e-Government. The opportunities for greater partnership in gathering data for benchmarking would seem to be significant.

Recommendation 23: Investigate opportunities for partnering with other data gatherers

Specific methods in use

We can offer a commentary on each of the identified data-gathering methods:

Official statistics are used relatively little because they tend to be non-e-Government-specific and (see commentary at Table 13.4) it can thus be hard to make the connection with e-Government. Probably their most appropriate use is in detailing the precursors to e-Government; something that only one major benchmarking study currently does (UN, 2005).

As noted above, there could be investigation of correlating e-Government indicators with governance indicators such as those collated by the World Bank (Kaufmann et al., 2005).

Internal self-assessment works well for some things, such as reporting of lessons learned. It works less well for others where there can be a 'public relations bias': the respondent is aware that their response will be publicly reported and will thus produce a good or bad reflection, such as in self-reporting the presence or absence of e-Government best practices. However, internal self-assessment does reach places that other methods do not: it is one of the few methods for gathering data to benchmark G2G e-Government.

Recommendation 24: Ensure internal self-assessment is used appropriately with minimal bias incentives

Third-party Web assessment divides into three different types:

1 *Categorisation*: Simple presence/absence measures, and classification from presence/absence into stage model ratings (UN, 2005; West, 2006). This approach is quite widely known and used.
2 *Quality assessment*: Evaluation via Web usage criteria such as content, functionality and design (Moore et al., 2005).
3 *Mystery user*: Replicating the user experience (Accenture, 2005). This is potentially a more subjective approach than the others but does come closest to reality since the assessor takes on the role of a user who, say, wishes to participate in an online debate or apply for a licence renewal.

Recommendation 25: Investigate the utility of mystery user techniques

Web metrics and crawlers may be a growth area for benchmarking given the relative ease with which they can be used. To date, they appear to be used mainly for e-services site quality assessment; for example, assessing the accessibility of sites to users with disabilities or assessing site privacy levels (e.g. see Choudrie et al., 2004; UN, 2005).

One area for further development may be the assessment of hyperlinks. These can be used to measure the quality (navigability, centralisation) of an individual site. They can also be used to measure the 'nodality' of an e-Government site: both its authority/visibility (the number of inlinks to that site) and its hubness (the number of outlinks from that site) (Petricek et al., 2006). (A 'quick-and-dirty' version of the former is to type consistent keywords into major search engines to see if the site appears on the top 10 hits: see Holliday, 2002.) Authority could be seen as one measure of value of external-facing e-Government. One could also look at the nature of nodality – for example, the number and proportion of links to and from CSOs as some measure of either G2N or of the recognised role of CSOs as intermediaries in delivery of government information and services in most countries (see Kuk, 2004).

To date, almost all benchmarking using Web metrics/crawlers has involved the use of externally applied tools. However, internally applied Web metrics (i.e. those available to e-Government Webmasters) offer an even richer source if they can be objectively reported. These include not merely usage indicators such as number of page hits or completed transactions but also proxies of outputs (e.g. measuring satisfaction in terms of repeat usage or cross-usage (usage of other information/services on a portal)) and even impacts (e.g. measuring benefits in terms of the extent of site use outside normal government office hours) (eGEP, 2006b).

Recommendation 26: Investigate relevance of automated assessment of site accessibility and nodality

Recommendation 27: Investigate potential for access to internally applied Web metrics

Pop-up surveys, or some equivalent automated method of questioning a random selection of site users, are generally seen as the preserve of site owners. However, there are examples of e-Government sites allowing 'foreign' pop-ups from a third-party organisation in order to enable independent comparative benchmarking (see Freed, 2006). Given the value of survey methods, this is worth further investigation though seems likely to be more acceptable to officials at national level, comparing across agencies, than at international level, comparing across countries (e.g. see Ramboll Management, 2004). As pointed out by those using these surveys, they provide a somewhat skewed response profile: non-users and potential users of e-Government are excluded; busy, less-confident and less-opinionated users tend to be under-represented. However, they do offer a fairly quick and easy way to gather e-Government data on use, outputs and impacts.

Recommendation 28: Investigate use of 'foreign' pop-up surveys

Focus group methods are very helpful for really understanding e-Government usage in depth. However, their strength is in generation of qualitative data and they rarely present data with the quantitative validity to allow cross-agency or cross-country comparisons.

Internal administrative records are rarely accessible directly by benchmarkers, and so they tend to suffer some of the shortcomings of internal self-assessment. Their variability also means they have little to offer cross-country benchmarking.

Mass user surveys can do things no other method can; for example, reach out to that vast majority of the world's population that has not yet been touched by e-Government. They are less skewed and allow for greater depth of questioning than pop-up surveys. They provide the statistically valid sample sizes that focus groups do not. Their main disadvantage is cost. However, given the large number of mass surveys currently undertaken, benchmarking studies can be built around the addition of a small number of questions into existing mass surveys. Some surveys specifically invite this (e.g. GI, 2005).

Recommendation 29: Piggy-back e-Government questions onto existing mass surveys

Less-used methods

Public domain statistics: While not quite falling into the category of 'official statistics', a number of benchmarking studies reuse e-Government statistics from publicly accessible e-Government or related reports. There is also public domain data from non-e-Government sources that could be of use in benchmarking either for direct use or as the basis for further calculations. For example, country-level data on:

- Internet access in schools (WEF Global Competitiveness Report).
- Extent of business Internet use (WEF Global Competitiveness Report).
- ICT expenditure as percentage of GDP (accessible via World Bank Knowledge Assessment Methodology site).
- Government prioritisation of ICT (WEF Global IT Report).
- Government procurement of ICT (WEF Global IT Report).
- Presence of ICT in government offices (WEF Global IT Report).
- Percentage of localities with public Internet access centres (proposed UN basic core ICT indicator that may become available (UNICTTF, 2005)).
- Percentage of individuals dealing with government/public authorities via Internet in last 12 months (proposed UN basic core ICT indicator that may become available).
- Percentage of businesses dealing with government/public authorities via Internet (proposed UN extended core ICT indicator; data for some countries is available on the current UNCTAD e-business database).

Recommendation 30: Ensure reuse of any appropriate public domain e-Government or related statistics

In addition, e-Government has really begun to take off as an area for academic study since the early 2000s, seeing an explosion in the amount of research being undertaken and outlets for that research. The outlets have risen from just two journals in 2002 with some remit to cover e-Government (*Government Information Quarterly*; *Information Polity*) to at least four more directly focusing on e-Government by 2008 (*Electronic Journal of e-Government*; *International Journal of Electronic Government Research*; *Journal of Information Technology and Politics*; *Transforming Government*) plus several annual e-Government conferences plus all the other information systems, public administration and e-business journal and conference outlets covering e-Government. Much of the written material is not of value to benchmarking being secondary research or focused on conceptualisation or reporting case studies. However, there is relevant primary research reported, including evidence from the most data-poor locations: developing countries (e.g. Kaaya, 2004; Abanumy et al., 2005).

Recommendation 31: Identify a national or regional collator to draw together all public domain research data on e-Government in their area

Intranet assessment: If access can be granted, then the techniques of third-party Web assessment can be applied to a sample of intranets within government, allowing the incorporation of G2G e-Government into benchmarking. Internally applied Web metrics and pop-up surveys can supplement this to provide data on use, outputs and impacts.

Recommendation 32: Seek access to intranet data

Public servant and politician surveys: Even a basic stakeholder analysis of e-Government (see Figure 13.14 for the DOCTORS stakeholder checklist) would identify two stakeholder groups almost entirely absent from data gathering for e-Government benchmarking: government staff and politicians. Yet government staff are central to the operation and data sourcing for most e-Government applications, and to the construction and receipt of output for many e-Government applications. Where they are included as sources of data for benchmarking, they provide a properly triangulated view of e-Government, and they deliver insights absent from other studies (e.g. see Jones and Williams, 2005).

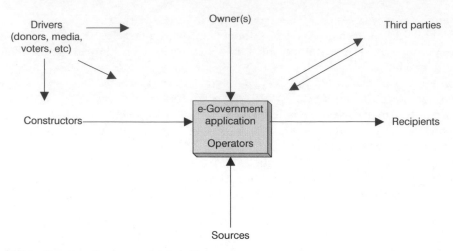

Figure 13.14 Generic e-Government stakeholder map

Equally, politicians are often the main owners or drivers (or third-party resistors) of e-Government. They are significant determinants of whether or not e-Government is providing public value (Horner and Hazel, 2005). And political legitimacy/support is seen alongside public value and operational capabilities as part of the 'strategic triangle' that determines the overall value and viability of public sector projects such as e-Government (see Figure 13.15: Moore and Khagram, 2004). Political legitimacy/support can therefore be surveyed both as an input and as an impact of e-Government projects. Yet politics and politicians – a central feature of public sector life – warrant hardly a mention in e-Government benchmarking studies.

Recommendation 33: Make greater use of public servant and politician surveys

Recommendation 34: Measure political legitimacy/support as both an input to and impact of e-Government

Intermediary surveys: In developing countries and in the disadvantaged communities of industrialised countries, access to e-Government is often intermediated; for example, occurring for citizens via a community or privately owned PC in a local telecentre, cybercafé or similar. These intermediary organisations are thus vital to e-Government – they form another part of the Figure 13.14 stakeholder map – yet have so far been overlooked in benchmarking. They could be included through direct surveys or through agreement to host pop-up surveys. For those intermediaries that have their own Web sites, these could be supplemented by either Web metrics/crawlers or third-party Web assessment. As noted above, automated measures of government Web site nodality can also be used to assess the extent of connectivity to service intermediaries.

Recommendation 35: Make greater use of intermediary (e.g. telecentre) surveys

Methods for specific issues

Here, the purpose is to reflect back on some of the priorities identified earlier, and look at ways to address those priorities. Rather than provide a specific recommendation for each issue, this section comes with a general point:

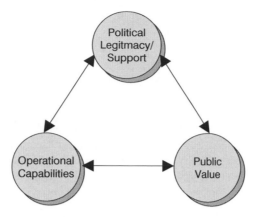

Figure 13.15   The public sector strategic triangle

Recommendation 36: Adopt methods appropriate to particular benchmarking interests

G2B: Most benchmarking exercises seem to fail G2B simply because it does not form part of the mental map of those commissioning or planning the research. It can fairly easily be added to third-party Web assessment and Web metrics by ensuring the inclusion of enterprise-relevant government agencies (e.g. Ministry of Industry or Department of Enterprise) and services (e.g. company registration, business development services, export support, public procurement, etc.) (e.g. see Capgemini, 2005). It can fairly easily be added to surveys by including a specific survey of entrepreneurs (e.g. see Graafland-Essers and Ettedgui, 2003).

G2G: Third-party Web assessment of intranets, cautious use of self-assessment and surveys of civil servants were identified above as key techniques for gathering data to benchmark G2G. A model questionnaire combining both front-office and back-office questions is available from NCM (2003).

e-Citizens – e-Democracy: The UN's (2005) e-participation approach provides a basis for measuring some elements of e-democracy using third-party Web assessment that focuses on citizen ability to influence policy-making. This is based on a three-stage model of: e-information (Web sites provide information on policies), e-consultation (presence of policy-related discussion forums) and e-decision-making (evidence of influence of citizen inputs such as presence of government feedback). Beyond this, there is potential for a 'mystery citizen' approach of assessing a test attempt to provide policy input or other forms of e-participation for each nation or agency being benchmarked. Third-party assessment can also involve content analysis of online discussion forums; for example, measuring the deliberative equality, rationality and interactivity of such discussions (Lyu, 2007). Real depth of understanding, though, can only come from survey work. This shows, for example, that the motivations of participants in e-democracy forums may relate much more to their desire to form and broadcast their own opinion to peers rather than to a desire to influence government policy (ibid.).

e-Citizens – e-Transparency: e-Transparency has five levels (Heeks, 2004):

1 *Publication*: Just providing basic information about a particular area of government.
2 *Transaction*: Automating some public sector process and reporting on that process.

3 *Reporting*: Providing specific details of public sector decisions and actions (e.g. via performance indicators).

4 *Openness*: Allowing users to compare public servant performance against pre-set benchmarks.

5 *Accountability*: Allowing users some mechanism of control (e.g. reward or punishment) over public servants.

This can be used as the basis for third-party Web assessment of those areas of government which are felt to be most important for transparency, such as budgets and other finances, procurement and contracts, and permits/licensing. Other methods that could be relevant include Web metrics/crawlers (assessing government nodality vis-à-vis key rights, anti-corruption and transparency CSOs) and citizen/entrepreneur surveys.

e-Society: Partnerships and linkages are probably best assessed by surveys of community, civil society and private sector organisations. Assessment via Web metrics/crawlers of nodality/ linkages of government Web sites to sites of these organisations is a supplemental possibility.

Sub-national tiers: Most sub-national governments in industrialised countries and growing numbers in developing countries are building Web sites that are assessable in various ways:

■ Simple visibility tests can be undertaken: what appears in the first 10 or 20 search engine entries when typing in '*Country* "state government"' or '*Country*"provincial government"' or '*Country*"district government"'.

■ Automated hyperlink assessment can measure the nodality of key local government sites such as the national Ministry/Department responsible for local government.

■ More directed searching can be undertaken – taking, say, the tiers of government for the largest city or for the most rural state/province – and assessing any Web sites that can be found using third-party Web assessment. Informant-based guidance can be used for identification of such sites, as per the approach used by Capgemini (2005).

Alternative channels including m-Government: Third-party Web assessment of provision for alternative digital channels can be used to assess these channels. For example, assessors can check for the presence/absence of WAP, SMS and PDA services on e-Government sites, and for reference to digital TV interfaces. Mystery user techniques can be applied to test out the utility of m-Government interfaces. For m-Government, this could be combined with public domain statistics on accessibility and use of mobile telephony to build an m-Government Index. Telephony can be assessed through means such as presence/absence of a phone contact number on government Web sites, use of phone contacts by mystery citizen researchers and by user survey. Integration between telephony and e-Government could be assessed by mystery citizen studies that investigate, say, whether a partially completed online transaction can be facilitated by subsequent phone contact.

Benefits: The benefits of e-Government fall into one or more of five categories (Heeks, 2001):

■ *Cheaper*: Producing outputs at lower total cost.
■ *More*: Producing more outputs.
■ *Quicker*: Producing outputs in less time.
■ *Better*: Producing outputs to a higher quality.
■ *New*: Producing new outputs.

The last two relate to effectiveness measures (see Table 13.6 indicators) and must generally be measured qualitatively. The first three relate to efficiency measures and may offer opportunities for quantitative, even financial, measurement. Where e-Government is cheaper, internal self-assessment may point to staff and other resource savings; user surveys may point to resource savings (e.g. postage, travel and intermediary fees) (Deloitte, 2004).

Where e-Government is quicker (and that is certainly the main benefit many users seek from e-Government: Accenture, 2004), financial benefits are not so immediately obvious. One approach – usable for any assessment of the user-side benefits of e-Government – is to assess how much users would be willing to pay for the benefits they perceive e-Government to deliver. This can produce an overall sense of e-Government's social value.

Alternatively, figures on usage levels and/or Web sophistication can be combined with evidence on user-side time savings to produce an estimate of the social benefits due to e-Government. For example, the proportion of citizens using transactional e-Government services in a country and their frequency of use of such services (estimates extrapolated from similar e-readiness countries can be used) can create an estimate of the total number of transactions per year in a country. This can be multiplied by case study data on the amount of time saved per transaction in moving from the most used traditional channel (typically telephone or in person) to create a total national annual time saving from e-Government citizen services. This can be valued in simple terms using average annual wage/income data. See Ramboll Management (2004) for an example of baseline figures (user time savings average just over 1 hour per transaction comparing online vs. offline) and calculation methods for European nations.

Equity and e-inclusion: There is a danger that e-Government will increase inequities in society, with US evidence that it 'helps people who already can help themselves' (Horrigan, 2005, p. 34). Hence the interest in 'e-inclusion', which means:

- 'Preventing digital exclusion, that is preventing disadvantaged people and groups from being left behind in the development of the information society. Here the focus is on access and basic ICT skills (digital literacy).
- Exploiting new digital opportunities, that is reducing existing disadvantages, providing new opportunities in terms of employability, quality of life, access to knowledge, etc.
- Fostering participation and empowerment, that is facilitating the use of ICT in order to allow individuals and groups to express themselves, to deepen and widen their social capital, to participate in democratic processes on a local as well as a wider scale' (EAG, 2005, p. 9).

Access rates can be determined by precursor studies looking at availability of ICT infrastructure, skills and other relevant resources within disadvantaged groups. Availability measures can also be used such as Web metric/crawler-based measures of e-Government site accessibility for the disabled, or third-party assessment of minority language availability (see West, 2001; Choudrie et al., 2004; UN, 2005). One can also look at the comparative maturity of e-Government domains of particular relevance to the socially disadvantaged, which are often held to be education, health, labour and social welfare (OECD, 2005; see UN, 2005 for use of this focus). These can be compared with generic domains or those appealing to non-disadvantaged groups (e.g. travel advice, higher education). Ultimately, though, benchmarking the second two elements of e-inclusion listed above will require

■ **Table 13.10**   Internet user gender and e-Government usage rates

Source	Female Internet users using e-Government (%)	Male Internet users using e-Government (%)
Multi-country (TNS, 2001)	89	78
Multi-country (TNS, 2003)	65	69
Singapore (Li et al., 2004)	67	73
South Korea (Lyu, 2007)	21	34

some form of survey work. It will also require recognition of the information chain (see Figure 13.5), which acts as a reminder of the non-e-Government-related resources that disadvantaged groups need in order to gain full benefit from e-Government.

As noted above, one can ask demographic questions in pop-up and mass user surveys. These provide an understanding of the equity of access and use of e-Government which, when related to income, can be presented in the form of Gini coefficient calculations and graphs. At present, though, there is relatively few statistics on the demographics of e-Government users, but there is a greater range of data on the demographics of Internet users indicating various divides of gender, age, education, income, etc. A question then arises: Can Internet user demographics be taken as an appropriate proxy for e-Government user demographics?

In relation to gender (see Table 13.10), there may be some sense of a greater tendency for male than female Internet users to access e-Government but there is no statistical validity to this sense from the data presented here.

The same can be said for age, education and income (see Table 13.11): there is some slight skew towards e-Government users being older, more educated and richer than the general Internet-using population but there is no statistical basis for making any differentiation.

On this evidence at least, there is no basis for differentiating between the demographics of Internet users and the demographics of e-Government users. Data for the former can therefore be used as a proxy for the latter in benchmarking issues such as equity and e-inclusion.

It was also noted earlier that data on Internet user numbers could be used to calculate the number of users of e-Government in a country or region. To do this, though, one requires a conversion factor on the percentage of Internet users who are e-Government users. Those conversion factors were used in the calculations for Table 13.2 but they were based on very limited data for developing countries; this area of evidence therefore requires strengthening, for example via more sample surveys of Internet users.

Public value: eGEP's approach to public value indicators for e-Government is rich and would require incorporation of many of the elements already described – public servant

Table 13.11   Comparative Internet user and e-Government user demographics

Indicator		Internet users	e-Government users
Average age	Multi-country (TNS, 2001)	<20 years (modal age)	25–34 years (modal age)
	Multi-country (TNS, 2003)	<25 years (modal age)	25–34 years (modal age)
	Singapore (Li et al., 2004)	34.1 years	33.6 years
	South Korea (Lyu, 2007)	32.4 years	33.5 years
Percentage of university educated	Singapore (Li et al., 2004)	23%	27%
	South Korea (Lyu, 2007)	61%	75%
Average monthly household income	Singapore (Li et al., 2004)	S$4246	S$4390

surveys, intermediary surveys, e-democracy and e-transparency measures, benefit and equity measures. Kearn's approach would also require a combination of methods to cover its nine indicators:

1 *Take-up*: Measure via user surveys (proxy via conversions from Internet user statistics).
2 *Satisfaction*: Measure via user or pop-surveys (proxy via internal Web metrics on repeat and cross-usage).
3 *Information*: Requires a new scale of information value, probably measured by third-party Web assessment (could be read as similar to e-Government site maturity).
4 *Choice*: Measure by third-party Web assessment or internal self-assessment in relation to choice of channels; may require internal self-assessment or survey to identify situations of choice of provider.
5 *Importance*: Requires a survey of user priorities (demand), matched against investment or availability (supply) of e-Government.
6 *Fairness*: Requires a survey of disadvantaged/excluded citizen priorities, matched against investment or availability (supply of e-Government); could also use survey figures on profile of use or outputs across disadvantaged vs. non-disadvantaged groups.
7 *Cost*: Measured by internal-self assessment.
8 *Outcome*: As argued above, needs to be proxied by impact or output measures, which are typically measured by survey.
9 *Trust*: Measured by user survey.

However, all discussions of public value agree that it is citizen preferences that determine the components of public value rather than one-size-fits-all approaches. As with other issues, there is some sense of these preferences and, hence, the meaning of public value for industrialised countries but much less sense of whether public value would mean something different for the majority, poor citizens of developing countries. One area, for instance, of particular concern to citizens in developing countries – and part of the good governance agenda – relates to personal security and the rule of law (Kaufmann et al., 2005). It would

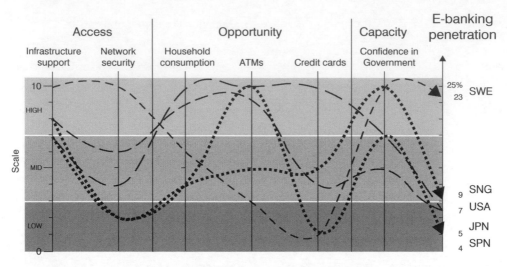

■ **Figure 13.16** Pathway diagram illustrating upstream–downstream relationship

thus be appropriate to consider two areas that have not appeared in any mainstream benchmarking study – e-Government in the judiciary, and e-Government in the police.

How to report?

It may be that much of the focus of benchmarking goes into the data gathering and analysis without considering in any detail how to then report and disseminate the benchmarking information. Such issues are rarely written about. Maugis et al. (2005) provide a discussion of innovative ways to report, and they make use of 'pathway diagrams' (see Figure 13.16, reproduced with permission). These select particular cases – agencies or countries – that have some important feature; this could be high levels of e-Government use or high levels of e-Government impact (or low levels). The precursors, inputs and intermediates for these particular cases are then plotted on a pathway diagram (Figure 13.16 provides an example for e-banking rather than e-Government, and focuses more on precursors and inputs than on use or impact). This allows analysts and decision-makers to visualise patterns fairly quickly and then identify what is and is not important in high (or low) e-Government performers. (Of course, this visual patterning is best checked statistically through analysis of variance techniques.)

Recommendation 37: Investigate use of innovative visualisation techniques to display benchmarking data

Discussion about dissemination of e-Government benchmarking is provided in Regional-IST (2004). This identifies three main 'pillars' for such dissemination:

1 Panels, seminars and other physical meetings that attempt to connect directly with as many appropriate decision-makers as possible.
2 Electronic discussion forums (though they note relatively poor levels of participation in those they used).

3   An interactive Web site that allows users to manipulate the data according to their own particular needs and interests rather than just presenting it in a static manner. This practice was adopted by the UN with the launch of its e-Government Readiness Knowledge Base (UN, 2007).

In addition, they note the value of a well-organised public relations exercise around the benchmarking report (such as press releases and interviews) to target a broader audience.

Recommendation 38: Make use of dissemination good practice

One assumption of benchmarking appears to be that results merely need to be put into the public domain and that users such as policy-makers will then be able to make effective use of them. However, this may not be true (RAWOO, 2001). It may therefore be appropriate to offer guidance, exemplars, even a training guide covering use of benchmarking data. Such guidance needs to work within the framework of the strategic triangle (see Figure 13.15): data users may have some aspect of public value in mind when they come to use benchmarking studies but they will be guided as much by what is politically (including personally) desirable and feasible, and by what is operationally feasible.

Recommendation 39: If necessary, provide guidance on use of benchmarking results

Finally, one may wish to evaluate the benchmarking study, which takes us full circle back to the issue of researching the usage of e-Government benchmarking. Formal evaluation could involve use of pop-up surveys on any benchmarking report Web site; plus telephone or other interviews of key users, focusing on issues such as user demographics, usage of benchmarking data, impact of benchmarking data, and user views on quality and improvements. As mentioned above, creation of a user panel would be appropriate for regular benchmarking studies. An example of a full evaluation of an IT-related benchmarking and information service is IST Results (2006).

Recommendation 40: Develop a mechanism for providing user feedback on the benchmarking study

Appendix 13A: Planning questions

Question checklist for those planning an e-Government benchmarking study

Why benchmark?

1   What is the internal purpose of this benchmarking study?
2   What is the external purpose of this benchmarking study?
3   Who is the intended audience for the study? Are there other likely audiences who will use the study?
4   What evidence of demand can be obtained from these audiences, to feed back into purpose?
5   What evidence of use can be obtained, to feed back into subsequent studies? Could and should a user panel be created?

What to benchmark?

1　Which components of e-Government (G2G, G2B, G2C, G2N) will you cover? Does this coverage reflect actual e-Government usage, priorities and benefits? Will biases arise if some components are omitted?

2　Which levels of e-Government (local, state/provincial, regional, national, international) will you cover? Does this coverage reflect actual e-Government usage, priorities and benefits? Will biases arise if some levels are omitted?

3　Which channels of e-Government (including m-Government) will you cover? Does this coverage reflect actual e-Government usage, priorities and benefits? Will biases arise if some channels are omitted?

4　Which value chain indicators of e-Government will you cover? Does this coverage reflect actual e-Government priorities and goals? Will biases arise if some indicators are omitted?

5　Will you undertake any correlations between your core e-Government indicators and other indicators of demand or impact?

6　Will you use any composite indicators? If so, how will you ensure their rigour and transparency?

7　Will you use any calculated indicators? If so, how will you ensure their rigour and transparency?

8　Will you use any standard public sector indicators? If so, how will you ensure their rigour and transparency?

9　Will you use any indicators of change over time? If so, how will you ensure their rigour and transparency?

10　Will you measure e-Government value chain change processes (e.g. strategy, development, adoption)? If so, how will you measure rigorously and transparently?

11　Will you measure e-Government's public value? If so, how will you measure rigorously and transparently?

12　Will you measure political legitimacy and support related to e-Government? If so, how will you measure rigorously and transparently?

How to benchmark?

1　How will the data-gathering methods you use rate in terms of cost, value, comparability and quality?

2　How transparent and objective should your data-gathering methods be?

3　Should survey methods be adopted in order to measure outputs and/or impacts and/or non-user groups?

4　Are there any opportunities for partnerships with other data gatherers?

5　Has the full potential of all different data-gathering methods, including less-used methods, been considered?

6　Will all data-gathering methods be used for appropriate purposes?

7　How will specific issues within the study (such as e-Government components, levels, channels, benefits, inclusion and public value) be benchmarked using appropriate methods?

How to report?

1　Can you make use of any innovative presentational techniques?

2　How can you make use of dissemination good practice?

3 Could and should guidance be provided on how to utilise the benchmarking study and its results?
4 How will you obtain user feedback on the study?

Appendix 13B: Evaluation questions

Question checklist for those evaluating an existing e-Government benchmarking study

Why benchmark?

1 Is there any sense of the internal purpose of this benchmarking study?
2 Is there any sense of the external purpose of this benchmarking study?
3 Is the audience for the study clear?
4 Is there any evidence of demand for this study? If so, is there any evidence of use of demand for this study?
5 Is there any evidence of use of this study?

What to benchmark?

1 Which components of e-Government (G2G, G2B, G2C, G2N) are covered? Does this coverage reflect actual e-Government usage, priorities and benefits? Do biases arise because some components have been omitted?
2 Which levels of e-Government (local, state/provincial, regional, national, international) are covered? Does this coverage reflect actual e-Government usage, priorities and benefits? Do biases arise because some levels have been omitted?
3 Which channels of e-Government (including m-Government) are covered? Does this coverage reflect actual e-Government usage, priorities and benefits? Do biases arise because some channels have been omitted?
4 Which value chain indicators of e-Government are covered? Does this coverage reflect actual e-Government priorities and goals? Do biases arise because some indicators have been omitted?
5 Have any correlations been undertaken between core e-Government indicators and other indicators of demand or impact? Are these causally and statistically credible?
6 Are any composite indicators used? Are they rigorous and transparent?
7 Are any calculated indicators used? Are they rigorous and transparent?
8 Are any standard public sector indicators used? Are they rigorous and transparent?
9 Are any indicators of change over time used? Are they rigorous and transparent?
10 Is there any measurement of e-Government value chain change processes (e.g. strategy, development, adoption)? If so, are the measures used rigorous and transparent?
11 Is there any measurement of e-Government's public value? If so, are the measures used rigorous and transparent?
12 Is there any measurement of political legitimacy and support related to e-Government? If so, are the measures used rigorous and transparent?

How to benchmark?

1 How do the data-gathering methods used rate in terms of cost, value, comparability and quality?
2 How transparent and objective are the data-gathering methods used?

3 Is output and/or impact measurement undertaken effectively (e.g. via survey)?
4 Are there other data-gathering methods, including less-used methods, that could be used but are not?
5 Have all data-gathering methods been used for appropriate purposes?
6 Are specific issues within the study (such as e-Government components, levels, channels, benefits, inclusion and public value) benchmarked using appropriate methods?

How to report?

1 Have good or innovative presentational and dissemination practices been used?
2 Is any guidance provided on how to utilise the benchmarking study and its results?
3 Has an effective means for eliciting user feedback been put in place?

References

Abanumy, A., Al-Badi, A. and Mayhew, P. (2005). 'e-Government website accessibility: In-depth evaluation of Saudi Arabia and Oman'. *Electronic Journal of e-Government*, 3(3), 99–106.

Accenture (2004). *eGovernment Leadership: High Performance, Maximum Value*, Accenture, Toronto, ON. Available at: http://www.accenture.com (accessed 22nd March 2007).

Accenture (2005). *Leadership in Customer Service: New Expectations, New Experiences*, Accenture, Toronto, ON. Available at: http://www.accenture.com (accessed 22nd March 2007).

Accenture (2006). *Leadership in Customer Service: Building the Trust*, Accenture, Chicago, IL. Available at: http://www.accenture.com (accessed 5th March 2007).

AGIMO (2005). *Australians' Use of and Satisfaction with E-Government Services*. Australian Government Information Management Office, Canberra.

Amis, P. (2001). Making a difference: What can municipal government do? *Insights*, 38. Available at: http://www.id21.org/insights/insights38/insights-iss38-art03.html (accessed 29th March 2007).

Anonymous (2006). Discussions with benchmarking study managers and government policy-makers, UN DPADM workshop, *E-Participation and E-Government: Understanding the Present and Creating the Future*, Budapest, Hungary, 27–28 July.

BAH (2002). *International e-Economy Benchmarking: The World's Most Effective Policies for the e-Economy*, Booz Allen Hamilton, London. Available at: http://www.itis.gov.se/publikationer/eng/ukreport.pdf (accessed 6th March 2007).

Bertelsmann Foundation (2002). *E-Government – Connecting Efficient Administration and Responsive Democracy*, Bertelsmann Foundation, Gütersloh. Available at: http://www.begix.de/en/studie/studie.pdf (accessed 4th July 2006).

Cabinet Office (2000). *e-Government: A Strategic Framework for Public Services in the Information Age*. Central IT Unit, Cabinet Office, London.

Cabinet Office (2005). *eAccessibility of Public Sector Services in the European Union*, Cabinet Office, London. Available at: http://www.cabinetoffice.gov.uk/e-government/resources/eaccessibility/index.asp (accessed 28th March 2007).

Capgemini (2004). *Does E-Government Pay Off?* Capgemini, Utrecht Available at: http://ec.europa.eu/idabc/servlets/Doc?id=19133 (accessed 28th March 2007).

Capgemini (2005). *Online Availability of Public Services: How Is Europe Progressing?* Capgemini, Brussels Available at: http://europa.eu.int/information_society/soccul/egov/egov_benchmarking_2005.pdf (accessed 28th March 2007).

Carbo, T. and Williams, J. G. (2004). 'Models and metrics for evaluating local electronic government systems and services'. *Electronic Journal of e-Government*, 2(2), 95–104.

Choudrie, J., Ghinea, G. and Weerakkody, V. (2004). 'Evaluating global e-government sites: A view using web diagnostic tools'. *Electronic Journal of e-Government*, 2(2), 105–114.

Cross, M. and MacGregor, J. (2006). *Cutting the Wires*, New Local Government Network, London Available at: http://www.nlgn.org.uk/pdfs/upload/cutwiressummary.pdf (accessed 30th March 2007).

Deloitte (2004). *Citizen Advantage: Enhancing Economic Competitiveness through E-Government*, Deloitte, New York, NY. Available at: http://www.deloitte.com (accessed 22nd March 2007).

DTI (2004). *International Benchmarking Study 2004*, Department of Trade and Industry, London. Available at: http://www2.bah.com/dti2004/ (accessed 29th March 2007).

EAG (2005). *e-Inclusion: New Challenges and Policy Recommendations*, eEurope Advisory Group, IDABC, Brussels. Available at: http://europa.eu.int/idabc/egovo (accessed 21st March 2007).

Edwards, M. (2003). *Civil Society*. Polity Press, Cambridge.

eGEP (2006a). *Compendium to the Measurement Framework*, eGovernment Economics Project, European Commission, Brussels. Available at: http://www.rso.it/notizie/Measurement_Framework_Compendium.pdf (accessed 3rd March 2007).

eGEP (2006b). *Measurement Framework Final Version*, eGovernment Economics Project, European Commission, Brussels, Available at: http://www.rso.it/notizie/D.2.4_Measurement_Framework_final_version.pdf (accessed 3rd March 2007).

ESCWA (2005). *Information Society Indicators*. Economic and Social Commission for West Asia, UN, New York, NY.

Flynn, N. (2002). *Public Sector Management*, 4th ed. Pearson Education, Harlow.

Freed, L. (2006). *E-Government Satisfaction Index*, ForeSee Results, Ann Arbor, MI Available at: http://www.foreseeresults.com/WhitePapers/ACSI_EGov_Commentary_Mar06.pdf (accessed 26th June 2006).

GI (2005). *Voice of the People Survey 2005*, Gallup International, London. Available at: http://www.voice-of-the-people.net/ContentFiles/docs/VoP_Questionnaire.pdf (accessed 23rd March 2007).

Goldkuhl, G. and Persson, A. (2006). From e-ladder to e-diamond: re-conceptualising models for public e-services. Paper presented at *14th European Conference on Information Systems* (ECIS2006), Göteborg, Sweden, June 12–14. Available at: http://www.vits.org/publikationer/dokument/588.pdf (accessed 5th March 2007).

Graafland-Essers, I. and Ettedgui, E. (2003). *Benchmarking E-Government in Europe and the US*, RAND, Santa Monica, CA. Available at: http://www.rand.org/pubs/monograph_reports/MR1733/MR1733.pdf (accessed 23rd March 2007).

Heath, W. (2000). *Europe's Readiness for E-Government*, Kable, London. Available at: http://www.dad.be/library/pdf/kable.pdf (accessed 29th March 2007).

Heeks, R. B. (1999). *Information and Communication Technologies, Poverty and Development*, IDPM Development Informatics Working Paper No.5, University of Manchester. Available at: http://www.sed.manchester.ac.uk/idpm/publications/wp/di/di_wp05.htm (accessed 5th March 2007).

Heeks, R. B. (2000). 'Why do most government IT projects fail?'. *ICA Newsletter*, 70, 26–31.

Heeks, R. B. (2001). 'Reinventing government in the information age'. In Heeks, R. B. (Ed.), *Reinventing Government in the Information Age*. Routledge, London, pp. 9–21.

Heeks, R. B. (2002). 'eGovernment in Africa: Promise and practice'. *Information Polity*, 7(2–3), 97–114.

Heeks, R. B. (2003). *Most eGovernment-for-Development Projects Fail: How Can Risks be Reduced?* IDPM i-Government Working Paper No.14, University of Manchester. Available at: http://www.sed.manchester.ac.uk/idpm/publications/wp/igov/igov_wp14.htm (accessed 5th March 2007).

Heeks, R. B. (2004). *Transparency Definitions Page*, eGovernment for Development project, University of Manchester, UK. Available at: http://www.egov4dev.org/transpdefn.htm (accessed 3rd March 2007).

Heeks, R. B. (2006). *Implementing and Managing eGovernment: An International Text*. Sage Publications, London.

Heeks, R. B. and Davies, A. (2001). 'Different approaches to information age reform'. In Heeks, R. B. (Ed.), *Reinventing Government in the Information Age*. Routledge, London, pp. 22–48.

Holliday, I. (2002). 'Building e-government in East and Southeast Asia: Regional rhetoric and national (in)action'. *Public Administration and Development*, 22(4), 323–335.

Horner, L. and Hazel, L. (2005). *Adding Public Value*, Work Foundation, London. Available at: http://www.theworkfoundation.com/Assets/PDFs/public_value.pdf (accessed 22nd March 2007).

Horrigan, J. B. (2005). *'On Demand' Citizens: E-Government at High Speed*. Pew Internet & American Life Project, Washington, DC.

IAB (2003). *High Payoff in Electronic Government: Measuring the Return on E-Government Investments*, Intergovernmental Advisory Board, Washington, DC. Available at: http://www.gsa.gov (accessed 22nd March 2007).

IMD (2006). *World Competitiveness Yearbook*, IMD, Lausanne. Available at: http://www01.imd.ch/documents/wcc/content/GO_List.pdf (accessed 23rd March 2007).

IST Results (2006). *IST Results User Survey 2005–2006*, IST Results, European Commission, Brussels. Available at: http://istresults.cordis.lu/pdf/User%20Survey%202005-Summary%20V2.pdf (accessed 4th March 2007).

ITU (2007) *Free Statistics*, International Telecommunications Union, Geneva. Available at: http://www.itu.int/ITU-D/ict/statistics/ (accessed 30th March 2007).

Janssen, D. (2003). 'Mine's bigger than yours: Assessing international egovernment benchmarking'. In Bannister, F. and Remenyi, D. (Eds.), *3rd European Conference on eGovernment*. MCIL, Reading, UK, pp. 209–218.

Janssen, D., Rotthier, S. and Snijkers, K. (2004). 'If you measure it they will score: An assessment of international egovernment benchmarking'. *Information Polity*, 9(3–4), 121–130.

Jensen, M. (2002). *Information and Communication Technologies (ICTs) as Tools for Improving Local Governance in Africa*, UNESCO, Paris. Available at: http://portal.unesco.org/ (accessed 29th March 2007).

Jones, A. and Williams, L. (2005). *Public Services and ICT*, The Work Foundation, London. Available at: http://www.theworkfoundation.com/Assets/PDFs/why_ict.pdf (accessed 22nd March 2007).

Kaaya, J. (2004). 'Implementing e-government services in East Africa'. *Electronic Journal of e-Government*, 2(1), 39–54.

Kaufmann, D., Kraay, A. and Mastruzzi, M. (2005). *Governance Matters IV: Governance Indicators for 1996–2004*, Policy Research Working Paper 3630, World Bank, Washington, DC. Available at: http://www.worldbank.org/wbi/governance/pubs/govmatters4.html (accessed 23rd March 2007).

Kearns, I. (2004). *Public Value and E-Government*, Institute for Public Policy Research, London. Available at: http://www.ippr.org.uk/uploadedFiles/projects/Kearns_Public ValueandeGovenrment_ippr.pdf (accessed 27th March 2007).

Kelly, G., Mulgan, G. and Muers, S. (2001). *Creating Public Value: An Analytical Framework for Public Sector Reform*, Cabinet Office, London. Available at: http://www.cabinetoffice.gov.uk/strategy/downloads/files/public_value2.pdf (accessed 22nd March 2007).

Kuk, G. (2004). 'Network Analysis of Disconnect in the Hollow State: The Case of e-Government Service Portals'. *Proceedings of the 12th European Conference on Information Systems*, Turku, Finland, June 14–16. Available at: http://csrc.lse.ac.uk/asp/aspecis/20040086.pdf (accessed 28th March 2007).

Kunstelj, M. and Vintar, M. (2004). 'Evaluating the progress of e-government development: A critical analysis'. *Information Polity*, 9(3–4), 131–148.

Li, H., Detenber, B. H., Lee, W. P. and Chia, S. (2004). 'E-government in Singapore: Demographics, usage patterns and perceptions'. *Journal of E-Government*, 1(3), 29–54.

Lyu, H.-S. (2007). *Understanding eParticipation in the Republic of Korea*, draft report, IDPM, University of Manchester.

Maugis, V., Choucri, N., Madnick, S. E., Siegel, M. D., Gillett, S. E., Haghseta, F., Zhu, H. and Best, M. (2005). 'Global e-readiness – For what? Readiness for e-banking'. *Information Technology for Development*, 11(4), 313–342.

Millard, J. (2006). eGovernance and eParticipation. Paper presented at UN DPADM workshop, *E-Participation and E-Government: Understanding the Present and Creating the Future*, Budapest, Hungary, 27–28 July.

Minges, M. (2005). *Evaluation of e-Readiness Indices in Latin America and the Caribbean*, ECLAC, Santiago. Available at: http://www.eclac.org/socinfo/publicaciones/default.asp?idioma=IN (accessed 4th March 2007).

Moore, D., McKeagney, M. and Fitzsimons, P. (2005). *Benchmarking eGovernment Websites in the U.K. and Ireland*, iQ Content Ltd, Dublin. Available at: http://www.iqcontent.com/publications/reports/article 43/ (accessed 23rd March 2007).

Moore, M. H. and Khagram, S. (2004). *On Creating Public Value*, Kennedy School of Government, Harvard University, Cambridge, MA. Available at: http://www.ksg.harvard.edu/m-rcbg/CSRI/publications/workingpaper_3_moore_khagram.pdf (accessed 22nd March 2007).

NCM (2003). *ICT Usage in the Public Sector: A Nordic Model Questionnaire*, Nordic Council of Ministers, Statistics Denmark, Copenhagen. Available at: http://www.dst.dk/upload/ictusagepublic.pdf (accessed 4th March 2007).

Nicoll, P., Robinson, J. and O'Hanlon, B. (2004). *Measuring the Efficiency and Effectiveness of E-Government*, Auditor-General, Canberra, Australia. Available at: http://www.anao.gov.au/uploads/documents/2004-05_Audit_Report_26.pdf (accessed 22nd March 2007).

NOIE (2003). *E-Government Benefits Study*, National Office for the Information Economy, Canberra. Available at: http://www.agimo.gov.au/__data/assets/file/16032/benefits.pdf (accessed 22nd March 2007).

OECD (1999). *Defining and Measuring E-Commerce: A Status Report*, OECD, Paris. Available at: http://www.oecd.org/dataoecd/12/55/2092477.pdf (accessed 24th March 2007).

OECD (2004). *E-Government: Making Change Happen – Country Papers*, OECD, Paris. Available at: http://ec.europa.eu/idabc/servlets/Doc?id=23330 (accessed 22nd March 2007).

OECD (2005). *Management in Government*, OECD, Paris. Available at: http://www.oecd.org (accessed 23rd March 2007).

OeE (2001). *Benchmarking Electronic Service Delivery*, Office of the e-Envoy, Cabinet Office, London. Available at: http://europa.eu.int/idabc/servlets/Doc?id=23244 (accessed 28th March 2007).

Page, S. (2006). Local government is key in development, *ID21 Viewpoints*, April. Available at: http://www.id21.org/viewpoints/PageApr06.html (accessed 3rd March 2007).

Paquet, G. and Roy, J. (2000). 'Information technology, public policy, and Canadian governance'. In Garson, G. D. (Ed.), *Handbook of Public Information Systems*. Marcel Dekker, New York, pp. 53–70.

Petricek, V., Escher, T., Cox, I. J. and Margetts, H. (2006). The web structure of e-government: Developing a methodology for quantitative evaluation. Paper presented at *WWW2006*, 23–16 May, Edinburgh. Available at: http://www.governmentontheweb.org/downloads/papers/WWW2006-Web_Structure_of_E_Government.pdf (accessed 26th March 2007).

Ramboll Management (2004). *Top of the Web: User Satisfaction and Usage Survey of eGovernment Services*, Ramboll Management, Copenhagen. Available at: http://ec.europa.eu/information_society/activities/egovernment_research/doc/top_of_the_web_report_2004.pdf (accessed 4th March 2007).

RAWOO (2001). *Utilization of Research for Development Cooperation: Linking Knowledge Production to Development Policy and Practice*, Publication No. 21. The Hague, Netherlands Development Assistance Research Council. Available at: http://www.rawoo.nl/pdf/rawoo21.pdf (accessed 22nd March 2007).

Regional-IST (2004). *Report on Decision-Makers Panels and on External Forums/Audits*, Regional-IST, Barcelona. Available at: http://www.uoc.edu/in3/regional/eng/deliver.html (accessed 4th March 2007).

Sipior, J. C. and Ward, B. T. (2005). 'Bridging the digital divide for e-government inclusion'. *Electronic Journal of e-Government*, 3(3), 137–146.

Stone, D. (2001). Getting research into policy? Paper presented to the third Annual Global Development Network Conference on '*Blending Local and Global Knowledge*', Rio De Janeiro, 10 December. Available at: http://www.gdnet.org/rapnet/pdf/Beyond%20Economics%20Stone.pdf (accessed 21st March 2007).

Streib, G. and Navarro, I. (2006). 'Citizen demand for interactive e-government'. *American Review of Public Administration*, 36(3), 288–300.

TBCS (2004). *Canada's Performance 2004*, Treasury Board of Canada Secretariat, Ottawa. Available at: http://www.tbs-sct.gc.ca/report/govrev/04/cp-rc2_e.asp (accessed 5th March 2007).

TI (2006). *Corruption Perceptions Index*, Transparency International, Berlin. Available at: http://www.transparency.org/policy_research/surveys_indices/cpi/2006 (accessed 23rd March 2007).

TNS (2001). *Government Online: An International Perspective*, Taylor Nelson Sofres, Melbourne. Available at: http://ec.europa.eu/idabc/servlets/Doc?id=23252 (accessed 4th March 2007).

TNS (2002). *Government Online: An International Perspective*, Taylor Nelson Sofres, Melbourne. Available at: http://unpan1.un.org/intradoc/groups/public/documents/APCITY/UNPAN007044.pdf (accessed 3rd March 2007).

TNS (2003). *Government Online: An International Perspective 2003*, Taylor Nelson Sofres, Melbourne. Available at: http://www.legermarketing.com/documents/TenInt/031219ENG.pdf (accessed 30th March 2007).

UIS (2003). *Measuring and Monitoring the Information and Knowledge Societies: A Statistical Challenge*, UNESCO Institute of Statistics, Montreal. Available at: http://portal.unesco.org/ (accessed 4th March 2007).

UN (2005). *UN Global e-Government Readiness Report 2005*, UN, New York. Available at: http://www.unpan.org/egovernment5.asp (accessed 21st March 2007).

UN (2007). *UN e-Government Readiness Knowledge Base*, UN, New York. Available at: http://www.unpan.org/egovkb/ (accessed 19th March 2007).

UNESCO (2005). *E-Government Tool-Kit for Developing Countries*. UNESCO, New Delhi.

UNICTTF (2005). *Measuring ICT: The Global Status of ICT Indicators*, UN ICT Task Force, New York. Available at: http://www.itu.int/ITU-D/ict/partnership/material/05-42742%20GLOBAL%20ICT.pdf (accessed 4th March 2007).

UNSD (2007). *Millennium Development Indicators*, UN Statistics Division, New York. Available at: http://unstats.un.org/unsd/mdg/default.aspx (accessed 3rd March 2007).

USA.gov (2007). *Awards and Recognitions*, USA.gov, Washington, DC. Available at: http://www.usa.gov/About/Awards.shtml (accessed 19th March 2007).

Wattegama, C. (2005). *Benchmarking National Telecom Regulatory Authority Websites*, World Dialogue on Regulation, Danish Technical University, Lyngby. Available at: http://www.lirneasia.net/wp-content/uploads/2006/02/Wattegama%202005%20Benchmarking%20NRAs.pdf (accessed 3rd March 2007).

West, D. M. (2001). *WMRC Global E-Government Survey*, Center for Public Policy, Brown University, Providence, RI. Available at: http://www.insidepolitics.org/egovt01int.html (accessed 21st March 2007).

West, D. M. (2006). *Global E-Government 2006*, Center for Public Policy, Brown University, Providence, RI. Available at: http://www.insidepolitics.org/egovt06int.pdf (accessed 5th March 2007).

World Bank (2007a). *e-Government Case Studies*, World Bank, Washington, DC. Available at: http://www.worldbank.org/egov (accessed 5th March 2007).

World Bank (2007b). *World Development Indicators*, World Bank, Washington, DC. Available at: http://www.worldbank.org/data (accessed 3rd March 2007).

World Bank (2007c). *Knowledge Assessment Methodology*, World Bank, Washington, DC. Available at: http://web.worldbank.org (accessed 24th March 2007).

WVS (2005) *2005–2006 World Values Survey*, World Values Survey. Available at: http://www.worldvaluessurvey.org/statistics/index.html (accessed 23rd March 2007).

Evaluating e-Government infrastructure through enterprise application integration (EAI)

M. Mustafa Kamal, M. Themistocleous and V. Morabito

■ Introduction

Local government authorities (LGAs) serve as agents to provide better and reliable services and information to citizens. Citizen-demand and advancements in Information Technology (IT) have contributed to the advent of electronic Government (e-Gov). Much emphasis has been placed on achieving this objective through the development of e-Gov Information Systems (e-Gov-IS). The authors support the theory that an e-Gov platform should not been seen as a stand-alone system but as a solution that communicates with back-office applications through an integrated infrastructure. An integrated e-Gov-IS can efficiently automate the business processes of LGAs and increase citizens' satisfaction. However, to achieve such a solution, LGAs need to integrate their IT infrastructure to provide a common and shared view of their information and services.

Nevertheless, literature indicates that LGAs have problems in meeting citizens' demands. This may be attributed to the limitations of LGAs' IT infrastructures that are not integrated and do not allow them to deliver end-to-end integrated services. Several LGAs have encountered difficulties in incorporating their e-Gov-IS, and have turned to the adoption of Customer Relationship Management (CRM) and Enterprise Resource Planning (ERP) software packages to improve their services. Nonetheless, many legacy systems have not been replaced and thus, the need for integrating their e-Gov-IS with their front desk and back-office systems still exists.

During recent years, Enterprise Application Integration (EAI) has emerged to support organisations to integrate their IT infrastructures and deliver high quality services. EAI can be used to piece together e-Gov-IS with packaged and legacy systems. Despite the fact that many other types of organisations, for example healthcare, multinationals, Small and Medium-sized Enterprises (SMEs) and large organisations have adopted EAI, its application by LGAs is limited. For this reason, LGAs need to realise the importance of EAI and speed up their decision-making process to adopt it. As a result, further research is required to support the decision-making process of LGAs when taking decisions for EAI adoption. Although existing models related to EAI adoption, for example Mantzana (2006), Khoumbati (2005), Chen (2005) and Themistocleous (2002) have been reported in the literature, the applicability and validity of these models in the public domain is arguable and under research, as these models were proposed to support the decision-making process in other sector organisations and not in LGAs.

The factors that influence the decision-making process for EAI adoption differ from one type of organisation to the other dependent among other things on the nature, and the size of the organisation (e.g. one set of factors is used to support EAI adoption in SMEs and another in large organisations). For this reason, these factors may not be applicable in LGAs. Thus, the authors postulate that it is important to investigate this area within LGAs and conduct research that contributes towards successful EAI adoption. The authors investigate EAI and illustrate, through a case study, how EAI can be used to develop an integrated e-Gov infrastructure. In doing so, and allowing others to relate their experiences to those reported herein it is hoped to aid other LGAs to integrate their disparate systems more efficiently and extend their e-Gov infrastructures.

The current domain

During the past two decades, several LGAs have focused on the use of e-Gov-IS to overcome their organisational problems and automate their business processes and functions. In addition, LGAs focused on e-Gov-IS to provide direct support to meet citizens' needs including housing, social services, and the management of a complex service infrastructure that supports communities and businesses (Johnson and King, 2005). However, e-Gov-IS developments within LGAs have resulted in non-integrated IT infrastructure (Beaumaster, 2002; Lam, 2005). The reason is that each LGA autonomously made its own IT operational decisions based on its individual needs (Aldrich et al., 2002; Di Natale et al., 2003; Janssen and Cresswell, 2005). Additionally, there was rarely a single approach for developing e-Gov-IS, as organisations have developed their applications without a common architectural plan (Markus and Tanis, 1999). Moreover, each LGA displays differences in the way: (a) their business processes are implemented to provide citizen services and (b) they make decisions in a different way than private organisations (Johnson and King, 2005). This evidence illustrate the fact that LGAs operate and function independently and do not share information and functionality with other LGAs (Gortmaker and Janssen, 2004).

The lack of common organisational-wide IT infrastructure has resulted in the development of a diversity of e-Gov-IS within LGAs. The disadvantages of such heterogeneous IT infrastructures are analyzed in the literature and include: (a) high maintenance costs and (b) data redundancy and inconsistency (Abie et al., 2004). LGAs have attempted to overcome these problems by manually interconnecting their disparate applications. But integration means much more than simply interconnecting all the disparate applications and connectivity is often insufficient due to the fact that individual applications were not designed to interoperate. There are two more basic problems for integration: (a) each application has its own organisational objects (e.g. citizens) and (b) each application has data that overlaps data in other applications. This partial redundancy generates significant data integrity problems.

In the 1990s the public domain turned to ERP implementations in an attempt to overcome the Year 2000 (Y2K) problem. Although ERP systems addressed the Y2K problem, they only provide a partial solution for the integration problem (Davenport, 1998; Vasconcelos et al., 2004). The reason is that ERP systems were not designed to integrate disparate systems but rather to replace them to achieve integration (Davenport, 1998). Themistocleous et al. (2005) report that there is an increasing demand to integrate the IT infrastructures in LGAs. This demand comes from disparate categories of stakeholders in LGAs like employees and managers, citizens and businesses. All of them seek to ease their transactions with other LGAs. In this context, LGAs have realised the limitations of their IT infrastructures and are seeking ways to improve their efficiency, and to provide better services to citizens. The limitations are summarised in Figure 14.1 with description.

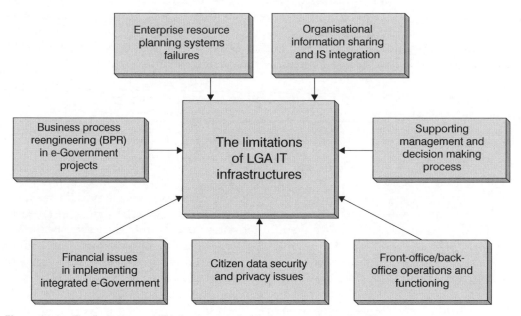

■ **Figure 14.1**   The limitations of IT infrastructure in local government authorities

ERP systems failures

ERP systems hold great potential to streamline inefficient processes and are reshaping business and government organisations in solving problems posed by autonomous applications (Watson et al., 2003). However, there are various examples where organisations were not gaining benefits (e.g. improvements in operational efficiency) that motivated them to make large investments in ERP systems (Songini, 2004). The failures theorised illustrate that ERP projects are set apart by their complexity and challenges posed by the accompanying large-scale organisational changes in transition to new systems and processes. Themistocleous and Irani (2001) noted that the complexity of ERP systems has forced organisations to collaborate with external consultants to adopt an ERP solution. Nonetheless, the discrepancy in ERP implementation approaches as well as cost overruns, customisation issues and ERP project delays often cause significant conflicts among organisations and consultants and may lead to failure (Wagner and Antonucci, 2004). Thus, the reported failures suggest that the move towards ERP has not reduced the need for integration, rather it has increased it (Vasconcelos et al., 2004).

Organisational information sharing and IS integration

Dawes (1996) reports that information sharing and IS integration, offers organisations the option to share information and make better-informed decisions. Gil-García et al. (2005) also reports that information sharing and IS integration allows managers to work with the same information drawn from multiple disparate sources. Within e-Gov perspectives, e-Gov initiatives are about the capture, management, use, dissemination and sharing seamless information (Gil-García and Pardo, 2005). To access seamless information, stand-alone IS needs to be integrated to enhance seamless interoperability. Nevertheless, in several cases the extent of information sharing and IS integration in LGAs does not go beyond the transfer of mandated documents (Gil-García et al., 2005). This may induce LGAs to adopt a single integration solution to effectively solve and support integration at data, object, interface and process levels.

Citizen data security and privacy issues

Enterprises require a secure environment with reliable technological solutions to function according to their requirements. Mwakalinga and Yngström (2004) report that the electronic provision of services is one of the main goals of several government organisations. In such an open and distributed processing environment, access control and authentication mechanisms are critical for government organisations. Therefore, a key obstacle in implementing e-Gov is citizens' concern for privacy and confidentiality of the personal data they provide (Signore et al., 2005). To date several privacy-augmenting technologies exit, for example Anonymizer (Osorio, 2001), Crowds (Reiter and Rubin, 1998), and TRUSTe (McCullagh, 1998). Analyzing these technologies illustrates that they have their own sets of considerations and each technology differs from other since their design is not focused on same parameters. Thus, there is a need for a technology that provides concrete security approaches to LGAs in securing and providing privacy of citizens' data.

Business Process Reengineering (BPR) in e-Gov projects

e-Gov projects have an increasing influence on how business processes evolve and change. Scholl (2005) reports that while early e-Gov projects focused on government-to-citizen information and interaction, the second and third wave of e-Gov projects also emphasized internal effectiveness and efficiency along with intra- and inter-departmental as well as intra- and inter-branch integration. With these increases in scale of e-Gov projects, existing business processes including core business processes become candidates for improvement and reengineering. In addition, realising better service provision for citizens and businesses is also a big challenge for governments at all levels (Gortmaker et al., 2004). In e-Gov, once the service and application potential of the early catalogue and transaction phases have been fully utilised, the next developmental step leads to the integration of services and business processes within and across government organisations and departments (Layne and Lee, 2001). Thus, better service provision requires the integration of business processes across LGAs.

Front-office/Back-office operations and functioning _____

Several government organisations have set up e-Gov systems, for example CRM and Geographic Information Systems (GIS) to improve the delivery of services to their citizens. Homburg and Bekkers (2002) note that these initiatives require information exchange through various networks available in the government organisation back-offices. Bekkers (1998) also reports that for e-Gov systems to be successful, back-office operations and functions, and, more specifically, back-office streamlining has to be taken care of, too. In the e-Gov literature, often the focus is on the interaction between government organisations and citizens via Web portals, call centres, physical offices and other interacting channels (Janssen and Wagenaar, 2003). Though, to exploit these channels in an efficient and effective way, the need to restructure the administrative operation, functions and processes is clearly felt to support coordination and cooperation between different LGAs. Legacy IS within LGAs often restricts the development towards new citizen-oriented processes. As a result, there is a need for an integration technological solution that enables seamless communication between front-office and back-office legacy IS and applications and across other LGAs.

Financial issues in implementing integrated e-Gov _____

Organisations tend to reduce costs to improve their financial capability. In LGAs, there is a need to reduce the costs of running a non-integrated IT infrastructure as well as to reduce the redundancy/inconsistency of data and systems (Abie et al., 2004, Gamper and Augsten 2003). Edwards and Newing (2000) report that EAI eliminates the redundancy of data and applications and thus, reduces operational costs since less effort is required to coordinate and maintain systems. Kalakota and Robinson (2001) suggest that a non-integrated infrastructure often results in a loss of sales that also has a negative impact on the organisation. In e-Gov, integration is needed to increase the performance and efficiency of LGAs that results in improvements of financial capacity.

Supporting management and the decision-making process _____

Zahavi (1999) reports the need to enhance the decision-making process and support management with real-time data that necessitates the development of integrated IT infrastructures. However, the limitations of existing LGA infrastructures inhibit management from taking accurate decisions. The reasons for this are: (a) systems heterogeneity (Janssen and Cresswell, 2005), (b) data redundancy and inconsistency (Abie et al., 2004), (c) low data quality (Gil-García and Pardo, 2005) and (d) lack of uniform citizen view. For instance, multiple applications store data for the same entity but there is often an inability to combine data and take decisions since there is: (a) data incompatibility (Gamper and Augsten,

2003), (b) communication problems, (c) interdepartmental coordination (Beaumaster, 2002) and (d) uniqueness of integration needs (Adams et al., 2003). Often, applications are developed at different times by different group of experts who operate independently and do not consider the interoperability constraints. Thus, LGAs need to integrate their financial, human resource, customer support and other disparate systems to support management and enhance the decision-making process.

The assessment of the literature above illustrates that LGAs need a technological solution to overcome their IT infrastructure limitations. However, in the past several efforts have been made to achieve integration at various levels of government such as: (a) AnalysePilot (Janssen et al., 2002), (b) SeamlessUK – PINPoint (Atherton, 2002), (c) PASSPORT (Gouscos et al., 2001), (d) CiTel (Signore et al., 2005). The authors report that these applications have their own sets of considerations and each of them differs from other since their design is not focused on similar parameters. Although these applications have provided significant benefits, they have not resulted in the development of an integrated IT infrastructure that efficiently automates and integrates LGA business processes and services. The reason is that they were developed to meet specific requirements and solve specific problems. While, these applications have not achieved the level of integration needed, they have contributed to better understanding of the limitations of LGA e-Gov-IS.

Due to these IT infrastructure limitations, LGAs are constrained and face difficulties: (a) overcoming their organisational and integration problems and (b) providing quality services to citizens. Thus, there is a need for a technology that provides a concrete solution to LGAs that attempts to meet organisations' requirements and integration problems. Clearly, the limitations presented in the previous section indicate the need for the adoption of EAI in LGAs. Since EAI is a new research area within LGAs, the authors attempt to review the literature on existing EAI adoption models.

Investigating existing EAI adoption models in the private and public domains

This section reviews EAI adoption in public and private domains and tries to understand how EAI might be used to support LGAs' IS integration and enhance their decision-making process. Due to limitations on EAI adoption literature in LGAs, a review of other areas supporting EAI adoption was performed. Examples of EAI adoption models are Mantzana (2006) and Khoumbati (2005) in healthcare, Themistocleous (2002) in multinationals, and adoption of emerging integration technologies in SMEs and large organisations by Chen (2005) are reviewed. This may assist the authors in building an understanding of different factors influencing EAI adoption in other areas.

EAI adoption in multinational organisations

Themistocleous (2002) established the scope by studying EAI area in multinational organisations. In doing so, he evaluated the adoption and impact of EAI on multinational organisations and proposed a conceptual model for EAI adoption in multinational organisations. The conceptual model proposed (Themistocleous, 2002) illustrates a number of factors such as: (a) benefits, (b) barriers, (c) IT infrastructure, (d) costs, (e) external pressures, (f) IT sophistication, (g) framework for evaluating integration technologies and (h) support. After addressing pragmatic outcomes, Themistocleous (2002) resulted in adding more factors such as: (a) internal pressures and (b) framework for evaluating EAI packages. However, Themistocleous (2002) also subdivided these factors, for example, classifying cost factors into three sub-factors such as: (a) direct cost, (b) indirect human cost and (c) indirect organisational cost. Then, explaining (a) operational, (b) managerial, (c) strategic, (d) technical and (e) organisational benefits and barriers, and clarifying organisational internal pressures, and external pressures into: (a) competitors and (b) trading partners. Similarly, dividing support factors as: (a) consultant support, (b) vendor global presence and (c) vendor support. These factors have been well researched and analyzed in the private and public domains.

EAI adoption in healthcare organisations

Khoumbati (2005) analyzed the literature in the EAI area and reported that the non-integrated IT infrastructure within healthcare organisations causes medical errors that are related to the loss of human lives. If the information needed is not available on time, errors may occur in prescribing, administering and dispensing drugs to patients. Therefore, accentuating the need for integration in the healthcare sector. By focusing on these problems, Khoumbati (2005) evaluated EAI and proposed a model for EAI adoption in healthcare organisations. Khoumbati (2005) adapted and revised Themistocleous' (2002) EAI adoption model. Khoumbati (2005) added specific healthcare related factors from EAI and healthcare informatics literature. In addition to the factors incorporated from Themistocleous (2002) model, Khoumbati (2005) included more factors such as: (a) patient satisfaction, (b) organisation size, (c) physician and patient relationship, (d) telemedicine and (e) compatibility. After practical results, Khoumbati (2005) revised the model and added two more factors: (a) education and (b) security and confidentiality.

Framework of actors and factors affecting EAI adoption in healthcare organisations

The literature indicates that IS adoption remains a time-consuming and complex process and issues associated with its management would appear to be of paramount importance (Irani and Love, 2001). However, not only technical and organisational, but also human factors need to be considered to reduce the complexity of EAI adoption and enhance its management (Fitzerald et al., 2002). The lack of awareness of human actors increases the actors' resistance to adopt EAI (Mantzana, 2006). Thus, decision-makers involved in the development, evaluation and adoption processes may need to consider the actors to successfully accomplish them (Turunen and Jan, 2000). In doing so, Mantzana (2006) utilised Khoumbati's (2005) EAI adoption model and extended the research area in the healthcare sector, by identifying the healthcare actors involved in EAI adoption process. Moreover, Mantzana identified the causal relationships among the healthcare actors and factors that influence EAI adoption.

Integration technologies adoption in SMEs and large organisations _____

Chen (2005) reviewed the literature on integration technologies adoption and reported that the findings derived from the study of large organisations cannot be applied in SMEs due to the distinct characteristics of SMEs. Thus, Chen (2005) identified the significant differences in the way that SMEs and large companies approach integration technologies, based on the existing literature, theoretical diffusion theories, and resource-based theory. In doing so, the factors used to explain the adoption of integration technologies in SMEs and large organisations are identified including: (a) nature of organisations, (b) company size, (c) integration needs, (d) time and (e) adoption factors for SMEs and large organisations. Additionally, adoption factors for SMEs and large organisations are found and classified into three categories: (a) adoption factors explicit to SMEs, (b) adoption factors explicit to large organisations and (c) common factors. Chen (2005) further extended these categories and added sub–factors, such as adoption factors explicit to SMEs including: (a) adopter characteristics, (b) IT sophistication, (c) dependency on trading partners and (d) government regulations; adoption factors explicit to large organisations include: (a) IT infrastructure, (b) IS complexity, (c) internal pressures, (d) perceived future prospects; and common factors include: (a) perceived benefits, (b) perceived barriers, (c) perceived financial goals, (d) external pressures and (e) competitive pressures. As a result, a revised conceptual model was proposed to explain different factors that influence adoption of integration technologies between SMEs and large organisations. The analysis of this model exemplifies that Chen (2005) incorporated several factors from the EAI model by Themistocleous (2002).

The aforementioned literature on EAI adoption in the private and public domains illustrates that Mantzana (2006), Khoumbati (2005) and Chen (2005) adapted numerous common factors (e.g. benefits, barriers, cost) from Themistocleous (2002) EAI adoption model. In addition, Mantzana (2006) identified different actors influencing EAI adoption in healthcare organisations, Khoumbati (2005) and Chen (2005) also presented domain-specific factors in their models. The authors argue here that although Mantzana (2006), Khoumbati (2005) and Chen (2005) validated several factors proposed by Themistocleous (2002), their models may not be applicable or generalised to LGAs. For example, in healthcare organisations, Khoumbati (2005) reported 'physician and patient relationship' as a factor for EAI adoption in healthcare organisations. The authors argue that this factor is not relevant for LGAs or other sector organisations. The rationale is that 'physician and patient relationship' signifies the relationship involved between two actors that are specifically related to healthcare and not others. In this case, the 'physician and patient relationship' factor cannot be considered in LGAs while taking decisions for EAI adoption.

On the other hand, although Chen (2005) adapted some common factors from Themistocleous' (2002) EAI adoption model, yet still Chen's (2005) model differs from the models proposed by Themistocleous (2002), Mantzana (2006) and Khoumbati (2005). The authors report that Chen (2005) did not specifically research EAI; instead Chen (2005) identified the significant differences in the way that SMEs and large companies approach integration technologies. The differences include: (a) availability of lower levels of resources, (b) substantially less sophisticated IS management, (c) the need for integration and (d) the quantity and quality of the environmental information. With such differences among SMEs and large organisations, the authors argue that the models developed for SMEs and large organisations may as well not be appropriate within LGAs.

Current research on EAI adoption in LGAs

LGAs are complex organisations and have developed their own structures and systems according to their requirements (Senyucel, 2005). Nye (1999) states that such LGA structures have been based traditionally on a bureaucratic model that emphasises decentralisation and specialisation in a mechanical and pre-planned approach. LGA service delivery and administration has also tended to be organised in the same bureaucratic manner (Senyucel, 2005). Due to their bureaucratic nature and the culture, LGAs have been experiencing what may be termed as – IT lag time (Beaumaster, 2002). The research indicates that LGAs have experienced approximately 10 years lag time between the adoption of new technologies and IS and its acceptance and routinisation across the organisations (Danziger and Kraemer, 1986). This shows that LGAs have been 'laggards' in adopting new technological solutions. The authors report that laggards can be summarised as those who adopt a technology only when they have no choice. In fact, many laggards do not explicitly adopt technologies at all, but rather acquire them accidentally when a particular technology is a component of a packaged solution (Rogers, 1995). Sometimes LGAs are forced to adopt new technologies, as other LGAs may require them to adopt them as well.

Thus, LGAs may be categorised in the 'late majority' group. There might be an exceptional case where LGAs might be considered as innovators, such as cases where LGAs (Singapore) that have proactively adopted sophisticated information technologies to boost their economy (Devadoss et al., 2002). Whereas, in other cases, LGAs wait till a technology becomes mature and then push the private sector to adopt this technology. The authors report that EAI adoption by LGAs does not significantly differ from other information technologies adopted within LGAs. However, today there are only a few published research case studies on EAI adoption in the LGA domain published in the normative literature (most of them discuss EAI in healthcare, SMEs and multinational organisations). The lack of published cases can be interpreted in many different ways. Some explanations may be that: (a) LGAs adopt new IT reactively compared to private organisations, (b) lack of skilled staff and reluctance to adopt new technologies, lack of understanding and knowledge of EAI in the LGAs, (c) LGAs have been very slow or even unprepared for technological transformations (Devadoss et al., 2002) and (d) LGAs are unable to act proactively as technologies constantly change and evolve around them (Beaumaster, 2002).

Additionally, several LGAs consider that the uncertainty about the costs and benefits of adopting EAI is a central problem (Janssen and Cresswell, 2005). The reason is that the information needed about costs and benefits may be incomplete or inaccessible to several LGAs. Carter et al. (2001) argues here that the access to information can be limited by organisational and functional boundaries that distribute knowledge of value-added activities such that no one, including top management, has complete knowledge of the processes. Due to lack of insight, LGAs are still reluctant to adopt EAI unless they are forced to do so (Janssen and Cresswell, 2005). Other reasons may also be that LGAs do not know whether and to what extent they should invest in EAI and they are unable to assess the return on these investments. The decisions taken in one LGA can have a profound influence on the activities, costs and benefits of other LGAs. Often the implications for other LGAs are not clear, consequently these other LGAs do not want to invest or change their processes to profit from EAI. There is a debate about how costs are divided and how benefits should be distributed over LGAs. The authors report that these barriers may impede the adoption of EAI in LGAs.

By studying the literature on adoption, Irani et al. (1999) report that there are difficulties faced by managers in the decision-making process during technology adoption and realisation of its maximum benefits. LGAs' top management is confronted with similar problems (Johnson and King, 2005). Collinge (2003) reports in this context that LGAs are in an *'awkward'* position. The reason is that central government is demanding to see a return on investment from LGAs. From below, citizens are demanding to see improvements in service delivery. LGAs have been required to submit planning statements, which set out how they are approaching the task of 'implementing e-enabled service delivery' (ODPM, 2004). Anecdotal evidence from the LGA breakout session of the Government UK IT Summit (2005) indicated a general recognition that, despite some great successes, many other e-enabled areas lacked service-depth. With such issues together with less literature support on EAI adoption in LGAs, LGA decision-makers seek answers for its adoption. For this reason, the authors analyzed the factors in the conceptual EAI adoption model proposed by (Kamal and Themistocleous, 2006). The model highlights several factors (organisational, pressure, technological, financial and support factors) and the authors attempt to evaluate the model through a case study conducted in a government organisation.

Research strategy and method

The role and the applicability of EAI in developing integrated IT infrastructures remains under investigation within LGAs. This paper attempts to study EAI to understand how public organisations use EAI technology to develop integrated IT infrastructures. The authors have followed an interpretive, qualitative case study approach to conduct this research. An interpretivist stance was adopted, as the aim of this paper is to understand how LGAs integrate their IT infrastructures. An interpretivist stance allows the authors to navigate and better explain this phenomenon. Also, the authors suggest that in the context of this research a qualitative approach is more appropriate as such an approach can be used to: (a) investigate little-known phenomena like EAI, (b) examine organisational and support factors, (c) examine the phenomenon in its natural setting and (d) learn from practice. In addition, the authors used a case study strategy to explore and understand the development of IT infrastructures in LGAs. In doing so, various data collection methods such as interviews, documentation and observation were used. The bias that is considered to be a danger in using a qualitative research approach is overcome by data triangulation. The use of multiple data collection methods makes the triangulation possible, which provides stronger substantiation of theory (Eisenhardt, 1989). For the purpose of this paper, three types of triangulation are used namely: (a) data (b) methodological and (c) interdisciplinary triangulation.

Case data

The case study organisation is a local government that serves citizens and businesses in a specified region in the United Kingdom (UK). For confidentiality reasons the authors use the coded name LGA. The case study organisation (LGA) is a big borough that aims to provide better and quicker services to its citizens. It employs a large number of staff and provides its services through various sectors including social and environmental services, property, education, health, etc. LGA relied on its software vendor expertise to develop and integrate its IT infrastructure. Since, the software vendor has an important role in this project, the authors refer to it as Softcom. Softcom is a large multinational company that employs over 40 000 employees in 145 countries. It provides integration solutions for LGAs looking to integrate various sectors (e.g. housing, property gazetteers).

Selection process

During the last three to four years, LGA has collaborated with Softcom to introduce a CRM solution that was incorporated with modules like complaints, street care, housing benefits and council tax. All these packages provided by Softcom have improved citizens' satisfaction, the efficiency and performance of LGA, and speeded up business processes. Nonetheless, there was a lot of scepticism regarding the integration of Softcom applications with non-Softcom systems. The CRM solutions can communicate with other ERP packages but have limitations, as they cannot exchange information with non-Softcom applications. The insufficient nature of the then existing IT infrastructure and the need for integration led LGA to revisit its e-Government, customer services and investment strategies. One solution was to phase out the non-Softcom applications and replace them with new ones. However, such a solution would have had cost LGA millions of pounds. There was less time and money and no proper justification to do so (such as eliminating the functionality of reliable systems). Also, the risks associated with such an approach were high. Conversely, the IT department was seeking possible solutions through integration. The IT management was persuaded that integration can deliver measurable business benefits to LGA that are worth the costs.

LGA relied on Softcom technical expertise to develop and integrate their e-Gov-IS and IT infrastructure. Softcom provides integration solutions for LGAs looking to integrate various applications and IS from different departments (e.g. housing, education). LGA follows a proactive approach when adopting IT solutions and aims to be amongst the first LGAs (in the UK) that will integrate IT infrastructure. For that reason, LGA took the decision to integrate its CRM and e-Gov applications with the back-office systems using EAI architecture and technologies. Since Softcom provides EAI solutions, LGA decided to collaborate with and integrate its systems. In doing so, LGA bought EAI software from Softcom without evaluating other alternative EAI packages. Such a decision differs from the practices of other organisations that evaluate EAI software before selecting one. When the IT managers were asked for the reasons that led their organisation to this action they reported that: (a) LGA lacks knowledge and expertise on EAI and (b) there is trust and close collaboration between LGA and Softcom. On the other hand, Softcom provides a solution, which is a mixture of some EAI technologies put together to promote the sales of their solution within various LGAs. Softcom has strategically invested in this project, as EAI is a new market in the public domain. Softcom, by designing and customising a solution for one LGA, can package this solution and easily sell it to other LGAs. Thus, it can easily gain a competitive advantage and market leadership.

Integration process

LGA was working towards a 'hub and spoke' methodology. The 'HUB' is a single Softcom database from which applications (the 'SPOKES') draw data and to which they return data.

The integration between LGA's Local Land Property Gazetteer (LLPG) and CRM system via Softcom HUB (i.e. Softcom InterConnect Integration HUB) will enable a two-way flow of data between LGA's LLPG and CRM system via Hub. For example, citizens will be able to request changes to addresses through the CRM system that will then update LLPG; and changes from other sources to LLPG will update the property elements of the CRM system.

The demonstration pilot project (DPP)

The demonstration pilot project (DPP) is a project within LGA where an integrated solution is being developed to provide multi-LGA access and sharing of information. (Figure 14.2) Currently, various LGAs own and manage their own applications and databases. LGAs are not aware of the information held on a specific citizen within another LGA. The DPP is based on integrating multi-LGAs to enable the LGAs involved with monitoring citizens to share information, track and monitor records of all citizen queries and take action when required. The problem is lack of communication between the LGAs, which could have resolved citizen problems. The need to integrate these systems is raised to avoid similar mistakes from the past re-occurring. The aim of the DPP project is to demonstrate to LGA officials and other LGAs that investing in a long-term programme of integration between Softcom solutions and non-Softcom solutions is necessary. On this basis the adoption of integration architecture within and among other LGAs will deliver measurable business benefits.

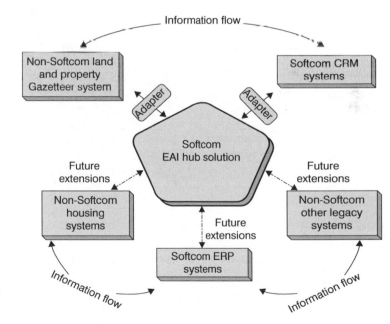

Figure 14.2
Demonstration Pilot Project (Kamal and Themistocleous, 2007)

The solution

The need for integration is to provide a common view of information from all the systems. There are different contact telephone numbers for each LGA and, for example, if a citizen wants to contact social services as well as the benefits department by telephone, a call is either transferred to the benefits department or the citizen has to call the benefits department specific line. This makes call handling difficult, slow and lowers the number of calls answered and dealt with. LGA planned that by using a CRM application as the front-office linked to the existing back-office applications, a common view of information held in all back-office applications could be achieved. In addition, using the call centre facilities of CRM, a single call from a citizen regarding various sectors can be handled by one agent. This will enhance quick, efficient provision of services, a higher number of calls will be handled and the long list of numbers (one for each sector) is reduced to 'single point of contact'. Citizen contact via mail or e-mail also needs to be directed to the required sector using a CRM application there are a variety of communication channels which can be used, and all information processed from the CRM application.

However, as reported earlier just using CRM applications is not enough, as it still needs to communicate with other applications at the back-office. To communicate with other applications there is a need to integrate CRM applications with the back-office applications. The reason is that CRM applications need integration with the other points of contact, leading to a single view of multichannel interactions including internal personnel as well as external customers. Figures 14.3 and 14.4 depict the scenarios of 'AS IS – Before Integration' and 'AS AFTER – After Integration' information flow. In both the Figures, (a) and (b) represents the message transmission steps, the dotted boxes represents the connectivity layer, arrows demonstrate the transportation layer, 123…abc illustrate translation layer and b…n represents the number of adapters. Figure 14.3 focuses on developing a design for the process of information flow from the CRM application to the back-office without applying integration technologies and architecture. Figure 14.4 focuses on developing a design for the process of information flow from the CRM application to the back-office applications using integration technologies and architecture. The authors employ EAI solutions to integrate back-office with the front-office applications. EAI solutions provide integration functionality through integration architecture using a variety of EAI technologies such as: (a) database-oriented middleware, (b) message-oriented technologies, (c) transaction-based technologies, (d) distributed object technologies and (e) interface-oriented technologies. There are four integration layers that are used to provide integration between CRM applications and back-office applications, for example (a) connectivity layer, (b) transportation layer, (c) transformation layer and (d) process automation layer (Themistocleous, 2002).

Description of information flow 'AS IS – before integration'

(a) Different stakeholders contact LGA through different communication channels (channels such as Softcom's interaction channel components of CRM) through Internet, telephony, call centre, kiosks, and face-to-face.
(b) Once the service request information is input in the CRM component an API is triggered to search the central database (central repository) for the information requested.
(c) If the service request information is available, it is relayed back to the employee/staff member, and communicated back to the stakeholder through different communication channels available.
(d) If the service request information is not available within the central database in the CRM, the information is then manually searched from the back-office systems/applications by the employees/staff member then follow step (c).

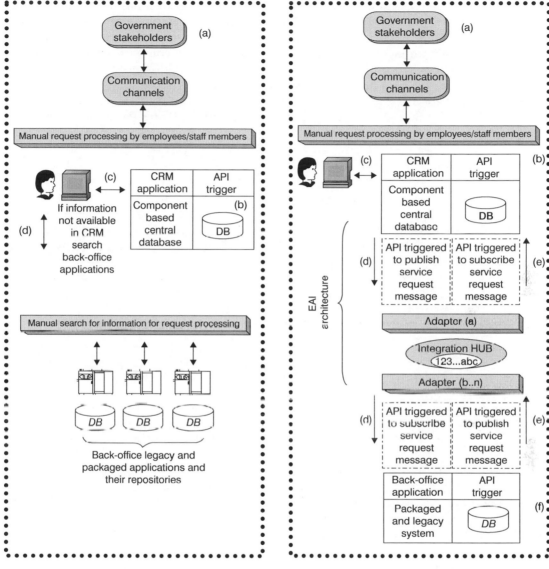

Figure 14.3 Information flow '**Before**' integration (Kamal and Themistocleous, 2007)

Figure 14.4 Information flow '**After**' integration (Kamal and Themistocleous, 2007)

Description of information flow 'AS AFTER – after integration'

(a) Different stakeholders contact LGA through different communication channels (channels such as Softcom's interaction channel components of CRM) through Internet, telephony, call centre, kiosks, and face-to-face.

(b) Once the service request information is input in the CRM component an API is triggered to search the central database (central repository) for the information requested.

(c) If the service request information is available it is relayed back to the employee/staff member, and communicated back to the stakeholder through different communication channels available.

(d) If the service request information is not available within the central database in the CRM, another API is triggered which publishes the service request message to the required back-office application through the integration hub. The connectivity layer within the integration hub provides the communication channel from the CRM application to the back-office applications. The service request message is then transported (through transportation layer) and transformed (through translation layer) by the adapter (a) to the required format of the receiver and is ready to be routed to the relevant back-office system through the integration hub. Adapter (b…n) then picks the service request message and sends it to the relevant back-office application, which subscribes the service request message. Depending on the type of back-office application, the adapter is selected from (b…n).

(e) Within the back-office application, another API is triggered to search for the service request information. When the information is found, it is published by the back-office application. Adapter (b…n) picks it up, transforms (through translation layer) it to the required format for the CRM, through the hub and adapter (a) picks it up and transports it (through the transportation layer) to the CRM application, which subscribes to the message. Then follow the step (c).

■ EAI selection process and adoption

The main issues derived from the case data presented are summarised in this section. The selection of EAI software is a complex and important process during an EAI project. As there is marketplace confusion regarding EAI packages and solutions, many organisations spend time and resources assessing and choosing appropriate EAI software. In this case study, LGA did not use any evaluation framework or other tools to assess EAI packages. The reason for this decision is that within LGA there were no clear procedures, norms and formal processes for selecting and assessing EAI software (i.e. no market knowledge on evaluating EAI software) and thus it took the decision to select EAI software by relying on Softcom expertise. This decision illustrates two significant issues, firstly, the manager's lack of knowledge on EAI area and thus took the decision to fully rely on Softcom for the selection of EAI packages. This also shows that managers also did not consider the risks associated with EAI technologies (e.g. EAI compatibility, complexity, etc.).

Secondly, as the literature indicates, the decision-making for technology adoption is typically concentrated at top-management level in the public sector (Ebrahim et al., 2004), hence, this decision was of high risk as the LGA top management chose an EAI package that was under development. The risky decision was that LGA fully relied on Softcom with experience on IT projects but with no clear view regarding the integration of its packages. Although, in this case study DPP was successful, the decision for selecting EAI software could have been the other way round. As mentioned above, the authors discussed six factors from EAI adoption model in LGAs (Kamal and Themistocleous, 2006) namely: (a) formalisation, (b) centralisation, (c) market knowledge, (d) evaluation framework, (d) technological risks and (e) managerial capability. The arguments on these factors indicate that these factors may have influenced EAI adoption in LGA and assist in extending e-Gov infrastructure.

In addition to these factors, the authors validated several other factors through this case study that also influenced the decision-making process for EAI adoption in LGAs. For example, as exemplified from the case study there was IT support from Softcom. Softcom consultants and integrators supported LGA's IT department to introduce EAI. In doing so, it supported and influenced the decision-making process. Moreover, IT support from Softcom also improved IT capabilities and enhanced the organisation's knowledge regarding applications integration and EAI. LGA top management and higher administrative authority initially recommended and supported the work on the DPP project and evaluation of the outcome. The reason for running the DPP project was the high cost of, and the limited success of, EAI applications in the public domain. The DPP project demonstrates that the integration (a) is technically feasible and (b) can deliver significant benefits to LGA.

As reported in the EAI adoption model (Kamal and Themistocleous, 2006) size can be categorised as the size of the community served and organisational size. The case study organisation (LGA) is a large organisation and serves a large community within a specific region of the UK. There were two reasons why LGA decided to run a pilot project. Additional reasons were: (a) to demonstrate to other LGAs that they could integrate with Softcom solutions, (b) to develop a better relationship with different vendors (in this case Softcom) to support the chances of technical support from Softcom in the future, (c) to develop expertise of working with Softcom technologies among the staff concerned and (d) to use the project as a lever for attracting additional funding for other similar projects.

Benefits extracted from the DPP project were: (a) reusability of systems, components and data, (b) reduction in data redundancy, (c) reliable data, (d) support in data sharing, (e) collaboration among departments and (f) improved management support for decision-making. Whereas, barriers extracted are: (a) reliance on Softcom for expertise, (b) no evaluation framework used to assess EAI tools, (c) lack of EAI knowledge, (d) low level of LGA IT infrastructure and (e) lack of business process reengineering (BPR).

Conclusions

While private companies have continued to take advantage of IT to improve their businesses, services offered by government organisations have remained deficient over the years. The concept of e-Gov has emerged as a credible solution to improve such services as it allows people to access public services from within their own homes or offices. The importance of e-Gov has been widely recognised with 30 European ministers agreed upon a plan to speed up the development of e-Gov-IS in an attempt to modernise the European public sector. During recent years public organisations have adopted CRM applications to improve their services and relationships with their citizens. The application of CRM is beneficial for LGA as it results in improvements in information sharing and cost reduction. Recently, many LGAs have attempted to link together their e-Gov and CRM applications to deliver better services. Nonetheless, public organisations have realised that they can gain significant advantages when they integrate their CRM and e-Gov-IS with their disparate back-office solutions. Thus, they are seeking ways to integrate their applications and IT infrastructures.

The authors suggest that public organisations can focus on integration technologies like EAI to incorporate their systems and processes, and thus, achieve their goals. Yet, the adoption of EAI by public organisations is still in its infancy within LGAs, researchers need to understand the issues surrounding this technology. In this paper the authors present and analyze one case study that focuses on the development of integrated e-Gov and IT infrastructures in an LGA. The case organisation has initially incorporated its e-Gov-IS with CRM to improve its services. Such interconnectivity has resulted in a partial integration solution, as there was no linkage between the front- (CRM, e-Gov) and back-office systems. Thus, the organisation collaborated with Softcom to apply an EAI solution and piece together its IS. The extracted results are based on one pilot case study only and, in addition, all factors reported by Kamal and Themistocleous (2006) were not analyzed in this one case study. However, it will allow the authors to take it as a starting point in comparing and analyzing EAI adoption factors when analyzing more case studies within LGAs. The authors assert that as the number of cases increase it will provide more harmonised results, and will allow better analysis and decision-making for EAI adoption.

■ References

Abie, H., Foyn, B., Bing, J., Blobel, B., Pharow, P., Delgado, J., Karnouskos, S., Pitkanen, O. and Tzovaras, D. (2004). 'The need for a digital rights management framework for the next generation of e-Government services'. *Electronic Government – An International Journal*, 1(1), 8–28.

Adams, N. J., Haston, S., Gillespie, N. and Macintosh, A. (2003). 'Conventional and Electronic Service Delivery within Public Authorities: The Issues and Lessons from the Private Sector'. *Proceedings of the Second International Conference on e-Government*, Prague, Czech Republic, pp. 129–134.

Aldrich, D., Berlot, J. C. and McClure, C. R. (2002). 'e-Government: Initiatives, development, and issues'. *Government Information Quarterly*, 19(4), 349–355.

Atherton, L. (2002). 'SeamlessUK – Building bridges between Information Islands'. *New Library World*, 103(11), 467–473.

Beaumaster, S. (2002). 'Local Government IT implementation issues: A challenge for public administration'. *35th Annual Hawaii International Conference on System Sciences*, IEEE Computer Society, pp. 1725–1734.

Bekkers, V. J. J. M. (1998). *Wiring Public Organisations and Changing Organisational Jurisdiction*. IOS Press, Amsterdam.

Carter, F. J., Jambulingham, T., Gupta, V. K. and Melone, N. (2001). 'Technological innovations: A framework for communicating diffusion effects'. *Information and Management*, 38, 277–287.

Chen, H. (2005). *Adopting Emerging Integration Technologies in Organisations*. PhD Thesis, Department of Information Systems and Computing, Brunel University, Uxbridge, Middlesex, UK.

Collinge, A, (2003). 'How and Where is Local e-Government Delivering Value to the Citizens?'. In *Local e-Government Now: Sustaining the Momentum*: Briefing on SOCITIM and I&DeA Report, APSE, Briefing 30/03 at: http://www.apse.org.uk

Danziger, J. N. and Kraemer, K. L. (1986). *People and Computers: The Impacts of Computing on End Users in Organizations*. Columbia University Press, New York, NY.

Davenport, T. H. (1998). 'Putting the Enterprise into the Enterprise Systems'. *Harvard Business Review*, pp. 121–131.

Dawes, S. S. (1996). 'Interagency information sharing: Expected benefits, manageable risks'. *Journal of Policy Analysis and Management*, 15(3), 377–394.

Devadoss, P. R., Pan, S. L. and Huang, J. C. (2002). 'Structural analysis of e-government initiatives: A case study of SCO'. *Decision Support Systems*, 34, 253–269.

Di Natale, M., Cucinotta, T. and Kolachalam, S. (2003). 'A Modular Open-Source Architecture for ICT Services in the Public Administration'. *Proceedings of the Second International Conference on e-Government Prague, Czech Republic*, Prague, Czech Republic, pp. 167–172.

Ebrahim, Z., Irani, Z. and Sarmad, A. S. (2004). 'Factors Influencing the Adoption of e-Government in Public Sector'. *European and Mediterranean Conference on Information Systems*, Tunis, Tunisia, pp. 1–10.

Edwards, P. and Newing, R. (2000). Application Integration for e-Business. London, UK.

Eisenhardt, K. M. (1989). 'Building theories from case study research'. *Academy of Management Review*, 14(4), 532–550.

Fitzerald, L., Ferlie, E., Wood, M. and Hawkins, C. (2002). 'Interlocking interactions, the diffusion of innovations in healthcare'. *Human Relations*, 55(12), 1429–1449.

Gamper, J. and Augsten, N. (2003). 'The Role of Web Services in Digital Government'. *Proceedings of the Second International Conference on e-Government*, Prague, Czech Republic, pp. 161–166.

Gil García, J. R. and Pardo, T. A. (2005). 'e-Government success factors: Mapping practical tools to theoretical foundations'. *Government Information Quarterly*, 22(1), 187–216.

Gil-García, J. R., Schneider, C. A., Pardo, T. A. and Cresswell, A. M. (2005). 'Inter-organisational Information Integration in the Criminal Justice Enterprise: Preliminary Lessons from State and County Initiatives'. *Proceedings of the 38th Hawaii International Conference on System Sciences*, Hawaii, pp. 1–10.

Gortmaker, J. and Janssen, M. (2004). 'Business Process Orchestration in e-Government: A Gap Analysis'. *Proceedings of the 15th International Resources Management Association (IRMA) International Conference*, New Orleans, LA, USA, pp. 1–6.

Gortmaker, J., Janssen, M. and Wagenaar, R. W. (2004). 'The Advantages of Web Service Orchestration in Perspective'. *Proceedings of the 6th International Conference of Electronic Commerce, ICEC*, Delft, The Netherlands.

Gouscos, D., Mentzas G. and Georgladis, P. (2001). 'PASSPORT: A Novel Architectural Model for the Provision of Seamless Cross-Border e-Government Services'. *12th International Conference on Database and Expert Systems Applications (DEXA 2001)*, Munich.

Government UK IT Summit (2005). A summary of the agenda and speakers can be found at http://www.cnetnetworks.co.uk/etf/govuk-it

Homburg, V. and Bekkers, V. (2002). 'The Back-Office of E-Government (Managing Information Domains as Political Economies)'. *35th Annual Hawaii International Conference on System Sciences, HICSS*, IEEE, pp. 1666–1674.

Irani, Z. and Love, P. (2001). 'The propagation of technology management taxonomies for evaluating investments in information systems)'. *Journal of Management Information Systems*, 17(3), 161–177.

Irani, Z., Ezingeard, J.-N., Grieve, R. J. and Race, P. (1999). 'Investment justification of information technology in manufacturing'. *The International Journal of Computer Applications in Technology*, 12(2), 90–101.

Janssen, M. and Cresswell, A. (2005). 'Enterprise Architecture Integration in E-Government'. *38th Hawaii International Conference on System Sciences*, Hawaii, pp. 1–10.

Janssen, M. and Wagenaar, R. (2003). 'Customer Relationship Management in e-Government: A Dutch Survey'. *Proceedings of the 3rd European Conference on e-Government*, Trinity College, Dublin, Ireland, pp. 227–238.

Janssen, M., Wagennar, R. and Beeren, J. (2002). 'Towards a Flexible ICT-Architecture for Multi-Channel e-Government Service Provisioning'. *36th Hawaii International Conference on System Sciences*, Hawaii, USA, pp. 148–157.

Johnson, O. A. and King, S. F. (2005). 'Best practice in local e-government: A process modelling approach'. *e-Government Workshop (eGOV05)*, 1–14.

Kalakota, R. and Robinson, M. (2001). *e-Business 2.0: Roadmap for Success*. Addison-Wesley, Boston, Massachusetts, USA, Addison-Wesley.

Kamal, M. M. and Themistocleous, M. (2006). 'A Conceptual Model for EAI Adoption in an e-Government Environment'. *European and Mediterranean Conference on Information Systems (EMCIS)*, Costa Blanca, Alicante, Spain, pp. 1–11.

Kamal, M. M. and Themistocleous, M. (2007). 'Investigating EAI Adoption in LGAs: A Case Study Based Analysis'. *Thirteenth Americas Conference on Information Systems*, Keystone, Colorado, USA, [CDROM Proceedings].

Khoumbati, K. (2005). 'Evaluating the Adoption of Enterprise Application Integration in Healthcare Organisations Using an Actor-Oriented Approach'. PhD Thesis, Department of Information Systems and Computing, Brunel University, Uxbridge, Middlesex, UK.

Lam, W. (2005). 'Barriers to e-government integration'. *The Journal of Enterprise Information Management*, 18(5), 511–530.

Layne, K. and Lee, J. (2001). 'Developing fully functional e-Government: A four stage model'. *Government Information Quarterly*, 18(2), 122–136.

Mantzana, V. G. (2006). 'Investigating The Adoption Of Enterprise Application Integration In Healthcare Organisations Using An Actor-Oriented Approach'. PhD Thesis, Department of Information Systems and Computing, Brunel University, Uxbridge, Middlesex, UK.

Markus, L., and Tanis, C. (1999). 'The Enterprise Systems Experience – From Adoption to Success'. *In Framing the Domain of IT Management: Glimpsing the Future Through the Past (Ed, Zmud, R.) Pinnaflex Educational Resources*, Inc, Oklahoma, USA, pp. 173–207.

McCullagh, A. (1998). 'The Establishment of Trust in the Electronic Commerce Environment'. *Proceedings of the Information Industry Outlook Conference*, Australia.

Mwakalinga, J. and Yngström, L. (2004). 'Integrated Security Systems for e-Government based on SAML Standard'. *ISSA Conference*, Gallagher Estate, Midrand, pp. 1–9.

Nye, Jr J. (1999). Information technology and Democratic Governance. Governance in Networked World, Hollins Publishing Company, NH, pp. 1–18.

Osorio, C. O. (2001). 'A New Framework for the Analysis of Solutions of Privacy – Enhanced Internet Commerce'. *eJeta-PRIVACY*.

ODPM (2004). 'Implementing Electronic Government Statements' at http://www.localegov.gov.uk

Reich, R. H. and Benbasat, I. (1996). 'Measuring the linkage between business and information technology objectives'. *MIS Quarterly*, 20(1), 55–81.

Reiter, M. and Rubin, A. (1998). 'Crowds: Anonymity for web transactions'. *ACM Transactions on Information and System Security*, 1.

Rogers, E. M. (1995). *Diffusion of Innovations*. The Free Press, New York.

Scholl, H. J. (2005). 'Interoperability in e-Government: More than Just Smart Middleware'. *Proceedings of the 38th Hawaii International Conference on System Sciences*, Hawaii.

Senyucel, Z. (2005). 'Towards Successful e-Government Facilitation in UK Local Authorities'. *e-Government Workshop '05 (eGOV05)*, pp. 1–16.

Signore, O., Chesi, F., and Pallotti, M. (2005). e-Government: Challenges and Opportunities. *CMG Italy – XIX Annual Conference*, Florence, Italy.

Songini, M. L. (2004). 'Australian Firm Faces ERP Implementation Woes'. *Computerworld*.

Themistocleous, M. (2002). 'Evaluating the Adoption of Enterprise Application Integration in Multinational Organisations'. PhD Thesis, Department of Information Systems and Computing, Brunel University, Uxbridge, Middlesex, UK.

Themistocleous, M. and Irani, Z. (2001). 'Benchmarking the benefits and barriers of application integration'. *Benchmarking An International Journal*, 8(4), 317–331.

Themistocleous, M., Irani, Z. and Love, P. E. D. (2005). 'Developing e-Government Integrated Infrastructures: A Case Study'. *38th Annual Hawaii International Conference on System Sciences (HICSS'05)* – Big Island, Hawaii, IEEE, pp. 1–10.

Turunen, P. and Jan, T. (2000). 'Stakeholder groups in the evaluation of medical information systems'. *7th European Conference on the Evaluation of Information Technology*, Dublin, Ireland, pp. 329–334.

Vasconcelos, A., Mira da Silva, M., Fernandes, A. and Tribolet, J. (2004). 'An Information System Architectural Framework for Enterprise Application Integration'. *Proceedings of the 37th Annual Hawaii International Conference on System Sciences, HICCS04*, Hawaii, pp. 225–233.

Wagnar, W. and Antonucci, Y. L. (2004). 'An Analysis of the Imagine PA Public Sector ERP Project'. *Proceedings of the Thirty-Seventh Annual Hawaii International Conference on System Sciences, Hicss 37*, Big Island, Hawaii, USA, IEEE Computer Society, Los Alamitos, California, USA. [CDROM Proceedings]

Watson, E., Vaught, S. and Gutierrez, D. (2003). 'ERP implementation in the state government'. *Annals of Cases on Information Technology*, 5, 302–319.

Zahavi, R. (1999). *Enterprise Application Integration with Corba.* John Wiley and Sons Inc, New York, USA.

t-Government for benefit realisation: A research agenda

S. Sahraoui, A. Ghoneim, Z. Irani and S. Ozkan

■ Introduction

This chapter will propose a model of t-Government and present a research agenda to increase understanding surrounding t-Government and the processes involved in furthering the agenda supportive of transformational government. In particular, the authors will propose both operational and conceptual models for the effective involvement of citizens and businesses in government functioning. This will help define an agenda for t-Government research that emerges from national UK strategy and policy for e-Government.

The main threads of t-Government encompass:

■ A citizen-centric delivery of public services or e-inclusion
■ A shared services culture to maximise value added to clients
■ The effective delivery and management of resources and skills within government- or professionalism

From the outset it is important to mention that t-Government is different from e-Government both conceptually and operationally. This will be drawn out in further developments. The above three threads of t-Government should be addressed principally from the perspectives of delivery, evaluation and participation in view of benefit realisation as envisioned by government strategic planning and policy directives (cf. Cabinet Office, 2005).

The research agenda needs to include the management of change dimension of these phenomena. In particular, research is needed to reshape the discourse towards emphasising a citizen-centric approach that defines, develops and benefits from public service. Decision-makers in government will need models of governance that fulfil transformational objectives. They will also need models of benefits realisation within a strategic governance framework. t-Government research should be addressing these relative voids as will be further explained.

The case for t-Government

Electronic Government often referred to as e-Government has reached a stage of maturity in that mandates set by central government have been achieved, at a cost of £184 per UK household, over a 7-year period from 2001–2008. This equates to a total e-Government expenditure of £3.9 billion between 2001 and 2008 (Kable, 2003). In context, UK local authorities are expected to deliver a total of £1.2 billion in accumulated efficiency savings by 2007–2008 through realising the benefits of e-Government (IDABC, 2005). Gershon (2004) calls (in his report) for £21.5 billion in annual efficiency improvements across the UK government by 2007–2008. The exploitation of e-Government such that benefits can be realised is the rationale being used to define transformational Government, within referred to as t-Government.

The 2006 Transformational Government Annual Report (Cabinet Office, 2007) identifies three distinctive themes integral to t-Government. These are presented in Figure 15.1 and include: customer-centric services; shared services and professionalism. Customer-centric services are explained in the 2005 *Transformational Government-Enabled by Technology Strategy* document (Cabinet Office, 2005) as being the transformation of public services for the benefit of citizens, businesses, taxpayers and front-line staff. The second dimension of t-Government is identified as shared services. These include the efficiency of corporate services and infrastructure of government organisations thus, supporting the freeing of resources for front-line delivery. The third dimension of transformational Government is

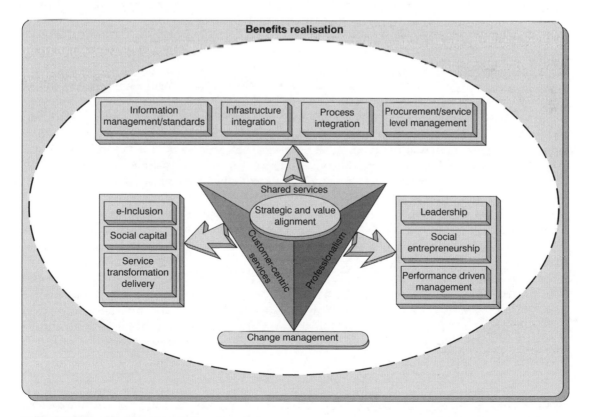

Figure 15.1 Tri-dimensional t-Government

professionalism, which includes the steps necessary to achieve the effective delivery of technology for government and nurturing capacity and skills in public administration. This area includes planning, delivery, management, skills and governance. Figure 15.1 extracts the three themes of t-Government, when set against a backdrop of change management for benefits realisation.

■ From e-Government to t-Government

The shift in focus from 'e-' to 't'-Government is the result of a logical realisation that the (information technology) IT trajectory of legacy e-Government systems and programs will not solve the lingering problems with public service delivery. The UK government seems to have realised that such a technology trajectory will not fulfil its ultimate objectives of transforming government services, and has opted for a strategic governance model based on the three axes presented in Figure 15.1. Hence, it has focused on redefining the role of IT in government:

> 'The challenge ahead is not just to 'do IT better' in the context of the past models for delivery of public services. It is also about 'doing IT differently' to support the next phase of public service reform' (Cabinet Office, 2005, p. 6).

Only the creation of a transformational dynamic within government will ensure that public services are systematically redesigned to fulfil client requirements, empower citizens and other clients through the development of a culture of shared services. Professionalism needs to be fostered as a system of management to ensure the sustainability of the trans-form-ational drive. By 2011, t-Government should be in place and the process made irreversible, such that a sustainable culture of change management would have been created (Cabinet Office, 2005). This will require that technology investments and service transformation must be directed towards a shifting of government and public services from the back-office towards the front-line and to the citizen and businesses, within a shared services framework. This framework will combine both a culture and an infrastructure to facilitate the delivery of shared and integrated services. Hence, current and planned investments will be evaluated from the standpoint of financial and service benefit realisation.

Change models will depend on the legacy e-Government systems and cultures in place. For some the transition will be almost an automatic growth from the transactional stage they are at now but for others, they will have to come out of their hibernation behind hollow front-ends, no matter how well designed they are. The key potential for innovation lies in addressing the reality that government can be transformed just like business. Although the principle objective of its business processes is not the creation of a revenue stream and commercial notions of 'value', 'good' or 'effective' systems may have only superficial relevance, the imperatives of efficiency and effectiveness are otherwise as important, though different in nature. This itself is a thought-provoking proposition that is expected to raise much debate within the research community.

Beyond the rhetoric of the UK government to put an end to e-Government and to shift to a t-Government strategy (cf. Ezgov, 2005), local authorities are left with a practical problem of analyzing their e-Government standing and deciding on a migration strategy. In extrapolating from the normative literature on e-Government it is evident that no clear models for t-Government benefit realisation have yet emerged, let alone a strategy for migration. Indeed, such literature has remained superficial in its treatment of the transformational potential of e-Government. Based on the vision for t-Government in the UK, an attempt is made below to outline an operational model that synthesises the major drives and stakeholders of the transformation process.

Operational model of t-Government

t-Government can be construed as the enactment of three perspectives: citizen-centricity, shared service culture and professionalism, in unison seeking to use Information Society Technologies (IST) to integrate citizen-customer feedback into the initial stages of policy development and the process of reengineering public services (Figure 15.2). For a local or regional authority this covers a wide range of different interfaces that will be channelled through GovConnect.gov.uk for citizens or, BusinessLink.gov.uk for commercial organisations. By November 2006, each department was required to have reviewed its Web sites in accordance with the Transformational Government strategy and its own overall communication strategy, and produce proposed trajectories for reducing its number of Web sites overall and converging on GovConnect and BusinessLink for the stated services[1] (Cabinet Office, 2006).

While Figure 15.1 represents a conceptual view of t-Government at the national/macro level, hence at a planning level, Figure 15.2 is a micro/local authority view of t-Government

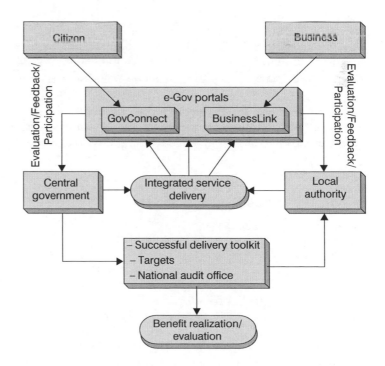

■ **Figure 15.2**
Operationalised t-Government

[1] 'Thus far, 951 Web sites have been considered and, of these, 90 have already closed and a further 461 are planned to be closed. 374 of the remaining sites would have been reviewed by June 2007, with a view to encouraging further rationalisation' (Cabinet Office, 2007).

implementation in terms of delivery, participation and evaluation such that an integrated perspective of central-and-local government through a common portal can be achieved. In terms of t-Government delivery, government services will become transparent to those that interact with it, as horizontal and vertical services will be integrated to develop and deliver improved public value. Indeed central government will support local authorities in the successful delivery of services through an implementation plan and a set of targets that have been developed by appropriate stakeholder groups (Cabinet Office, 2006). As t-Government implies, active participation when seen in the context of Figure 15.2 provides the impetus for the development and delivery of integrated services where the client engages through a pull process (Irani et al., 2004), first, participating in the planning and implementation of e-Government services; secondly, through a pull-model of service delivery, clients manage the delivery process to fit their peculiar requirements, and lastly, they are at the centre of the evaluation of benefit realisation through providing feedback and taking up services that benefit them the most. This is echoed in the original t-Government strategy document as bringing a

> 'strong and reliable customer voice into the design of individual services; and (at a more general level) to get a better understanding of the service expectations of citizens, businesses and public servants' (Cabinet Office, 2005, p. 8).

and further emphasised in the first annual review through evaluating the impact of IT-enabled services on people's daily lives and not merely the take up of these services (Cabinet Office, 2007).

The process of operationalising t-Government evaluation is both front-office and back-office. In the former it involves the benefits, costs and risks associated with service provision whereas in the latter evaluation is often external and is subjected to escalating levels of scrutiny involving disparate bodies like the National Audit Office and a Gateway Review Team (Perrin, 2006) to explore efficiency gains and benefit realisation.

Based on the operational view of t-Government as depicted in Figure 15.2, the authors have drawn a list of the critical variables differentiating e- from t-Government and the consequent actions needed for an effective migration process (Table 15.1).

Strategic governance model

Several models for e-Government maturity and growth exist (Layne and Lee, 2001; Watson and Mundy, 2001; Chen, 2002; UN, 2003; World Bank, 2003). These models have several stages associated with them. However, as Anderson and Henriksen (2006) claim, such models remain essentially focused around technological capability and are thought to be linear extrapolations of ICT growth models in general such as Nolan's stages of growth model (cf. Beynon-Davies, 2007). This technological rationalist paradigm (Sahraoui, 2007) held by e-Government providers, namely the public administrators and the technologists in charge of channelling the delivery of their services, keeps at bay e-Government clients, citizens and businesses alike. Thus, to become a meaningful agent of transformation for public service delivery and modern governance, t-Government providers must abandon their technological bias and focus on socio-cultural transformations yielding the desired inclusion

Table 15.1 Differentiation between e-Gov and t-Gov and migration strategy

	e-Government	t-Government	Migration from e-Gov to t-Gov
Objective	Putting government services online	Making the government transformational through IT	Transformational leadership
Citizen involvement	Access and accessibility	Build social capital	e-Democracy
Business involvement	Online transacting	Supply chain integration	Supply chain management
Service delivery	Push-model	Pull-model	e-Inclusion
Evaluation	Stage model growth	Benefit realisation	Meta model of evaluation and benchmarking
Resource management	Resource allocation	Professionalism	Empowerment
Integration	Shared services IT platform	Shared services culture	Cultural change
Business model	Technological capability	Strategic governance	e-Citizenship
IT role	Enabling online delivery	Enabling the transformation of the business of government	BPR

(Leitner, 2003). One of the most important areas of change is the reconsideration of the citizen as partner rather than service recipient. Though public service is different and is deeply entrenched into a culture of one-way service provision, sophistication of clients and especially citizenry, is accentuating the pressure on government to deliver on demand and as per the exact requirements of clients:

> 'Of course public services are different. Their values are different. But today people won't accept a service handed down from on high. They want to shape it to their needs, and the reality of their lives...' (RT Hon Tony Blair, MP, 2006).

It is nonetheless very difficult to redirect bureaucracies to rethink the role of citizens and accept the principle of total transparency and accountability and engage in equitable partnership (Drake et al., 2004; Sahraoui et al., 2006). This is further complicated by the fact that most public services have been operating as monopolies for a very long time.

The model of Figure 15.3, dubbed a strategic governance model, purports to palliate insufficiencies of growth models and illustrates how t-Government integrates citizens and businesses into its inner-workings, wherein they are not anymore at the margins of an e-Government model that dealt with clients like external entities. Rather, clients, both citizens and corporate, are bracketed within the value-chain of t-Government and become integral to the inner workings of the value network of government (Beynon-Davies, 2007).

Contrary to the models of Figures 15.1 and 15.2 which represent working models of t-Government, hence accounting for all aspects of the t-Government edifice, both human and

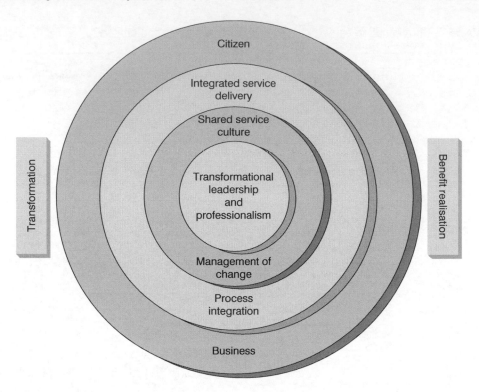

technological, the strategic governance model outlined above is restricted to human activity system infrastructure as defined by Beynon-Davies (2007), hence constituting 'the organization of activity supporting the creation and distribution of value' (p. 16). As such it is rather a meta-model underlying a grand theory of t-Government and could thus account for a myriad of configurations of t-Government implementation models.

The model is premised on transformation of key activities and processes within a strategy of multi-stakeholder benefit realisation. As indicated in Table 15.1, the latter is best appraised through meta-models of evaluation and benchmarking (cf. Beynon-Davies, 2007) as opposed to linear evaluations deriving from the stages of growth models. On the outer layers of the government value network, both citizens and businesses play a role throughout the t-Government value-chain. Given the central role of clients for benefit realisation, resources are shifted to the front-line to ensure a sustained integration of clients into t-Government. This shifting of resources, for it not to be dispersed, requires the concentration of the delivery process into very few front-ends as 'the number of operational centres of shared services should be measured in tens rather than hundreds' (cf. Cabinet Office, 2006). However, contrary to e-Government, the concentration of shared services is not an artefact of Web design or IT integration but rather built on a genuine ontology of integration or semantic Web that derives from the integration of business processes which, in turn, derive from a shared services culture:

> 'The semantic Web and ontology-based approaches seem to promise a support for administrative processes crossing borders of organizations, systems and infrastructures' (cf. Sabol and Mach, 2006, p. 10).

Shared services are developed within an organisational culture premised on capacity building and professional networks where public service can foster skill and career building among its employees (cf. Ezgov, 2005). Human resource management in t-Government becomes a shared function rather than the prerogative of distinct administrations (cf. Cabinet Office, 2006). This assuredly represents a major cultural shift for the wider public sector and underlies the drive for professionalism, wherein back-office administrative processes are transformed into front-office, pull-based, value-added services (cf. Irani et al., 2004). The whole edifice is made possible through transformational leadership and management of change as the inner core of the strategic governance model. Transformational leadership has been identified elsewhere as of the essence to manage public servants through transitioning from e- to t-Government:

'Transformational leadership and investment in effective communication and change management will be essential, particularly when staff involved in delivering legacy back office services sense a threat of redundancy or a transfer to front office work' (Smith, 2006).

e-Government research

Despite the prominence of the official discourse on t-Government, academic and practitioner-based research is still struggling with coming to grips with e-Government, let alone t-Government. However the issue has not been completely evaded. It was rather approached with different denominations. If one refers to the three axes of the government's transformational strategy, research support exists in current literature, namely e-citizen and e-inclusion for the citizen-centric axis (Bertot, 2003; UN, 2005); automation vs. transformation (Heeks, 2003), and efficiency vs. effectiveness (O'Hara and Stevens, 2006) for the process reengineering aspect, but much less has been written about the professionalism aspect that is integral to t-Government. Another key aspect that has been only tangentially dealt with is the fostering of a shared services culture (cf. Drake et al., 2004). It was mostly approached from a common service platform perspective mainly technological rather than social or cultural. Andersen and Henriksen (2006) notice that the e-Government wave was not accompanied with fundamental new research perspectives and that predominantly it continued along the investigative lines of IT in government that has been around since the 1970s. They go on to suggest new research aimed at

'more dimensions than simply integration issues and supportive functions of formal Government primarily provided by technology.... After more than thirty years of use of IT in the public sector, these benefits are, however, self-evident and Government should move beyond these benefits focusing more on streamlining core processes and reaching customers in a more efficient manner' (p. 237).

The real challenge comes not from the latest developments in technology but the paradigm shift away from push-based to pull-based public services (cf. Irani et al., 2004). t-Government is the central phenomenon engendered by that paradigm shift and local agencies need 'flag pole' research to understand the change models that they need to put in place to integrate their citizenry in the work of government. It is here that research is needed to support local authorities in the 'carving' out of study and evaluation areas and bringing together appropriate expertise to frame sound research proposals.

e-Government research continues to privilege the technology and transactional side of e-Government at the expense of transformation and social inclusion among other key variables. Rose and van Rossum (2005) in their review of European e-Government research assert that researchers either focused on the technology model or the governance model, but seldom were they able to integrate the two. They also pinpoint a clear bias and prioritisation of technology-driven research over governance-driven research, yielding technology systems that are not very reflective of underlying social models or how communities learn and create knowledge. They propose as a result that cooperation be developed between technology and governance style researchers, software developers, industry, regional and national government. The authors further assert that 'technology and community models of learning and knowledge creation are hard to reconcile, and coordinating the efforts of researchers working in the two paradigms is a significant European challenge' (Rose and Van Rossum, p. 13).

A research agenda for t-Government

There is a clear need for a novel approach to the development and delivery of public services within a new paradigm of government functioning, namely transformational government or t-Government. The speedy planning and implementation of t-Government in the UK makes it all the more urgent that the system of innovation in the country rides the bandwagon to help achieve government objectives. In particular, the background above identifies the development of models for **e-citizen**, service reengineering with the accompanying institution of a **shared services culture**, and building capacity and skills as part of the **professionalism** drive as key areas where research is needed. A t-Government research drive or agenda is further justified as follows:

- t-Government is a new phenomenon, and thus an exploratory approach – discussion – is needed while reflecting on the achievements of e-Government. Although the problems of transformational cultures have been around with the e-business phenomenon, government works under different constraints and looks at value beyond its instrumental aspects of revenue streams. Likewise, local agencies work under distinctive constraints and need to use distinctive notions of value such as social capital. The e-business client does not nearly hold the same esteem by its provider even within the most integrated of supply chains. No models could be identified to detect the new 'business model' of government. However, and just like e-business, t-Government is an end in itself and not a means to an end (The Computer Bulletin, 2005). This alone mandates a focused approach.
- The issues are multi-faceted, and need to address social and organisational factors as well as technology itself as enablers of t-Government. Research efforts must be moved away from the classical IT trajectory of public service delivery. Cross-disciplinary expertise, with access to a wide range of empirical data from individual organisations and projects, is needed.
- Although the vision and strategy are nationally driven, no research framework has been proposed to accompany the implementation of the t-Government strategy. The Chief Information Office Council (CIO) has pledged to work with the academic sector 'to help implement the strategy and deliver innovative solutions' (Cabinet Office, 2005, p. 30). Academics should help define a joint research and evaluation framework for t-Government.
- Research should examine the emerging paradigms in mobile and communication technologies in improving citizen involvement in the working of government. Case studies of

innovative uses of citizen access technologies or IST within the t-Government framework are particularly needed.

While an endless number of research topics and areas could be derived from the three models outlined in this paper and likewise from research frameworks or meta-models that have been developed in the literature (cf. Beynon-Davies, 2007), only central research questions will be of interest here. Central research questions have been defined by Scholl (2007) as justifying the existence altogether of the discipline of e-Government or its basic epistemology. These are transformation, integration, participation and preservation. On the other hand, research topics that are mono-disciplinary represent the off-shoot of reference disciplines into the practice of t-Government and do not constitute a native epistemology warranting a new disciplinary perspective. Whilst a pluridisciplinary approach seems to dominate in current research, an interdisciplinary and integrative strategy seems to be the most promising way for the field to develop. Interdisciplinarity has characterised highly regarded disciplines in the natural sciences in particular (e.g. Biosciences). However, in developing central research questions for t-Government, the proposed framework goes beyond the four central research areas that were identified by Scholl (2007) and combines them with the three threads of t-Government discussed earlier to yield central research questions within each of the threads. Finally, evaluation will be retained as an additional central research question for t-Government. Indeed, it has been argued before that benefit realisation within t-Government is non-linear and adopts a meta-model and benchmarking approach that is specific to t-Government. However, it should be noted that no attempt is made here to distinguish between t-Government and e-Government in terms of epistemological foundations as central research questions from e-Government were retained as those for t-Government as well. From this point of view, t-Government could be construed as the trend towards interdisciplinarity in e-Government research. Indeed, e-Government has mostly developed along mono- and pluri-disciplinary lines in the past, and as a result has somehow come short in developing its own theories (cf. Scholl, 2007).

The sub-division of t-Government research, hence of its central research questions, has the obvious advantage of coalescing research efforts into the critical threads of t-Government. However, the risk in doing so is the dispersal of research efforts into separate threads. While this might be true, the government agenda, hence t-Government practice, mandates that the three threads be studied separately and not simply lumped under the general umbrella of an overarching t-Government. This does not preclude, however, areas of investigation that cut across the three threads. In Table 15.2, an attempt is made to develop central research questions at the intersection of central areas and t-Government threads. Whenever available, existing research that has albeit partially investigated core questions is listed in the last column of the table. The table is by no means exhaustive and is only meant to map out the epistemological field of t-Government. Further grounded research is needed to pinpoint research questions before they can be investigated.

Methodological considerations

While the above research areas necessitate a wide variety of research methods and techniques, key methodologies are recommended during the early stages of t-Government deployment. Until that time when the research agenda acquires the status of an epistemology

■ Table 15.2 Core research issues in t-Government

	e-Inclusion	Shared services culture	Professionalism	References
Transformation		Transformational leadership	Transformational capacity building in public services	Bretschneider (2003)
		Management of cultural change		Fontaine (2001)
Integration	Integration of business clients into the e-Gov supply chain		Reengineering for process integration across the silos of public administration	Beynon-Davies (2007)
			Government supply-chain management	Millard (2003)
Preservation		Ontology and semantic Web for t-Gov	IS Alignment	Sabol and Mach (2006)
				Klischewski (2004)
Participation	Building social capital among citizens			Lenk and Tranmuller (2002) Balutis (2001)
Evaluation			Quality assurance in government supplier management	Mele (2003)
				Jones et al. (2006)

within one or more threads, some methodological considerations have to be adopted. Three core areas of research that are derived from Table 15.2 are evoked below with appropriate methodological considerations. These were not tied to the specific threads but derive from which core area of research is being investigated.

Transformation and integration

The whole t-Government endeavour relies on a critical assumption about public service; that it is willing to shift to a shared services culture. The culture of sharing is indeed alien to public administration. The government strategy is not very explicit about how cultural interventions will be done to bring public administration in line with the requirements of a shared services culture. This will not be achieved by technological integration alone as e-Government has worked on that premise. 'Interventionist' research as in action research, for instance, will be a prime channel to bring about cultural change. Transformational leadership at the top, whenever it exists, will not suffice to push down the changes. Long serving public administrators in charge of relaying change within their departments will be very likely so imbued with the local culture and its embedded practices that they will fail to create the necessary dynamic for change. Recourse to external consultants alone will not be effective either. Internal consultants or action researchers will be a key ingredient for successful steering of cultural changes. The corporate culture literature is replete with models for effective cultural change through transformational leadership (cf. Kilmann, 1989; Schein, 2004).

Participation

Participation is an all encompassing framework for the involvement of a variety of stakeholders at all levels of the government value network. By drawing in stakeholders that were traditionally considered external to the mechanics of e-Government, namely citizens and businesses, the whole dynamic of participation is altered. This necessitates, as Scholl (2007) advocates, an integrative interdisciplinary perspective to gauge the effect of a more proactive citizen on say the culture of government and the subsequent behaviour of public servants. Hence measurements of citizen satisfaction or degree of participation in the development of e-Government which primarily draw from mono-disciplines like Marketing and Information Systems (IS) become not adapted to t-Government participation. As participation entails building social capital through nurturing deliberative processes in public policy making, a combined perspective that draws from both political science and IS is necessary. Such integration does not exist at the moment as political science struggles to accommodate the study of IST that are changing the landscape of public policy (Becker, 1998). While this represents a real challenge for t-Government research, it also represents a great opportunity to establish its own epistemology independently from the reference disciplines. In methodological terms, benefit realisation within a t-Government perspective goes beyond measuring the degree of customer satisfaction with e-services and encompasses the study of new governance structures that include citizens and businesses as proactive partners.

Benefit realisation

One key distinction of t-Government from e-Government is how it is evaluated. Benefit realisation is a multi-stakeholder approach to measuring the effectiveness and efficiency of t-Government. While for efficiency, government seems to be content to determine efficiency gains through standard accounting methods, effectiveness measurement on the other hand is more problematic as it entails measuring not only customer satisfaction as with e-Government but more nebulous constructs such as enhanced social capital and public value, enhanced skills and capacity among public service personnel, etc. Traditional accounting methods are not suitable for measurement here. More complex research designs based on focus groups, qualitative investigation and the like are required for measuring t-Government effectiveness. The objective is not only to gather data about whether t-Government is effective or not on different counts but first and foremost to understand the intervening processes in ensuring such effectiveness.

Evaluation is further complicated by the conflicting objectives that central government and local authorities might have. t-Government is primarily centrally led by the UK government and largely imposed as a normative model for e-service delivery. While this creates an appropriate framework for implementation studies driven by the normative framework of t-Government implementation, the adjustment process to this normative model both at the level of central government and local authorities will inevitably deviate from the planned framework. This should not be perceived negatively but rather studied inductively to feed-back into the normative model of implementation. The use of *grounded research methodologies* is essential so not to assume reality. Benchmarking of successful experiences should not be rushed, but rather subjected to a rigorous process of ascertaining benefit realisation.

Though practitioners can turn to a variety of independent organisations and business-support groups for guidance, no critical stock of best practice in t-Government has yet been developed. Local Government Associations that have much wider ranging research portfo-lios do not muster the necessary visibility to establish, exploit and disseminate best prac-tice throughout the UK. Specialists such as the Society for IT Managers (SOCITM), with its Information Age Government Group together with CIPFA and its e-Government Forum Group, both offer specialist training/consultancy services and have accumulated a signifi-cant amount of literature over the past few years. However, with the change of paradigm from e-Government to t-Government, it will take them time to adjust to the new reality of things and develop appropriate models and benchmarks.

■ Conclusion

Other than developing a t-Government epistemology, the principle beneficiaries of a t-Government research agenda will be the government itself and especially local gov-ernment agencies as they shift paradigm in their dealings with citizens and businesses. Research findings will help the public sector better utilise resources and improve their position vis-à-vis central government targets. Likewise, the academic community would bene-fit from a coherent framework for t-Government research and the establishment of a clear focus for t-Government IST within the research funding agencies.

In meshing with the new social and cultural orientation of the t-Government drive, a thor-ough review of work undertaken by public administration scholars, public policy analysts, political scientists, and democracy theorists holds the promise of infusing much needed value-added to the narrower IT rationalist perspective that has so far predominated in the e-Government discourse. Research can significantly reshape the area of t-Government through building bridges between the disciplines and harnessing a variety of tools and methods that could be adopted in the t-Government context. However, and as urged by Scholl (2007), theory building in e- or t-Government should develop based on the integra-tive science model, whereby central research questions are defined and appropriate unify-ing theories are developed to investigate the core questions. Anything short of that, and in continuing to draw from mono-disciplines like IS or multiple disciplines but with research questions belonging to the reference disciplines, t-Government will carry forward the weak epistemological legacy of e-Government. This paper has attempted to define a research agenda around core questions that relate to the three threads of t-Government, hence anchoring t-Government epistemology development into the practice domain and avoiding the risk of pursuing an epistemology at the expense of rigorous and relevant research.

References

Andersen, K. V. and Henriksen, H. Z. (2006). 'e-Government maturity models: Extension of the Layne and Lee model'. *Government Information Quarterly*, 23, 236–248.

Balutis, A. P. (2001). 'e-Government 2001, Part I: Understanding the challenge and evolving strategies'. *The Public Manager*, 30(1), 23–34.

Becker, T. (1998). 'Governance and electronic innovation: A clash of paradigms'. *Information, Communication, and Society*, 1(3), 339–343.

Bertot, J. C. (2003). 'The multiple dimensions of the digital divide: More than the technology 'haves' and 'have nots'. *Government Information Quarterly*, 20, 185–191.

Beynon-Davies, P. (2007). 'Models for e-Government'. *Transforming Government: People, Process and Policy*, 1(1), 7–28.

RT Hon Tony Blair MP, Speech to Labour Party Conference, Manchester, 2006.

Bretschneider, S. (2003). 'Information technology, e-Government and institutional change'. *Public Administration Review*, 63, 738–741.

Cabinet Office (2005). *Transformational Government-Enabled by Technology Strategy Document.*

Cabinet Office (2006). *Transformational Government 2006 Implementation Plan.*

Cabinet Office (2007). *Transformational Government 2006 Annual Report.*

Chen, H. (2002). 'Digital government: Technologies and practices'. *Decision Support Systems*, 34, 223–227.

The Computer Bulletin (2005). 'Ian Watmore' Vol. 47, No. 2, March, pp. 14–15, Oxford University Press.

Drake, D. B., Steckler, N. A. and Koch, M. J. (2004). 'Information sharing in and across government agencies – The role and influence of scientist, politician, and bureaucrat subcultures'. *Social Science Computer Review*, 22(1), 67–84.

Ezgov (2005). *Beyond the Form*. http://www.ezgoveurope.com/

Fontaine, J (2001). *Building the Virtual State: Information Technology and Institutional Change*, the Brookings Institution, Washington, DC.

Sir Peter Gershon, CBE (2004), Releasing resources to the frontline: Independent review of public sector efficiency, July, HM Treasury, London, UK. Available on-line http://www.hm-treasury.gov.uk/media/C/A/efficiency_review120704.pdf

Heeks, R. (2003). *Most eGovernment-for-Development Projects Fail: How Can Risks be Reduced?* IDPM i-Government Working Paper no.14, http://www.idpm.man.ac.uk/publications/wp/igov/index.shtml (accessed 30 December 2004).

Idabc (2005). *UK: UK local councils to start reaping e-Government savings in 2006–2007* http://www.ec.europa.eu/idabc/en/document/3856/345 (February).

Irani, Z., Themistocleous, M. and Ghinea, G. (2004). 'Developing Infrastructure Guidelines to Support Pull/Push E-Government Information Technology (DIG-IT)', Research Note, *European and Mediterranean Conference on Information Systems*, 25–27 July, Tunis, Tunisia.

Jones, S., Irani, Z., Sharif, A. and Themistocleous, M. (2006). 'e-Government evaluation: reflections on two organizational studies'. *Proceedings of the 39th Hawaii International Conference on System Sciences*, pp. 1–8.

Kable (2003). Kable's Government Computing, *e-Government will cost more than it saves*, http://www.kablenet.com/kd.nsf/Frontpage/1630A7F2B9A7B96680256D40002 EC027?OpenDocument

Kilmann, R. H. (1989). *Managing Beyond the Quick Fix*. San-Francisco, Jossey-Bass.

Klischewski, R. (2004). 'Information integration or process integration? How to achieve interoperability in administration'. In Traunmuller, R. (Ed.), *Electronic Government: Third*

International Conference, EGOV 2004, Zaragoza, Spain, August 30–September 3, Proceedings. Springer, New York, NY.

Layne, K. and LEE, J. W. (2001). 'Developing fully functional e-Government: A four stage model'. *Government Information Quarterly*, 18(2), 122–136.

Leitner, C. (2003). *eGovernment in Europe: The State of Affairs*, European Institute of Public Administration, Maastricht, the Netherlands.

Lenk, K. and Tranmuller, R. (2002). 'Electronic government: Where are we heading?' In Traunmuller, R. and Lenk, K. (Eds.), *Electronic Government: First International Conference, EGOV 2002, Aix-en-Provence, France, September 2–6: Proceedings*. Springer, Berlin.

Mele, V. (2003). *Evaluation and Benchmarking of e-Government: Status and Perspectives. Issue Report No.34*, September, Databank Consulting, pp. 1–42.

Millard, J. (2003). *ePublic services in Europe: Past, Present, and Future*. Danish Technology Institute, Copenhagen.

O'Hara, K. and Stevens, D. (2006). 'Democracy, Ideology and Process Re-Engineering: Realising the Benefits of e-Government in Singapore'. In Huai, J., Shen, V. and Tan, C. J. (Eds.), *Proceedings of Workshop on e-Government: Barriers and Opportunities*, www06 (in press), Edinburgh.

Perrin, W. (2006). *Benefits Management and Realisation: UK Approach*. eGovernment Unit, Cabinet Office.

Rose, J. and van Rossum, M. (2005). 'A Roadmap for European Research in Learning and Knowledge Creation in e-Government'. *ECEG*, pp. 343–348.

Sabol, T. and Mach, M. (2006). 'Semantic Web in e-Government'. *AAAI Spring Symposium Series*, Stanford University, CA, USA, March 27–29.

Sahraoui, S. (2007). 'e-Inclusion as a further stage of e-Government?'. *Transforming Government: People, Process, and Policy*, 1(1), 44–58.

Sahraoui, S., Gharaibeh, G. and Jboori, A. (2006). 'Saudi e-Government: Can it overcome its challenges'. In *Proceedings of the Workshop on e-Government Research*, Brunel University, West London, UK, September.

Schein, E. (2004). *Organizational Culture and Leadership*, 3rd ed. San-Francisco, Jossey-Bass.

Scholl, H. (2007). 'Central research questions in e-Government, or which trajectory should the study domain take?'. *Transforming Government: People, Process, and Policy*, 1(1), 67–88.

Smith, P. (2006). A blueprint for transformation. *E-Government bulletin*. Available at http://www.cio.gov.uk/documents/news/pdf/ABlueprintForTransformation.pdf

United Nations (2003). *World Public Sector Report: e-Government at the Crossroads*. United Nations, New York.

United Nations (2005). *Global e-Government Readiness Report 2005: From e-Government to e-inclusion*. United Nations, New York.

The World Bank (2003). *A Definition of e-Government*. The World Bank, Washington, DC.

Watson, R. T. and Mundy, B. (2001). 'A strategic perspective of electronic democracy'. *Communications of the ACM*, 44(1), 27–30.

Index